S0-DFR-130

The Drama of Fallen France

THE DRAMA OF FALLEN FRANCE

Reading *la Comédie sans Tickets*

Kenneth Krauss

STATE UNIVERSITY OF NEW YORK PRESS

Published by
State University of New York Press, Albany

© 2004 State University of New York

All rights reserved

Printed in the United States of America

No part of this book may be used or reproduced in any manner whatsoever
without written permission. No part of this book may be stored in a
retrieval system or transmitted in any form or by any means including
electronic, electrostatic, magnetic tape, mechanical, photocopying, recording,
or otherwise without the prior permission in writing of the publisher.

For information, address State University of New York Press,
90 State Street, Suite 700, Albany, NY 12207

Production by Diane Ganeles
Marketing by Anne M. Valentine

Library of Congress Cataloging-in-Publication Data

Krauss, Kenneth, 1948–
    The drama of fallen France : Reading la comédie sans tickets / Kenneth Krauss.
    p. cm.
    Includes bibliographical references and index.
    ISBN 0-7914-5953-5 (alk. paper)
    1. French drama—20th century—History and criticism. 2. Government,
Resistance to, in literature. 3. France—History—German occupation, 1940–1945.
4. Theater—France—History—20th century. 5. World War, 1939–1945—France—
Theater and the war. I. Title.

PQ558.K73 2003
842'.91209358—dc21   2003042558

10 9 8 7 6 5 4 3 2 1

To the memory of Eleanor Richman
who, even when it might have been forgotten,
kept alive in me the idea of France
and gave so much to everyone.

Contents

Illustrations   ix

Acknowledgments   xi

Overture   xiii

Chapter 1:
A Queer Premiere: Jean Cocteau's *The Typewriter*   1

Chapter 2:
Collabo Beefcake and Resistant Reception:
Ambiguity in André Obey's *Eight Hundred Meters* and
   The Suppliant Women   35

Chapter 3:
French Identity:
The Intended Audience for Jean Giraudoux's *The Apollo of Marsac*   61

Chapter 4:
The Limits of Opportunism:
Simone Jollivet's *The Princess of Ursins*   81

Chapter 5:
The Politics of Intention:
Jean Anouilh's *Antigone* via *Oreste*   105

Chapter 6:
The Politics of Reception:
Jean-Paul Sartre's *The Flies*   129

Chapter 7:
A Politics of Sexuality:
Henry de Montherlant's *Nobody's Son*   145

Chapter 8:
The Politics of Impersonation:
Casting and Recasting Paul Claudel's *The Satin Slipper*   175

Epilogue:
Catching *The Last Métro*:
François Truffaut's Portrayal of Occupation Drama and Sexuality   191

Finale   207

Notes   211

Bibliography   235

Name Index and Literary Works   249

Illustrations

———

Cartoons of Cocteau and cast of *The Typewriter*   xxiv

Breker's Sculptures at l'Orangerie   37

Photo spread of *The Suppliant Women*   48

Set designs for *The Apollo of Marsac*   76

Simone Jollivet around 1928 and 1943   95

The Princess of Ursins meets her nemesis   103

Near the final curtain of *Nobody's Son*   167

Acknowledgments

There are many thanks I must make for the help that I received for this project. The National Endowment for the Humanities (NEH) and the Société des Professeurs Français et Francophones d'Amérique both provided monetary assistance for research in France. The NEH also gave me the opportunity to participate in a seminar at Harvard University (under the direction of Susan Suleiman). The College of Saint Rose has, since 1991, repeatedly awarded me funding for research as well.

I would like to thank *George Sand Studies*, *Journal of Dramatic Theory and Criticism*, *Simone de Beauvoir Studies*, *New England Theatre Journal*, and *Paul Claudel Papers*, in which early versions of pieces of this book appeared. I would also like to express my gratitude to the Theatre, French, and History Departments at Southern Illinois University, which invited me to give a talk on "Collaborationist Beefcake."

Emotional support over the period during which I worked on this project came from a number of sources. The English Department at The College of Saint Rose consistently listened to my problems and several of my colleagues, including Debra Young, Kate Cavanaugh, Hollis Seamon, and Barbara Ungar, allowed me to subject them to drafts of what would become this book. My mentor at Columbia University, Martin Meisel, and my cowriter on an earlier project, Nancy Hazelton, encouraged me when I became discouraged, and they and Eileen Allman kindly read pieces of the book as it evolved and commented on it. During her year at Columbia, Carol Rosen urged me to pursue this project. My old friend David Burke read through an earlier version of the manuscripts and offered advice. Dr. Susan L. Cox helped me to understand some of the psychodynamics involved in Montherlant's abuse of children.

Throughout this book, I note people, many of them in France, who aided me in my attempt to find and understand certain material. Here I would like to acknowledge, in particular, Edmond M. Desportes de Linières, founding president of the Association Charles Dullin, who guided much of my research, who gave me access to several important collections, and who introduced me to Paul-Louis Mignon. M. Desportes de Linières helped me to experience France and its theatre and took care of me as if I were his son. Serge Added talked to me about facts and ideas. My dear friend from graduate days, Christine Biélazka-DuVernay, and her husband, Fréderic, put me up in Sèvres for several weeks and sent me photocopies. My friends in Brunoy, Claire and Alain Chevolleau, Marie-Luce and Bruno Varin, and Sophie and Haddou Aït Naceur, continue to make me feel welcome in a place where foreigners may not always be well received.

At the NEH seminar at Harvard, I was helped by the participants, particularly by Elizabeth Houlding and Ray Bach, whose work I had read beforehand, and Jocelyn van Tuyl, whose own writing on André Gide helped me better understand the career of Henry de Montherlant. Mary Ann Witt, with whom I appeared on an MLA panel, and Josephine Arnold, who happened to be visiting New York's Capital Region, both discussed with me their ideas about the theatre during the War, as did Yolanda Astarita Patterson of the Simone de Beauvoir Society, who offered ongoing friendship and validation and put me in touch with Dennis Gilbert, who gave me very helpful criticism and direction.

Several College of Saint Rose students helped find and reproduce research, especially the late Scott Ryan, Carol Gage, John Hunter, and Aine Ellrott Greamey. My former colleague in art history, Stuart Curtis, and his successor, Lucy Bowditch, helped me with illustrations, and Luigi Benincasa at the Saint Rose public relations office and David Seiler at Skidmore College library assisted me by creating electronic versions of them.

Finally, my completion of this project could not have been accomplished without the support of two very important individuals, my schnauzer, Olivia, and my partner, Joe Pickul.

Any innaccuracies and deficiencies in this book are due solely to me and not to any of the preceding. I hope that anyone whom I have, because of my waning memory, left out will forgive my carelessness.

Overture

———

Between June 1940 and August 1944, France existed under two separate though associated administrations, the first, the German military authority headquartered in Paris and the second, a French regime established under Maréchal Philippe Pétain at Vichy. How one describes this four-year period inevitably reveals one's view of it: To call it "The Occupation" implies a defeated France held hostage, and to refer to this time as "the Vichy Years" suggests that France under Pétain acted largely on its own volition and without much prodding from the Germans. Yet the power dynamic, both cooperative and competitive, between these two official centers was significant, and labeling the nation as either "captive" or "fascist" France tends to simplify the complexity of the actual circumstances. The way in which everyday life was lived reflected the maddening, often dizzying, contradictions that resulted from the ongoing accords and conflicts between Paris and Vichy. People in the Occupied Zone were acutely aware of the need to go along with what their governors—both German and French—demanded and of their opportunities (whether great or small) to defy them. And as the months wore on and Vichy lost power, real and spiritual, to Nazi-ruled Paris and to various groups working against the Germans, deeper divisions among the population continued to fragment a country that each splintering group struggled to represent.

Among the beneficiaries of the relationship between the German Occupiers and the French State were the state-run and private theatres that flourished in the former French capital during these four years. The Germans in the summer of 1940 encouraged theatres to reopen (even as they censored them) while Vichy offered ample subsidies for performances and playhouses. After the Second World War, many believed that what had appeared on the Paris stage was at worst innocuous and at best reflective of audiences' sympathies or even identifications with the Résistance; such a belief was consonant with a widespread postwar notion that those involved in collaboration were exceptional and few, that they could be purged from a society, which, once cleansed, might pick up and go on. After 1968, however, many began to question the role played by the theatre during the War, asking how much the theatre's economic and artistic collaboration with the regimes in power led to a political collaboration; such questioning was consonant with a growing doubt about what the French in fact did before, during, and after the War.

In France, where the investigation and interpretation of these years remain a vital part of an assessment of the current cultural climate, studies on "Occupation" or "Vichyite" theatre clearly reflect contemporary trends. After the War, there is a romanticization of the topic, which eventually turns to a head-on embrace of the nostalgia of the wartime stage; by the 1970s and early 1980s, however, a critical distinction between "resistance" and "collaboration" on (or via) the stage has been drawn; in the 1990s more rigorous research yields data that support the notion that the theatre, along with French culture as a whole, functioned in a collaborationist mode throughout the four-year period. This ongoing discussion has resulted in a polarization of discourse on the topic, one side emphasizing that to a significant extent the theatre allowed French audiences to identify themselves as anti-German and/ or anti-fascist, the other persisting in uncovering information that repudiates virtually all notion of a "théâtre résistant."

While the antithetical argument has been useful in realizing the complexity of the topic, the resulting contentiousness has created a certain animosity and bitterness among the opposing participants. Most seriously, the very evidence that has gone into supporting the idea that the theatre was not a medium of collaboration has, perhaps necessarily, been attacked by those who assert that it was exactly that. This is particularly troubling in that much of the former comes from personal experience, from the human document, which by its very nature is fragile, ephemeral, highly subjective. Indeed, to dismiss or discount firsthand knowledge, whatever possible distortions it may include, is always risky. And as those who directly experienced the wartime theatre in Paris leave us, the remaining evidence begins to grow heavier on the side of those whose experience of the period has been largely, if not entirely, vicarious.

The essays in this book are attempts to reconcile the two disparate positions. True, in a broad sense, the Paris theatres during the War were, more or less, sites of collaboration, but they were also (perhaps less often though nevertheless quite genuinely) in specific moments—some of them longer, sustained moments—sites of resistance. Still, even if there were substantial instances when audience members were moved against the prevailing regimes or toward those who risked their lives to thwart them, there were moments too when spectators were encouraged to view the fall of their country as acceptable, natural, even desirable. The French theatre during the war was not a totally shameful institution, nor was it by any means one that played a thoroughly heroic role.

Was the drama that played on the stages of wartime Paris collaborationist or was it resistant? The answer is not easily given with concision—or rather, the question requires a long and very complicated reply. In order to understand what happened on- and off-stage during the period, one must delve carefully into the circumstances of dramatic and theatrical production and of audience reception within the precise context. Furthermore, one must discuss those two crucial terms.

We tend to look back on and to locate politically those who lived through the Occupation by situating them somewhere between the poles of resistance and collaboration; but in the first year following the Defeat, these terms, which are now familiar to us, had only begun to evolve into what they have come to signify. As Robert O. Paxton makes clear, the armistice document between France and Germany, signed June 22, 1940, itself called for "French officials and public services 'to conform to the decisions of the German authorities and collaborate faithfully with them' "; forever altering the use of "collaboration," a once innocent word that had meant "working together," the armistice was merely the first step that would take "many Frenchmen down a path of everyday complicity that led gradually and eventually to active assistance to German measures undreamed of in 1940" (18–19). As this path and its destination became apparent, the term took on more explicit denotations of betrayal.

Similarly, "resistance," as Henry Rousso astutely reminds us, was initially brought forward at about the same time by the "man of June Eighteenth [1940]," Charles De Gaulle, who, just four days before the signing of the armistice that demanded collaboration (18), declared from London via the BBC, "Whatever happens, the flame of French resistance must not and shall not go out" (Lacouture 225). John F. Sweets eloquently recommends a redefinition of what the term eventually came to mean (at least for some)— i.e., "the activities of the organized resistance movements, and . . . the bombings, assassinations, robberies, sabotage, and guerilla attacks that dramatized their presence"—to one that takes into account the general atmosphere that nurtured and encouraged such activities (224) (and perhaps in some way identified with them), an atmosphere that was most pervasive toward the end of the Occupation. Yet for many, "resistance" persists either as an extremely precise term, applicable to relatively few, or a troublingly general term, easily disputed. Thus, one cannot merely label something as an example of resistance or collaboration; one must explain how and why.

The exercise of identifying the allegiances of artists and their work from this period has not been limited to theatre. In relating the term "resistance" to the visual arts of the Occupation, Michèle C. Cone mentions two (or three) "models of self-expression from the viewpoint of resistance-writers" (xx). In the first, "the classical model . . . 'the truth' is uttered between the lines more or less furtively but *un*ambiguously—at least for those sympathetic to the views expressed in disguise" (xx–xxi). In the second, "used [by writers] in Eastern Europe under communism," an "official message is resisted and garbled by an internal modification of its material parts that renders its meaning totally opaque yet has the appearance of a typographical error. . . ." In the third, "Derridian" model (which Cone does not find credible), "the official views in the writing can be interpreted in conflicting ways . . . ," which make it possible "to read irony into the voice that spells out the official view" (xxi).

The problem with these models is that each relies heavily on interpretation. With the first, we must wonder how a text that is read "*un*ambiguously" by "those sympathetic to the views expressed in disguise," will be read by those who are not sympathetic with the disguised views. Does their lack of sympathy also ensure another reading—or another unambiguous reading? And how much do the circumstances surrounding the writer's conscious (or even unconscious) resistance also figure in the ambiguity (which of course is necessary for the text to mean more than one thing) and the lack of ambiguity (which the model definition suggests is necessary in order to make it genuinely resistant)? How much do (and/or should) the intentions of the writer (in as much as they can ever really be knowable) figure in the interpretation of the text? And are readings of a text that are completely unanticipated by the writer wrong or ought they to be considered viable and valuable interpretations? This interpretive dilemma becomes so pointed in the third (Derridian) model—to what extent is the reading "of irony into the voice that spells out the official view" a complete invention of the reader?—that Cone altogether rules it out.

Although the second model seems somewhat less dependent on readers' sympathies, for readers presumably would be able to point concretely to the "appearance of a typographical error," problems of interpretation remain: The "official message . . . garbled by an internal modification of its material parts" only appears resistant when readers can make sense of the garbling as something other than random or accidental typographical (or other) error and can thus construe subversive meanings from the apparent "official message" carried in, and in some ways dominating, the text. Again, even with typographical proof, the "resistant" meaning of the text must be located by readers. In all three models, the eye of the beholder determines what is and is not resistance writing; thus, the nature of the text (as either resistant or not) is relative (as are the terms "resistance" and "collaboration").

What is objective, however, are specific acts of interpretation, response, reception: Written texts and painted canvases do not in themselves signify;

their significance, in large part, emerges from their interaction with readers or viewers. In the theatre, where reception itself can (and sometimes does) become performance, response is often palapable, concrete, tangible. An audience may erupt against a particular stage piece, laugh at a comic turn, applaud a line of dialogue, grow restless during a scene; even if one contends that spectators are wrong to react as they do (an argument that usually seeks to silence or invalidate the evidence of reception), one cannot deny the actuality of that reaction.

Early in the four-year period during which the Nazis occupied Paris, the phrase "comédie sans tickets" was coined by Robert Brasillach, an occasional drama critic and also the editor of the racist weekly, *Je suis partout*. Translated literally, the phrase means "comedy without ration coupons," and was meant to describe the type of supposedly realistic play, often a frivolous comedy (especially prevalent in the first season following the Defeat) that avoided depicting all aspects of the recent crisis. Such plays, Brasillach felt, in their attempts to entertain, dodged the common experiences of the Occupation, such as the omnipresent ration coupons required to purchase the basic necessities of life and virtually all other goods (Le Boterf 185). Thus, he mocked the "myth" of realistic theatre. A right-wing intellectual before the War and a major pro-German ideologue after the Defeat, Brasillach proclaimed that under the new order art should support the struggle toward fascism. (He and his fellow critics also believed that the highly successful though frivolous "boulevard" comedies, which had dominated the prewar stage and to which these comédies sans tickets bore a close resemblance, had largely been the work of the Jews.)[1]

In ultra-right-wing, pro-German terms, Brasillach's phrase carried the insinuation that the theatre of the Third Republic was not merely flighty but irresponsible and dishonest, both representative of and a part of the decadence that had led to the Defeat. The New France demanded, or so he was insinuating, a dose of the New Reality, with which by now conventional and bourgeois stage realism had nothing to do. According to the collabo press, the most successful of the new dramatic pieces of the period were set either in a foreign past (ancient Greece, Spain's Golden Age) or in a very generally constructed present. Thus, Brasillach and others in the pro-fascist press praised the plays of Jean Anouilh, whose wartime scripts were located either in a nonspecific contemporary setting (such as *Léocadia* and *Le Rendez-vous à Senlis* [*The Rendez-vous at Senlis*]) or in another time and place (such as *Antigone* and *Eurydice*). Ironically, the shift in time and place allowed Anouilh (as well as Sartre and other playwrights) to refer to what was going on in the present. In the case of *Léocadia*, written before the Defeat but staged after, this script, like virtually all "present-day" works from the Occupation, offered a completely unidentifiable contemporaneity and made no concessions to those timely ration coupons. Still, *Léocadia* was such a great success during the barren first season after the Defeat that *Je suis partout* printed it in one of its issues. (Well after the Liberation, a translation of the same play—again, without any concessions to the specifics of time—became a hit on Broadway as *Time Remembered*.) Even as Brasillach complained about those "comédies sans tickets," remarkably few plays, even those celebrated in the collaborationist press, referred directly to current conditions and events.

Thus, if Brasillach's call for referentiality seems a narrow, if not an arbitrary, way of determining whether or not a play reflects its times, we should also understand comédie sans tickets as an attempt by an extremely politicized critic to impose some order on a potentially unwieldy and dangerous art form. "Comédie sans tickets" was a convenient epithet with which to vilify those whose work did not conform to Brasillach's expectations of what a play ought to be and do. Yet even Brasillach was sufficiently susceptible to good theatre to appreciate a piece that was not only written by someone whose political views he loathed but whose script (which was clearly set in the present) seemed to ignore direct references to the present: In 1944, he could not hide his admiration for Jean-Paul Sartre's *Huis Clos* (*No Exit*), which he found dramatically brilliant. Thus, in spite of his simplistic call for new works that literally represented the New France, Brasillach and other reviewers in the collaborationist press sometimes welcomed plays that, though seemingly un- or apolitical, were artistically compelling; in fact, these critics appear to have imposed their own right-wing values on some of the very works in which other audience members saw themes of resistance.

The contemporary critics' interpretations are well documented in print. Yet the circumstances surrounding newspaper and magazine publication, including (though not limited to) direct censorship by the Germans, heavily influenced what could be and thus what was written. There were underground papers that offered theatre reviews, but these were few and intermittent; moreover, the circumstances surrounding resistance publication also influenced what could be and thus what was written. The most prominent instance concerns *Antigone*, a play by Anouilh that received very positive notices in the censored press and a damningly negative review in a Résistance newspaper; yet *Antigone* was one of the plays that the population came to believe had included a dramatization of resistance. While some have argued that this was a postwar belief imposed by those who wanted to see France as a nation of resistors, there is enough anecdotal evidence to suggest that the truth was much stranger, that despite all the accolades from the collabo press and the condemnation of one Résistance critic, there were spectators who watched *Antigone* during the Occupation who indeed heard the call to resist clearly sounded.

To assert that *Antigone* advocated the Résistance would be wrong, but to discount and ignore the reactions of spectators who construed that it did would be equally erroneous. One way to judge a script is by its author's intentions, but these are extremely difficult to locate, especially during a time when playwrights (such as Sartre in an interview about *Les Mouches* [*The Flies*]) deliberately masked their motivations. Of course, one may examine an author's life, his or her behavior, actions, and thoughts at the time of composition, but even here we can only guess at how truly revealing these may be. Furthermore, authors are not necessarily always conscious of their own intentions.

Yet a play is much more than its author's intentions (whether they be conscious or not); a play comprises not only a dramatic text (a script) and a theatre text (the stage elements brought into play through production) but also a text of response, a matrix of spectator reactions, and a history of reception. Without an audience a play is merely a rehearsal; with an audience it is a significant or at least a signifying work of art. Moreover, the gap between the playwright's intended audience and the actual audiences may make for interpretations that are, although surprising and unexpected, nonetheless valid.

Throughout the chapters that comprise this study, I attempt to examine the playscript and the production of several plays written and/or produced during the Occupation and also to explore the role played by the theatre audience and/or the role expected of them. In chapter 1, I look at the uproar that broke out during the premiere of Jean Cocteau's *La Machine à Écrire* (*The Typewriter*) at the Théâtre Hébertot in the spring of 1941; the brawl has long been understood to have been extraneous to what was happening on stage—as a reaction not to the play but to the playwright. Research, however, suggests that such an explanation is a simplification that robs both the performance and its reception of their meaning. The riot at the Hébertot may have been (as others have indicated) in part focused on Cocteau, who was seen as the epitome of the decadence of the Third Republic, but at the same time, *The Typewriter* played an important role in its audience's violent eruption.

In chapter 2, I turn to another work that has been misconstrued, André Obey's *Huit Cents Mètres* (*Eight Hundred Meters*). Although some postwar writers have inferred that this Vichy-subsidized performance (along with Obey's version of Aeschylus' *The Suppliant Women*) performed in the summer of 1941 at Roland-Garros Stadium was highly collaborationist, a study of the dramatic text and its performance suggests that response to the work was probably more ambivalent than previously supposed. Even the fascist glamorization of "the body beautiful," apparent here in athletic display, was no straightforward presentation. Some among the collaborationist press, who eyed such a display suspiciously, did their best to neutralize the homoerotic implications in the production's presentation of beefcake: The production received mixed reviews. Yet the audience could and did come away with highly divergent impressions of what they had experienced.

After the Defeat, the great French playwright before the War, Jean Giraudoux, saw his artistic partner, actor/director Louis Jouvet, leave for South America. In 1942 Giraudoux sent him (from the safety of Switzerland) a new one-act that Jouvet premiered in Rio in the spring of 1942. Although many have seen in *L'Apollon de Marsac* (*The Apollo of Marsac*), as it was originally titled, a light, whimsical comedy, the play contained both references to the current situation in France (including, quite literally, Brasillach's "tickets") and a broader message about what it meant to be French. Still, this message would have been largely lost on spectators in the New World, and when Jouvet premiered the play in France in 1947, the Occupation was over, and the other play that was performed on the same bill—Jean Genet's *Les Bonnes* (*The Maids*)—created so much controversy that critics found Giraudoux's play trivial. Yet the script appears to be intended for an Occupation audience of French spectators, who would have responded with a very different interpretation.

In chapter 4, I move to a work of which neither reviewers nor audiences approved, *La Princesse des Ursins* (*The Princess of Ursins*). In an era when females were increasingly and systematically excluded from public life and the professions, Simone Jollivet's play chronicles the ascent of a woman whose sheer audacity and conniving nearly manage to thwart the misogynist heirarchy. Jollivet herself attempted the same rise in the male-dominated theatre of the Occupation; she was the mistress of actor/director Charles Dullin and was well situated to promote and push her own script into production. She had also been the first great love of Jean-Paul Sartre, and ironically, it was his subsequent long term companion, Simone de Beauvoir, who perpetuated Jollivet's memory. Although Beauvoir may have rationalized that her dislike for her former rival was due to Jollivet's naïve and throughly nasty statements of political opportunism, Beauvoir also sensed in her a strategy for subduing the opposite sex (the very strategy glorified in *Princess*), which was clearly the opposite of feminism: *Princess* was and remains a self-defeating script about self-defeat.

In chapters 5 and 6, I look at two plays that survived the Occupation with international reputations. Anouilh's *Antigone*, as noted earlier, has been a topic of much debate. To contemplate the author's intentions, I examine an unfinished, little-discussed script on which Anouilh worked shortly before he began writing *Antigone*, the fragment *Oreste*, published in 1947. The differences between the piece that Anouilh abandoned and the one he brought to the stage are meaningful and offer some insight into some of his conscious aims in writing the later play. Sartre's *Les Mouches* (*The Flies*), which after the War became for many the paradigm of resistance (and even of Résistance) theatre, has nonetheless also been the source of considerable contention. Even a superficial perusal of the script suggests that Sartre was very deliberately satirizing Vichy. But is such an interpretation the result of our postwar awareness or did spectators during the Occupation recognize what appears so obvious now? In this case, the author's intentions seem indisputable: It is the reception of the play that has been debated. Both scripts are at the very center of any discussion of whether stage plays actually did generate meanings that audiences saw as contrary to the current regimes.

As I mention earlier, few dramas of the period were actually set during the Occupation. Henry de Montherlant's *Fils de Personne* (*Nobody's Son*), set in Nice after the Defeat, is a notable exception. In chapter 7, I trace the problematic intentions of Montherlant's text and question why general audiences were unable to decode its extremely subversive messages. The subversive messages here, however, are not adequately described (as would be appropriate in the case of *The Flies*) as political or resistant: Montherlant was advocating his own brand of sexual politics, and he aimed this message at those who shared his particular sexuality. The cultural elements that framed the audiences' reception of this play were especially powerful in masking the playwright's agenda or at least in disabling spectators from articulating what they may have suspected.

The great theatre event of this era was the epic presentation of Paul Claudel's *Le Soulier de Satin* (*The Satin Slipper*), which Jean-Louis Barrault (who had directed *Eight Hundred Meters*) staged and starred in at the Comédie-Française during the Occupation's last theatre season. As with Cocteau in 1941, Claudel himself was the object of some harsh condemnation by reviewers; his anti-German sentiments were apparently well known and his skepticism regarding Vichy made him, in spite of his conservative, ultra-Catholic political position, a target for the collaborationist press. Barrault convinced Claudel to allow the play (written years before) to be performed, and both worked on a shortened version (which ran about five hours). Barrault, whose politics always seemed disconcertingly elusive, injected his own sense of "total theatre" into what might have been a very long and devout evening. Even in that bastion of state approval, the Comédie-Française (which was directly financed by Vichy), the stage version of *Le Soulier de Satin* managed—despite its deeply reactionary themes—to break new theatrical ground. In addition to his innovative production techniques, Barrault's casting to some extent questioned, perhaps even undermined, some of Claudel's certainties about life and love. The director was able to use the theatrical text to comment on the dramatic text so that audiences might regard the play with more thoughtfulness and detachment than Claudel might have intended.

The occupiers, though they strove to keep the City of Light as festive and diverting as possible, insisted on a curfew. Thus, plays began earlier in the evening so that spectators could catch the last métro that would take them home. This mad dash for the train while the final curtain was falling gave its name to François Truffaut's 1980 film, *Le Dernier Métro* (*The Last Métro*), which is perhaps the best known representation of the Paris theatre during these grim four years; a discussion of this film forms the epilogue to this study. Truffaut had been influenced by the films and film critics of the Occupation and had written on both; his own criticism discounted the idea of a defiant French cinema even as he acknowledged that audiences had construed an intentional message of resistance in some films. On one level, *Le Dernier Métro* questions the dynamics of the wartime stage performances and their reception and offers, true to its director and to the time when the film was made, an interestingly mixed and evasive reply. On another level, however, the film tries to rewrite the Occupation to make it appear an eerily miscolored version of the present: Truffaut incorporates a panoply of period details with literary, theatrical, and cinematic allusions to bring forth a depiction of how, regardless of the differences, life and love (especially love) are really much the same now as they were then.

Ironically, Brasillach's "comédie sans tickets" may be construed in quite another way: "comedy without ration coupons" may also be interpreted to mean "theatre so plentiful as not to require rationing." Indeed, one of the few commodities during the war that was not in short supply and was not limited by coupons was dramatic performance. There was more theatre in Paris under the Germans than there had ever been before, and box offices, overall, took in more money than they had collected before the Defeat.

More than half a century after the Liberation, readers are far less ready to embrace the glorious image of a courageous theatre operating in defiance of the invaders. Yet the legitimate theatre was a place that could and sometimes did offer audiences a sense that they were in a space that was uniquely French. Although Germans had their own cinemas and tended to visit the more visually oriented venues, such as nightclubs, the opera, and the Grand Guignol, they often appeared in the audiences of the more serious venues; yet here their presence, made plain by their uniforms, identified them as foreigners. The French language and culture united French spectators, and in spite of their political differences, spectators in Paris sat through plays with a sense that they were not in a territory of the Third Reich but once again in France. For better and for worse, the theatre played a significant role during the Occupation.

That haunting question as to the nature of that role—collaborationist or resistant—is difficult to answer if only because there is so much that must be included in response. The prevailing characteristic of the Paris theatre during these years was its ambiguity. There is no simple truth here: It is my hope, however, that this book, fragmented as it may be, will at least demonstrate the truth's necessary complexity.

De gauche à droite : Jean Cocteau, Jean Marais, Gabrielle Dorziat
Jacques Baumer

Cartoons of Cocteau and cast (top) and of the cast in a stormy scene from
The Typewriter *(Bibliotheque Nationale de France).*

1

A Queer Premiere:
Jean Cocteau's *The Typewriter*

Introduction

Late in April 1941, toward the close of the first Parisian theatre season following the Defeat, Jean Cocteau's *La Machine à écrire* (*The Typewriter*)
opened, then closed, then reopened at the Théâtre Hébertot. Written in the
style of a detective drama, the play starred the actor generally known—at
least in the entertainment world at the time—as Cocteau's sometime lover
and perpetual companion, Jean Marais, as identical twin brothers. The reviews are curiously reticent about what exactly occurred at the Hébertot, and
historians and critics offer sometimes contradictory pieces of a puzzle that,
even when carefully put together, forms an incomplete picture.

   The fragments are, however, intriguing. Merrill Rosenberg describes
how, on the evening of April 29, 1941, the dress rehearsal (répétition génerale),
sponsored "as a gala" by the daily *Paris-Soir* and attended by various "dig-
nitaries," caused in the Hébertot's auditorium a demonstration by members of
the Parti Populaire Français (PPF). This disruption prompted Vichy's ambassador to Paris, Fernand de Brinon, to order the withdrawal of the production
("Vichy's Theatrical Venture" 136). Francis Steegmuller describes the disorder that greeted the *Typewriter* premiere and the revival of *Les Parents Terribles*
(at the Gymnase later that year): "stink bombs exploded in the theatres, and
hoodlums filled the aisles and climbed onto the stage, shouting obscenities at
Cocteau and Marais as a couple" (442).[1] Patrick Marsh too notes that these
plays "were seriously disrupted by violent scenes fomented by fascist sympathizers and members of the Parti Populaire Français" ("Le Théâtre

Français . . ." 231) and adds with regard to *The Typewriter* that "violent protests succeeded in the withdrawal of the piece from the bill" (232).[2]

Several accounts, though, entirely omit the riot and describe instead other significant aspects. Neal Oxenhandler never mentions disturbances by the PPF and/or hoodlums (in this case, one does not exclude the other) but indicates that the play "immediately after the dress rehearsal, . . . was banned" and that this ban "was the signal for the beginning of those attacks against Cocteau and Jean Marais, which reached their climax with the revival of *Les Parents Terribles*" (216). Similarly, Serge Added, in *Le Théâtre dans les années Vichy*, tells how on April 29, 1941,

> a commissioner acting on instructions from the police prefect banned the performances. The day after, the same, under instructions from the same, suspended the previous ban. In the mean time, the Propaganda Abteilung intervened to make the prefect go back on his original decision in the name of artistic freedom! Fernand de Brinon, the [Vichy] French government's ambassador to Paris, was at the origin of the ban. (43)[3]

Jean Marais, who was on stage in one of his two roles much of the time, recalls the affair differently. Not only does he fail to report an uproar in the auditorium, but he suggests that the April 29 ban came from the Germans. When Jacques Hébertot, owner of the theatre, approached the Nazis, he was told that once he had paid all the required fees, the play could run. Two days later, after some stage business, including an epileptic fit by one of the Marais twins in Act II, and some dialogue in Act III, were cut, the play reopened (134). Several reviewers remarked that the seizure was offensive, but Roger Sardou in *Les Nouveaux Temps* mentions that it "greatly affected certain spectators and caused, in the house, several different commotions."[4]

This much seems clear: After its dress rehearsal, *The Typewriter* was closed on April 29, probably by the Paris police, who were presumably acting on behalf of the Germans. Although Brinon may have instigated it, Ingrid Galster suggests that Suzanne Abetz, French wife of German ambassador Otto Abetz (who was apparently far more liberal than she), called for the ban (222)[5]; Brinon was in fact present at the opening, but so was Mme Abetz; thus, the impetus behind the suppression may have come from both, either separately or together.[6] In any case, the Germans reversed the interdiction a few days later and allowed the police to save face with the excuse that certain fees had to be paid. The censors—either Vichy's or the Germans' or both—insisted that specific passages be omitted before the reopening. There was probably some protest by the PPF, though perhaps not as violent as the brawl that would bring down the curtain midway through *Les Parents Terribles* the following autumn: Definitely there were some negative reactions to the play in the press. Nonetheless, *The Typewriter* was reinstated and ran through June 1941 (Florisoone, Cogniat, Bonnat 41).

The causes for the outcry against and for the closing and reopening of *The Typewriter* have never been adequately explored. Rosenberg asserts that the play "offered an incisive critique of the pettiness and hypocrisy of French provincial life" ("Vichy's Theatrical Venture" 136) but goes on to agree with Roger Lannes that Cocteau himself, "who epitomized the spirit of nonconformity to the French public," and not his work, was the actual object of the PPF's protests (137). Patrick Marsh implies the same, indicating that *The Typewriter* was hardly a masterpiece ("Le Théâtre à Paris . . ." 230) and that the attack launched against it by the newspaper *L'Appel* was clearly against Cocteau (232). Added quotes a letter from Cocteau (to Gaston Bâty) in which the playwright declares that he himself was the cause of the ban, not the play; this declaration confirms the conclusion that the suppression was due to the author's identity and behavior rather than to his script (43). For the most part, historians who have examined the period concur that the author was the actual object of censure, and with few exceptions, literary critics seem to share Oxenhandler's view that the script is a failure (216–220).

To present-day readers, the hostile response to *The Typewriter* may appear typical of the repression of artistic freedom that might be expected during the German Occupation. Modern sensibilities easily envision the entire episode in a way that follows a stock scenario: The nonconformist, homosexual dramatist, whose play was promoted by a French newspaper, is ostracized and censured by collaborators and the Nazis (who we know imprisoned and murdered male German homosexuals). However, such a rendering is very far from the truth.

This chapter examines the dramatic, theatre, and audience texts of *The Typewriter* in light of those years in which the play was originally performed. Written toward the end of the drôle de guerre (or "phoney war"), as Cocteau and hundreds of thousands fled the German advance, and staged near the end of the Occupation's first season, *The Typewriter* occupies a significant time and space—a unique moment when diverse cultural and political forces came together and clashed. This chapter explores why and how the events described above—the Hébertot "riot," the withdrawal of the play and its reinstatement—occurred, and goes on to propose, contrary to those who have previously examined the dramatic text, that the playscript around which these events swirled was neither the meaningless potboiler that many have called it nor the "incisive critique . . . of French provincial life" that Rosenberg suggests it was; *The Typewriter* was the actual site of the dispute to which it has previously been only incidentally linked. The play was not merely theatre scripted by a homosexual but an expression of its author's subculture; to some degree, *The Typewriter*, in spite of its attempts to resemble a conventional piece, was (wittingly or unwittingly) perceived as a discernible expression of contemporary homosexual sensibility.

The Typewriter may be, as Jacques Guicharnaud contends, "generally considered [Cocteau's] worst play and one that he himself repudiated" (63), but its role in its own prohibition and restoration was hardly irrelevant. Indeed, the puzzle piece that has always been missing from the broad picture has been the one containing the play itself.

Paradoxical Politics, Newspapers, Plays

Readers unfamiliar with the political climate of Occupied Paris may have little notion of its heterogeneity. Of course, only right-wing and for the most part extreme right-wing politics played out publicly, but even among this bloc, one might encounter diversity. The idea that the government at Vichy was a solid front was a myth; indeed, throughout his remarkable study, *Vichy France: Old Guard and New Order, 1940–1944*, Robert O. Paxton documents how, in spite of a desire to appear a monolithic corporatist entity, the Vichy regime was a hotbed of disagreement and that, even with Pétain as ongoing Head of State, the government changed a number of times. In Paris, too, various factions among the ruling Germans, including the SS, the embassy, and the army's various departments, all vied for control, and each competed in courting various political and other groups within the former capital.

Vichy France, strictly speaking, was not genuinely fascist in itself; Roger Griffen calls it *Ersatz* fascist or parafascist. Griffen observes, "although the façade of national regeneration was maintained, the State, as the representative of the interests of the traditional ruling hierarchy, repressed rather than encouraged those aspects of fascism which it rightly saw as threatening to its interests." Both Franco's Spain and Vichy France managed to co-opt or marginalize fascism. Such regimes "aped some of the superficial aspects of the Fascist and Nazi apparatus and style of power" (19). The Pétain regime's traditionalism lacked the aggressive, dynamic approach evident in Italian and German movements. Although Vichy spoke of a New France, the idea of an actual fascist revolution, the notion of which had been established by Mussolini and imitated by Hitler, was clearly perceived as "threatening to its interests."

Caught between the Nazi occupiers and the Vichy French, both unstable vectors of power, people constantly wondered how to reconcile their ideas of France with its current dilemma. To be genuinely French—always an implicit and sometimes the explicit subject of most of the plays performed during this period—might mean being in favor of De Gaulle and the Free French in London, but, especially during the first year of the Occupation, it more than likely meant being for Pétain, which was not necessarily the same as being pro-Vichy. One could define oneself politically as pro-Vichy and anti-German, pro-Vichy and pro-German, pro-Pétain and anti-Vichy, pro-German and anti-Vichy, even pro-Gaullist and pro-Pétain (though probably, in this case, anti-Vichy and almost certainly anti-German). And one's self-definition probably changed over the period.

The Parti Populaire Français, whose members have been accused of disrupting the first performance of *The Typewriter*, nicely illustrates how such confusions over national and political identity played out. The PPF was created by Jacques Doriot, who before the War had been Communist mayor of Saint-Denis, the working-class suburb to the north of Paris, and who eventually fought with and was then expelled from the Party. "In the elections of 1936," writes Alfred Cobban, "he managed to hold his fiefdom of Saint-Denis against his former party, in rivalry with which he founded the Parti Populaire Français" (151). Doriot was impressed with Hitler, and as the 1930s advanced, the PPF veered further right and became progressively more anti-communist. Following the Defeat, Bertram M. Gordon recalls, the PPF was "[t]he most active and probably the largest of the collaborationist parties" (10). Paxton estimates that it had "300,000 members, 4,000 of them active, in 1941" and received its funding from Germany's Ambassador to Paris, Otto Abetz (253).

Paxton further notes how the PPF, while nominally loyal to Pétain, was distrusted by the Vichy government, which Doriot (and other French fascists) criticized for its traditionalism and disinterest in the fascist revolution. Vichyites Pierre Laval and François Darlan convinced Doriot's Nazi backer, Abetz, to keep Doriot from "becoming an alternate German candidate for [French] prime minister," but the Nazis refused to shut down the PPF, and there were even "active centers of PPF activity in the Vichy Zone" (253). The PPF pursued its own program, often distinct from Vichy's and the Nazis,' and it was, as Gordon points out, "[o]nly with the attack on the Soviet Union" by Germany on June 22, 1941, that the PPF became "a vigorous partisan of collaboration" (11).[7] Thus, on April 29, 1941, almost two months before the German assault on Russia, the PPF toughs who broke up the theatre gala sponsored by *Paris-Soir* considered themselves members of a fascist revolutionary front, positioned separately from other French fascists and the Nazis.

The collaborationist press was similarly heterogeneous: The daily that sponsored Cocteau's gala, *Paris-Soir*, though published in Paris before the war, had closed after the Defeat and was then, as Donna Evleth puts it, "relaunched by the Germans." Evleth adds that "the 'real' *Paris-Soir* . . . retreated to the south zone" along with the *Le Figaro*, *Les Temps*, and a few other Paris papers. Some of these, like *Le Figaro*, "suspended publication when the Germans occupied the south zone" in 1942 (193). The Occupiers,

Galster explains, used the press, in part, to reassure French readers that nothing had changed, and thus, rather than starting new periodicals (which they did to a limited extent), favored the reappearance of newspapers that existed before the armistice, although in such cases, and Galster mentions specifically *Paris-Soir*, the only thing preserved was the paper's name (94). As for the contents of Paris newspapers, Marsh summarizes:

> Virtually all news, both foreign and domestic, was filtered through the Agence Française d'Information, which was organized and came under the control of the Propagandastaffel. Newspapers were subject to the Propagandastaffel not only for what they published, but also for such details as the lay-out of the paper, the number of columns per page and even the characters to be used. Thus newspapers were completely controlled throughout the war, both at source and distribution levels.

Reopened by the Germans on June 22, 1940 (the day the armistice was signed), the new *Paris-Soir*, Marsh observes, was one of several reborn papers that "supported Pétain's government" ("The Theatre: Collaboration or Compromise?" 155), but as noted above, loyalty to Pétain did not always mean loyalty to Vichy.

A less easily revived paper from before the war was Robert Brasillach's *Je suis partout*, which Evleth characterizes as "anti-Semitic but intellectual" and which, she notes, Robert Brasillach, who would be executed after the war for collaboration, edited until 1943 (193). This weekly had articulated its ultra-rightist views beginning in the 1930s, and it was closed down as France entered the War. Despite its blatantly fascist voice, it had not been allowed to reopen until February 1941, at which time Alain Laubreaux resumed his post as theatre critic (and, as such, came to play a leading role in the events surrounding *The Typewriter*).[8] According to Marsh, Laubreaux, who also wrote for *Le Cri du Peuple* and *Le Petit Parisien* (both run by the PPF's Doriot), "was an arch-collaborator, and wrote reviews which were often vindictive, frequently unfair, violently anti-Semitic and wildly prejudiced—nevertheless he must be regarded as one of the most influential drama critics of the war" ("The Theatre . . ." 155).

There were, as Galster notes, other smaller political–literary weeklies founded by other factions, such as the pro-Vichy *L'Appel*, representing the Ligue Française (97), but few were as successful as *La Gerbe*, funded by Ambassador Abetz (96) and thus, Marsh indicates, "hostile to Pétain and Vichy" under the directorship of "Alphonse de Chateaubriant, a fervent Nazi, a champion of collaboration and admirer of Hitler" ("The Theatre . . ." 155). "While the majority of political articles and editorials in *La Gerbe* suggest that the review was little more than a crude propaganda sheet plugging the Nazi line," observes Richard J. Golsan, "Chateaubriant's own ambitions for the journal were much more grandiose. . . . *La Gerbe* would seek an 'armistice de l'esprit' to match the military armistice signed by Pétain" (31). Its regular drama critic, André Castelot (brother of the actor, Jacques, who would eventually appear in *La Princesse des Ursins*), had a well-earned reputation for nastiness.

Perhaps the example of *Comœdia*, an arts weekly that had existed before the Defeat and was subsequently "relaunched," best illustrates how all publications, no matter what their political orientation or purpose, were in some way controlled by and supportive of the occupiers and their French adherents: The paper, Herbert Lottman affirms, attracted some of the best minds in France, much as the *Nouvelle Revue Française* had done before the War, and appeared to be apolitical. To some, this weekly, which limited itself to cultural matters, seemed neutral, but others sensed in its coverage of the arts across (German-occupied) Europe a strong measure of Nazi propaganda. Yet the most effective role that *Comœdia* performed for the Germans was, as Lottman puts it, presenting the arts world "as if cultural life could be carried on as usual on streets patrolled by Hitler's army" (163–164). Even as *Comœdia* was viewed as being "different" from publications directly funded by Abetz or by a French fascist party, the paper inevitably served a double purpose.

Like the press, the theatre was co-opted by the occupiers. Although in January 1945 a few foreign visitors, such as Philip Toynbee, might believe that "[t]he Germans appear to have interfered very little with the freedom of the Paris stage, and there has been a varied and fertile dramatic activity" (156), the theatre in occupied Paris came very much under the control of the Germans, who, as Leo Forkey points out, "not only allowed the theatres to reopen, but encouraged them as an integral part of their program to make Paris a recreation center, and France an agrarian state" ("Theatres of Paris" 299). Little by little, Hervé Le Boterf recalls, beginning slowly in July and August, and then more rapidly through the fall of 1940 and into the winter of 1941, established theatres reopened and new playhouses, such as the Monceau, Edward VII, and Avenue (formerly cinemas) and the Noctambules (formerly a cabaret) opened their doors (166). "At the end of 1940," Marsh specifies, "thirty-four theatres, fourteen music-halls, two circuses . . . , six cabarets and about thirty cinemas were open" ("The Theatre . . ." 144).

Yet what Toynbee calls "varied and fertile dramatic activity" was hardly apparent during this first year of theatre when, as Le Boterf indicates, revivals outnumbered new plays seventy-five to thirty-five (169); Le Boterf calls the 1940–1941 season "Le Temps des 'Réprises' " (174–179). Rosenberg adds that "[o]nly one theater, the Hébertot [where *The Typewriter* would eventually open], presented the work of an unpublished author as its initial production. Together with this play, Jean Anouilh's *Léocadia* and Sacha Guitry's *Le Bien-Aimé* were the only new plays put on in Paris during the last six months of 1940" ("Vichy's Theatrical Venture" 131). Just a few of the new works of the second half of the season stood out, such as Jean Anouilh's *Le Rendez-vous de Senlis* (written before the war), Stève Passeur's *Marché noir*, and Cocteau's *The Typewriter*.

Part of the control exercised by the Germans came in the form of direct censorship. Marsh describes how, for productions at private theatres in Paris, playscripts "were first read by the Vichy censor and then sent on to the German censor at the Propagandastaffel," all texts having been submitted "well in advance so that the authorities would have ample time to give their decision about the suitability of any particular work" ("The Theatre . . ." 149). Vichy retained control over state-run theatres, the Comédie-Française, Odéon, Opéra Comique, and Théâtre National Populaire although, here too, the occupiers had more than a little influence. Initially, Rosenberg tells us, "The Germans appointed Roger Capgras, husband of Alice Cocéa (manager of the Théâtre des Ambassadeurs), as liaison between themselves and the [private] theaters," but his fascist sympathies prompted his replacement by three respected stage directors, Charles Dullin, Pierre Renoir, and Gaston Bâty in January 1941 ("Vichy's Theatrical Venture" 129).

While Added observes that censorship was central to the theatrical project of the Vichy government (37), which he capably illustrates subsidized many of the private theatres and private productions (his table, "Subventions des Beaux-Arts au théâtre dramatique," specifies the extent and amounts: 82–83), he also provides instances (among them the reinstatement of *The Typewriter*) when the power of the Nazis' censors superseded that of Vichy's. Added concludes that no matter how fervently Brinon might assure Dr. Karl Epting (director of the German Institute and Abetz's cultural attaché) that Cocteau's work was contrary to their efforts toward the regeneration of the youth and art that must come with collaboration, the Germans were clearly not interested in Brinon's program (43).

In fact, the Germans seem to have been interested in achieving the direct opposite of Brinon's goals—in promoting the complete degeneration of French youth and art. The collaboration that the armistice demanded applied to the French (whose institutions—their government, presses, playhouses—had been co-opted) and not to the Germans, who followed a very different course in France than in the Fatherland.

Gay Paris Under the Germans

On June 18, 1941, educator and writer Jean Guéhenno noted in his diary:

> Sociological problem: why so many pederasts among the collaborators? C . . . , F . . . , M . . . , D . . . (who, as they say, likes to go both ways). Are they waiting for the new order to legitimatize their loves?[9]

This observation, made while *The Typewriter* was still playing at the Hébertot, offers a clue to one of the ways through which the Nazis pursued their program of degeneration in Paris.

Yet, in describing this phenomenon, I am obliged to differentiate it from previous discussions that have sought to conflate homosexuality and fascism. As Andrew Hewitt demonstrates in his analysis of reactions to works by Jean Genet, in postwar politics, "the linkage [between homosexuality and fascism] permeates a popular culture that has long understood decadence as effeminization and effeminization as homosexuality" ("Sleeping with the Enemy" 119). As I note later in this chapter, condemnation of the enemy as homosexual and vice versa was never limited to the Nazis and their sympathizers; in liberated France, the Left as well as the Right were capable of seeing the invert as culprit and the culprit as invert, as Jean-Paul Sartre's famous post-war essay, "Qu'est-ce que c'est un Collaborateur?" makes clear. Yet Guéhenno's remark, written a year into the Occupation, seems to be asking something else, not why all collaborators were homosexual but why, astonishingly, there were any homosexuals among those who collaborated. And Guéhenno's surprise is understandable in light of the Nazi's very public hatred of "pederasts."[10]

In spite—and, ironically, because—of the Germans' well known abhorrence of inverts within the Reich, homosexuals in what remained as France were neither legally penalized nor rounded up by the Germans. "Nazi-occupied Europe was largely to escape this homophobic persecution," writes Antony Copley (153).[11] Heinrich Himmler, head of the SS and, as George L. Mosse in *Nationalism and Sexuality* explains, the most outspoken Nazi leader for the "extinction [*Auslöschung*] of abnormal life" (169), was himself responsible for this peculiar policy of acceptance:

> Himmler argued that Germany's interests lay in encouraging the degenerating consequences of homosexuality amongst the subject peoples, hence accelerating their decline. Homosexuals in [occupied] France had more to fear from homophobia within. (Copley 153)

Summing up an address to the SS leadership at Bad Tölz in November 1937, Mosse points out Himmler's belief that "[t]he conspiracy of homosexuals must be viewed side by side with the world Jewish conspiracy" for the two were "bent on destroying the German state and race as the implacable enemies of German virtue and will" (168). Thus, Himmler's reasoning in permitting homosexuality outside Germany, as bizarre as it may seem today, perhaps made perfect sense to his fellow Nazis: This policy would allow the "slave nations," to the benefit of the Reich, to destroy themselves from within.[12] In the Reich, homosexuals were placed in concentration camps and eventually exterminated;

in what Nazi Germany regarded as France, they were tolerated and in some cases even recruited.

Of course, in those parts of France that were incorporated into the greater Reich, homosexuality was viewed quite differently. The awful history of Pierre Seel illustrates how in Alsace those suspected of homosexuality were imprisoned and murdered. Yet Seel's chilling description of being summoned to the Gestapo and his ensuing confinement, remind the reader that he, like all in Alsace and in other areas directly appropriated by the Germans, was regarded as German, not French; in Germany being a homosexual remained a crime.

In Paris, however, the Nazis found a subculture of homosexual men who might be of use to the Reich's master plan, for from the beginnings of modern times, homosexuality had always had a strong presence in the metropolis. Unlike Germany, Austria, and England, where homosexual acts had remained outlawed, homosexuality was legal in France: The Code Napoléon did not criminalize such acts except, writes Robert A. Nye in *Masculinity and Male Codes of Honor in Modern France*, for "forcible rape, child molestation, and 'outrage' " (108). Yet during the first three-quarters of the nineteenth century, despite the liberalized laws, the Paris police relentlessly sought and harassed men for practicing various forms of homosexual behavior.

Although, as Copley describes how, with the advent of the Third Republic, medical researchers in France, as in other European countries, began to regard homosexuality as a pathological problem (135ff), the Paris police persisted in their "crackdown . . . on offenses against public decency, with consequent court appearance for men of all ages and all backgrounds" (147). In other words, Nye clarifies, the police were able to use what the Code called "public outrage" in order to criminalize and punish what were ostensibly legal but immoral acts (168). Even after the First World War, with the translation of Freud into French (Copley 149) and the widespread belief that homosexuality ought to be treated psychiatrically, the culture continued to regard inversion as shameful, and the police went on with their arrests. Thus, in spite of an apparent legalized permissiveness, the prevailing atmosphere in Paris through the end of the 1930s remained, at least for males, somewhat repressive. Formally, homosexuality might not have been a crime, but homosexual behavior had become criminalized.

Nevertheless, a large part of this repression was cultural rather than legal and focused on issues related to gender and gender roles. To be thought of as being capable of performing homosexual acts meant being thought of as *a* homosexual: as Nye puts it, "a *behavior* was converted to an *identity*" (102). Hence, the male who discreetly engaged in sexual acts with other males, had "little need to fear direct police intervention in his private life"; however, even the most wary of men "had much more to fear . . . from the judgments of his fellow citizens about the *quality* of his masculinity" (107). George Chauncey, in his study of gay[13] male sexual identity in New York City, explores a similar contemporary phenomenon. He is able to discern analogous cultural attitudes toward males whose effeminacy labeled them as homosexual and males who, in spite of their sexual attraction to other males, because of their lack of effeminacy, were viewed as "normal" (65–97). "Only in the 1930s, 1940s, and 1950s," asserts Chauncey, "did the now-conventional division of men into 'homosexuals' and 'heterosexuals,' based on the sex of their sexual partners, replace the division of men into 'fairies' and 'normal men' on the basis of their imaginary gender status . . ." (13). Chauncey also offers evidence that men who performed sexual acts both with women and other males were identified (and identified themselves) not as homosexual but as "normal" "so long as they played the 'man's part' [the dominant role] with both" (119). Thus, in this period of transition, not just one's partner but one's "role" in the sexual act and one's social behavior were key elements in determining one's sexual identity.

Such distinctions had considerable influence on popular and private views of homosexuality in France. Indeed, the whole problematic notion of "the man's role," that social construct culturally assumed to incorporate maleness, lurked (and perhaps still lurks) behind every discussion of homosexuality. To speak broadly, homosexuality in France remained a threat to what had come (or what was coming) to constitute masculinity. Therefore, those who had been designated through their actions as "homosexual" were subjected to some of the culture's more repressive measures and were in this sense criminalized.

Of course, "repressive" must be admitted as a relative term. There had always been, in spite of cultural and other prohibitions, a lavender underground or demi-monde in Paris. True, in the 1920s Berlin was regarded as the gay capital of Europe. "For a brief moment in 1929," writes Klaus Müller, "the burgeoning gay and lesbian movement even seemed likely to abolish" the German anti-homosexual laws; "[a] parliamentary commission that was rewriting the nation's moral code voted to drop the anti-sodomy statute" (9). During the Weimar Republic, homosexual men and women made a major assault on the legal and cultural restrictions against them, and generally, in spite of the existing legal restrictions, the atmosphere in Berlin was more tolerant than in Paris.

However, after Hitler's ascent, Magnus Hirshfeld's Institute for Sexual Research and his efforts to repeal the sodomy laws came to a halt. After the Nazi takeover in 1933, recounts Copley, Ernst Röhm, commander of the SA and himself a known homosexual, unleashed his "stormtroopers—ironically themselves to become victims of the same homophobic campaign— . . . on the gay community." While any evidence of homosexual behavior was now highly punishable in Germany ("a lewd glance would do," notes Copley) and men labeled homosexuals were cruelly hunted down and detained (153), France, where the legal system and moral attitudes remained the same, now seemed less repressive to homosexuals, in the same way that it suddenly seemed more tolerant to Jews. After the Defeat, of course, Jews born in France and foreign Jews who had fled there would find a change of policy, but French homosexuals might discover a mixed though not always unwelcoming reception in the City of Light.

Vichy, which stood for traditionalist values, the family, and motherhood, was hostile to homosexuality. Statutes passed in 1941 restricted homosexual behavior (Nye 106). In August 1942, the regime would pass the first legislation since the Code Napoléon (which, as specified earlier, already punished the corruption of children) to deal explicitly with the punishment of such behavior. "This related," explains Copley, "to 'les délits d'excitation habituelle de mineurs à la débauche' " and referred to seductions (by males or females) of a minor between fifteen and twenty-one years of age; "it made no difference," Copley adds, "if both partners were under age" (203).[14] There is, nonetheless, a certain irony here, for the Vichy Minister of Education (1942–1944), Abel Bonnard, was well known to be a homosexual. Moreover, whenever they could, French (and German) fascists were eager to claim celebrity supporters, even "maverick" novelist Henry de Montherlant, whose clandestine but untiring penchant for cruising pre-adolescent boys during the Occupation would play an important role in his new career as playwright. (My analysis of his play, *Fils de Personne* [*Nobody's Son*], follows in chapter 7.)

Yet what is significant here is not so much the Vichy government's hypocrisy, which was pervasive and remains well documented, but the need of this weakening regime to delimit in its own way that which it perceived to be a danger and offense. On the surface, the Vichy decrees may seem rather feeble in comparison with the Nazis' approach to controlling homosexuality in Germany through mass imprisonment and murder, but the laws' invidiousness clearly lies in their statutory differentiation of the homosexual and lesbian from others in society and in their characterization and outlawing of specific acts and practices that were already prohibited socially. In spite of their apparent limitations, the decrees mark an attempt to legitimize cultural prejudices that had not since the French Revolution carried genuine legal weight.

The Vichy decrees seem to have come partially in response to the apparent flourishing of homosexuality in German-occupied Paris. Although there has yet to be a full-length study on gay Paris under the Occupation, some of its shadow may be glimpsed. Edmund White's masterful *Genet: A Biography*, written from an openly gay point of view, presents a wealth of detail about the homosexual demi-monde in Paris during the War. A world of nightclubs and clandestine pick-ups, with a select pornographic book trade among gentlemen with money and a steady traffic in male prostitution; an urban arts center of discrete cafes, bars, and clubs; a place where homosexual men held positions across society, including in the government, police force, and judicial system—occupied Paris witnessed not merely the sort of collaboration to which Guéhenno refers but in some cases (as in Genet's) to a literal coupling with the enemy.[15]

In White's cityscape, there lurk gay fascist sympathizers and traitors: Maurice Sachs, the half-Jewish poet who had converted to Catholicism with Cocteau and after the Defeat "sided with the Nazis and was then killed by them," (266)[16] is notable. Indeed, Sachs himself has left "Suite au sabbat," an uncompleted memoir featuring glimpses of the gay underworld just after the Defeat. In addition, there were homosexual men whose association with Dr. Epting's German Institute and other cultural organizations would later be viewed as collaborationist, such as Montherlant, Marcel Jouhandeau, and Cocteau himself (176). André Gide, a longtime progressive thinker on homosexuality, was in the Free Zone when France fell and eventually left for North Africa. Daniel Guérin, who would become a gay activist, though in Paris during the Occupation, would not begin to address the topic seriously until after the War.[17] White's sketches of occupied Paris, however, do not focus clearly on 1940–1941 for two crucial reasons: First, much of the first year of the Occupation Genet spent not at large in Paris but in jail; and second, although Genet's relationship with Cocteau (who opened the doors for him into the noncriminal, literary–artistic homosexual world) began during the Occupation, they did not meet until 1943, well after the curtain had come down on *The Typewriter*.

The relative freedom with which homosexual males moved through Paris seems perhaps no greater than before the War, but in many significant ways it does not appear to have been very much less. Yet the very survival in Paris of a gay subculture—as Michael Bronski defines it, a "group excluded from the dominant culture" whose "outsider status allows the development of a distinct culture based upon the very characteristics which separate the group from the mainstream" (7)—was not just an offense to Vichy, which postured moral righteousness no matter what its proponents did on the sly, but, more important, an outright affront to French collaborationists in Paris, like Doriot and some of the ultra-rightist journalists who would attack *The Typewriter*. After all, the PPF and other radical fascists had modeled themselves on the Nazis; they had already eagerly begun promoting the occupiers' hatred for the Jews (with which they had no quarrel), and they were no doubt distressed and annoyed that the Germans, who so energetically punished homosexuals within their own borders, should allow these degenerates such liberty in Paris.

Marais versus Laubreaux

Jean Marais appears frequently in the sections of *Genet: A Biography* that
deal with the Occupation: Marais's lover (whom Cocteau allowed to move in
with Marais and himself) around the time *The Typewriter* opened, was water-
polo player Paul Morihien, who would become the publisher of the first
edition of Genet's *Notre Dame des fleurs* (*Our Lady of the Flowers*) (204; the
book was originally printed in a limited edition and clandestinely distributed
during the Occupation). Moreover, Marais's relationship with Cocteau ensured that Jeannot (as Cocteau called him) would frequently meet and sometimes even come to the rescue of Genet.[18] Although Marais's gay life in
occupied Paris is perhaps more discernible in White's 1993 book than in the
actor's own *Histoires de ma vie*, published in 1975, Marais chronicles in
detail an incident precipitated by the closing and reopening of *The Typewriter,*
which illuminates how, in the juxtaposition of Nazi Paris and Pétainist Vichy,
frictions generated by various rival forces within French culture caused sparks
to ignite and, if only momentarily, burst into flame.

Marais narrates the incident, which has been described by various historians and critics and (as noted in this book's epilogue) was fictionalized and
transposed to François Truffaut's 1980 *The Last Métro*, as follows:

> A few days before opening night [of *The Typewriter* . . .], a journal-
> ist from *Le Petit Parisien* informed me that Alain Laubreaux, critic
> for both that paper and *Je Suis Partout* and a veritable *Führer* of
> dramatic literature, was getting ready to "tear Cocteau to pieces."
>
> "He hasn't seen or read the play," I said.
>
> ". . . [J]ust the same, his mind is made up."
>
> "Well, you can tell Laubreaux that if he goes through with it, I'll
> bash his face in."
>
> . . . . The day after the dress rehearsal—which for once had gone
> without incident—the production was banned. Hébertot went off to
> the Germans and pointed out the inconsistency of their ban. . . .
>
> Two days later, the performances were allowed on condition
> that we suppress the epileptic fit at the end of the second act. The
> Germans were trying to save face.
>
> Alain Laubreaux didn't show up. Nonetheless, what a vicious
> review! Not content with tearing the play and actors to shreds, he
> indulged in vile attacks both on Cocteau's writing and on his private
> life. I was obliged to live up to my word: whatever the price, I had
> to strike.
>
> . . . We dined every night after the show at a little restaurant
> nearby. . . .   . . . I was having supper with Cocteau and Michèle Alfa

when I was advised that Hébertot wanted to see me. . . . I went up. . . . At first I didn't see a thing. In the glimmer of the lightning bolts, I recognized Hébertot's bald skull. I held out my hand to him. . . . [t]hen someone else, to whom I introduced myself. He didn't give his name. Hébertot said to me "That's Alain Laubreaux.". . . .

"If it is, I'll spit in his face. Sir, are you Alain Laubreaux?". . . .

He said yes. And I spit. He got up. I thought he wanted to fight.

The little restaurateur, who had followed me, separated us: "Not in my restaurant!. . . ."

I went down the stairs. . . .

"Laubreaux is with the Gestapo," Jean said to me. "We'll be shot."

"This is not your affair," I answered. . . .

. . . . At last I see [Laubreaux], followed by Hébertot. . . . I follow them.

Laubreaux has a big square cane. I grab it from him. If I use the cane on him, I run the risk of killing him. I toss the cane. . . . I attack Laubreaux with my fists. He falls. His brow is cut open. He screams, "Help! Police!" I can't take any credit; he didn't defend himself. And I continue to pummel him, in time with my cries, rhythmically: "And Jean-Louis Barrault? What did he ever do to you? And Berthau? And Bourdet?"

In my crazed litany, I invoke all his victims. ("Confronting a Critic" 182–184)

I quote this at length to present the story as told by its protagonist. According to Marais, this incident was widely known within the theatre community, and indeed there have been a number of retellings of what occurred, some predating Marais's version, others (including Truffaut's in *The Last Métro*) postdating it. Marais's anecdote is particularly theatrical, its narrator cast in a role as masculine as any he would play on stage or screen; his swagger and devil-may-care heroics accompany his manly, if somewhat showy, efforts to avenge the critic who sought to ruin Cocteau and other thespians.

Nonetheless, as Marais indicates, Laubreaux's attacks and some of those by others against *The Typewriter* appeared to be more personal than theatrical. Although his first review (in *Le Petit Parisien*, 3 May 1941) was negative, it is relatively polite, even as it damned Cocteau's dramaturgy and Marais's acting ability. Another reviewer, writing in *L'Appel* (8 May 1941), was more pointedly vicious, calling the dramatist "a notorious invert; seeking his inspiration (?) in opium and other illegal drugs. Mr. Jean Cocteau is nothing less than that," and adding that Cocteau's genius derived from acclaim of the prewar elite (Rosenberg, "The French Theatre" 168).[19] If only by contrast, Laubreaux's initial notice was almost decorous.

Although Laubreaux was not only the drama critic for two dailies, *Le Petit Parisien* and *Le Cri du Peuple*, but also for *Je suis partout*, Lucien Rebatet (writing as François Vinneuil) was first to review *The Typewriter* for the weekly (12 May 1941). Again, the attack against Cocteau was made on a personal level, though Rebatet's charges are more skillfully extended to the play itself:

> *The Typewriter* is the same type of inverted theatre. . . . It is too easy to see at its center the same watermark of physical and intellectual perversions in which its author does not cease to contort himself. (9; 21)[20]

Laubreaux's second review of the play, which appeared in the next issue of *Je suis partout* (19 May 1941), includes the same gay bashing but adds an ample helping of anti-Semitism and accuses the play's director, Raymond Roulleau, of being "a purveyor of pornography" (9). Laubreaux even went on in a later issue to defend Rebatet's and his own reviews and to abuse Cocteau again.

Thus, the sort of ruination Laubreaux and others had in mind was to defame Cocteau by provoking, as Nye puts it, "the judgments of his fellow citizens about the *quality* of his masculinity" (107). Marais, of course, would have been guilty by association. His assault and battery of the critic dramatizes another question, one that had perhaps become every bit as urgent by the spring of 1941 as the question, What does it mean to be French? Indeed, Marais's behavior asks, in its own belligerent way, What does it mean to be a French*man*? Although different playwrights would respond to this question in different ways, Marais, who was an actor, could only act out his answer. The melodramatic nature of the vignette takes for granted the machismo Marais felt it necessary to deploy in order to contradict the critic: In his own telling of the incident, Marais emasculates Laubreaux by first taking, then disposing of his cane, and then wounding him and exacting revenge, first physically, then psychically.

Up to now, Marais had been assured protection from such personal criticisms through that cultural system that had identified him not so much by his choice of sexual partners—Cocteau, Morihien, and others—but by his sexual role and social (as well as stage) presentation of himself. Marais's close friend, former lover, and patron, was generally perceived not just as a flaming aesthete but as an effeminate, and as Steegmuller acknowledges, "the nature of [Cocteau's] sexuality was always well known to be passive" (18). Thus far, Marais's sexuality had escaped public scrutiny. Now, with his film career poised for success, Jeannot needed to maintain the identity of a handsome young man who was attractive (and attracted) to females. While the attack may appear to have its basis in the politics of culture, economics seems to have been a cause as well. The power of the collabo press did not harm Marais the movie star: Cocteau complains throughout his wartime journal how teenage girls relentlessly follow Marais on the street and wait for him outside their apartment in the Palais Royal.[21]

This issue of masculinity was important not just to Marais, who perhaps felt obliged to demonstrate his manhood, but to Laubreaux, who belonged to an ultra-conservative elite that had in fact, either consciously or unconsciously, displayed a penchant for the homoerotic while at the same time maintaining a fierce homophobia. Mosse detects such a trend in the writings of collaborator and homophobe Drieu La Rochelle, in which the pursuit of love and praise of war "were accompanied by consciousness of the beauty and strength of the male body." Drieu's work, Mosse surmises, "was the written equivalent of the nude statues that guarded Nazi buildings [such as Arno Breker's male nudes flanking Hitler's Chancellery] . . . ; but here [in Drieu's writings] the male eros remained intact" (175). At the same time, Drieu "lumped homosexuals together with Jews as creatures of the city, unhealthy and rootless." Reviewing the works of Montherlant and Robert Brasillach along with those of Drieu, Mosse concludes, "French fascism almost flaunted homoerotic, if not homosexual, attitudes that other fascisms sought to suppress. Here the consequences Himmler wanted to abort seemed to emerge into the light of day" (176). Perhaps the real difference may have been that in Germany much fascist art took a graphic and plastic form, whereas in France it was almost exclusively literary.[22] Only to the extent that linguistic representation could be more explicit than painting or sculpture, then, can the homoerotic be seen as being "flaunted."

At the same time, "Any discussion of fascism and sexuality," notes Mosse, "must always return to the worship of masculinity and to the community of men as the ruling élite" (176). The masculinity that fascist Frenchmen had been "celebrating," was, at least in part, an expression of what Eve Kosofsky Sedgewick has called "homosocial desire," which refers to "social bonds between persons of the same sex" (1). Sedgewick, in discussing "homosocial desire," hypothesizes about "the potential unbrokenness of a continuum between homosocial and homosexual—a continuum whose visibility, for men, in our society, is radically disrupted" (1–2). For French fascists, then, whose control over Paris was mocked daily by the very presence of the Germans (who had brought the French fascists to prominence), the pervasiveness and tolerance of male homosexuality made evident a major link between two points that for them were supposed not to be connected at all—the worship of masculinity and homoeroticism. Thus, that men (or, as the ultra-rightists might have put it, males) such as Cocteau and Marais were left to do as they pleased, posed a bitter reminder that, despite all their collaborative efforts, the French fascists had been effeminized by those whom they would have liked to think of as their German allies. Freud hypothesized what later experiments seem to have shown to be true, that extreme homophobia is manifested by men who are themselves aroused by homosexual thoughts; in such instances the denial of same-sex attraction becomes all the more vehement and violent.

Unfortunately, hatred of homosexuals was never the exclusive franchise of the fascists. While homosexuals were rounded up by the Germans, "antifascists attempted," writes Mosse, "to prove that the homosexuality of Ernst Röhm had infected the whole [Nazi] movement" (186). Heger explains how "[d]uring the 1930s and 1940s, homophobia would become one of the most frequently used tools of both Nazi and Stalinist propaganda to portray the other side as morally degenerate" and that "[p]ostwar films about the Nazi regime often included these homophobic posturings without challenging them" (10). Copley looks skeptically at Jean-Paul Sartre's "description of the sexual opportunities opened for his character, Daniel, in *Les Chemins de la Liberté*, by the presence of German troops" (203); but after the Liberation some would see, in the real or alleged willingness of some homosexuals during the war to collaborate, a reason not to repeal Vichy's anti-gay laws. Ironically, even though Marais was maligned by Vichy and the French fascists, he was also denied entrance into an actor's unit of the Résistance because, as one of its members, Louis Jourdan, later put it, "Cocteau talks too much" (Steegmuller 445), an idea that Marais himself had uttered to Cocteau (Cocteau, *Journal* 551).

Lottman, chronicling the intellectual life on the Left Bank in the 1930s and 1940s, adds an interesting twist to Marais's clash with the press:

> When Cocteau complained to his German friends about the attacks on him in *Je Suis Partout*, they replied, "It's the French who are attacking you; you're not liked by your colleagues." Marais physically assaulted the distasteful collaborationist critic Alain Laubreaux and was saved from arrest, it is said, by a phone call from Cocteau to Breker—the German had given his private number to Cocteau for just such an emergency. (169)

Although Marais never refers to any help from Breker, Cocteau had been a friend of the sculptor since the 1920s and would continue as one throughout the Occupation and after. His recurrent mention of the gratitude he owed Breker, who performed a number of services on his behalf (some of them to benefit Marais), has led the editor of Cocteau's wartime journals to infer that the sculptor may indeed have been responsible for quelling Laubreaux's efforts against Marais (112n). This may help explain Cocteau's loyalty to Breker, for whose May 1942 opening at the Orangerie Cocteau composed a highly flattering address, which was later published and which in part prompted many to charge Cocteau with collaboration. Whether or not the phone call that Lottman mentions ever occurred, such an event is credible and could easily have taken place.

The curious cultural links and ruptures between fascist aesthetics and homoeroticism are further examined in chapter 2. The question remaining here, however, regards Cocteau as a person and an author. Exactly who was Jean Cocteau, or perhaps more significantly for this study, who was Jean Cocteau during the German Occupation of Paris? During the four years that followed the Defeat, the Cocteau who seemed to embody so much of Vichy's enmity and who would bear the burden of so many fascist French attacks, became, despite his increasing time in the public eye, ever more elusive.

Cocteau in Occupied Paris

In addition to being a poet, novelist, screenwriter and director, artist, painter, and designer, Jean Cocteau (1889–1963) was a dramatist of some repute. Of all the arts in which he worked, the theatre perhaps came most naturally to him. On the claustrophobic and often treacherous social stage of the Occupation, he managed to transform his vast social circle into a cast who supported him through the War. As a widely known homosexual trapped in a "situation limite," Cocteau played to whatever part of the audience might best appreciate him, no matter who might be seated in that section of the house.

Although a biographical sketch that would do justice to Cocteau is beyond the range of this study, a number of aspects about him are pertinent here. For example, although brought up in a proper middle-class family, a teenage Cocteau apparently ran away from home and lived in hiding for about a year (or so he told people) in the Old Port district of Marseilles (which the Germans destroyed during the War). Steegmuller refers to a monologue written for Edith Piaf (probably during the Occupation), itself based on a short story Cocteau published in 1933, in which "a young [male] thief, having disguised himself as a female prostitute to escape the police, allows himself to be courted by an elderly gentleman—with fatal consequences" (17). During the 1920s, his affair with the young writer, Raymond Radiguet, who died in 1923, caused him to return to smoking opium, an addiction—described in detail in his memoir *Opium* (1929)—that he would never completely shake, except perhaps during the Occupation, when narcotics were impossible to buy (Steegmuller 440). Among his earlier important dramatic works are *Orphée* (1926), *La Machine Infernale* (1934), and *Les Parents Terribles* (1938), which he attempted to revive after *The Typewriter*. He had already written and directed the film *Le Sang d'un Poète* (1931) and would go on to write the screenplay for the 1943 classic, *L'Eternel Retour*.

His relationship with Marais, which lasted until Cocteau's death, began in 1937, when Marais was cast in the chorus of Cocteau's *Oedipe*. By the time *The Typewriter* had been produced, their romantic connection seems to have cooled (both having found other love interests) but not the intensity and intimacy of their friendship; they continued to live together for many years.

Cocteau's homosexuality was publicly and tacitly recognized, but his confessional novella, *Le Livre blanc*, was published anonymously, first in 1928 (by Maurice Sachs), and again in 1930 (this time with illustrations obviously by Cocteau), as was the 1953 edition (published by Paul Morihien). In an English translation, brought out in 1957, Cocteau admits to composing the drawings and writing the preface, in which he declares,

> I have even, yes, in several preceding editions accompanied this text with drawings which are patent evidence of the fact that if I do not specialize in a taste for my own sex, I do nonetheless recognize therein one of the sly helping hands fond nature is wont to extend to humans. (8)

Cocteau's original explanation for his denial of having written the book, offers Margaret Crosland, was "that he did not wish to upset his mother," but Mme Cocteau died in 1943 by which time, if she had looked at any of the reviews that her son's plays had received over the past three years, she could not have helped but be aware of his sexual orientation. "His reasons for not conceding authorship, even in 1957," Crosland suggests, "seem to constitute a game he was playing both with himself and with his readers" (9).

This "game," as Crosland calls it, was played out according to cultural and legal rules: Cocteau's anonymity had probably more to do with the same impulses that had caused Marais to thrash Laubreaux. Even after the war, the Vichy decree against pederasty stayed in place and attitudes about sexuality had not greatly changed; the same cultural repression of homosexuality that had operated during the Third Republic and the Vichy regime lingered into the 1960s. Certainly, Mme Cocteau had more than enough opportunity to recognize her son's sexual preferences, but what is clear from Marais's behavior, as well as Cocteau's, is that *being* a homosexual was rather different from *being called* a homosexual. Unlike Montherlant, both Cocteau and Marais appear to have been able to accept being known for who and for what they were so long as the who and the what went unnamed. In an age when even widely known gay figures, such as Gide and Jouhandeau, remained married, Cocteau and Marais were uniquely "out," although, during the war at least, a portion of the public (including Marais's female fans) may not have understood the implications of their identities. Thus, if Marais battered Laubreaux for identifying him, and Cocteau shied away from acknowledging his novella, it was perhaps because existing attitudes toward sexuality seemed to require them to do so.

In order to survive and succeed as a homosexual in Occupied Paris, a feat difficult enough for those who were discreet but an ongoing struggle for those few who were more frank about their sexuality, Cocteau drew on the human resources available to him and did what he felt he had to do or at least what he was able to. Although Lottman's reference to Arno Breker's intervention on Marais's behalf is admittedly rumor, Breker's memoir is nevertheless disturbingly indicative of Cocteau's ambivalent position during the Occupation:

> Cocteau and I got in touch immediately, in the autumn of 1940, at the time of the first sojourn that I made to Paris under the Occupation. It gave us heart to preserve a climate of "entente," in spite of the events. (292)

Indeed, Cocteau's entente with Breker, renewed now not merely in spite of but because of the "events" of 1940, included his attending the opening of the sculptor's show at the Orangerie, just a year after the troubled debut of *The Typewriter*, and composing for Breker a few lines of high praise (to be delivered as a speech). His "Salute to Breker," intended to be read aloud at the gallery, was instead published, enraging many of Cocteau's friends; the "Salute" is predictably nonpolitical, praising Breker's depictions of limbs and veins (*Journal* 133), but even here Cocteau's careful adulations are mixed with an almost bland tactfulness that implies an underlying ambivalence. Cocteau confides to his *Journal* his appreciation of the "giant statues with a close-to-sensual flavor of detail and sense of mankind and of their hair and veins"; he also inserts a quip made at the exhibit by a fellow thespian, the reputedly gay Sacha Guitry[23] (who also after the war would be charged with collaboration): "If these statues had come in with erections, no one would be able to move about here" (125). Cocteau seemed to like Breker genuinely, and after he and Marais met the sculptor at the exhibition one evening at closing time, he notes, "Marais being the type of person Breker is, I wanted him to make his acquaintance" (130). Ten days later, recalling a tête-à-tête with Breker on the Champs Élysées, Cocteau observes that his own relationship with Marais resembles Hitler's relationship with Breker: "He loves him. He's an adopted son." At the same time, he notes that on the "Jewish question," Breker becomes very formal, reflecting Hitler. "No possible exception," Cocteau paraphrases the sculptor. "A duel to the death" (138). Breker left Paris shortly after this conversation, and his presence in Cocteau's life diminished but never completely waned. The two remained on friendly terms until Cocteau's death.

Even Francis Steegmuller, who on the whole admires Cocteau, is forced to admit,

> The courageous French writers who eschewed publication under these conditions did not include Cocteau. Cocteau had no hesitation about seeking German-approved authorization to produce his plays; he saw Germans constantly, though not in his own home; in 1944 he published a volume of poems he said he had written in German. . . . (440)

Steegmuller's understatement only heightens the apparent ease with which Cocteau socialized with the Germans, whom he clearly preferred (and with apparent good reason) to the fascists of his native land. He developed a friendship with German novelist Paul Jünger, now a Wehrmacht officer stationed in Paris, and was acquainted with Ambassador Otto Abetz. He visited the German Institute, spoke on German-run Radio Paris, and throughout the Occupation habitually dined at that haven for Nazis and their affluent sympathizers, Maxim's—all of which brought him into close contact with those in a position to help him.

Still, not everything Cocteau did can be interpreted as pure opportunism: It was, in fact, directly to Ambassador Abetz in February 1944 that Cocteau sent his petition protesting the internment at Drancy (the half-built public housing project that was turned into a concentration camp for Jews who were to be deported) of poet Max Jacob, who would die there (Steegmuller 444–447). Moreover, Cocteau was, "along with many other bystanders, beaten up by right-wing rowdies [of the Ligue des Volontaires Français contre le Bolchévisme] because he refused to salute their flag during a 1943 anti-Bolshevist demonstration on the Champs-Elysées" (White 191); such a refusal was not only guaranteed to infuriate the French fascists but the Germans as well. After the Liberation, Cocteau was attacked in the press but was cleared by a tribunal of all charges of collaboration.

Because of who Cocteau was and what he did, the connections that many (including Cocteau himself) have drawn between the attacks against *The Typewriter* and its dramatist are understandable. Indeed, the denigrations themselves (like the one quoted previously from *L'Appel*) seem to point toward the person, rather than to the play. In addition to Added (43), Rosenberg (137), and Marsh ("Le Théâtre à Paris . . ." 230, 232), Steegmuller suggests that Cocteau was widely associated with the alleged decadence of the Third Republic: Moreover, his authorship of "an anti-racist article in a newspaper" prior to the invasion and "the supposed incest theme of *Les Parents Terribles*," which had premiered in 1938 (441), may have been additional causes for the angry reaction. To an extent, of course, these writers are correct in seeing Cocteau as the reviewers' target.

Yet Lucien Rebatet, who was disgustingly bigoted but sometimes acutely intelligent, makes an important point in identifying Cocteau's drama as "inverted theatre." Because *The Typewriter* does in fact emerge from what we may now recognize as a gay sensibility, the play itself was not merely a vehicle that happened to suffer due to its writer's reputation.

Inverted Theatre: Une fausse intrigue policière

On the surface, *The Typewriter* appears to be a detective drama in the vein of a typical commercial—or as the French would say, *boulevard*—potboiler. Yet in a short Préface printed in the original program[24] (and also, in a slightly different form, in the mise en scène[25] and all subsequent published editions), Cocteau not only admits that his play seeks to court approval of "the ordinary Public" by utilizing the "boulevard" style but adds that it is in fact "une fausse intrigue policière," or as Ronald Duncan translates it, "a pseudo-detective play," which,

> has enabled me to draw a picture of the terrible humbug of the provinces before the crash ["le débacle," perhaps better translated as "the Defeat"]; it was a provincialism whose vices and hypocrisy forced some to justify themselves as best they could, and others, the romantic youth, to become political idealists. (5–6)

Cocteau, in writing the melodrama, tried to exploit the popular murder-mystery genre and at the same time attempted to use the established form for his own purposes, to articulate serious social statements (or so he claims). Such a mix of commercial and serious drama was problematic, for audiences of the former often scorned the latter and vice versa. Furthermore, to defy the familiar conventions that apply to a murder mystery while in the process of delivering them, may have been more than what Cocteau calls the "ordinary Public" was willing to accept. A summary of the play reveals the difficulties Cocteau encountered in trying to write *The Typewriter* (the plot of which he had altered a dozen times, 6) and why he felt obliged to insert the word "fausse" before "intrigue policière."

Set in an unnamed provincial town, *The Typewriter* follows the criminal investigation of an anonymous letter campaign. The letters publicize some hidden misdeed in an outwardly respectable person's past, and because of them, several recipients have taken their own lives. Fred, a police detective near retirement, has been secretly assigned to the case, and comes to the town, where he stays at his old friend Didier's home, in order to find the culprit who signs each letter, "La Machine à écrire" ("The Typewriter"). He meets Didier's upright son, Pascal, his capricious ward, Margot, and an older, attractive widow, Solange, from the nearby chateau of Malemort. After the death of his first wife, an actress, Didier had considered marrying Solange, but Pascal's objections that it would be improper (a view shared by the townsfolk) stopped him. Alone, now that her own son has gone off to school, Solange has fallen in love with Pascal's twin, Maxim, who has just been released from prison and has secretly returned to town. Maxim has fallen ill while hiding in the woods and has been taken in by Solange at Malemort.

In his search for the criminal, Fred is guided by an important clue: Each typewritten letter uses uppercase Ms rather than lowercase, suggesting some special significance of the capitalized letter. In fact, at the close of Act I, set at Didier's house, Margot, an aspiring dramatist, who is bored with her country life and impending marriage to the proper Pascal, confesses that she has sent the letters. However, in Act II Fred arrives at Malemort and confides to Solange that a number of people have already confessed to the crime and that Margot could not possibly be guilty. Fred has already guessed that Solange is harboring the reckless Maxim, who soon enters. Fred realizes immediately that Solange has become Maxim's mistress, but he has understood from observing Margot that she (though engaged to his twin) has always been in love with Maxim and that he loves her in return. The detective's questioning brings about an unexpected admission: Maxim confesses to being The Typewriter but again, Fred rejects the confession. Maxim's rage at this rejection seems to precipitate an epileptic convulsion.[26]

In Act III, Fred returns to Malemort and confronts Solange with the fact that Maxim and she cannot go on as lovers because Margot and Maxim—no matter how much they argue—are destined for each other; he knows that Solange is in fact the perpetrator of the crime (the M, he has deduced, stands for Malemort). Yet Fred has arranged everything tidily. Because he himself is in love with Solange and even sympathetic with her desire to seek revenge from the town's moralistic hypocrites who ruined her own happiness, he has prepared someone else to take the fall: Monique, the girl who works in the post office and has already happily confessed to sending the letters. Monique arrives and promises to turn herself in. She also announces, quite unexpectedly, that she and Pascal have been lovers for years. When Margot learns that Pascal has been the postmistress's paramour, she sees that her fiancé's uprightness has been a fraudulent pose; she announces her love for Maxim. With everything put together neatly, Fred offers to take Solange away from the town. Yet Solange, unable to go on with her deceptions and unwilling to accept Fred's pity, shoots herself.

This summary makes clear some of the problems in the play. Overly contrived and ultimately not very convincing, *The Typewriter* fails to live up to its genre's promise of a sleuth solving an exciting mystery. True, Fred eventually exposes the culprit, but the audience is never privy to his deductive process. Moreover, the "subplot" of Pascal and Monique, which eventually releases Margot to marry Maxim, seems like a later addition. Indeed, Cocteau's Préface implies that the idea that "tied up" the plot apparently came at the last moment (6). In any case, little dramatic groundwork is laid earlier in the play to prepare the audience for this startling turn.

As for the script's supposed social statements, although a few have taken Cocteau at his word and construed in the play some serious social criticism, the supposed exploration of provincial hypocrisy is never particularly deep and in the final analysis seems oddly incidental. The presence of such hypocrisy is necessary in order to motivate Solange to write the letters and Fred to vindicate her, and yet the hypocrisy itself is not dramatized but merely referred to. For some in the audience, Fred's view that Solange's letter-writing has been justified may absolve her of her crime: She has lashed out in a valiant attempt to revenge herself on those who have harmed her. Those who still find her actions abhorrent might be chastened by her merciless punishment of herself, a penalty far harsher than what the law would demand. Still, Solange's confession and suicide feel like empty, theatrical gestures because the closest we get to experiencing actual hypocrites comes at the very end—the scene revealing Pascal's and Monique's secret affair. Yet, as noted above, this scene feels uncomfortably tangential to the work as a whole.

The anonymous letters in *The Typewriter* may remind readers of another important work from the Occupation, Henri-Georges Clouzot's *Le Corbeau*, the 1943 film that was in fact based on the same torrent of hate mail that erupted during the 1920s in Tulles, where Cocteau had visited. Louis Chavance's screenplay, begun in 1931, had been completed by 1938 (Ehrlich 178), but in spite of its prewar scenario, the film was viewed by some, in part because it had been produced by German-subsidized Continental,[27] as deliberately anti-French. Like *The Typewriter*, *Le Corbeau* looks at the dishonest respectability of the French middle class. However, its indictment of what Evelyn Ehrlich calls "French hypocrisy" (185), in itself intensely bitter, was perhaps less offensive to the Résistance than its insinuations that people are only human and that moral questions have no simple, black-or-white answers (186–187). Its moral relativism posed a problem to those in the process of fighting the Germans, and therefore, explains Ehrlich, "To those members of the Resistance who still cannot forgive him, Clouzot's *Le Corbeau* was the most dangerous film of its time" (187). For better and worse, *Le Corbeau* brilliantly transcends the thriller format to which it might easily have adhered. Yet *The Typewriter*, written allegedly to entertain the "ordinary Public," who, Cocteau says in his preface, are "more or less similar to a twelve-year-old child whose interest is difficult to hold except with laughter and tears" (5), sinks under the weight of its unwieldy plot and its overly theatricalized attempts to tug on the audience's emotions.

Cocteau's infantalization of his audience gives way to his curious statement of intent, to expose the provincial "vices and hypocrisy" before the Defeat and the resultant self-justification of some and the political idealism of "the romantic youth." The implication here is that the playwright is depicting some of the causes for the fall of France. This seems a signal sent, if not toward Brasillach, then at least toward the collabo press, which continued to attack the degeneracy of the Third Republic (with which Cocteau himself had become identified). Of course, the script was written before the armistice, well before the regime in Vichy launched an assault against its predecessor; this prefatory claim was tacked on to allege that the play was both timely and consistent with the artistic aims of the New France. As far as time period is concerned, though, *The Typewriter* offers no references to when it is set and, like most detective plays, takes place in an unspecified present; in short, it is an "intrigue policière" sans tickets. Thus, *The Typewriter* fails to realize its author's stated intentions and does not function credibly as either a detective play or a social critique. What does emerge from the script, however, is Cocteau's own peculiar sensibility, which derives from his personal and subcultural experiences as a homosexual.

Michael Bronski raises several important and related concerns regarding the overlap of the theatre community and the gay subculture:

> Who can come out and who remains closeted raises the important issues of what and how society allows gay artists to create, how this informs the creations, and how this affects gay sensibility. An interesting measure of social tolerance is the ratio of actual homosexuality portrayed to the number of gay people involved in the theater, and the appearance of covert aspects of gay sensibility in popular plays. (111)

In occupied Paris, the number of explicit, on-stage portrayals of homosexuality was, not surprisingly, extremely low (with Sartre's Inez in *Huis Clos* the best known, if not the only, example) while the number of gay people working in the theatre probably remained about the same; what Bronski calls "the appearance of covert aspects of gay sensibility in popular plays," however minimal its occurrence, can only have been heavily encoded. Few appear to have read much homosexual (or pedophilic) significance into Montherlant's plays, but of course his sexuality, though suspected, was never publicly discussed. Cocteau, on the other hand, was more widely "out,"[28] and his plays would consequently be perceived by some spectators, both friendly and hostile to the gay subculture, as the work of a homosexual playwright.

Although the public, or at least a significant part of the public, might think of Cocteau as homosexual, his openness on this subject was, as noted

earlier, limited by various cultural factors. He might, behind a pose of anonymity, depict homosexuality explicitly in his fiction and in erotic sketches,[29]
but writing for the stage was a different matter. The public nature of attending
a play, unlike the private act of reading a novel or examining published
drawings, restricted how much a dramatist, especially a homosexual dramatist, might directly express about homosexuality on stage.[30] Moreover, the
rigidity of French culture—and most other cultures until the late 1960s—on
this aspect of sexuality kept many gay writers' personal and artistic lives
separate and only covertly connected.

The problems confronting an outright stage portrayal of homosexuality
become apparent by contrasting the fiction of Genet, which—like its author—
was openly and admittedly gay, with his early plays; and which at most either
suggest a certain homoeroticism (as with *Haute Surveillance*), or imply that
a character may have committed homosexual acts (as with *Les Bonnes*), or
may have homosexual tendencies (as in *Le Balcon*). These dramas confront
a world that is predominantly and oppressively heterosexual, and Genet's
own role as one who had been excluded, even outlawed, makes his analysis
especially acute; no matter how much his plays maintain their focus on straight
society, their point of view is noticeably gay. In a similar and somewhat
analogous way, in the United States, Tennessee Williams, whose homosexuality was, at least in the 1940s and 1950s, rarely mentioned but often suspected, aimed his dramas at the "normal" world, which his own "abnormality"
allowed him to deconstruct; what comes through in Williams's plays is not
just a critique of the seemingly unchangeable sexual roles of males and
females, enforced by a highly phobic culture, but the voice of the ostracized,
the pariah. Of course, the plays of both Genet and Williams present themselves as serious drama while *The Typewriter* presents itself as a commercial
thriller. Nonetheless, even at their most frivolous, the stage pieces of Cocteau,
discoverer and friend of Genet and admirer of Williams (whose *Streetcar
Named Desire* he would later adapt for the French stage) explore what appears to be a heterosexual world from a homosexual perspective.

As I note earlier, French culture drove homosexuals to hide their sexuality; an analogous need to maintain a cover surfaces in Cocteau's script
through repeated depictions of characters engaged in role-playing, often in a
broadly theatricalized manner, to mask their true identities. Margot is constantly playing the dramatist, frequently dressed in the stage costumes left by
her stepmother, Didier's deceased actress wife, and looking for drama in this
dreary environment. In Act I, after a joke about poisoning Pascal's food (10),
Margot exits and re-enters dressed as Lucretia Borgia (20). Appropriately, she
is first to play the role of the confessed letter-writer in her confession at the
close of Act I. Fred plays the part of a benevolent relative (throughout he is
referred to as "oncle"). Maxim deliberately enacts the prodigal son. Didier,

though supposedly quite proper, is underneath (as Fred assures him) a child (11). Both Solange and Pascal create parts for themselves that are familiar to the townspeople (the suffering widow and the moral son, respectively), assuming public masks of respectability while privately committing forbidden acts. Postmistress Monique, like the others who confess to the crime, is content to play the perpetrator and to hide her affair with Pascal.

The construction of *The Typewriter's* world of performers dramatizes the struggle of having to hide who one really is, a practice which, for homosexuals in particular, French culture more than the law necessitated. Some of the role-playing, like Pascal's, requires one to pretend to be highly moral in order to violate the very code one allegedly endorses—no doubt a more than familiar situation for the majority of gay males at the time. More meaningfully, perhaps, are those roles which to some degree allow the "actor" to express his true self without full disclosure of his real identity: Fred, for example, by masquerading as a kindly uncle is able to make negative statements about the police—statements in which he genuinely believes but which his actual role as detective would invalidate (as we see in Act II, when Maxim learns who Fred is and is thus able to disregard such criticisms); likewise, Maxim, playing the part of the bad boy, is able to let some of his actual kindness come through. In this way, the play implies that hiding one's true self may in some way be liberating, another notion with which homosexuals in occupied Paris might easily identify and which Cocteau himself even seems to endorse through his denial-admission in the 1957 preface to *The White Book*, "I do not specialize in a taste for my own sex. . . ."

Perhaps more significantly, these role-players seem quite willing not just to hide their deeds but to admit to acts that they have not committed and yet on some level may have wished to commit. This seeming contradiction implies that one's fantasies, even when they remain unrealized, are a major factor in one's self-definition; one is described by one's desires rather than by one's actual deeds, and one in turn obscures one's own forbidden acts but, through fantasy, lays claim to even worse ones. Contemporary reviewers of *The Typewriter* found this willingness to confess especially bewildering or repugnant: Laubreaux complained in *Le Petit Parisien* that the heroic figures of Cocteau's theatre works accused themselves of the worst cowardice due to their more than ignoble mental depravity, and added, "Il vaut mieux rire." Perhaps Laubreaux's puzzlement was due in part to his rejection of Freudian (i.e., "Jewish") psychology. Yet in the experience of those who comprised contemporary gay culture, the notion that desire determined identity had been firmly implanted by the view that homosexuality was a psychological problem, not a criminal tendency, and that identity might be the result not so much of what one did but what one wanted to do. As in Genet's brothel in *Le Balcon*, satisfaction may come from taking on the part of, rather than actually being, the criminal. Thus, the staged performance of the apparent act, rather than the actual commission of the authentic act, provides the actor (that is, the person who is both performing and not performing the act) with an experience as good as, perhaps better than, the actual.

To some degree, critics and censors found the whole notion of false confessions objectionable. In fact, while the promptbook for the original production supports the recollection of Marais and others that the epileptic fit (which in the script gives its name to Act II) had to be taken out, a much longer scene toward the end of Act III, in which Monique, Pascal's secret love and the town's postmistress, is happy to "take the rap" for Solange, seems to have offended as well. This excision required that Monique's role be entirely cut from the play. According to the stage manager's notes, after cuts were made, Act I lost five minutes, Act II three minutes, and Act III sixteen minutes. The epileptic seizure, which might strike a modern audience as melodramatic, may have been considered ugly (as Sardou suggests in his review in *Les Nouveaux Temps*), but the self-accusation held an even uglier implication: that committing a crime might be a desirable act.

Indeed, the attitude in *The Typewriter* toward criminality is interestingly complicated. Rather than focusing on provincial hypocrisy, the play depicts ordinary townspeople attracted to the writing of cruel letters and to the violent consequences of this activity (such as inflicting psychological pain or driving others to suicide). The play sets up an ambivalent relationship between hunter and hunted. As mentioned above, Fred's own feelings about his police work are conflicted, and his sympathy for the culprit, even before he discovers that it is Solange, is strong. Moreover, Solange's own motivation in resorting to the poison pen—or in this case, the venomous keyboard—comes from her own powerlessness to control her life in this pitiless town; her acts of vengeance thus take on an almost heroic stature when, at the end of the play, in a fit of histrionic heroics, she commits suicide. The result of the play's often contrived plotting, then, is not the emotional suspense and relief of a thriller but an unsettling and conspicuous decriminalization of the criminal: In "gay" terms, *The Typewriter* dismantles the culture's (and maybe even the genre's) assumptions about right and wrong, questioning what should be punishable and what ought to go unpunished.

Even with the deletion of Monique, *The Typewriter* continued to offer an ongoing commentary glamorizing, even vindicating, criminality. Fred, who hunts criminals, manages to find an innocent purity in them: "Children don't compromise," he tells Didier in Act I. "To them the criminal is always right" (12). He even compares the poison pen to divine justice: "These smug little towns deserve a plague of locusts, or anonymous letters to blast their hypocrisy. And the mysterious informer who signs himself 'The Typewriter' has all my sympathy!" (19). A few minutes later he admires Margot in costume: "I think you're magnificent as Lucretia Borgia" (21). As the first-act curtain falls, Margot (still dressed as the poisoner) tries to invent her confession as the letter-writer and improvises a tale laced with revenge against a soldier who spurned her (44–45). In Act II, the audience meets a supposedly genuine criminal, the allegedly evil twin, Maxim, with whom both Solange and Margot are in love. Solange wants him, rather romantically, to disregard his previous troubles, urging him to "forget your past and your life in prison" (48) and "say . . . to yourself every night: 'There's no such thing as prison. Prison is a myth. I'll never think of prison again' " (49). Yet according to Maxim, his time behind bars remains unforgettable:

> Solange: . . . . You were sentenced by mistake, but you went through with it.
>
> Maxim: What else could I do? Do you know grown men there even lick the boots of the governor for fear of never getting out of that terrible place? I've worn myself out with being obedient, being a coward, doing what I couldn't bear.
>
> Solange: Till it's become a part of you?
>
> Maxim: Yes, for ever. . . . (48–49)

Of course, Solange believes that the crime and punishment, in spite of Maxim's innocence, is written on his soul. She even tells Fred, "I sometimes forget he is free with nothing threatening him, except himself!" (51). On some level, Maxim's criminal behavior and his status as a pariah have attracted Solange to him; her loneliness and her own clandestine activities find refuge in his. During Act II, while Fred is interrogating Maxim, Solange exits to type out another hate letter (and later re-enters only to exit for the post office).

Throughout *The Typewriter*, Cocteau's characters present attractive images of the transgressor. Maxim's appeal is evident in his responses to Fred's cross examination: He starts by describing how he escaped after his arrest in Toulon, was helped by some girls (who were unsuccessful in removing his handcuffs), and later recaptured. As soon as he suspects Margot may be implicated, he transforms what actually occurred into a confession so that he may take on the blame himself. As Solange has already revealed (25–26), after his release Maxim returned and, while hiding in the woods, convinced local boys to bring him food and clothing, even organizing them into a secret club of sorts. Now, in an attempt to persuade Fred that he is The Typewriter, Maxim embellishes the story, inventing how he forced the club members to spy on their families and deliver scandalous secrets (60).[31] He used their information, he assures Fred, in his letters. However, Fred has already told Maxim (who of course cannot trust him) that Margot and the seven other young people who have confessed cannot be considered suspects. He explains,

> I suppose the newspapers, detective novels and gangster films are at the bottom of it. These kids see themselves as some sort of hero and dramatise themselves in some way, and in order to get publicity they'll even confess to a crime they've never even imagined. (57)

This idea of the criminal as hero, insinuated in Act I by Fred, is described in Act II by Maxim, who has captured the admiration of the girls at Toulon and won the sympathy of the boys in his home town, of his own stepsister, and even of the beautiful mother of one of the boys in his gang.

In *The Typewriter*'s full text, the notion of the criminal-hero is most clearly articulated by Fred, whose knowledge of the law allows him (in a section of Act III later removed) to guarantee Solange, Maxim, and Margot that Monique will not hang because "she's mad. . . . A town like this drives anybody mad" (89). By implication, Fred is acquitting not Monique, who of course has not done anything wrong, but Solange, both for her letter writing and for her allowing Monique to accept the blame. This absolution was, along with the entire scene, cut from the play, and yet in dialogue that survived in the performance script, Maxim consoles Solange at the end of her own confession: "I'm no more innocent than you. Criminals are all alike. Everything conspires to drive us from society—that I haven't the guts to do any harm doesn't make me innocent; on the contrary" (95). Thus, Solange's actions may be seen as laudable under the circumstances, even by the hardened detective, who asserts, "for the best of reasons, you have committed the worst of crimes. . . . My verdict is 'Not guilty' " (98).

Perhaps Cocteau's most revealing line is Maxim's "Everything conspires to drive us from society. . . ." The playwright might have said much the same for both the felon and the homosexual; both had been criminalized, for their actual or their fantasized deeds. Beneath the dialogue lurks a subtext, which, at least now, seems to speak in a particular way to the homosexual spectator. And when, less than two years later, Cocteau first encountered Genet's writing, which joined its author's real and invented thievery with his (homo)sexuality, Cocteau evidently recognized the conflation as such. In his first journal entry to mention Genet (February 6, 1943), he notes that *Le Condamné à mort* (*The Man Condemned to Death*) is an erotic poem dedicated to the glory of a young assassin, executed four years earlier; the poem is "a splendor" (261). About a week later, he meets Genet and records how he had been marked by the prison system, to the point of seeming maniacal;

at the same time, Cocteau delights in the unpublishable eroticism of Genet's newest poems (269). A week later, Genet has read to Cocteau from his novel *Our Lady of the Flowers*, which at first Cocteau despises, but then understands is the very expression of what he himself has tried to imply but has been unable to write explicitly:

> Three hundred incredible pages in which he pieces together the mythology of "queers." At first such a subject is repellent. . . . Subsequently I wanted to ask his forgiveness for my stupidity. . . . One dreams of possessing the book and making it famous. On the other hand, that's impossible. . . . The true example of blinding and unacceptable purity. . . . Genet is a thief and wanted by the police. One trembles at the thought that he might disappear and that his works might be destroyed. They should be published, just a few copies to be sold under the counter. (quoted by White 196–197)

Six days later, Cocteau has read the whole book and confides,

> For me it's the great event of the epoch. It disgusts me, repels me, astonishes me, it poses a thousand problems. . . . Jean Genet's eye embarrasses and disturbs you. . . . I've reread *Our Lady of the Flowers* line by line. Everything is hateful and worthy of respect. (197–198)

The initial tension, which so delighted Cocteau in *The Man Condemned to Death*, between homoeroticism and criminality must have seemed overwhelming in the novel. Cocteau had avoided writing about his own homosexuality for fear of distressing his mother; any direct statement about the crime against nature could be made only in pornographic or underground literature (like *The White Book*). Eventually, Cocteau did promote Genet's writings, even as he continued to find their explicitness deeply troubling.

In his own way, Cocteau had tried to fuse the distinct images of malefactor and invert. In *The Typewriter* he came close enough to offend a homophobic segment of the audience, who were predisposed to combing his script for their own purposes; unlike his more liberal fans (the educated, the artistic, the socially brilliant—some of whom were homosexual), the PPF and the Vichy loyalists were quick to identify their objections and to articulate them volubly. Perhaps these ultra-rightists would not have subjected this imitation detective drama to such scrutiny had they not known that a well-known "pervert" had written it. Perhaps its subtext would have gone unnoticed except by those whose experience would allow them more readily to comprehend it. Yet those who condemned *The Typewriter* because they had managed, for whatever reasons, to read between the lines, to read past its puportedly conventional surface, and to decode its underlying messages, were not wrong: As much as they loathed it, they had indeed discerned Cocteau's subtext.

Conclusion

In a variety of ways, Cocteau's play puts on stage, in what had been under the Third Republic an acceptable manner, elements of contemporary homosexual subculture. Cocteau had written it as he and the Third Republic fled Paris. Yet when the play finally opened, times had radically changed: Not only had the unspoken subject matter become a major bone of contention between French fascists in Paris and their supposed German allies, and anathema to everyone except the Nazis in Paris, but the very style of the play, which Cocteau himself calls "boulevard," was now symbolic of the previous regime and all it was now supposed to stand for; Georges Champeaux succinctly summed it up (May 15, 1941) in the pro-German *La Gerbe*, calling *The Typewriter* reminiscent of Bataille, Bernstein, and (curiously) Pirandello and concluding it was "a cocktail" of boulevard theatre and avant-garde theatre. Although Champeaux largely upheld Cocteau's reputation (André Castelot would later castigate him in the same paper), the very mention of Bernstein not only summons up associations of the boulevard but also insinuates the assumption (which Simone de Beauvoir would hear in Simone Jollivet's retorts near the end of 1941[32]) that the popular theatre had long been overrun by Jews. In a similar but less vicious way, F.R.D., the reviewer in *La Semaine à Paris* (7–12 May 1941), describes the play as a divertissement, a prewar cocktail. "But will we ever be serious?" he asks in closing.

Significantly, not all the negative reviews harped on Cocteau's sexuality. For example, Maurice Rostand, son of the author of *Cyrano* (and a childhood friend of Cocteau), in *Paris-Midi* (4 May 1941) found the plot unbelievable, as did Georges Pioch in *L'Œuvre* (4 May 1941). Jacques Berland in *Paris-Soir* (4 May 1941) enjoyed the play up until its weak ending, but Armory in *Les Nouveaux Temps* (6 May 1941), particularly repelled by Marais's convulsions at the end of Act II, deemed the entire piece to be epileptic. *The Typewriter* was hardly a smash hit, yet its notoriety had sufficiently preceded it to allow the melodrama to run until the season's end.

Like the ending of the plot, Cocteau's Préface seems to have been added well after most of the script was written. As mentioned above, this short piece, included at the beginning of the program, gives an explanation for the play's style and content; it is an apologia to a potentially hostile press. And although it attempts to specify the play's intended audience, that "ordinary Public" whom he calls "similar to a twelve-year-old child," the script itself is hardly commercial fare. Cocteau's theatre successes before the Defeat were artistic: Some, like *Parade* and *Orphée*, were avant-garde while others, like *La Machine Infernale* and *Les Parents Terribles*, were highly charged, innovative, and controversial drama. *The Typewriter*, whether or not the script itself is any good, is too flawed and too intelligent a play to be boulevard material. Cocteau was used to writing for a cultural elite, who might have been a better, if not ideal, audience for *The Typewriter*.

Yet by now audiences in general were somehow different than before the armistice. As much as the press and the theatre itself told spectators that nothing had altered, spectators knew that everything was utterly changed. The auditorium had become more politicized and would remain so beyond the end of the Occupation. Even the innocuous comedies of the boulevard had come under attack. People seated in the house were listening more carefully. If someone on stage uttered some disparaging remark about a character named "Adolphe," as occurred in Labiche's *29 Degrés à l'Ombre* (Rosenberg, "The French Theatre . . ." 194), audiences seized on it and exploded into laughter. (The line was promptly changed.) Collaborationist critics felt a responsibility not merely to chastise any work that offended their values and political ideals but also to appropriate, from any work, whatever they could. In the case of *The Typewriter*, they found absolutely nothing to help their cause. The Germans obviously felt differently.

While to a few, like Laubreaux and the unnamed reviewer in *L'Appel*, the mere presence of inverts in the theatre was objectionable, Rebatet made the point that the play was clearly the product of an invert's mind. Although we may today find Rebatet's attack on Cocteau entirely without merit, I cannot discount his connection between the dramatist and the script. One may say all kinds of things, good and bad, about this play, but perhaps the most valid point in understanding it and the uproar it inspired is best summed up by that fascist aesthete who, for the worst of reasons, wrote in *Je suis partout*, that *The Typewriter* was nothing more than "inverted theatre."

2

Collabo Beefcake and Resistant Reception: Ambiguity in André Obey's *Eight Hundred Meters* and *The Suppliant Women*

Introduction

About two months after the premiere of *The Typewriter* at the Hébertot, Roland-Garros Stadium served as a theatre for an unusual double bill: André Obey's version of *Les Suppliantes* (*The Suppliant Women*) of Aeschylus and Obey's original "drame sportif" *Huit cents mètres* (*Eight Hundred Meters*), a poetic drama, written partly in verse, which simulated an 800-meter race. Promoted in a full-page advertisement in *Comœdia* as "THÉATRE—MUSIQUE–SPORT," the paired plays were presented—along with a half-time gymnastic show by the Paris firemen's special regiment—on the afternoons of Saturday, July 5, and Sunday, July 6, 1941, with the support of the Vichy government's Ministry of Education and Sport to profit the National Assistance for "Athletic Prisoners of War and their Families."[1] Both plays were directed by a rising member of the Comédie-Française, Jean-Louis Barrault, an actor-director who before the War had made his name among the avant-garde.

The same collaborationist press that had, at the end of April, vilified Cocteau's melodrama by labeling it boulevard drama in the effeminate style of the Third Republic, now excitedly anticipated the Roland-Garros events, which perhaps more than any other performance during the Occupation's first season, would successfully combine the modern with the classical, as if the two represented an embodiment of the traditionalist yet robust present era and its National Revolution. Although the reviews in the censored dailies and weeklies would be mixed, this production—as a number of recent historians and critics have pointed out—clearly benefited the cause of French fascists.

Yet even while *The Suppliant Women* and *Eight Hundred Meters* may easily be regarded as in some ways consonant with fascist or para-fascist ideology, they also, in the complicated environment in which they were presented, seem capable of suggesting ideas about France, the Defeat, and the country's subsequent crisis that were contrary to their own apparently "fascist" content. Such seemingly disparate meanings certainly were possible during the Occupation, when all scripts performed in public had to be passed by the censor. Indeed, significant claims have been made about how such dramatists as Claude Vermorel (who wrote *Jeanne avec nous* [*Joan Among Us*]), Jean-Paul Sartre (who wrote *The Flies*), and Jean Anouilh (who wrote *Antigone*), whose scripts had been approved by the German censors, had subtly but clearly signaled to their audiences some messages of resistance; some have insisted that the directors of such plays helped convey some of these messages. Furthermore, producers might look upon such ambiguity as desirable because plays needed to appeal to a wide range of Occupation audiences, whose political and cultural allegiances were diverse. Nonetheless, whatever the intent of the playwright, director, and producer, and whatever possible readings a dramatic and a theatre text might be able to offer, the times and their circumstances made some interpretations more likely than others and to some degree determined what a theatre text might mean.

One particular factor that figures prominently in the original productions of both *The Suppliant Women* and *Eight Hundred Meters* is the display of the male physique. As I will discuss in chapter 8, Barrault had already incorporated the body (his own included) into his direction of earlier projects. As noted in chapter 1, intolerance of homosexuals by fascists and Nazis perpetuated the illusion that what Sedgewick calls "homosocial desire" might easily be separated from homosexual desire. At the same time, as Mosse has explained, fascism and Nazism both aspired to idealize males as the ruling elite and manifested such aspirations through "the worship of masculinity" (176). German art had manifested this worship visually in Arno Breker's sculpture (as well as in film, painting, and graphic design), while in France, Mosse observes, pro-fascists had produced "the written equivalent" (175). Even though the worship of the masculine in France may have found literary, rather than visual, expression, the literary texts of these plays formed the basis of a daytime spectacle that was, like Breker's sculptures, very tangibly homoerotic.

In this chapter, the 1941 production of these plays will be examined in an attempt to understand how and what they meant in context. First will come an exploration of the ways through which collaborationists and French fascists of the period connected their own political views with sports, ancient Greece, and theatre. Following this, there will be an analysis of some of the possible meanings of these plays, meanings that may seem contradictory but

Two of Breker's sculptures shown at the Orangerie (top). Breker's vision of the classical kouros (bottom left); Cocteau and Breker at the Orangerie exhibition (bottom right).

which might have been identified by spectators whose sympathies neither coincided with nor even paralleled those of the censors, those of the Vichy subsidizers, and those of the collaborationist press who reviewed the production. Finally, what and how the production of these plays signified in the midst of contemporary Occupation culture will be considered.

Performance in Sport and Theatre

What are the performance dynamics of the sport arena? To an extent, the playing area of a field or stadium, by its foundation on presenting sporting events in which struggle, as well as victory and defeat, are (within the rules of the game at least) actual, is easily identified as a or perhaps *the* site of αγον (agon)—meaning struggle and conflict or even the arena where these take place.[2] It is not enough that the events presented be physical; a circus, for example, may offer any number of acts (trapeze, balance, demonstrations of strength) that require physical skill, but what is missing is a sense of conflict and outcome, of competition and of winning and losing, all of which are crucial to agon. Even definitions of sport that emphasize its performance rather than its outcome specify some objective measure of performance, and thus imply a requisite victory or defeat. Hence, the sportive event, as Eleanor Metheny describes it, is "a self-chosen and rule-governed task [the performance of which] produces a conception of honorable behavior, a conception of the performance of the task, and a score which denotes the quality of that performance in quantitative terms" (61–62). Of course, as Michel Foucault would have pointed out, the notion that agon is or can be confined to one (or one type of) location is in itself duplicitous, for if we look carefully, we find numerous sites of struggle throughout a culture. Nonetheless, we may agree that there remains a distinct difference between watching a genuinely competitive sporting event, like gymnasts contending for the highest score, and one that utilizes similar physical abilities, such as trapeze artists performing at staggering heights, for entertainment.

Still, as Roland Barthes insists in his essay, "The World of Wrestling," included in *Mythologies* (15–25), our engagement in sportive events may be just as visceral and full of meaning as our involvement while watching stage drama. Metheny sees legitimate sports reception as drawing an emotional response from construed (though often subconscious) meanings: "even if the spectator cannot explain the meanings he finds in watching the performances of the champions . . . [,] [h]e has made those meanings his own by experiencing them within the innermost reaches of his own feelings" (82).[3] Brian Pronger adds, "Athletics is a traditional theater for the acting out of myths" (15); the spectator thus becomes involved in emotionally decoding what Barthes calls the "intelligible spectacle" (20):

> In wrestling, nothing exists except in the absolute, there is no sym-
> bol, no allusion, everything is presented exhaustively. . . . What is
> portrayed by wrestling is therefore an ideal understanding of things;
> it is the euphoria of men raised for a while above the constitutive
> ambiguity of everyday situations and placed before the panoramic
> view of univocal Nature, in which signs at last correspond to causes,
> without obstacle, without evasion, without contradiction. (24–25)

An event that we assume is authentically competitive in nature—a professional
basketball game, a college football game, an amateur tennis match—inspires in
its spectators many of the same feelings that Barthes describes above. On a
very basic level, spectators may easily convert a team or individual for whom
they are rooting into a representative of their "own community, educational
institution, or some socially organized group" (Metheny 81–82) and thus take
a victory or a defeat as indicative of something far larger and more meaningful
about their social identities and thus about themselves.

By implication, then, as those engaged in the athletic event start to
downplay genuine struggle and to emphasize the enactment of struggle, as the
wrestlers have begun to do in the matches that Barthes describes, the audience's
interest shifts away from their responses to the competition and outcome and
instead gravitates toward the performances of the participants. Events that are
acknowledged to be far more staged than the matches that Barthes discusses—
such as the American "pro" wrestling matches on television, for which audiences assume that the outcome is predetermined and for which the wrestlers
arrive fully made-up and costumed, with distinct characterizations—such pseudo-
sportive events depend more heavily than do legitimate sports events on their
ability to succeed as what Barthes calls "a duration, a display" and to "[take]
up the ancient myths of public Suffering and Humiliation: the cross and the
pillory" (21). In other words, as sport moves closer to drama, audience response becomes more intensely theatricalized; less depends on the outcome (as
with Oedipus, the audience already knows the ending) and more on the enactment of "myth" through the participants' performances.

Just as a genuinely sportive event can accentuate its own theatricality
(through, for example, the players' fights during a hockey game or the half-
time pageantry of a football game), a drama may try to exploit a sense of the
agon of sport. For the most part, of course, drama is quite openly everything
that the sportive event alleges not to be: Drama is quite openly (as Barthes
puts it) "a duration, a display" and from its inception has blatantly striven to
reenact ancient myths; even though action and conflict form the spine of
dramatic structure, Aristotle reminds us in the *Poetics* that drama displays an
imitation or representation of an action and, by extension, offers merely a
mimesis or representation of conflict. A play that attempts to cross over from
the world of drama into the world of sporting event thus seeks to intensify

its representation of conflict through a synthetic version of an athletic contest, which imitates the mechanics of the genuine sportive agon. This sort of crossover is familiar enough in dramatic films, in which settings necessary to the depiction of such events are easily achieved, but due to reasons of staging and space, is relatively rare in theatre plays.

Much of the above has been argued in terms that allude to ancient times. In addition to *agon*, which I have used (rather than *conflict* or *struggle*) in order to make obvious the classical grounding of this discussion, and to other words derived from the Greek (like *stadium*) and Latin (like *arena*), the discussion itself has proceeded in language and ideas derived from ancient drama. This comingling of the sportive with the classical—particularly of the classical theatre—is of long standing. In France the tradition of staging classical and sportive plays in a sports setting had its roots long before the Occupation: During the 1919–1920 season, Firmin Gémier, who had played Jarry's Ubu and later founded the Théâtre Ambulant and later the Théâtre National Populaire, produced at the Cirque d'Hiver an adaptation of *Oedipus Rex*, along with a modernized Provençal nativity pageant, *La Grande Pastorale*. Although as Frederick Brown indicates, this *Oedipus* was a vulgarization of Sophocles (300) in which the spectacle dwarfed the dialogue (which was, in turn, reduced to octosyllabic verse) and even sounded to some to have been "rewritten for illiterates" (294), Oscar Brockett and Robert Findley note that the spectacle was in fact particularly impressive: "Perhaps the most striking scene was that in which two hundred supernumeraries, many of them trained gymnasts, javelin throwers, and jumpers, staged an athletic contest" (360). Gémier had produced other Greek plays (by Aeschylus and Aristophanes) in the open air and with athletic spectacle, and thus, as a commentator in *L'Œuvre* (17 July 1941) points out, his work served as a model for the double bill of *The Suppliant Women* and *Eight Hundred Meters* and the athletic entr'acte. Gémier's influence on this double bill may be glimpsed both through its use of stadium presentation before a mass audience and for its attempt to synthesize and exploit the sense of agon associated with classical sport.

The link between the two productions, though extremely complex, is traceable. In fact Bradby sees Gémier's efforts to create theatre en masse (both on a massive scale and in the name of the masses) as laying the foundation for such plays as J. R. Bloch's *Naissance d'une cité*, a vast pageant commissioned by the Popular Front government for the 1937 International Exhibition. Bloch's attempt at "total theatre" (11) was performed at the vast indoor cycling stadium in the fifteenth arrondissement, the Vélodrome d'Hiver, which seated 15,000 (Marrus and Paxton 251). As Bradby observes, Bloch's work and other similar dramatic pieces (such as the composite show *Vive la liberté*) were "inspired, to some extent, by socialist trade union gatherings in Germany in the twenties," which had themselves "been superseded by the Nazi mass rallies" that were so meticulously captured by Leni Riefenstal (11–12).

In the rally at Nuremberg, which Riefenstal documented and intensified in her 1934 film, *Triumph of the Will*, we can discern both athleticism and drama. Nazi ideology or perhaps sentiment is quickly translated into theatre: movements, sounds, images that communicate far more effectively than the Führer's Sturm und Drang oratory (which in the film takes up thankfully little time). Simultaneously, the arena setting not only accommodates the masses but lends to the entire enterprise the tradition and significance of agon. The "struggle" (and we should recall that Hitler entitled his autobiography *Mein Kampf*) played out here does not pit one team inside the arena against another but juxtaposes those within the stadium (both on the field and off) and those outside, solidifying into a team those who are present and pitting them against all who have been excluded.

Later, in *Olympia*, released in 1938, Riefenstal aimed her cameras directly at the spectacle of sport, depicting the conflict and struggle aesthetically, some of the time more as a statuesque display than as a contest. Indeed, as I will try to show later in this chapter, the well-muscled effigies caught by Riefenstal's lens are cinematic cousins of the sculptures of Arno Breker (whose statues adorned Berlin's Olympic stadium). Breker's male nudes, which would eventually be placed on prominent display in occupied Paris, attempted to combine the beauty of ancient Greek art with ideals of Aryan superiority. Similarly, Riefenstal illustrates how the Greek-inspired Olympiad in Berlin turned the traditional opening parade into a political march of bodies-beautiful, most of them sieg-heiling, before Hitler. Riefenstal's two films illustrate the Nazi technique of exploiting the concept of agon associated with the arena setting and infusing the mass event, whether sportive or political, with dramatic conflict. What makes *Olympia* most informative here is how clearly the fascist choreography (at odd moments only a few steps away from the congenial and self-aware absurdity of Busby Berkeley's) tried to present and reveal itself as classical in origin.[4]

It is crucial to recall that in France (which in the 1930s was far more politically diverse than Germany) the same arena might host the left-wing dramatic event one night and the right-wing political rally the next. In fact, around the very time Bloch's *Naissance d'une cité* was performed at the Vélodrome d'Hiver, an especially notable mass rally utilized this site. Michael Marrus and Robert Paxton describe the event:

In addition to sporting events, the Vel d'Hiv [as the stadium was popularly known] had seen its share of political rallies, including xenophobic and antisemitic demonstrations. When Charles Maurras [head of the right-wing and heavily bigoted *Action Française*] was released from prison in July 1937 (the directness of his attacks upon premier Léon Blum having won him a sentence for incitement of murder), the Vel d'Hiv was the site of a large demonstration attended

> by Xavier Vallat, Darquier de Pellepoix, Léon Daudet, Philippe Henriot, and other notable antisemites. (250)

The dynamic here is similar to that mentioned above with regard to the Nazi rallies: The mentality of *us* (in the stadium) versus *them* (beyond the stadium) prevails, redirecting the sense of agon, which is traditionally confined within the stadium walls. The emphasis then falls on deploying theatrics in order to convince the spectators that the struggle, which seemed intangible, has become concrete and thus real. As suggested earlier, this is essentially the same task to which drama aspires, the creation of the illusion—imitation, representation, *mimesis*—of conflict. Admittedly, the Maurras rally may have lacked the same outright display of classical muscularity that marked the 1936 Olympiad. Yet if André Zucca's photos of some of the right-wing rallies that took place at the Vel d'Hiv during the Occupation reflect at all the style of this prewar gathering,[5] the 1937 fête must have consisted of much of the same orderly movement and ritualized coordination and display of symbolic artifacts (flags, emblems, uniforms, speakers), which are depicted in Riefenstal's earlier film and which *Olympia* makes clear are supposedly founded on classical models.

Vichy and Sport

During the Third Republic, athletics in France conformed to the view of "sport, culture, and the state," which Richard Gruneau sees as commonly held in liberal pluralist theories:

> First, institutionalized sport is seen to be an expression of a consensus that has been developed, and is currently shared, by voluntary actors. Secondly, sport is not seen to be a formal part of the state system. . . . According to this view, sport should be an area of life that is somehow set-off from the "realities" of politics and government. (19)

Such notions are idealistic and perhaps ultimately meretricious, for as Lincoln Allison maintains, "[S]port, by its very nature, generates political resources" (15). Thus, the Popular Front government had begun a program to reform sport and physical education, first under Léo Lagrange and then Jean Zay, even while it upheld the ideas Gruneau articulates above. The program changed under the Vichy regime. As Jean-Louis Gay–Lescot asserts, just as physical education under Vichy was definitively installed as part of the education ministry, the sportive movement (like everything else) became an affair of state (112).

D. W. Halls describes how only three days after Pétain's assumption of power, Jean Borotra, a former tennis pro, was appointed to take charge of sport and of the physical education of French youth (188). Distinguishing the present government from the one that had failed France, Borotra "drew a direct connection between physical fitness and the defeat" (189).[6] True, the democratic state had earlier made efforts to improve sports education, but now Vichy made its physical training program a part of its National Revolution. Although Halls argues strenuously that Borotra was a patriot who hated the Germans (who, suspecting that he was a Gaullist or a potential organizer of French rightists against them, tried to find evidence to use against him), he admits that Borotra's program of athletic renewal (though not Borotra himself) prompted some to associate with physical education "the rather un-French concept of race" (189–190).[7] No matter what his private beliefs, however, the head of athletics under Vichy was hardly able to subvert either the ideals or the enactments of bigotry for which the regime he served had come to stand.

Sportive and athletic events began to adhere to a ritualized format. At meets and contests, participants under Borotra's program were made to swear an "Athlete's Oath"; Gay-Lescot describes how in the shadow of the tricolor and with the singing of the Marseillaise, contestants would avow, "Je promets, sur l'honneur, de pratiquer le sport avec désintéressement, discipline et loyauté pour devenir meilleur et mieux servir ma patrie" (89). Ceremonies in which "thousands of youngsters swore the oath before the local prefect" were, Halls tells us, held annually. "Sometimes," he adds, "the grand march that preceded the competition gave rise to comparisons with Nazi youth rallies, although Borotra had in mind the Greek rather than the Nazi ideal" (192). It was Borotra who subsidized Barrault's double bill of Greek tragedy and "drame sportif" at Roland-Garros and who later, Frederick Brown reveals, "asked Barrault to help organize a Festival of Youth on behalf of the new order" (427); Brown offers an extract from Robert Cardinne-Petit:

> Barrault accepted with enthusiasm. . . . The impresario he was knew no bounds: he saw things writ large and his zeal, which made him chafe at the modest budget allocated him, did wonders in the manipulation of the masses. All the youth leaders and monitors of physical education participated in the open-air demonstration at Bagatelle . . . which unfolded after the fashion of the national revolution with fanfares, choruses, parades, ensemble movements, all the rhythm of the popular hymn "Maréchal, nous voilà!" (427–428)[8]

Sports and athletics became subsumed by a state that predicated itself on the regeneration, spiritual and physical, of the French nation. The financial support, which, in a precarious economic time, promoted such activities, ensured that they would become living advertisements for Pétain's National Revolution; they were very blatantly Vichyite propaganda.

That pro-French, anti-German Borotra's pregame marches were viewed as Nazi-inspired may seem ironic, but we have already seen how the "Nazi ideal" was easily mistaken for the "Greek ideal" because Nazi ideology had tried to superimpose the classical upon itself. Beneath Riefenstal's statuesque images and Breker's muscular sculptures lay idealizations of Aryan male beauty founded upon decades of German thought. Summarizing more than a century of aesthetics, Mosse explains,

> The evolution of bourgeois morality was contemporaneous with the rediscovery of classical sculpture. J. J. Winckelmann, describing Greek male statuary as the paradigm of beauty for all time . . . in 1774, made this art acceptable to the middle classes by raising nudity to an abstract plane. . . . Such beauty was perceived as somehow sexless, a conviction shared by others at a later date, aided by the belief that the almost transparent whiteness of these figures raised them above the personal and sensual. Male symbolism could not be stripped of all physicality; the beauty of the Greek youths—lithe and supple, muscular and harmonious bodies—lay in their nakedness. It was precisely the corporeality of the sculpture that expressed strength and harmony, order and dynamism, in other words the ideal qualities of both burgher and nation. . . . For the Nazis such men symbolized the true German upon whose commitment the Third Reich depended. ("Beauty without Sensuality" 27)[9]

Yet even as National Socialism argued for the depiction of its own ideals in painting and sculpture, it promoted neoclassical art because, Mosse insists, "in its effort at self-representation . . . [it] simply appropriated long-standing popular tradition and taste" ("Beauty without Sensuality" 25). The seemingly harmonious marriage between accepted traditional styles based on Greek models and Nazi philosophy, though an unstable one (a point to which I will return later in this chapter), helped make the classical itself seem an extension of fascism. Hence, the staging of Greek and Greek-based plays in occupied Paris drew praise from the collaborationist press; in addition to revivals of the Attic tragedians and new works by contemporary French dramatists, the presentation of *Iphigénie en Tauride* by Goethe and *Iphigénie à Delphes* by Gerhardt Hauptmann allowed drama critics with pro-German sympathies to wax eloquent about these "classical" tragedies. The 1943 revival of Giraudoux's *Electre* might be eagerly viewed by the Nazis as what Agnes Raymond calls "a defense of order" (18) and "an apology for dictatorship" (118n) while Sartre's rendition of Oreste's return, *Les Mouches*, (*The Flies*) with its "decadent staging" by Charles Dullin—and a philosophic message (and an author) that collaborationist critics eyed distrustfully—seemed to desecrate its Greek prototypes.[10]

Borotra might have rationalized that "the grand march that preceded the competition" and "gave rise to comparisons with Nazi youth rallies" was in fact part of a very French neoclassical athletic tradition, which included, through the efforts of Baron Pierre de Couberton, the reinstatement of that pinnacle of Greek sport, the Olympics, which were eventually held in Paris in 1924. He might have argued too that the first play on the double bill at Roland-Garros, *The Suppliant Women*, was a bona fide Greek tragedy and that *Eight Hundred Meters* had, as Obey disclosed, been based on an actual event that had occurred during the 1924 games. He could, as well, have pointed to Gémier's production at the Cirque d'Hiver (which had fused Greek drama with athletic event) as the, or at least a, precedent for this one. Yet given the context, the prevailing cultural forces and the political circumstances, Barrault's theatrical production of Obey's texts seems to fit well with Borotra's program in which sports and athletics were appropriated by a parafascist state that was clearly, by financing this theatrical presentation, investing in its own legitimization.

Beefcake on Parade

What is generally written about *The Suppliant Women* and *Eight Hundred Meters* is that they were performed at the Stade Roland-Garros in Paris as a "représentation exceptionnelle." With one notable exception (Frederick Brown, who never directly names the modern play but does refer to it), recent critics tend to pay more attention to the "drame sportif" than to the ancient tragedy; such a tendency is understandable: Obey's "foot-race tragedy" offered a certain novelty rare during the Occupation and even today the play remains something of a curiosity. Moreover, if the Occupation press coverage provides any indication, many—though not all—who witnessed the double bill were more excited by *Eight Hundred Meters* than by Aeschylus' work.

Yet, if this production is to be glimpsed in context, *The Suppliant Women* must also be seen in its contemporary light. In the 1940s, the play was thought to be the oldest of the surviving Greek tragedies—Bernard Knox reminds us that *The Persians* of Aeschylus has only relatively recently been thought to be the earliest (7); in fact, Armory, in a lengthy critique in *Les Nouveaux Temps* (15 July 1941), calls the play "a work that was, for centuries, considered the masterpiece of tragedy." In true antique fashion, Aeschylus' *The Suppliant Women* is carried not by its brief, awkwardly handled episodes featuring two actors but by its ample chorus, the fifty daughters of Danaus, who arrive as suppliants at a grove near Argos. Fleeing their fifty Egyptian cousins, who wish to force them into marriage, the girls beg King Pelasgus for sanctuary; he leaves to ask his people for permission to grant it; however, when he returns to convey their consent, Danaus arrives and tells his daughters that their cousins have landed. Their herald comes to take the girls away, but Pelasgus has armed his own forces. So the herald, threatening war, departs, leaving Danaus to counsel his daughters to be grateful to the Argives and the gods. The suppliants sing a hymn of deliverance (Bernadette 2–3). The plot proceeds with stark simplicity; the choral passages are powerful. In its own way, Aeschylus' ancient script offers a sublime example of a very austere classicism.

The venerability of *The Suppliant Women* and the accuracy of its production were stressed in the preopening press coverage. Short articles in *Les Nouveaux Temps* and *Le Petit Parisien* (both from 4 July 1941) emphasize the authentic masks and cothurnes to be worn for the play, while a longer piece by Jean-Marie Roche in *Le Pays Libre* (5 July 1941) raves that the play, one of the most famous works by the father of Greek tragedy, successfully evokes the monuments of ancient Greece. Rehearsal shots, one of which accompanied the piece in *Les Nouveaux Temps* and another in *Le Matin*, show male actors rehearsing in large Greek masks.[11] Thus, Aeschylus' play lent some of its authenticity as a venerated art object to the afternoon's program: In a piece entitled, "La Tragédie du 800 mètres," which was published twice in *Comœdia*,[12] Obey asserted that *Eight Hundred Meters* qualified as an actual tragedy under the definition given in Aristotle's *Poetics* and then compared his play to Aeschylus' *Seven Against Thebes* and *Persians*. Barrault, in a brief interview about the production in *Paris-Midi* (4 July 1941), even assumed a classically heroic tone:

> I must render homage to the courage of all the artists. Thanks to the compliance of the national theatres and thanks to the good will of everyone, we will come close on Saturday to giving our lives, for three hours, beneath the sun.[13]

In some way, then, *Eight Hundred Meters* benefited from the legitimacy of the antique play. Perhaps the playwright and the actor/director—or perhaps Borotra himself—worried that without the link to ancient Greece, this production might be associated with Nazi extravaganzas.

Of course, not only did the Greek connection itself serve as an immediate reference to Nazi art, but the very spectacle that would emerge from the dramatization of these scripts was inevitably laden with imagery that was (like Borotra's "grand march that preceded the competition") quickly and perhaps not altogether inaccurately construed as Nazi in origin. As John M.

Hoberman reminds us, "The dream of dynamic virility, prominently featuring the perfected body as a symbol of force, has been a theme of every fascist culture" and "the Nazis promulgated a 'virile' ideal of the Aryan warrior" (*Sport and Political Ideology* 84).[14] Therefore, such a construction ought to have been predictable from the half-time athletic display by the Paris firemen and from the text of *Eight Hundred Meters*, which utilized the same kind of display of male physiques as seen in the opening sequences of *Olympia* and the sculptures by Breker; a photograph that appeared after the play opened shows the runners in skimpy shorts, racing bare-chested and with convincingly competitive form.[15] Another photo, which accompanied the brief review in *L'Atelier* (12 July 1941), shows Barrault directing, running fully clothed alongside three of his nearly naked actors.

Yet Barrault's penchant for showing the body, which had figured so prominently in his earlier work, was even more noticeable in *The Suppliant Women*. The photograph in *Le Matin*, with five male actors in masks, depicts these muscular firemen—several showing off their washboard abs—in shorts. Although the rehearsal shot that ran in *Les Nouveaux Temps* has the actors in masks and costumes, their wardrobe consists of togas that reveal their shoulders, arms, and legs.

Most spectacular, however, is the spread in *La Semaine* (3 July 1941), with two large rehearsal photos of the firemen-actors, again shirtless and in shorts, as the Egyptians who are carrying off the chorus (who are dressed in shorts, tops, and modern high-heeled shoes): in the first picture (captioned "The 'Suppliant Women' daughters of Danaus have a Greek Beauty. Spectators will regret that they won't retain their rehearsal costumes"), the women are lifted overhead by their abductors and appear as long, bare legs and high heels, while their ravishers, who are mounting a wide staircase and have been caught by the camera from behind, show off their broad backs and well developed arms as they hold the maidens aloft; in the second (captioned "These firemen repeat the gesture made by Greek athletes in 461 B.C."), the legs and heeled shoes of the Suppliant Women are glimpsed at the top of the picture, but the physiques of the two males supporting them are portrayed almost completely and in clear detail: bulging muscles, chest hair, provocative flesh tones. While the caption writer nudges an elbow into the ribs of the heterosexual male reader ("You'll be sorry the girls won't be keeping their rehearsal costumes"), the eye, guided by the lens, is directed not to the disembodied Chorine-Suppliants but to the full-bodied Firemen-Egyptians.

That the entire program for the afternoon would provide an exhibition of beefcake seems to have been evident before performances had begun. Georges Pioch, reviewing in *L'Œuvre* (12 July 1941), had warily anticipated the "nudité juvénile" of the firemen's half-time athletics demonstration. Indeed, a caricature featured in *La Semaine à Paris* (3 July 1941) depicts the

Photo spread showing firemen and chorines rehearsing The Suppliant
Women *(Bibliotheque Nationale de France).*

double bill as consisting of the determined runners of *Eight Hundred Meters*
and combatative warriors of *The Suppliant Women,* all in black shorts, with
an elongated and sinewy Barrault, striking a graceful but manly pose in the
foreground, clad only in white briefs.

Two modern critics have commented on the importance of the implications of these physical displays. David Bradby notes how *Eight Hundred Meters*

> demonstrates very clearly Barrault's continuing belief in the central-
> ity of the human physique for the act of theatre, but also his political
> naïvety, since the times had changed dramatically between the Popu-
> lar Front and 1941: the cult of the body had acquired sinister
> overtones. . . . Early in the war he put his enthusiasm for physical
> training with youth groups at the disposal of Vichy. . . . (24–25)

Patrick Marsh, who infers a tendency even more insidious than what Bradby
calls "naïvety," places *Eight Hundred Meters* among "a number of plays
[that] were written and staged which, to varying extents, mirrored the ideals
of the new order" ("The Theatre . . ." 157) and concludes,

> This somewhat unusual theatrical event must be considered as hav-
> ing a clear affinity with the cult of the body beautiful which the Nazi
> propagandists promoted through the pages of the daily press; the
> publicity for the play in *Comoedia* was surrounded by a series of
> statements written by none other than Jean Giraudoux. . . . (157–158)[16]

In this context, "the cult of the body beautiful," to which Barrault was seemingly so attracted, was readily viewable not so much, as Marsh argues, "as
having a clear affinity with" that "which the Nazi propagandists promoted
through the pages of the daily press" but as being identical to it.[17] And even
though this physique worship certainly had, as Bradby explains, "acquired
sinister overtones," the adjective here may be somewhat anachronistic: More
precisely, the "overtones" that "the cult of the body" had acquired represented
the shift from the Popular Front to Vichy and to the German occupiers; in the
summer of 1941 this shift was not necessarily "sinister" for all French people.

To some degree, many in occupied France might try to claim the classics and sports as neutral ground. Yet in Paris, after a little more than a year
of the Occupation, and in this culture, as it was being redefined and recon-
structed, precious little territory was genuinely nonaligned. The best that one
might do was to claim an allegiance to France, but the choice remained
between that France in which sportive displays "unfolded after the fashion of
the national revolution with fanfares, choruses, parades, ensemble movements,
all the rhythm of the popular hymn 'Maréchal, nous voilà!' " and the France
of the Marianne, of "Liberté, Égalité, Fraternité," of genuine tolerance and
acceptance. Although for some the full implications of the former might not
yet have seemed clear, even early during what has come to be called "the
Vichy years" the choice was there.

Possibilities of Interpretation

To understand what this theatrical event may have meant to those who experienced it when it played in July 1941, requires an investigation of how the
dramatic texts were realized by the theatre text (the scripts put into production) and then some attempt to consider their reception. Although above I
emphasize the prominent display of the male body, which press materials
support, a number of other production aspects should be mentioned especially
with regard to *The Suppliant Women*: In addition to the use of ancient-
inspired costumes and cothurnes (designed by Marie-Hélène Dasté and L.
Coutaud) and masks (designed by Collamarini), the performance featured
music by Arthur Honegger and sets reflecting Greek architecture (by Calsat)

with classical decorations (by F. Labisse) and sculptures (by Leclerc, Charlet, and Giovanetti). The staging at Roland-Garros of this ancient tragedy, which by modern standards may seem a static and uneventful script, was extensive and, at least technically, engaging.

Critics responded more to the theatrical than to the dramatic text. In *Les Nouveaux Temps*, in a scathing dismissal of both Obey's translation and the very idea of presenting the play in this context, Armory devotes much attention to the details of the production, if only to dispute their legitimacy. And in the piece in *L'Œuvre,* which compares Gémier's stagings with Barrault's (championing the earlier director), the writer admits that "the music, the dances, and the sportive exercises suffice to create the atmosphere of a pleasing spectacle." Both the reviewer in *La Gerbe* (10 July 1941) and Jacques Berland in *Paris-Soir* (12 July 1941) refer to the elements of production in positive terms, and Georges Pioch in *L'Œuvre* discusses the sights and sounds of the event with admiring care; Marcel Dellanoy, however, in *Les Nouveaux Temps* (15 July 1941), complains that the text was buried under the vast spectacle.

Perhaps the most explicit and substantial discussion of the dramatic text came from Roland Purnal, writing in *Comœdia* (12 July 1941). After a careful summation of the events in the play, Purnal arrives at the following interpretation:

> Thus triumphs without break that lofty idea of justice which, always, hangs over Aeschylean tragedy. And the drama terminates on an act of grace: the daughters of Danaus disown the gods of Egypt to render homage to those of Hellas, who after all, are their *true* gods, if one can well remember that Argos is the birthplace of their race.

Purnal's reading makes the Danaids' transfer of allegiance from the false Egyptian gods to the *true* gods (the gods of their true racial forebears) an enactment of the triumph of ideal justice; by implication, suppliant France is saved by Germany, and the gods of the Allies, who failed to protect the nation during the drôle de guerre, are replaced by the gods of the Axis. For Purnal, the ancient play becomes a modern parable. Much of his interpretation is prompted not only by what seem to be his own sympathies but also by the larger setting, which frames the stage setting—by the wider theatrical experience. The reviewer in *Le Petit Parisien* (6 July 1941) expresses this big picture most vividly:

> Four o'clock! The sun for two hours strikes the thousands of faces and suddenly necks become immobile when the start of the spectacle is announced by the trumpets. On the stadium ground, beneath the gaze of the Gods, the scene shines purely: tall columns the color of rust and blue break away into a scene of temples and

mountains. At the other end of the arena, on a low platform, the orchestra of the Conservatory Society of Concerts. . . . At the side of Jean Borotra, Mr. Jean-Louis Vaudoyer, administrator of the Comédie-Française, and personalities of letters, theatre, and music. I imagine that hidden among the spectators are the great poets on sport. Montherlant, and Giraudoux, who once wrote . . . "the only time in which the French senators busied themselves with sports, it was to take up this famous decree: Buses, horses, trucks must march in step around the Senate. Ideas too." Has something changed, then? Because over Roland-Garros stadium today rules a younger generation that is healthy, vigorous, full of enthusiasm.

The grandeur of the event, with its thousands of sun-drenched spectators, its heralding trumpets, and its columns and a panorama of classical temples and mountains, and with Borotra, and near him Vaudoyer, Montherlant,[18] and Giraudoux, as well as other celebrities from the literary, theatrical, and musical worlds—the sequence of these details brings to mind the skillful montage in *Triumph of the Will*. In an environment in which the audience is itself a part of the theatricalization, one might find it easy to decry the lazy, flabby senators of the Third Republic and applaud today's healthy, vigorous youth, brimming with enthusiasm. In a way, the grand spectacle helps to form and inform the point of view from which Purnal regards *The Suppliant Women*.

Of course, there are—and more important, were—perspectives other than Purnal's from which to regard Aeschylus' tragedy. For example, instead of identifying the Argives, whose constitutional monarch must ask his citizens to approve protection of the Suppliant Women, with the Germans, the spectator might connect the Egyptian rapists with the Nazis. In this light, the Argives may be seen as the democratic powers—the Allies, who represent salvation. If one wished to pursue the myth beyond the play (and into the two lost tragedies that completed the trilogy that *The Suppliant Women* began), the ravishers eventually force the daughters of Danaus into marriage and are then all murdered by their captive wives (except for Hypermnestra, who refuses to kill her husband); in this reading, Germany, in spite of temporary victory, is doomed to defeat, and the war is bound to continue. Thus, a spectator conversant with the classics might have been able to see past the production and form a totally different interpretation, but such an audience member would have had to be able to read through the theatre text, which reviewers like Purnal and others found "made" the play, or which a skeptic like Armory insisted was just too big to get beyond. To resist the grand spectacle must have required an audience member to have held, before entering the arena, well formed beliefs about the play itself that differed radically from those of the collaborationist press.[19]

The question still lingers, however, as to whether or not *Eight Hundred Meters* was capable of being read in ways that might differ politically from the fervent appreciations of the fascist critics. Recent critics have, with good reason, seen the play as a dramatization of a fascist or para-fascist agenda, but could spectators have found in this play anything other than a dramatization and celebration of fascist values? Again, only some exploration of how the script, by way of production, was experienced by the spectators can lead to an answer to this question.

Unlike *The Suppliant Women*, a substantial work of literature that had been read and studied for centuries, the dramatic text of *Eight Hundred Meters* was brief and unpublished. As noted earlier, Obey had tried in an article, which ran twice in *Comœdia*, to stress that his sports drama was a tragedy in its own right; he had gone on to reveal that the play had been inspired by Paul Martin, a Swiss runner in the 1924 Paris Olympics, who had been expected to win the 800-meter race but had fallen ill in the final lap and thus came in second "—and that was tragic," declares Obey. Readers familiar with *L'Orgue du Stade*, Obey's 1924 account of the Paris Olympics, might have recalled that he had already described the event in a climactic essay entitled, "Le huit cents mètres de Paul Martin" (191–215). Beyond this, however, little else about his new script was known prior to its premiere, and as I will make clear shortly, even more than with *The Suppliant Women*, most critics were far more interested (both before and after they had seen the play) in the spectacle. Nevertheless, the script of *Eight Hundred Meters* is in itself of considerable interest, in part because it offers some concrete evidence of what was behind something that has always been regarded as a primarily theatrical event.[20]

Eight Hundred Meters was written to be staged as a race: The seven contestants—played by, among others, Jean Marais, Alain Cuny, Michel Vitold, and Barrault himself (as the favored runner who falters)[21] —were situated on the track; Fernand Ledoux, of the Comédie-Française, read the role of Le Speaker, which was broadcast over a public address system, and in one of the stadium's audience sections sat Le Chœur, a chorus of young spectators, each carrying a small flag representing a country. As Le Speaker offered a poetic and occasionally ironic narration, Le Chœur might echo his remarks or strike up a chant that somehow differed. The dialogue alternated between verse and prose. Coordinated with the interplay of sight and speech was a percussive score composed especially for the production by Honegger.

After calling the stadium to attention, Le Speaker silences Le Chœur with a long speech extolling the contest and the stadium itself. "The stadium," he announces, "is a free place!" and Le Chœur reply, "The stadium is a free place!" (9–10) Their interchange builds to a back-and-forth incantation in which Le Speaker and choir praise the sun, the wind, clouds, air, water, and earth (but not fire), with final praise for sport itself and the playing field, the soil of the cross-country run and the mud of the rugby match (11). Le Speaker next turns to the combat of "the big naked young men" (14) who will compete in this "summer's tragedy" (15). Initially, the six participants are named according to origin, one each from the north, northeast, east, south, northwest, and west (15–16); they eventually enter and are identified, respectively, as Lundgren (a Scandinavian), Marva (a Finn), Heltzer (a German), Ramondès (a Spaniard), Stallard (a Briton), and Richardson (an American) (17–19). Finally "Jean, notre homme" (21), that is, a Frenchman, arrives.

Le Speaker describes "our man Jean" as a man alone, "divided . . . in two parts," and adds,

> . . . Like you and me!
> Like the sons of this earth!
> Heart of sun, soul of mists.
> Half action, half dream.
> Soul of the gray North sea,
> And heart of the Mediterranean.
> . . . .
> Half male, yes, and half female.
> But—by what strange inversion?—
> the male, in us, is reason;
> the heroism is female! (23–24)

Le Choeur splits in two, one choir made up of males, the other of females, to echo in response. A single male and a single female voice emerge, representing the two sides of Jean (and by extension, of the audience), and as the race begins, each urges him on. At first, Jean lags behind, torn by these two voices. Unable to get ahead, he laments,

> Unjust! Unjust! This is unjust!
> I needed some free ground!
> Some free space! That was my right! (29)[22]

He shouts that being so far behind in the race feels like being in prison (31). Gradually, Jean pulls ahead. The female voice spurs him on, but the male voice predicts his ruin. Finally catching up, he cries, "Ha! I am free! I am free!/I have gained my freedom" (35). Yet the heroics of victory go to his head and get the better of his reason; he runs close to the cheering audience, eager to hear their acclaim (37). Although the female voice and Le Choeur exhort Jean to struggle on—"Be a man!" they shout (38)—this momentary distraction allows Marva to win. Le Speaker and Le Choeur conclude with a chant on the primacy of the contest, the ancient tragic ritual common to Man (42–44).

As implied earlier, much in the script of *Eight Hundred Meters* seems to articulate the ideals of the Vichy government, which subsidized the production and whose ideals themselves, as indicated above, reflected Nazi ideology. The identification of characters by place of origin ("The man of the North," etc.) sounds very much like "the rather un-French concept of race," which Halls tells us, under Borotra, some had by now come to associate with physical education (189–190).[23] Quite literally engendering "opposing" aspects of the central character's personality, so that action and reason are represented as male and dreams and heroism are represented as female, smacks of the same symbolism that Mosse traces through fascist German culture, in which the male body, epitomized by the Greeks, "symbolized the true German upon whose commitment the Third Reich depended" (27); indeed, as noted earlier, the image of the naked male body is specified by the script, which defines the competition as one between "the big naked young men." And the notion of agon, the sportive struggle, which embodied in such high Nazi art as the films of Riefenstal and the sculptures of Breker the way of the world, rings through this dramatic text loud and clear.[24]

Yet the play remains problematic, if only because at its center there lurks the troubling spirit of defeat. Unlike Nazi art, which champions victory and achievement, romantically pulling triumph from the jaws of disaster, *Eight Hundred Meters* focuses not on the big winner of the foot race but on the big loser. Unlike the Swiss runner Paul Martin, who inspired Obey's play, Frenchman Jean is not suddenly stricken with illness but smitten by pride. His failure results directly from hubris. To an extent, he is redeemed: After a tense moment, he embraces Marva, and they rejoin the other runners who have by now crossed the finish line. This acceptance is hailed by the female voice, who cries, "He has won!" (42), and then Le Speaker and Le Choeur celebrate what they have just witnessed as basic to the condition of humankind. Jean fades into the group of young men who have come to represent youth as "the triumph of life" (44).

From the perspective of July 1941, spectators would have quickly associated the defeat of "notre homme," Jean, with the fall of France. Interpretations might have gone in two directions: one toward equating Jean's reconciliation with Marva as symbolic of France's need to accept her own defeat (due to foolish overconfidence in her own ability and, of course, republican decadence) in order to rejoin the community of European (that is, fascist) nations; the other toward viewing the Defeat in the drôle de guerre as only one loss in a longer, ongoing combat.

Although the first view seems the more likely, particularly in light of the script as a whole, such a reading seems less inevitable when one considers that the winner is Marva and not "the man of the East," Heltzer; Obey could have easily made the German the victor over the Finn.[25] Why did the playwright so clearly avoid such an outcome? One answer might be that audiences would not have tolerated it. Even for those who collaborated or espoused the Nazis' cause, the actual Defeat carried with it a certain humiliation and shame; more important, even in 1941 there were potentially enough people in a Parisian audience who did not look favorably upon Germany that a director would have been wise to avoid over-determining a play's message in favor of the occupier. Moreover, even while the theme of collaborationism might appear to flow throughout the script, such a notion was one that Borotra, in spite of his post in the Vichy government, probably would not have paid to publicize. As Halls reminds us, suspected and scrutinized by the Nazis, the patron of this "représentation exceptionnelle" may have intended it not only as good publicity for his physical education program but also as a demonstration that there would always be another race to run.

Of course, contemporary critics in the press do not offer either interpretation; predictably, there is no mention of the Defeat. Yet what they say is informative. Some condemn the dramatic text, calling it "pretentious" (*La Gerbe*) and "a farce" (Armory in *Les Nouveaux Temps*); "I believe immediately in the Argive gods," complains Purnal in *Comœdia*, "but I never come to believe in the 800-meter race." Others find much to praise, including the reviewer for *Le Petit Parisien*, Maurice Rostand in *Paris-Midi* (9 July 1941), and Pioch in *L'Œuvre*. Pioch, in observing that the play's static moments were more interesting than its frenetic ones, describes how one runner eclipsed the others—Jean Marais, "whose athletic nudity, foreshadowed in the statuary, is a magnificent spectacle."[26] And Armory, who pans the play, confesses he could not help admiring the splendid and very sculptured group of actor-runners headed up by Jean Marais. That two critics, one pro, the other con, should note Marais's masculine beauty is significant, for their remarks for the first time in this discussion articulate the palpable homoeroticism latent but nonetheless present in this particular theatre imagery.

This homoeroticism underlies much of my previous discussion. Homoeroticism, for example, lingers beneath the display of the firemen's physiques in *La Semaine*, and the caption, "Spectators will regret that they won't retain their rehearsal costumes," which obviously refers the (male) reader to the legs of the actresses held aloft, only partially mitigates and sanctions the exhibition of attractive men to other men. Much the same goes on around the other photographs of the actors in *The Suppliant Women* and *Eight Hundred Meters*: In the pictures the male bodies are displayed in clear, appealing detail even as the captions try to discount or at least minimize their erotic allure. The imagery and its insinuations are even satirized in the caricature of Barrault and company in *La Semaine à Paris*.

As I suggest earlier, no matter what the political affiliations of the pur-veyors of this beefcake (pro-Vichy, delusionally neutral, or simply naïve), the imagery of the naked male physique could not escape association with the Nazi cult of the body. And beneath the sacred objects of this cult flow the same homoerotic undercurrents. Mosse may talk of a "beauty without sensuality" (25) but in actuality the tension between the content and form (in a Riefenstal film, a Breker statue,[27] or any of the works, which pictorially or otherwise portrayed the male physique) was never sufficient to extinguish completely sparks of the sexually or, more problematically, the homosexually suggestive. As Hoberman deduces, the "combination of 'Germanic strength' and the 'Greek ideal of physical beauty' is an unstable one" (*Sport and Political Ideology* 103). Yet while Hoberman offers complex ideological reasons for this assertion, I would explain it more simply: A highly homophobic culture (such as Nazi Germany or fascist France) that tries to appropriate as its own the iconography of a homophile culture (such as ancient Greece) can never, in spite of however many purges and denials, fully suppress that iconography's ability to signify. Some signs seem to have a durability that transcends a culture's attempts to alter or recode them; just as a blazing sun can never be completely made to stand for frigidity, so is it impossible to create a beautiful human form that is entirely distinct from its human, and thus sexual, dimension.

Rather than return to a discussion of Nazi Germany's ongoing attacks against the ever present threat of homosexuality,[28] I will turn to Jean Marais, whose physical appearance in *Eight Hundred Meters* was viewed by Pioch and Armory as significant enough to mention. What exactly might Marais have signified to them? As members of the theatre community, both critics were no doubt familiar with Marais's romantic connection to Cocteau. And they would have known, too, that on April 29, Marais had opened (in the role of twins) in *The Typewriter*; that after the ban on the play, Cocteau had been attacked in the press, particularly by Alain Laubreaux, not just for *The Type-writer* but for the homosexual private life that Cocteau did little to hide; and that during that same spring Marais, who had continued with the play (which reopened a few days later and ran through June) had attacked Laubreaux with his fists outside a restaurant. To two drama critics, this recent history, coupled with his sexuality,[29] might have made Marais's appearance more meaningful than their references to his gorgeous physique would suggest.

Marais the actor was (and was by some known to be), in a variety of ways, the antithesis of what he portrayed in *Eight Hundred Meters*. He was not the wholesome heterosexual athlete so prized by Nazis, pro-fascists, Vichyites, and Borotra but—at least to some in the collaborationist press—a decadent queer who represented the worst degeneracies of the Third Repub-lic. Thus, his inclusion in the cast provoked an evident irony, which is expressed in the two critics' comments. His presence in the play might have signaled to some, as it did to Armory, that the real purpose of the presentation was not to re-create a race but to show off handsome male flesh, which in itself (and particularly in the case of Marais) might be pleasing but did not make for great drama. To others, such as the unathletic Pioch (who admitted that he had no interest in sports), the statuesque sight of the muscular Marais reminded him that the whole event worked not as sport but as drama. For both reviewers, mention of Marais is a way to articulate how the play could not seriously sustain the agon that it had attempted to synthesize.[30] For some audience members, the theatre text of *Eight Hundred Meters* appears to have worked against and even perhaps subverted the dramatic text's fascist implications in a curious way. Perhaps the negative reviews that *Eight Hundred Meters* received are in some way indicative of the critics' distrust for the play's ambiguities and possible readings, which loomed, formless yet subversive, beyond the dramatic text.

For finally, there is also, flowing subterraneanly through the script, a subtle thematic current—some may argue it is too subtle to be discerned—of thoughts and emotions regarding freedom and confinement. Early in the script, the stadium is celebrated as a free space ("The stadium," says Le Speaker, "is a free place!" 10). As he struggles ahead, Jean cries for "Some free space! That is my right!" (29). Still behind, he talks of his position as "This prison!" (31), and only when he does catch up can he shout, "Ha! I am free!" (35). Jean's ultimate defeat, then, is difficult to see as a call for getting along with the conqueror, except perhaps in the way in which inmates are forced to "get along" with their jailers.

At the same time, though, we must remember that actual audience response is highly diverse and individualized. Bradby notes how amateur sportsman Gabriel Cousins, who would later become a playwright but, in 1941, had never attended a play before, was profoundly influenced by the Roland-Garros double bill. Yet the "resonance" that *Eight Hundred Meters* set up in him was not at all political but aesthetic; the familiar context of the stadium helped Cousins comprehend the physicality of theatre (25). And one of the more avid and politically sensitive theatregoers of the period, Simone de Beauvoir, remembered Obey's sports drama as "an insipid little paean to the glories of athletics" (*Prime of Life* 485) although, admittedly, she had come to see her friend Olga in *Les Suppliantes*.

Conclusion

In a sense quite different from the one Robert Brasillach had intended, the double bill at Roland-Garros constituted a genuine comédie sans tickets: The plays contained no direct references to the current era. Yet many reviewers in the Nazi-controlled papers praised these pieces, which in many ways fulfilled their expectations of what drama ought to be. Still, the need for a new vocabulary that might be deployed to castigate those works that did not coincide with the fascist agenda remained. If spectators could interpret *The Suppliant Women* and *Eight Hundred Meters*, which had been approved, promoted, and produced by the Vichy government, as anything other than pro-Vichy, then there was always the danger that audiences of other works might construe them in a similarly erroneous way, or at least in one that proved contrary to what the current regime desired. Throughout the War, the press tried to control response, and to that end coined and recoined phrases—"comédie sans tickets," "boulevard comedy," "inverted theatre," "pre-war cocktail," "purveyor of pornography"; the list would grow.

The attempted rechanneling of the homoerotic implications in Nazi art is neatly summed up by Helmut Lehman-Haupt on Breker, who "not only models the muscle of a male body to recapture the classic Greek image but also shapes each part so as to express a paroxysm of wrath and vengeance" (quoted by Cone 65). Yet how much chiseled cruelty is needed to divert the male observer's apprehension of eros in a depiction of someone of his own sex? In spite of and because of the careful and controlled display of masculine beauty, packaged to be sensed but not savored, homoerotic imagery inevitably emerges. All the "wrath and vengeance" in the world cannot totally efface human reception of what is intrinsic to a representation. In the case of these plays, the muscled male bodies belonged to the fierce ravishers of women (the fire-fighter Egyptians in *The Suppliant Women*) and to the driven competitors (the actor-runners in *Eight Hundred Meters*); still they were appealing.

But perhaps the chief lesson that this "représentation exceptionelle" offered the French under the Occupation had less to do with the body beautiful than with the body politic. The plays, after all, concerned themselves with the vanquished and the also-ran, the ravished victim and the over-confident participant whom all expected to come in first but who emerged the loser. In short, *The Suppliant Women* and *Eight Hundred Meters* attempted to soothe the humiliation of their French audiences even as they reminded them of their own defeat.

Almost exactly one year after the presentation of *The Suppliant Women* and *Eight Hundred Meters* (and just five years after the Maurras rally and Bloch's *Naissance d'une cité*), in July 1942, the Vélodrome d'Hiver became the collection point in operation Vent Printanier (Spring Wind), in which Paris city police rounded up Jewish families; by the end of the first day of the police action (July 16), 7,000 Jews, more than half of them children, had been interned in the stadium (Josephs 62). The use of this facility for detention had its precedents: as Marrus and Paxton point out, "in 1939, internees of German nationality—mostly Jewish refugees—were assembled there before being sent to concentration camps in the Paris region" and "[in] May 1940 the stadium was used for interned women, who in some cases huddled in the cold. . . ." The conditions for the women at the Vel d'Hiv were "reportedly even worse than those of interned foreign men at the Roland Garros Stadium" (250). The next stop for the Jews who in 1942 had been interned by Vent Printanier, was the housing project in the working-class suburb of Drancy, now a concentration camp from where nearly 70,000 would be carried by train to the east and to their deaths.

3

French Identity:
The Intended Audience for
Jean Giraudoux's *The Apollo of Marsac*

Introduction

As Marsh tells us, extracts from the writings of Jean Giraudoux, diplomat, government minister, and France's most celebrated playwright, framed the publicity for *Eight Hundred Meters* and *The Suppliant Women* in the collaborationist arts weekly, *Comœdia* ("The Theatre . . ." 157–158). These quotes were reprinted to enhance the legitimacy of the double-bill spectacle and even to imply a certain sympathy on the part of Giraudoux for this project sponsored by the Vichy Ministry of Education and Sport. Here are a few:

> The peoples who have the most considerable percentage of art reviews are those who count the strongest in sports: Germany and Finland.

> A doctor who is not athletic is a chemist whose instruments are soiled.[1]

> There isn't a hero in Racine who isn't athletic.

> There isn't a great man whose image might be diminished by the attribution of an achievement in sports.[2]

And in *Le Sport*, Giraudoux declared,

> He who neglects the rapture of the body, neglects the health of his country. ("Le Théâtre . . ." 236)[3]

Yet Marsh adds, "It is very ironic that these words had been cited in this context: they had been written by a man profoundly hostile to The National Revolution and the Germans" (237)[4], and he wonders why Giraudoux allowed these extracts to be published on behalf of *Eight Hundred Meters*. Giraudoux was in fact a complex man, indeed one of the few French dramatists between the wars who was both artistically respected and commercially successful, even widely admired by the public.

Although Giraudoux's only new play produced in occupied Paris, *Sodome et Gomorrhe* (*Sodom and Gomorrah*), opened to mixed notices, it ran from October 1943 through May 1944 (by which time he had died). Yet the playwright's reputation would live on after the Liberation through the posthumous production of *La Folle de Chaillot* (*The Madwoman of Chaillot*), written during the War and produced at the end of 1945 by Giraudoux's longtime director and friend, Louis Jouvet. In this seemingly fanciful view of modern society, the men who control various financial interests that destroy the beauty of life are tricked into sacrificing themselves, lured to their deaths by the very greed with which they would not hesitate to ruin all else. Not only were the reviews superlative, but *Madwoman* went on to become an international hit (and, more than two decades later, a film). In more recent years, David Bradby has come to view the play as "clearly meant as an old man's valedictory attack on all that is petty and self-seeking in the modern world" and concludes, "it has dated very rapidly and now seems almost irresponsibly naive" (20). Jeffrey Mehlman makes more serious accusations, seeing in the play (in the context of the dramatist's body of writings) an expression of Giraudoux's xenophobic anti-Semitism (34–64).

However, during the Occupation Giraudoux completed at least one other play, about which Bradby and Mehlman—and indeed, about which most critics—have remarkably little to say. This whimsical one-act comedy, generally known as *L'Apollon de Bellac* (translated into English as *The Apollo of Bellac* or *The Apollo de Bellac*), was first written and produced (and published) under the title, *L'Apollon de Marsac* (*The Apollo of Marsac*).[5] Regarded by theatre reviewers and literary critics as a congenial minor work, the piece, when considered in light of its intended enactment and audience response, both of which must be grounded in the context of the Occupation, presents a pointed commentary on the self-esteem of defeated Frenchmen.

Giraudoux's political affiliations and beliefs were complicated, far more so, perhaps, than his plays suggest. The works that he composed between the wars, those that received popular and critical acclaim, belong to a large degree to a now-defunct genre: the drama of ideas. Likewise, in the tradition of French neoclassicism and romantic comedy, Giraudoux brings characters on stage who speak beautifully, and his wit, charm, and intelligence, as well as his occasional servings of sentiment, made his plays appear highly polished.

Still, lurking beneath the seemingly scintillating conversations and glittering debates are issues that are not merely raised but also ultimately resolved—never crudely, through mere disputation, but theatrically, through that "poetry of the theatre"—the poetry of visual and other nonverbal images about which Cocteau spoke—and tidily. Perhaps the relative lack of interest in Giraudoux's works since the late 1960s, at least outside of France, is due not so much to his whimsy and sense of enchantment but to his tendency toward easy closure. The complexity evoked by so many of his contemporaries is ultimately purged from his dramatic works, which remain brilliant but flawed by their own perfection.

For all his artistry and privacy, Giraudoux was always a very public person. He not only wrote plays but published poetry, novels, and nonfiction books; during the Occupation he completed two screenplays. After a career in the diplomatic service, he became Minister of Information in the Daladier government, and following the Defeat, after serving briefly in the same position (White 194), he held a minor but ministerial post under Vichy. During the drôle de guerre he had been a familiar presence, speaking on the radio, giving interviews, writing for newspapers and magazines; even with Paris under the Germans and his eventual retirement, he remained well known. In February 1943, when Cocteau first become acquainted with Jean Genet, he noted in his Occupation journal that he had gone to get his coat and met Giraudoux (whom he knew well) in the cloakroom; after the two emerged, Genet took Cocteau aside and asked, "You know Giraudoux? . . . But . . . he's not a poet!" (269; translation White 193). Genet detested Giraudoux but was clearly impressed that Cocteau knew him. And ironically it would be Genet's fate to have to suffer comparison with the older playwright when *Les Bonnes* (*The Maids*) was first produced with Giraudoux's *Apollo* (White 194).

Perhaps the reason *Apollo* has been so easy to dismiss or ignore is that it was never presented under the circumstances for which Giraudoux had intended it—performed by Louis Jouvet and Madeleine Ozeray and company before a Parisian audience in the winter of 1942. Perpetually removed, first by place, then through time, the play's intended meaning easily fades. In order to understand this curious one-act, we must consider it in its original, though unrealized, form and in its probable intended context.

While discussing Jean Cocteau's *The Typewriter*, I was able, by drawing on reports of people's conduct (and misconduct) in the auditorium, to gain a glimpse of what this detective drama may have meant when originally presented. Although Cocteau included in the script and the program some indication of the play's intended audience—that "ordinary Public," who are "more or less similar to a twelve-year-old child whose interest is difficult to hold except with laughter and tears" (5)—this intended audience did not show up for the premiere. Instead, the discrepancy between his intended audience and the actual, unanticipatedly diverse audience was nearly fatal to the production. Examining André Obey's *The Suppliant Women* and *Eight Hundred Meters*, I could use press descriptions of spectators and their placement in the stadium-turned-theatre, as well as reviewers' own reactions, to help me arrive at some understanding of how and what the plays may have signified to those who saw this double bill. However, an Occupation play that never found an Occupation audience proves more difficult to interpret in terms of the Occupation, if only because there can be no tangible evidence of how actual audiences responded to a real production during the period. *The Apollo of Marsac* is just such a play.

Just how important is it to consider contemporary spectator response in order to arrive at a responsible interpretation of an Occupation play—that is, an interpretation that takes into account what and how the play meant (and was meant to mean) when first written and/or presented? One may, with apparent justification, argue that a number of Occupation plays have been successfully produced since 1944; yet the reception of such revivals has obviously been quite different from how the plays were originally received (or in this case would have been received). One may, for example, conclude that plays written during the Occupation but presented afterward might do very well if one thinks of Giraudoux's *The Madwoman of Chaillot* as an example. However, *Madwoman* is hardly typical of Occupation drama, for its playwright, who died in January 1944, had anticipated the Liberation and deliberately written the fantasy for post-Occupation performance. Similarly, Albert Camus had begun *Caligula* during the Occupation, but the script, which would play so brilliantly during the first postwar season, had been substantially revised after the Liberation.[6] One may even find well known dramas—Jean-Paul Sartre's *No Exit* and Camus's *Le Malentendu* (*The Misunderstanding*)—that opened during the Occupation's fourth and final season, then closed as the Nazis fled and the Allies entered Paris, and subsequently reopened, continuing their runs. Still, contemporary reviews show clearly how Occupation and post-Occupation critical receptions differed, and there is evidence too that the same is true for spectator response.

The need to locate meaning in contemporary Occupation audiences remains imperative, for even though Occupation dramas may seem to make sense to modern spectators and readers, in a straightforward and an uncomplicated way, the sense that they make, or rather the sense that *we* modern spectators and readers make of them, is very much contingent upon the way that we recognize and construe the time and place from which the dramas emerged.[7] As I will show in chapter 5, many who looked at Anouilh's *Antigone* in the 1950s and 1960s, when the Gaullist myth of a France-résistante formed the prevalent historical perspective, tended to see the play as a vehicle of resistance; more recently, those who regard what happened after the Defeat from a post-resistancialist point of view tend to perceive the play as carrying a distinctly collaborationist or even profascist message.

Modern interpretations are too often distorted by modern values and prejudices: When I first examined *The Typewriter*, I was (not unlike the reader whom I anticipated in chapter 1) expecting the play to be the brave outcry of a forbidden minority, in part because my own times have taught me to sympathize with the plight of oppressed gay men and women; likewise, my first look at *The Suppliant Women* and *Eight Hundred Meters* was guided by a revulsion for the kind of fascist pageantry that the spectacle resembled. In both cases, my first attempts toward interpretation had more to do with how I perceived my own world than with how I could come to terms with the Occupation's.

Such interpretations, molded by present conditions, are bound to distort; to do justice to a playscript, readers must be able to imagine it in the context of what I will call the *intended* play. The intended play may be thought of as the playwright's notion of how the script, when performed in a theatre, will play in front of the audience whom the playwright has in mind. I must, then, divide the intended play into two separate but intimately related components: *the intended production* and *the intended audience*. Both take on obvious importance when a play remains unproduced for a significant period of time. Attempts to formulate the responses of an imagined audience, a group of spectators who in reality never saw the play, to an imagined production, one that was never mounted, can move a reader closer to an understanding of what the play, at least in its playwright's own terms, may have been meant to mean.

Responses to the Dramatic Text

Apollo was written sometime between mid-summer 1941 and the winter of 1942. During this period, Giraudoux, who had served as Director of Historical Landmarks under Vichy, retired (November 1941) to write. He completed this one-act by February 1942: in a lecture (posthumously published in *Visitations*), which he gave at the end of that month in Lausanne, Switzerland, he quotes rather freely from an early version of the play (*Visitations* 27–44), a revised draft of which he then mailed from Geneva to his longtime collaborator in the theatre, Louis Jouvet, who was then in Brazil (Giraudoux and Jouvet 110). *Apollo* opened in Rio de Janeiro in June 1942 and formed part of the repertory with which Jouvet's company toured Latin America.

As I shall discuss in detail later in this chapter, there is much to indicate that Giraudoux wrote the play especially for Jouvet and his company; thus, one may argue that the Rio production in part realized at least one component of the intended play—that is, the intended production. Yet that other component of the intended play, the intended contemporary French audience, was clearly absent. Even though *Apollo* had been produced with the cast whom Giraudoux had in mind while writing the play, it was performed in French for Latin American audiences who were, for reasons of language, culture, and history, far different from the spectators whom the playwright had in mind. In fact, the discrepancies between the intended and actual audiences had a clear and concrete impact on the visual appearance of the Rio production; this impact will become all the more evident at the conclusion of this chapter through a comparison of the stage set used in the Rio production and the one used in Jouvet's subsequent production of the play in Paris.

When, in February 1945, Jouvet returned to France from Latin America, Giraudoux had been dead for more than a year. The following December, Jouvet produced *The Madwoman of Chaillot*; not until a year and a half later did he stage *Apollo* in Paris. By this time, Ozeray and he had parted company.[8] In the role of Agnès, Jouvet now cast a young actress, Dominique Blanchar; for the set, he retained the designer he had used for the Rio production, Eduardo Anahory. To complete the evening, Jouvet settled on a playscript by Jean Genet, which Cocteau had encouraged him to read.[9] After requesting specific cuts, Jouvet agreed to use a shortened version of Genet's *The Maids* as a curtain-raiser for *Apollo*.[10] The plays opened at the theatre at which Jouvet had presented so many of Giraudoux's works, the Athénée (by this point known too as Théâtre Louis Jouvet), in April 1947.

In contrast to Genet's masterpiece of role-playing and ritualized violence, *Apollo* seems exceedingly tame: Agnès, a girl looking for work, arrives in the waiting room of the International Bureau of Inventors Great and Small. While trying to get past the male Receptionist, she is advised by a nondescript Man from the village of Bellac (or in the original version, Marsac[11]), who suddenly appears that, to get what she wants from the men in power here, she must tell each that he is handsome—as handsome as the made-up statue, the Apollo of Bellac. With coaxing and practice, Agnès praises the Receptionist, Vice Président, Président, and board members. The Président brings out his secretary, Mlle Chevredent ("Goat's-tooth"), who insists the Président is ugly; he hires Agnès in her place. The Président's mistress, Thérèse, enters; she maintains the Président is *not* a handsome man, argues with the Président, Agnès, and the Man from Bellac, then leaves. The Président places the diamond engagement ring intended for Thérèse on Agnès's finger.

Still, Agnès feels uncomfortable having complimented these men, who have all believed her. Rather than succeed through flattery, she tells the Man, who she pretends *is* Apollo, that she wants a man whom she finds truly handsome. As they converse, she is asked to close her eyes, and then she suddenly begins to believe that the Man from Bellac is in fact Apollo; confronted now with the image of divine beauty, she must admit that she is only human and thus chooses to live on a far more human scale. Yet upon opening her eyes, she declares that the nondescript Man *is* really handsome. He quickly departs, leaving a saddened Agnès to face the dubious success of her new job and wealthy suitor, while the bureaucrats on stage search for Apollo.[12]

Though interesting, the plot of *Apollo* pales beside *The Maids*.[13] In fact, recalling Claire and Solange, their real and imagined attempts against Madame and their bizarre end, modern readers may find the double bill of *The Maids* and *Apollo* utterly incongruous. Perhaps it seemed so too to Jouvet, whose associate, Léo Lapara, who appeared as the Receptionist in both the Rio and Paris premieres of *Apollo*, maintains that the director had ample misgivings about this odd coupling and that the audience more than shared this uneasiness.[14]

In any case, in 1947 critics found this a disconcerting evening in the theatre.[15] "Certainly, one understands and approves Jouvet's intentions in wishing to precede the Giraudoux play with a work of a newcomer," complained René Lalou, who went on to ask, "But what did he have in mind in choosing *The Maids* by Jean Genêt [sic]?" (4). Having sat through the Genet piece, some critics found the Giraudoux play rather light-weight. "A dessert by Giraudoux . . . [,] a little insipid, terminates the evening," commented Robert Kanters (86). "It is simplicity, innocence, candor," wrote Roger Lannes, ". . . transparent as the air" (6). Gabriel Marcel thought its charm "a little too insistent" (10).

Some reviewers implied that the double bill should have been reversed: Thierry Maulnier, for example, went so far as to call *Apollo* "nothing more than a light comedy in one act, a 'curtain raiser' in which the dramatic substance is rather slender . . ." (42). Francis Ambrière concurred that *Apollo* was nothing more than an "incomparable curtain-raiser" (1). J.-J. Rinieri, who thought it "a perfect curtain-raiser," was incredulous that one could "seriously think that it was for this [Giraudoux] entertainment that the production [double bill] has been created" (158). Interestingly, even most of the reviews that preferred Giraudoux's play to Genet's tend in some way to subordinate it—perhaps inevitably—to *The Maids* in their discussions of the two. And while *The Maids* has gone on to become a classic of the modern theatre, *Apollo*, in spite of its subsequent successes on stage, in both France and other countries, has remained a decidedly slight piece.

Similarly, critics writing in English, responding largely to their readings of the written text rather than to performances of the play, illustrate a tendency to diminish the importance of the work. Reviewing Giraudoux's career in the first number of *Yale French Studies* to be devoted entirely to drama, Georges May summarily dismisses *Apollo* as "mediocre" (93). Far kinder, Donald Inskip calls the play a "witty, light-hearted fantastication" (148). Robert Cohen, who finds some serious matter in it, admits that much of *Apollo* is "a frothy jest" (76). Agnes Raymond offers a penetrating biographical approach to the play but refrains from critical judgment (93–95).[16]

Significantly, a number of writers on modern French drama, including Joseph Chiari (114, 131, 234), Wallace Fowlie (298), Jacques Guicharnaud (312, 324), Bettina Knapp (*French Theatre* . . . 184), and Bradby (19, 54), mention *Apollo* but say nothing at all about it.

It is perhaps a little too easy to declare, with all the certainty granted by hindsight, that *The Maids* pointed toward the future, what Bradby calls "The New Theatre" (54ff), while *Apollo*, as Robert Cohen puts it, "was profoundly of the past" (77). We must remember that in 1947 "the past" amounted to a mere five years, a relatively short time for a work by a major dramatist— who during the previous season had posthumously scored an enormous success with *The Madwoman of Chaillot*, itself written a little after *Apollo*—to seem antiquated. Of course, the reason these five years made such a vast difference was because the production as Giraudoux had conceived it was no longer producible and because the audiences for whom *Apollo* had been written had ceased to exist. As noted previously, by 1947 Ozeray had left Jouvet's troupe and thus could not play the role of Agnès, which had been written for her; the Jouvet troupe, so triumphant before the fall of France, had (along with France itself) altered.

More important, though, the audience's reception of the play, even if Ozeray and Jouvet could have performed it as intended, could never measure up to what Giraudoux had anticipated: the feelings of humiliation and deprivation of 1942, though not completely forgotten, were by 1947 in the process of being revised. During the Occupation, people came to the theatre with a great hunger for inspiration and ideas. Yet the passage of time and the inevitable influence of the present on memories of the past had seriously transformed the sensibilities of the spectators. The subtle references in the script to the Occupation and the strong but guarded thematic content, which had been carefully and sufficiently understated, as if to slip past the censors, seemed to audiences after the Liberation so slight as to be unremarkable.

Reflections and Responses

In 1947 French audiences failed to see themselves as an intrinsic part of the play. Such involvement was crucial, as Giraudoux had meant the play, because on both a thematic and a theatrical level, *Apollo*, at least the *intended play*, is about mirrors, about images of oneself presented by others. This reflection motif is obvious even on a basic "storyline" level of this "frothy jest." Throughout the play, we watch as Agnès throw back to the men of the Bureau images of themselves that are positive—images that they not only like but that they choose as their own. We are, moreover, told that the board members, whom Agnès has praised, have all taken out their pocket mirrors, and we even hear them (offstage) cheering when a member proposes a three-way mirror for the men's washroom (934).[17] Choice is perhaps most evident in the Président's rejection of Thérèse in favor of Agnès. As Cohen puts it,

> [R]eality is too difficult to define by any one mirror: that being the case, the president may as well accept Agnès's version as Thérèse's. Neither woman is telling "the truth," both are reflecting what they see through the filter of what they want to see. . . . The President has the right to pick the mirror that flatters him the most. . . . (80)

In the end, the Man from Bellac too serves as a mirror for Agnès. Through him she comes to confront an image of herself—of the person she no longer is and the person she has become.

Yet on another level, one more related to the audience and their role in the play, *Apollo* sets about cracking the very mirror on which this and all plays rely, the metaphorical mirror of the stage. The decided lack of realism, which prompts Inskip's "witty, light-hearted fantastication" and Cohen's "frothy jest," is present in *Apollo* not merely for the effect of whimsy. As in many of Giraudoux's works, the playfulness in the drama is included to remind the audience that they are indeed watching a play.

The metatheatrical experience is extended by the author's insistence on specific actors to play the lead roles. As I have stated earlier, there is ample evidence that Giraudoux wrote *Apollo* especially for Jouvet's company. The lecture on theatre that the playwright delivered in Lausanne, Switzerland in February 1942, just before he sent the manuscript to Jouvet in Rio, includes a passage of the work in progress, which uses Jouvet's name instead of the character's (*Visitations* 27–44). Pointedly, the manuscript sent to Rio instructs, «Cher Jouvet, Cher Louis, trouvez-vous même le nom d'Apollon . . . » ("Dear Jouvet, Dear Louis, find the name 'Apollo' your own . . ." (*Cahiers* 110).[18] Giraudoux further notes in his lecture (though not in the published versions of the play) that Agnès "singularly resembles Madeleine Ozeray" (*Visitations* 27). This second casting cue harkens back to Giraudoux's earlier *L'Impromptu de Paris* (*The Impromptu of Paris*) (1937), a one-act in the tradition of Molière's *L'Impromptu de Versailles*, in which the actors of Jouvet's troupe play characters bearing their own names; Ozeray is cast as Ozeray playing Agnès in *L'École des Femmes*. In Molière's role of Agnès, both Inskip (78) and Cohen (78) attest, Ozeray scored one of her greatest successes. Thus, in the intended play of *Apollo*, Madeleine Ozeray is every bit as much Agnès as Louis Jouvet is M. de Marsac and/or Apollo.[19]

Having identified at least two of his characters with specific performers, Giraudoux obviously felt that he had to give his play to those for whom he had intended it. He felt the same about *Sodom and Gomorrah*, a play completed about the same time as *Apollo* (Giraudoux and Jouvet 110): Written for Edwige Feuillère, who had remained in France (and for whom he also wrote about this time the screenplay of *La Duchesse de Langeais*), *Sodom and Gomorrah* was staged in Paris in 1943, the last new play by Giraudoux to be performed during his lifetime. Having learned his craft as dramatist from his director, Jouvet, with whom his relationship had always been highly collaborative, Giraudoux (unlike Claudel, who for years had refused to allow productions for many of his plays) had always felt an intense connection between his scripts and their realizations—or, to put this more in the terminology with which I began this chapter, Giraudoux wrote his dramatic works with a strong sense of the intended play. Thus, the dramatist believed it vital to his intended play that *Apollo* be produced with Jouvet and Ozeray. As with *The Impromptu of Paris*, this one-act was designed to exploit the self-conscious interplay between the actors/characters and the audience.

This metatheatrical experience, which Giraudoux seems to have considered so crucial, is palpable even in the published versions of the playscript, both "Marsac" and "Bellac," in which M. de Marsac and M. de Bellac have, respectively, replaced Jouvet's name. In its published versions, *Apollo* is a play that comments self-reflectively on itself and on theatre in general. Raymond implies as much about all of Giraudoux's wartime dramaturgy when she observes:

> After the defeat of 1940, [Giraudoux] saw the theatre as a radiant confessional where [and here she quotes from the Lausanne lecture] "the crowd comes . . . to listen to its own confessions of cowardice and sacrifice, hate and passion." (95)[20]

The ambiguity of the stage, on which confession masquerades as fictive dialogue, allows the crowd to listen; at the same time, the sanctioned pretense of drama permits the crowd (if they so wish) to dismiss the play as "just a play." And ambiguity was, indeed, heightened during the Occupation, when, as is clear from what happened with Cocteau's *The Typewriter*, the Vichy and German censors carefully scoured scripts for subversive references and audiences looked for and sometimes invented verbal or other signs that in any way might somehow allude to the current crisis.

Giraudoux reminds the audience of this paradox when, toward the conclusion of *Apollo*, the Man from Bellac/Jouvet (or Apollo/Jouvet) tells Agnès/Ozeray, "Let's pretend that what happens in a traditional play happens to us . . ." (943). By gesturing toward the expected happy ending (which the audience will be denied), the playwright calls attention to the conventions through which audience members are usually able to separate themselves from stage plays. Thus Giraudoux warns the audience—the intended, Occupation audience—that the words they have heard and the images they have glimpsed, in spite of the seeming levity of the dramatic action, must not be discarded.

Occupation Significances

In order to understand *Apollo*, then, it becomes crucial to consider those for whom Giraudoux wrote the play—the people of German-occupied Paris. If we shift away from the actual productions (the Latin American of 1942–1945 and the Parisian of 1947) and those who attended them and imagine a house of French people in the spring of 1942 responding to a Jouvet-Ozeray production of the play, *Apollo* begins to change, to expand. From this perspective, the play begins to seem more substantial, more relevant to the dire circumstances that existed when the play was composed. Indeed, the significance of *Apollo*, even as I have so far discussed it, begins to deepen through the responses of its intended audience of Parisian theatregoers of the 1941–1942 season.

These were people who had lived under Nazi rule for a year and a half. As David Pryce-Jones describes them, they were familiar by now with rationing and shortages: coal, cloth, leather goods, food—most of all food. They had no oil for heating, and as gas reserves dwindled, they resorted to kerosene, also in short supply, for cooking. Anti-Semitism was on the rise: Jews, this audience knew, had to register with the authorities. By the end of May 1942 these registrants would be made to appear visually different from their fellow French citizens by being required to wear yellow stars on their clothing (82–131).

Compelling Jews to wear yellow stars was only the most blatant of a variety of ways to exclude them from French society. Summarizing the period from the summer of 1941 to the late spring of 1942, Jeremy Josephs begins with the August 31, 1941 discriminatory measures denying Jews radios, telephones, and bicycles and goes on to enumerate the many public places that were shortly thereafter closed to Jews, including parks, museums, cafés, cinemas, concert and music halls, and, of course, the theatre (39–40). By February 7, 1942 Jews would have had a difficult enough time getting to and leaving the theatre because of the curfew that restricted them to their homes between eight at night and six in the morning (Lubetski 186). What Marsh calls "[t]he most infamous policy that the Germans imposed on the French theatre by means of the COES" (the Comité d'Organisation des Enterprises de Spectacle, which effectively controlled the theatre in occupied Paris) was the June 6, 1942, anti-Jewish legislation banning Jews from working in the theatre ("The Theatre . . ." 147–148). Thus, by the end of the 1941–

1942 season, Jews could not be part of either the on-stage performance or the audience. As described in chapter 2, by the following July, some would be briefly contained in that site of sports events, political rallies, and theatrical spectacle, the Vel d'Hiv, only to be transported to Drancy.

The City of Light was darkened, figuratively and literally. The thirty-four playhouses opened by 7:30 so that customers might dash for the last métro. As noted in Chapter I, the previous season, the first following the Defeat, saw many revivals and only a few new plays. In addition to a handful of meaningful premieres, there were also Michel Duran's *Boléro*, Germaine Lefrancq's *Vingt-cinq ans de Bonheur*, and *L'Amant de Bornéo* by José Germain and Roger Ferdinand, to all of which Hervé Le Boterf applies Brasillach's phrase, "comédie sans tickets." Célia Bertin describes how coupons needed to purchase food were allotted according to each person from three years of age and older, and she details the amounts of each commodity permitted for adults, who were issued ration coupons according to their profession (38–39). One of the very few commodities of which there were no shortages in occupied Paris, was theatre: During the first season of 1940–1941, in spite of censorship and limited funds, some theatres reported their highest receipts since the early 1930s (Forkey 301).

The following season, 1941–1942, brought more revivals, several of them memorable: Cocteau's *Les Parents Terribles* caused a riot at the Gymnase; Jean Sarment's adaptation of Schiller's *Don Carlos* opened at the Odéon; and Jean-Louis Barrault starred as Hamlet at the Comédie-Française, where Goethe's *Iphigénie en Tauride* played in French and two weeks later (performed by the Munich State Theatre) in German. There were, however, also a few significant new plays. In December, Anouilh's *Eurydice* premiered at the Atelier. Charles Dullin, who a few years before had moved from the Atelier to the Theatre de Paris and then on to the Sarah-Bernhardt (renamed Théâtre de la Cité), opened in January in *La Princesse des Ursins*, written by his mistress, Simone Jollivet (see chapter 4). Around the same time, Claude Vermorel's *Jeanne avec nous*, appeared at the Comédie des Champs-Elysées; written before the war, this drama based on the life of Jeanne d'Arc was praised by some in the fascist press but would be remembered by many (including Beauvoir) as evoking the sentiment of resistance. In March, *Les Pirates de Paris: L'Affaire Stavisky*, by Michel Daxiat, that is, by Alain Laubreaux, the critic who had attacked Cocteau's *The Typewriter* and had in turn been physically assaulted by Jean Marais, played at the Ambigu.

The very same critics and audiences who were going to see these and other new plays and revivals were the ones who, in the late winter or early spring of 1942, would have come to Giraudoux's seemingly fanciful one-act. What would they have made of *Apollo*?

Certainly, they would have seized upon a number of references that other audiences would have missed, most notably perhaps this insult, which the Président flings at Thérèse: "On ne les [les femmes] a pas arrachées au fer de notre propre côte, pour qu'elles achètent des bas sans tickets . . ." ("Women were not torn from men's ribs just so that they could buy stockings without coupons . . .").[21] This remark, which would no doubt have sounded obscure to a Latin American house in 1942[22] and curiously dated to Parisians in 1947, would inform Giraudoux's intended audience that this was no "comédie sans tickets." Certainly all women and most men in occupied Paris would have grinned at the notion that hosiery could be purchased without ration coupons. Thus, in spite of the play's fantastical setting and plot, Giraudoux's intended audience would have understood immediately that its author was indeed commenting on the present.

They would have noted some irony too in the Man from Bellac's invention, the "légume unique," which he claims can serve as meat and bread, wine and chocolate (all of which were now rationed) to feed the world (920); they would have no doubt construed in it a reference both to the current Parisian obsession with food, which, as Pryce-Jones tells us, the well-to-do preferred not to discuss (100), and also a satirical comment on the frequent (and highly unsatisfactory) use of food substitutes, like the "loathsome ersatz coffee called *café national*," which Collins and Lapierre recall was "made from acorns and chick-peas" (16). Similarly, the statuette of the Dying Gaul, which Thérèse keeps on her mantle and which the Président says he will have melted down (940), would have reminded this audience of how many of the bronzes that had adorned Parisian parks and squares were being transported to the Reich to be turned into shell casings (Collins and Lapierre 15). Even the depiction of the Bureau in which *Apollo* is set, bland as it may appear to us, might have conveyed to these spectators some parody, even a send-up, of the bureaucratic and technocratic hierarchy built by the German occupiers and by the Vichy regime.

All of these small but pointed references were perhaps innocuous enough to slip past the German censors. Nonetheless, the references would have been heard by a Parisian audience in 1942 as scattered yet persistent signals indicating that this play was on some level clearly addressing the world in which they, the spectators, found themselves. The metatheatrical dimension, which I note earlier, would have both verified and amplified the audience's suspicions that the play was carefully, perhaps even cautiously, gesturing to them amid what might otherwise have been mistaken for pure whimsy, pointing toward important and very contemporary concerns.

Let us return to the whole notion of the mirror, so central to the play's action, both dramatic and theatrical. We may suppose that after France's defeat in the "phoney war" of 1940, many in France had had some difficulty confronting themselves in the glass; this certainly may be inferred by what Giraudoux himself reveals in a book begun in 1942 but not published until 1973:

> June, 1940.
> Is this the first time I've ever been defeated?
> A friend entered my room.
> He was the first defeated Frenchman whom I saw, for I hadn't yet taken a look at myself in the mirror. (*Souvenir de deux existences* 75)

In keeping with the mirror imagery in *Apollo*, Giraudoux suggests that we see ourselves through others. Even before he can gaze at himself in the glass, the playwright manages to catch a glimpse of his country's and his own personal defeat in the face of a friend. The friend becomes the instrument through which he recognizes a reflection of reality and beholds the truth about himself.

As Cohen points out, mirrors are obviously subjective in *Apollo*; each must choose which mirror he is to believe. Yet for a Parisian audience in 1942, the scene in which the Président decides to believe Agnès's view of him and to reject Thérèse's would have carried both strong public and private implications: Thérèse's apartment is stiff and formal and above her hearth stands that bronze of The Dying Gaul, which would have easily been perceived as a symbol of an enslaved and moribund France; Agnès's small flat, however, is simply yet comfortably decorated, and over her mantle hangs (of course) a mirror (940). Thus, the Président takes Agnès's positive image of self-confrontation rather than the defeatist one offered by his mistress. For the French in 1942, choosing a mirror becomes a personal and political act, which seems nothing short of existential.

On this level, then, we may imagine a Parisian house in 1942 drawing from this play a strong statement about what it truly meant to be French, what it truly meant to view oneself as the subject of the Nazi occupiers. Read from this perspective, *Apollo* suddenly appears to be arguing against the self-image of defeat and the breast-beating propagated by Vichy in Pétain's public speeches—speeches that had, Agnes Raymond reminds us, been published in book form in 1941 (under the title *La France nouvelle*) and with which Giraudoux, having served in the Ministry of Information, was very familiar. If, as Raymond contends, "all of Giraudoux's writings during this period reflect his reactions to the Marshall's public utterances" (100), we may surmise that in direct contrast to Pétain's instructions on self-portraiture, Giraudoux in *Apollo* offered the public a very different set of directions: Create your own self-image, and base it upon a positive notion of what it means to be a Frenchman, the playwright appears to be telling the house, at least those in the intended house who might have been able to hear him.

The house may not, however, have discerned much difference between Giraudoux's image of women and the official view coming out of Vichy. Indeed, the very line the Président flings at Thérèse, the one that suggests that this play is not a comédie sans tickets—"Women were not torn from men's ribs just so that they could buy stockings without coupons . . ."—is drawn from a rather revealing tirade:

> What a woman! A true woman! Hear me well, Thérèse, for the last time. Women were placed in the world to tell us what Agnès tells us [that is, that all men are handsome, intelligent and brave]. They were not pulled from our own ribs so that they could buy stockings without ration coupons, lament the poor quality of nail-polish removers, or say bad things about their fellow women. They were put here on earth to tell men that they are handsome.[23]

Women's job is to reflect for men their proper images; their petty feminine habits are tolerable only when they serve as positive mirrors. As the Président soon tells Thérèse, Agnès can tell him he is handsome because she is beautiful, but Thérèse can only tell him he is ugly because she is ugly. This may, as Cohen suggests, be just a matter of relativism: "Neither woman is telling 'the truth,' both are reflecting what they see through the filter of what they want to see." Yet even in this description, there is the implication that each is prevaricating. Whether all is, as Cohen would like to assure us, relative or the right woman simply needs to know how to say the right things to the right person at the right time in order to grab some power ("«L'Apollon de Marsac» apprend aux femmes comment mener les hommes" says the headline over the brief review in *L'Epoque*[24]), remains a matter of interpretation.

I will have more to say in chapter 4 about women's plight during the Occupation; for now, it is perhaps worthwhile asking if there is any evidence that the meaning I have ascribed to the play was shared by anyone else. I believe so: In fact, if we consider Eduardo Anahory's set designs, we may find that my reading is not totally unfounded. His first set, for the 1942 production, appears highly functional but rather unrevealing.[25] The use of French windows, two at stage left, two at stage right, and two upstage, each framed by Ionic columns, is neatly balanced, even classically symmetrical. The scene feels light—doors left and right are hung between flats—and, in spite of the way it harkens back to conventional box sets, stylized. This set was, of course, designed to travel throughout Latin America with Jouvet's troupe.

Significantly, when Jouvet opened the show in Paris, he kept Anahory as scene designer (although he gave *The Maids* to Christian Bérard), but he requested a change in set. The French windows were retained as a motif,

Set for the Rio premiere of The Apollo of Marsac, *1942 (top). Set for the Paris premiere, 1947 (bottom).*

though without the Ionic columns; those windows hung at stage left (without glazed panes and thus more like doors) and at stage right (without door handles and thus more like windows) were increased in number; Anahory's sketch for the 1947 production seems vague about exactly how many, there being seven stage right and six stage left. Yet even as drawn, the later plan brings into play the use of perspective, for the two lines of French windows converge at a central point.

The difference between the two designs is remarkable. Implicit in the 1947 sketch is a reference to an architectural site with which virtually everyone in France would have been familiar: the Hall of Mirrors at Versailles. And although this room is not named directly in the script itself, such an association is indeed implied; when Agnès reveals that, in contrast to Thérèse's Dying Gaul, there stands over her mantle a mirror, the Président replies,

> Thank you, mirrors. Thank you, reflections. Thanks to all that which hereafter throws back my image or my voice. Thank you, reflecting ponds of Versailles! Thank you, echo! (940)

To a French, rather than to a Latin American, audience this allusion would, of course, have offered yet another sign that the play was preoccupied with French reflections. Thus, through the 1947 set, Jouvet was attempting to offer a visual interpretation of the play that he had read back in 1942 and to put on stage—as well as he could—for a later French audience a rather pointed reminder of what he recalled as the intended Occupation production.

A Parisian house in 1942 would have associated Versailles with a positive and powerful image of France and of things French. Images of the golden age, of the pomp and power of the rule of Louis XIV and the classical French theatre would have posed a marked contrast to the then-current image of the Vichy regime, which in an age of shame and of vanquished agonizing (epitomized by the image of the Dying Gaul), desperately tried to deny its own powerlessness. And of course, as the director must have hoped, the very thought of Versailles would have carried with it the memory of the end of the previous war, when a conquered Germany had been forced to sign a treaty named for the great palace.

Giraudoux's intended audience of 1942 would no doubt have seen more in the play than I can begin to relate here. Certainly, however, as the reviews of the 1947 production in Paris suggest, the Parisian audience who attended the curious double-bill of *Apollo* and *The Maids* saw a lot less. Without the active context of the Occupation, the play might easily be mistaken for froth.

Conclusion

As we move back through time, to the production as Giraudoux envisioned it and to the spectators whom he imagined seeing *Apollo*, different meanings begin to emerge. For the 1942 audience, whose responses I have attempted to construct, this play would have carried some message of hope. At its most meaningful, *Apollo* does not shrink from dramatizing how self-respect—notably French self-respect—can be achieved only through the active pursuit of French choices. In context, it is neither froth nor jest.

At the same time, the play can hardly be viewed as one that would have been construed as advocating resistance. While Giraudoux's play seems to suggest that German influences should be discarded, we would do well to recall that the playwright himself had always, although rather conflictedly, felt drawn to them. On trial for collaboration, Brasillach (who was later executed) complained that during the Occupation he and Giraudoux had lunched many times at the German Institute and that now he, the critic, was being tried as a traitor while the playwright had virtually become a saint (Pryce-Jones 42); although Brasillach's argument is self-justifying and reductive, it nevertheless contains a germ of truth. Jacques Body, in his extensive assessment of Giraudoux's lifelong interest in Germany, explains how French intellectuals were compelled for official documents, such as passports into the Vichy-controlled Free Zone, gasoline vouchers, and food coupons, to go to the Institute (where they might more easily be pulled into collaborating on German-financed cultural events), and that in spite of his lunches there (which he eventually curtailed), Giraudoux never participated in any of the official receptions (*Giraudoux et l'Allemagne* 435–436). Nonetheless, Body's evaluation of Giraudoux's relationship with Germany may be summarized by the adjective "ambivalent."

More seriously, however, Michael Marrus and Robert Paxton identify a very tangible strand of anti-Semitism that manifested itself even before the Occupation in Giraudoux's 1939 book of "political reflections," *Pleins Pouvoirs*: their analysis of his elitism and prejudice (52–53) sheds light on views that the dramatist to some degree shared with Brasillach and other anti-Jewish collaborators. Body's assertions that Giraudoux was never a proclaimed anti-Semite but had, as a member of his class and culture, inherited his bigotry (*Giraudoux et l'Allemagne* 329) seem a little feeble in this context. And Mehlman, who is the most willing to connect Giraudoux the ideologue with Giraudoux the playwright, offers a rather chilling (and as he believes, "representative") passage from *Pleins Pouvoirs*, some of which I include, as follows:

> There have entered into our land, through an infiltration whose se-
> cret I have in vain attempted to discover, about one hundred thou-

sand Ashkenasis, escaped from the ghettos of Poland or Rumania. . . . Trained as they have been for centuries to work in our worst conditions, they eliminate our compatriots . . . from all the crafts of artisanry . . . , and, piled up by tens in single rooms, escape every investigation relating to the census, taxes, and labor. . . . A horde which manages to be deprived of all its national rights and to defy every expulsion and whose precarious and abnormal physical constitution sends it, by the thousands, into our hospitals, that it encumbers. (47)

These words speak for themselves.

Nonetheless, it would be as reductive (and fallacious) to think Giraudoux a collaborator as it would be to label him (as Brasillach reminds us many were eager to do after the liberation) a resistor. The man who lunched at the Institute and expressed such despicable feelings about Jews was the same man who drove his son across Spain so that he could join De Gaulle in London; this is the very complex person who wrote *La Folle de Chaillot*.

As noted earlier, Marsh points to comments written by Giraudoux and printed in the arts weekly *Comœdia* in the summer of 1941—comments that certainly appear consonant with "the cult of the body beautiful which the Nazi propagandists promoted through the pages of the daily press" and, at least out of context, sound rather pro-Aryan and even anti-French. Such "attitudes and opinions which, in the rapidly changing circumstances," he concludes, Giraudoux might not have expressed had he known how his writings would eventually be viewed ("The Theatre . . ." 161). Indeed, he is right to mention "the rapidly changing circumstances," for the Occupation was not a static time. Circumstances changed enormously, not only from the Defeat (when many believed Germany would quickly and easily win the War) to the Liberation of Paris (by which time almost all knew the Allies would attain victory), but from week to week, even from day to day.

In order to understand what Giraudoux wrote, we must come to terms with the playwright and his play. We must accept that the playwright, in the context of this period during which his life (though not his career) came to an abrupt halt, remains rather problematic. Given this, we must look not to the bare text of *Apollo*—that is, to the playscript out of context—but to the play intended, comprised the intended production and the intended audience, in order to consider the play's meaning.

4

The Limits of Opportunism:
Simone Jollivet's *The Princess of Ursins*

Introduction

Rather than duplicate the Occupation's initial "season of reprises," theatre producers during the following seasons sought fresh material. Well known writers, including Sacha Guitry and Jean Anouilh, would turn out a series of new scripts. The often tradition-bound Comédie-Française would commission during the war years a comedy from Jean Cocteau, whose *Renaud et Armide* managed to erase the scandal caused by *The Typewriter* and by the revival of *Les Parents Terribles*, and a tragedy from Henry de Montherlant, *La Reine Morte* (*Queen After Death*). Also for the Comédie Paul Claudel would allow Jean-Louis Barrault to help him bring his mammoth poetic drama, *Le Soulier de Satin* (*The Satin Slipper*) to the stage. Jean-Paul Sartre and Albert Camus would start their playwrighting careers. There was, if nothing else, extraordinary opportunity for dramatists.

If the Germans and Vichy had resurrected the theatre at least in part to provide entertainment, Parisians seemed in need of entertaining. The usual boulevard comedies continued in popularity, and those pro-fascist critics, whose condemnations of the lighter fare had little if any impact, strove to incorporate their political values into their reviews, sometimes lavishing compliments on those plays in which they thought they could discern their own views. Sometimes they imposed interpretations on dramas that others saw very differently. For example, while Beauvoir and others recalled Claude Vermorel's *Jeanne avec Nous* (*Joan Among Us*) as conveying a deliberate heartfelt message of resistance, commentators in the collaborationist press in 1942 gave it, on the whole, a highly favorable reception.[1] As described in the next chapter, Jean Anouilh's *Antigone* received high praise from the Paris critics while some in the audience believed Antigone's refusal to obey Creon was symbolic of anti-German defiance; the conflict of opinion was further complicated by an article in an underground paper that denounced Anouilh and his play. No matter what the political climate, however, Parisian reviewers and spectators still expected to be diverted and engaged.

Of course, their standards were high. Even avidly pro-Nazi critics would not embrace a script solely on its political merits, and audiences, no matter what their affiliations, would get up and leave a performance they found unsatisfying. Thus, *Les Pirates de Paris: L'Affaire Stavisky* (*The Pirates of Paris: The Stavisky Affair*), which opened in April 1942 at the Théâtre de l'Ambigu, failed to impress anyone in spite of its obvious fascist appeal. Although attributed to Michel Daxiat, the play's actual author was none other than Alain Laubreaux, who (as described earlier) had the spring before written attacks against Jean Cocteau and Jean Marais and was then later physically attacked by Marais outside a restaurant.[2] The play was based upon the financial scandal that had rocked the Third Republic in the winter of 1934 and in part precipitated an unsuccessful rightist coup. *Pirates* consisted of fourteen scenes, stretching from 1897 until 1934, ending with the apparent suicide of the Russian-Jewish swindler Serge (Sacha) Stavisky (played by Paul Œttly, who also directed). It was rabidly anti-Semitic and anti-republican, but reviewers, who were well aware of who Michel Daxiat really was, reacted negatively to this melodrama. Indeed, the only unabashedly positive notice that *The Pirates of Paris* received was from Laubreaux himself in *Je suis partout*; yet even Laubreaux's raves about Daxiat's work and the repeated advertisements in his fascist weekly could not keep the play on stage for more than a few weeks. Whatever the press might say, audiences did not appreciate *Pirates*.[3]

The script for *The Pirates of Paris* has not survived, and for some its disappearance is not entirely sad, for the play marks a low point in playwriting under the Occupation and remains the prime example of collaborationist theatre. Yet the melodrama's failure also exemplifies how, even under the circumstances of the Occupation, in both society and the theatre, a man like Laubreaux, who was intelligent and well-placed, might easily miss the opportunity to have his work become a bona fide hit. Perhaps if the script were extant, we might learn exactly what about *Pirates* made it so unpalatable to so many. Yet we do have the script for another play, which was written by someone who has been said to have espoused fascist ideas and who, like Laubreaux, was not only intelligent and well-positioned but was willing to use whatever was necessary to bring a play to the stage: Simone Jollivet, the notorious "Camille" of Simone de Beauvoir's memoir *La Force de l'age* (*The Prime of Life*) and later volumes. Beauvoir, who had good reason not to like Jollivet, recalled how throughout the Occupation "Camille" would utter heinously pro-Nazi statements, seemingly convinced that under the new regime she would finally make her mark. Jollivet's *La Princesse des Ursins* (*The Princess of Ursins*) was one of the few plays by a female playwright to be produced under the Occupation.

A reading of the script more than fifty years later suggests that this odd work about the Spanish succession was more than just the visually beautiful but awkwardly written historical drama which many took it to be: Indeed, amid royal intrigues, vulgar jokes, and moments of exaggerated emotion, *Princess* depicts Jollivet's personal struggle in a society in which exceptional women, secretly and often ruthlessly, tried to compete with men. In retelling the conflict between the title character, a noblewoman sent to Spain by Louis XIV to advise the new Bourbon monarch, and the men who eventually succeeded in exiling her, Jollivet expected to attain celebrity. The story had attracted her, for in it she no doubt sensed her own story, and she firmly believed the moment had arrived for its dramatization; she eagerly positioned herself to reach for the laurels that had heretofore eluded her. Yet Jollivet's confidence in her writing was clearly disproportionate to her skill as a dramatist. Indeed, she was crushed by the play's reception. When it opened at the Théâtre de la Cité on January 16, 1942, directed by and starring Jollivet's lover, the brilliant Charles Dullin, *Princess* received largely unfavorable notices and closed on February 17, 1942.

Jollivet may have believed consciously or felt intuitively that her historical drama would, under the new political order, find a supportive audience. It was exciting and interesting, and on analysis, despite the daring of its heroine, it appears to present a fable that might seem consonant with the Nazi and Vichy ideals of womanhood; as if to demonstrate that women do not belong in the public arena, an unscrupulous female protagonist schemes and connives in order to rule but in the end is overcome by the males whom she has usurped. It may be argued that the heroine's career of treachery takes on an almost Marlovian twist when, in a final scene, she faces the man who brought about her downfall: In spite of her monstrousness and subsequent punishment, the Princess in her final moments on stage may have been intended perhaps to solicit from the audience some degree of sympathy. Yet, the fascist moral about women's roles in society is neither seriously called into question nor contradicted.

As Stephen Greenblatt asserts, at the beginning of *Shakespearean Negotiations*, "[W]orks of art, however intensely marked by the creative intelligence and private obsessions of the individual, are the products of collective negotiation and exchange" (vii). A discussion of authorship, then, and on authorial intention must focus not only on the dramatist's conscious efforts in writing a play, but on the context—the time, place, and conditions—in which she wrote and on the forces that shaped her knowledge of the world. In this regard, Jollivet accurately transmitted the plight of women within her own culture, inscribing into the script echoes of the misogynistic oppression that was then being practiced and enacted into law; at the same time, however, her own view of the way things were and had to be, was heavily influenced by her individual choices and responses to this oppression. Ironically, Jollivet's method of coping, her acceptance of the male-dominated system that she perceived and of the role allotted her within that system, both appear in *The Princess of Ursins* and, in effect, predict the playwright's inevitable failure.

Women, Vichy, and the Occupation

The composition of *The Princess of Ursins* (like that of *The Typewriter*) belongs to the drôle de guerre and to the early months of the German Occupation. Of course, the issues surrounding women in France after June 1940 are as complicated as those of the Occupation as a whole. Once the Third Republic had capitulated, France became sadly divided, not only along the very obvious geographical lines that the Germans drew on the map in 1940 (by which a northern Occupied Zone was separated from what was called— at least for the first half of the Occupation—the southern Free Zone), but politically and culturally as well. The French government, now headed by Pétain, was situated at Vichy, the Germans ruled from Paris, and what and where the real France might be found was a complicated and persistent issue.

Certainly, as suggested earlier, the presence of two governments complicated the official world. As Herbert Lottman characterizes "the two Frances":

> One of them centered on Paris, under direct control of German military authorities, with only the token presence of a French government. The other was a fully structured "French State" whose capital was Vichy, whose leader was a World War I hero, Marshal Philippe Pétain, with nominal authority over a so-called unoccupied or "free" zone. In Paris, the Germans were concerned with maintaining order while carrying on their war: this could mean tolerating a certain degree of cultural and even political pluralism. In Vichy, where Pétain had been voted full powers on July 10, 1940, by what survived of the prewar Third Republic, a coalition of ideologues relished the opportunity provided by defeat to promote a certain philosophy of the state and of the citizen's duty. (151)

France was a country in two zones, the Free Zone, until 1942 ruled by the Vichy government, and the Occupied Zone, ruled by the Germans from Paris. Even within the so-called Free Zone, where Vichy legislated the alleged revitalization of France, life varied tremendously according to location; thus, terms one associates with the Occupation, such as "collaboration" and "resistance," take on a geographical meaning. As Richard Cobb describes it, "If Vichy remained, predictably, *vichyssois*, Montpellier never was. Both the history of collaboration and that of resistance can be studied only in local or, at most, regional terms." Moreover, notes Cobb, within the Occupied Zone, "the Germans had ensured that the experience of occupation should differ radically from place to place" (40). Thus, to generalize about what Frenchwomen endured during this period becomes reductive.

Nonetheless, what came out of Vichy, both legally and ideologically, offers a distinct reflection of the official attitude toward women by those who, if not in complete power, at least believed themselves to be at the center of the French National Revolution. At the Free Zone's capital, as in Berlin, women were regarded as wives and mothers. John F. Sweets quotes a government brochure distributed to French schools in 1943, "School and the Family," which insisted, "The greatest threat to France is depopulation."[4] In keeping with this emphasis on maternity, elaborate Mother's Day ceremonies (some hosted by the Maréchal himself) were held at which women with many children were awarded medals; more practically, their households received special tax benefits (42–43). To secure marriage and the family, remarks Paxton, a 1941 law "forbade any divorce during the first three years of a marriage," and Justice Minister Barthélemy "instructed the courts to interpret the divorce law as strictly as possible" (167). Paxton adds, "contemplating the different elementary education offered girls by the 15 August 1941 school program, for example, one is forced to conclude that Vichy preferred women barefoot and pregnant in the kitchen" (168).[5]

What Vichy promulgated was often more easily put into print than into practice. For example, even with legislation that, as Paxton indicates, was intended to limit the number of women in the work place (167–168),[6] Sweets reminds us how, with labor shortages caused by the relocation of male French workers to Germany, such intentions could not be enacted. Similarly, the virtuous Vichy campaigns against such "threats" to marriage and the family as prostitution and abortion were miserable failures (43).

In the former French capital and current German command headquarters, where Vichy's pronouncements, like Pétain himself, may have counted morally but not practically, women were also suppressed. True to the occupiers themselves, women in Paris were excluded from all lucrative and powerful posts. Arguing that collaborationism "tended to be masculine and adult," Cobb explains that women had little of what the Germans could put to ready use:

> There were no women railway engineers and very few women in the police, there were no *miliciennes* nor any fascist *amazones*, there

were more waiters than waitresses, *chauffeuses de taxi* were extremely rare . . . , men drove the *métro*, women clipped the tickets at
the barriers . . . , and women were not even subjected to the *Relève*
[movement to volunteer for work in Germany in exchange for French
POWs], nor, later, to those of the *STO* [compulsory labor service in
Germany for Frenchmen]. . . . Within [the] generous, expansive
confines [of collaborationism], women could only be assigned to
secondary rôles: typists, telephonists, secretaries, chambermaids.
There were no women publishers or printers; even the most famous
woman journalist, Geneviève Tabouis, had left France for New York
in July 1940. (107–108)

With more than a million French prisoners of war held in Germany, allowing
women to enter the work force would have made good economic, though
apparently not good ideological, sense.

Although Cobb's survey is in itself bleak, and while it may be argued
that during the Occupation women were far worse off than they had been
under the Third Republic, the fact remains that many of the positions mentioned by Cobb that had existed prior to the War (railway engineer, police
officer, taxi or métro driver, publisher, printer, journalist) had never been very
open to women. French feminists, Steven Hause recalls, who had rallied
toward suffrage during the First World War, believing "that the end of Hos-
tilities would bring legislative attention to the rights of women" (99), were
blocked by the Senate throughout the interwar years. Even as he concedes
that Léon Blum had in 1936 given two minor cabinet posts to women, Paxton
reminds us that women in France did not get the vote until 1946 (168).

The issue of the changing role of women, "emerging now as individuals capable of playing a role in public life," writes Alfred Cobban, belongs
to the "post-war scene" (232).[7] During the War, French culture and society
on the whole gave women little encouragement to improve their lot. Only
in the Résistance, notes Paula Schwartz, were women allowed an active
role "from positions of leadership to the base" (141) and involvement in
various underground movements "politicize[d] some French women for the
very first time" (153).

More significantly, however, following the Defeat, many of these
unofficial practices, which had kept females in subservient positions before
1940 were, with the advent of German and Vichy rule, legitimatized. Whatever barriers women encountered in their fight to have a career or merely to
earn a living were, under the Occupation, not merely personal or even cultural; they were now official policy and law. Even collaboration for women
restricted them to function within the narrow limits prescribed by Vichy and
Nazi ideology, and because German soldiers were forbidden to marry for-

eigners, French women could become not their wives but only their mistresses, though certainly mothers of their children; within the Occupied Zone alone, writes Cobb, 80,000 French women claimed to have given birth to half-Aryan children (66–67). As Célia Bertin in *Femmes sous l'Occupation* bluntly puts it, "The collaboration of women most often began by that which designates a vulgar expression that clearly shows the hatred attached to it: 'Horizontal collaboration' " (101).[8] No one needed to paraphrase Sartre's famous question into "Qu'est-ce que c'est une collaboratrice?" In an important sense, the Occupation made worse the cultural suppression against which women had been struggling throughout the Third Republic.

In short, everywhere in France during the Occupation, women's prospects worsened. As the rulers who followed the Third Republic attempted to make official their beliefs, the necessities of wartime decreed some wide disparities between what was said to be real and what in actuality occurred. Still, whatever problems Frenchwomen had encountered between the wars—and there were many—seem minimal in contrast to what the succeeding regime would bring.

What was true in general of society was true too about the theatre. Just as Vichy had made exceptions in the workplace for women "in 'traditionally feminine' industries" (Sweets 43), the theatre assigned only a few of its jobs, most notably those involving acting on stage, to women. Although the legitimate theatre in France had a long tradition of females playing males, the custom of males portraying females had been limited to certain authors and specific performers, and perhaps this, along with what Cobb terms "the politics of 'virility' " (108), which permeated the period, bringing with it both antifeminism and homophobia, necessitated women playing women with few exceptions (the best known of which are discussed in chapter 8). Other backstage "traditionally feminine" roles (in wardrobe or makeup, for example) might go to females as well. Theatre professions from which women appear to have been largely if not completely excluded, both before and during the Occupation (and for some years after), include the powerful roles of director and dramatist.[9]

Simone Jollivet, who aspired to become a recognized dramatist, was indeed fortunate to play consort to one of France's most important and creative stage directors. Charles Dullin, one of the Cartel des Quatre (the Coalition of Four directors, who had all worked under Jacques Copeau), had founded his Atelier in Montmartre in 1922. Here, until 1940, he mounted and often performed in a succession of extraordinary productions, remaining true to the text of his scripts but at the same time providing strong visual and sound effects in their presentation. The most influential thinkers of the next generation, Barrault, as actor and director, and Antonin Artaud, whose theoretical writings would have a major impact on drama all over the world, were both trained by Dullin. His varied repertory included classics by Aristophanes, Shakespeare, Calderon, and Molière, as well as contemporary plays by Cocteau, Pirandello, Achard, Salacrou, Romains, and Passeur (Brockett and Findlay 366–370). For the 1940–1941 season, Dullin moved from his small studio theatre to the considerably larger, municipally funded Théâtre de Paris, and the following season he was scheduled to open at the Théâtre Sarah Bernhardt (which was renamed, because of the actress's Jewish ancestry, Théâtre de la Cité).[10]

Because of her immediate access to and strong sway over Dullin, Jollivet was perhaps perfectly situated to become France's leading female dramatist. In 1932 Dullin had directed her unsuccessful play, *The Shadow* (*L'Ombre*), at the Atelier and brought to the stage her adaptations of Balzac's *Le Faiseur* (1936), Shakespeare's *Julius Caesar* (1937), and Aristophanes' *Plutus* (1938). These last two were highly successful; she would go on to adapt Shakespeare's *King Lear* (1945) and Balzac's *La Marâtre* (1949). In addition, she had directed one of Artaud's favorites, John Ford's *T'is Pity She's a Whore*. However, now that Dullin was about to set up in a larger, more recognized playhouse, Jollivet may well have seen the coming season as the precise moment when she might grasp success.

Yet the Occupation, at least in retrospect, hardly seems the optimal time for a female playwright to make her mark. Under the intensified misogyny of the current authorities, perhaps only a woman who felt comfortable playing a Nazi-sympathizer but who, behind the scenes, through her ability to seduce and influence men in order to create appropriate opportunities for her own advancement, would set upon such a career. Simone Jollivet was, for the most part, such a woman.

Simone on Simone: Toulouse, Camille, and Others

Who exactly was Simone Jollivet?[11] One of the important sources on her life is Jean-Paul Sartre, who, in an interview with John Gerassi, related a story about his "first serious affair." Gerassi recounts how Sartre noticed, in the dressing room of the woman he loved, five bottles of perfume:

> and the fifth was marked *J-P*. Each contained a different perfume. Sartre blew his stack, demanding [she] immediately discard her four other lovers.
>
> "What? Do you own me?" she fired back. "Am I supposed to sit here and wait for your *occasional* appearances? How dare you expect me to conform to your wishes; do you conform to mine? Are you prepared to abandon l'Ecole Normale? To move to Toulouse? To take me around the world?"

Sartre hesitated. "I paced back and forth in her lush, heavily scented bedroom thinking over what she had said . . . but not too long, for she was right, of course, and I knew it. I concluded that jealousy *is* possessiveness. *Therefore*, I decided never to be jealous again." (79)[12]

This woman who taught Sartre the connection between jealousy and possession was someone whom he addressed as "Toulouse" (the city from where she originally came) and sometimes referred to as "Camille"; performing on stage as Simone-Camille Sans, she would later become known as a translator and writer in Paris under her given name, Simone Jollivet.

The first thirteen of Sartre's collected letters were written to Jollivet, spanning the years 1926 to 1928, during which time she and Sartre pursued their affair. In the letters Sartre develops his thoughts and interests, recommends books, and describes his impecunious daily life; he also offers a glimpse of this woman to whom he confesses, "I love you with all my heart and soul" (15). She is his "dear little girl," who can be "selfish, frivolous, and cowardly to boot" (9) and who refers to his letters as "little lectures" (19); he does not like her claiming that she loves him "passionately, like *La Marietta* [in Stendhal's *Charterhouse of Parma*], who was after all just a slut with a crush on Fabrice" (24), nor is he complacent when she wires him on a Friday, "Not free, pointless to come on Sunday" (8).

Unfortunately, although Sartre would recall her with fondness, he has left little about Jollivet. Instead, their frequently turbulent, sometimes passionate affair is more fully described by that other Simone who came into Sartre's life in 1928, after he had split with Jollivet, who had gone on to her relationship with Dullin (and apparently many others). In her memoirs, Beauvoir presents a portrait of Jollivet, which to some extent amplifies and in many ways completes the sketch that Sartre's letters to his dear Toulouse delineate.

Most of what is known about Simone Jollivet in fact comes from this other Simone. Yet as Beauvoir is herself first to admit, her view of Jollivet— whom she calls Camille in *The Prime of Life*—was, from the very start, highly subjective. At the beginning of their acquaintance, around 1930, Camille inspired in Beauvoir feelings like those that Sartre told Gerassi he himself had endured—"the most unpleasant emotion that had ever laid hold on me, and which, I believe, is most often described as jealousy" (74).[13] Perhaps Beauvoir's jealousy of Camille is understandable, for she felt Sartre "frequently set her up as an example" to her; Beauvoir also notes, "Sartre had a higher regard for her than me" (71). Thus, Beauvoir confides, "for a long time" her own "attitude toward Camille remained ambiguous" (75), and she sums up her ambivalence with a certain irony:

> How unpleasant it is to feel doubts concerning one's motives! From
> the moment I brought my accusation [that Jollivet distorted the truth]
> against Camille I myself became suspect, since it would give me far
> too much satisfaction if she were proved in the wrong. I floundered
> in a morass of indecision, not daring openly either to pronounce her
> guilty or acquit her; I would not glory in my prudery, nor yet would
> I discard it. (71)

This ambiguity of emotion was not diminished in 1932, when Beauvoir learned
of the failure of Jollivet's first play (which she both wrote and appeared in
under her stage name, Simone-Camille Sans), *The Shadow*: "When I thought
about her," recalled Beauvoir, "my mind was split between astonishment and
impatience" (108).

Beauvoir's ambivalent response might have been validated by the way
the papers reacted to *The Shadow*. In general, the piece was dismissed. Edmond
Seé complained, "This medieval drama larded with philosophical consider-
ations, and in which Freudian psychoanalysis plays a primordial role, delivers
only a very uncertain meaning!"[14] René Wisner referred to it as "a worthless
show." Yet reviewers also tended to focus their disdain on the woman who
wrote and starred in the play rather than on the play itself. René Lalou in
Nouveau Lettres sneered at Jollivet's inexperience: "Not to be needlessly
cruel, it is necessary to remember that this piece was played under the auspice
of the 'Theatre for studious young actors.' . . ." James de Couquet, in spite of
"the youth of the author," preferred her dramaturgy to her acting ("Her inexperience on stage is flagrant"), but Charles-Henry felt the reverse: "we recognize our preference for the actress over the woman of letters. . . ." Robert
Destry in *Figaro* managed to mangle her pseudonym as he quipped, "Mlle
Camille-Simone Sans is, in effect, a young blonde from Toulouse, and this is
her premiere." Perhaps Beauvoir never noticed to what extent the critics
maligned the fact that the other Simone was a woman.

Eventually Beauvoir came to believe that Jollivet's own "narcissism
and her coquettish tricks" had robbed Jollivet "of all her former power" over
Beauvoir and that Beauvoir could now simply enjoy Jollivet's company,
"without any ulterior motives to worry" her (189). As the 1930s faded into
the 1940s, Jollivet and Dullin became friends with Sartre and Beauvoir. As
Sartre's relationship with Dullin (who would produce and direct *The Flies* in
1943) grew closer, his later letters to Jollivet remain affectionate though
clearly less passionate than his early correspondence;[15] yet Beauvoir refers,
both in her memoirs and her letters, to various visits, to apartments in Paris
and to Dullin's country house at Ferrolles near Crécy-en-Brie during this
time, so that the relationship between the four clearly continued.

In fact, one such visit to Crécy, in September 1939, is described in some detail, both in Beauvoir's wartime diaries (45–50) and *The Prime of Life* (391-394),[16] and in even greater detail in a long letter sent to Sartre (62–69). The journal (47) and memoir (392–393) entries mention[17] only that Jollivet gave Beauvoir the prologue and first draft of a play about the Princess of Ursins and that Beauvoir stayed up late reading them, finishing them the next day. Yet Beauvoir's letter to Sartre is (perhaps typically) more revealing:

> [Toulouse] handed me the prologue and first act of her play, which I started to read yesterday evening in bed and have just finished [around noon the next day]. It's neither ridiculous, nor clumsy, nor even very boring; but despite a certain liveliness of the dialogue I find it dreadfully flat. I didn't expect that at all. It's sober and lacklustre—impossible to know without the remaining acts how it would turn out on the stage. It's definitely better than *Plutus*, but one can't conceive why it was ever written. (65–66)

The letter does indicate precisely when Jollivet started working on the play: Begun at the onset of the drôle de guerre, *Princess* was probably finished around the time that France fell, in June 1940. By July 24, 1940, when Beauvoir wrote Sartre that Jollivet was "hoping to act in her own play this winter" (338), it appears to have been completed. Yet Beauvoir's early appraisal, of what was probably an early draft of the beginning of *The Princess of Ursins*, is her only critical comment here; her references to the play in *The Prime of Life* reveal only that Dullin's move to the Théâtre de la Cité was "at Camille's insistence" and that *Princess*, which was the first new play of Dullin's first season there, "was not a success" (508), yet they imply that her opinion of the work never improved.

Perhaps one reason for Beauvoir's dislike of the piece was that her feelings toward Jollivet had once again become far from benign. In fact, her reference above in her letter to Sartre, to Jollivet acting in her own play, occurs in a context that is disturbing:

> We went to dinner with Toulouse. She was all in white, with a long dress, a burnous and long tresses—she looked like a Valkyrie. She was enthusiastically making plans for the future, since she thinks the moment of her glory—and the flowering of her genius—has finally come. They're hoping to play her version of *Plutus* in the Arènes de Lutèce in September, and she's adapting Aristophanes's *Knights* too, which is a satire against demagogy. She's also hoping to act in her own play this winter. She seems to hold Dullin in the palm of her

hand. She was eager to get me (and you by proxy) to share her point of view. (338)

In this excerpt from a letter to Sartre (who was now a prisoner of war), Beauvoir seems to be implying that Jollivet saw the German victory as an opportunity to pursue her own success as a playwright.[18] The distastefulness of the scene to Beauvoir seems rather strong.

Significantly, several of the elements of this anecdote reappear in *The Prime of Life* in a remembrance of another dinner. The time, as Beauvoir places it, is sometime between December 20 and 28, 1940, about four months after the episode mentioned above:

> The last few times I had seen Dullin he had held forth at length about the shortcomings of the "Boches," no doubt inspired by the chauvinistic patriotism proper to an old soldier. But one night I was dining with him and Camille in the grillroom of the Théâtre de Paris [where Dullin was then directing], and halfway through the meal Camille made a most categorical declaration, which he listened to without uttering so much as a word. Since Nazism was in the ascendant, she said, we should rally to it; if she, Camille, was ever to make a real name for herself it was now or never, and how could she use her own epoch as a pedestal if she rejected it? She was convinced that her hour had struck, and stuck to this position with passionate intensity. I interrupted her with what seemed to me an unanswerable argument: the persecution of the Jews. "Oh, that," she said. "Well, Bernstein's been running the show for quite long enough—time to give someone else a chance." At this I really started to let loose, but she put on her haughtiest expression and said, hands fluttering, a delicate smile on her lips, "People with something inside them will always get it out, persecutions or no persecutions." In our present situation I found the futility of this infantile Nietzscheism quite intolerable, and I nearly left the table. In the end Dullin's kindness and embarrassment prevented my doing so, but I got up and went the moment I had swallowed my last mouthful, feeling both hurt and angry. It was a long time before I saw them again. (472–473)

Although this description is clearly about a different incident, it sounds startlingly similar to the earlier dinner (the public location, the topic, Jollivet's attitude and her attempt to convince Beauvoir). Perhaps it was the ongoing frequency of such arguments that had led Beauvoir to write Sartre, in late October 1940, "Have I told you that the last time I saw Toulouse and Dullin we had a real shouting match, for the same reasons as ever—though at the same time they're quite besotted with friendly feelings for you!" (346) The irony here, the tug between politics (a direct reference to which the military censor would not have permitted) and personal fondness, is notable.

The account of the dinner at the Théâtre de Paris grillroom is written into the memoir with great conviction. Yet in reality the mixture of anger and affection was now, as before, difficult for Beauvoir to regulate. While Beauvoir concludes in *The Prime of Life*, "It was a long time before I saw them again," her letter to Sartre of February 21, 1941 makes clear that seven weeks after the dinner incident she had already seen Dullin and was going to see Jollivet, whom she acknowledges with sadness has the wrong sympathies (371).[19]

The ambivalence Beauvoir felt toward Jollivet, both on first meeting her and again during the War, was no doubt justified. Indeed, the disapproval by one Simone of the other places Beauvoir in good company. As Frederick Brown points out, Dullin's sister, after his death in 1950, lamented the women who had betrayed Dullin in love, foremost among whom would have been Jollivet (363), who was in fact not present at his funeral and virtually shunned at his memorial. On a personal level, especially with other women and particularly with one like Beauvoir, who became so acutely aware of women's conditions under the Occupation, Jollivet was in some ways out of her element.[20] She was a wonderful conversationalist and utterly charming though self-centered and self-destructive. Although a sometimes-skilled adapter and translator, Jollivet does not seem to have been a very good writer. Ultimately, her narcissism and alcoholism would ruin her.

In *Tout Compte Fait* (*All Said and Done*), the final volume of her memoirs, Beauvoir spends several pages summing up Camille, her life and death: "Our relationship chilled at the beginning of the occupation," she recalls. "Camille went over to Nazism, accepting the persecution of the Jews without turning a hair" (65). Yet there had always been a cold wind that blew through the space between the two women. In truth, Jollivet and Beauvoir had been set against each other early on, and there is ample evidence (some apparent in quotes above taken from *The Prime of Life*) that Sartre did not mind their competitive struggle. Indeed, some of Beauvoir's anecdotes suggest that what Camille did best was to provoke her determinedly rational (and at times humorless) opponent. Such provocative behavior was part of what Jollivet had come to recognize as her "charm": It had worked with Sartre and Dullin and many other men, but it was less successful with women. Yet no matter whom she was with, male or female, Jollivet was always on the lookout for opportunity.

Jollivet's opportunism is quite palpable in the publicity that preceded *Princess*. In a preopening article written for *La Gerbe* (funded, it may be recalled, by Otto Abetz and heavily pro-German in its editorial policies),

"S. Jollivet" attributed her dramatic accomplishments to something far higher than herself, and as if to avoid taking any credit for any of the brilliance of her own script, concluded, "And from me, a little ambitious and very humble vow at the time: not to have deserved too much more than that original creator: History." And in an interview feature, Yvon Novy, writing in *Comœdia*, the arts weekly, which first appeared in 1941 and had extolled the wisdom of Vichy,[21] paints a portrait of the playwright very different from Beauvoir's, of a "young blonde woman with clear eyes, whose smiling and courteous affability which hides an avid imagination, a taste for rendering life in all its intensity. . . ." Fawningly, Novy pronounces that "conciseness is in her manner" and that she has "the modesty of her beginnings, of her work, of her personality." Jollivet, of whom *Comœdia* printed a 1928 photograph to accompany the piece, was obviously on her best behavior.

Nonetheless, the word that resonates throughout the *Comœdia* interview, written while *Princess* was in rehearsal, is *chance*. True to the playwright's grandiose conception of "History" (and her place in it), Mme Jollivet, as Novy calls her, the adapter of Shakespeare, Balzac, and Aristophanes, came to the theatre carrying the manuscript of her first play—Novy does not seem to know about *The Shadow*—and by happy chance, Dullin chose it to premiere at his new theatre. His conclusion, no doubt prompted by Jollivet herself, is most revealing: "Chance? Maybe. Simone Jollivet, in any case, is well prepared to make good." Here, in spite of the interviewee's attempt to make the best impression and the interviewer's willingness to gloss over what he surely knew about her,[22] is the Toulouse who "thinks the moment of her glory—and the flowering of her genius—has finally come," the Camille who, if she "was ever to make a real name for herself it was now or never," in short, the by now desperate opportunist whom Sartre had once loved and whom Beauvoir had come to admire and despise.

The Princess of Ursins: *Women Behind the Scenes*

The beginning episodes of Jollivet's *The Princess of Ursins* would probably invite from modern readers many of the same comments that Beauvoir, after she had perused it in draft, conveyed to Sartre in 1939. Indeed, the prologue and first act, in spite of their intriguing plot and characters, as well as a good measure of irreverence and sensationalism, do seem very long. Perhaps the length of the typescript (the prologue alone goes on for nearly twenty-two pages and the first act another sixty-five) contributed to Beauvoir's sense of tedium.[23] Nonetheless, there is ample indication even in the early part of the play (that is, the part that Beauvoir had seen in manuscript) that Jollivet is writing about a world in which women are routinely excluded from power

Simone Jollivet around 1928 (top). Simone Jollivet around 1943 (bottom).
Courtesy Association Charles Dullin.

and must rely on cunning to manipulate those men who are firmly in control—a world which, in spite of its historical setting, bears a frightening resemblance to the occupied Paris that Jollivet herself inhabited.

The play begins in a chamber at Versailles: Saint-Simon speaks directly to the audience of the crisis in Spain, then promptly hides as Louis XIV and his mistress, Mme de Maintenon, enter, disputing whether or not his grandson Philippe should wear the Spanish crown. What they debate matters less than how they go about debating: Mme de Maintenon seems the Sun King's equal, and in the end she and the Princesse de Bourgogne triumph. Louis, against his better judgment, calls for his grandson Philippe, whom he promises to send to Madrid.

Mme de Maintenon has already chosen as companion for Marie-Louise (Philippe's young wife) an older woman who can guide them past the perils of assuming this throne: Anne-Marie de Trémouille, later known as the Duchess of Bracciano, now Princess of Ursins, is sent for. In the interim, Saint-Simon steps from the shadows to gossip with Louville, a general and friend of Philippe who will accompany the French forces into Spain. Louville, gossiping about the military leader Vendôme, describes the general's habit of rising late and giving audiences as he sits on the commode. One cleric who was especially eager to ingratiate himself was treated to a full display of the general's posterior:

> and when finally, Vendôme arising presented the full moon of his behind, our man [the priest], putting his hands together, cried out "culo d'angelo" [ass of an angel] and hastened to kiss him. (Prol., 17)

This buffoon, the ridiculously ingratiating Abbé Albéroni (whom Dullin himself portrayed), now enters just as Mme des Ursins arrives too. She mistakes the fawning cleric, who bows himself out, for a member of the Italian commedia del l'arte troupe; little does she suspect that he will become her nemesis. Finally, Mme de Maintenon enters, entrusting the young royal couple to the care of Mme des Ursins, who agrees to go with them to Madrid and to keep in constant touch with Versailles.

Act I opens in the Palace du Buen Retiro at Madrid[24]; Mme des Ursins comes into the dark royal bedchamber, to the annoyance of King Philippe and to the amusement of the new Queen. Philippe wishes to hunt, but Marie-Louise wants him to remain at the palace. Mme des Ursins, by reminding him of state business he must conduct, prevails upon him to stay. Once she is alone, however, she wonders when this "schoolboy" will decide to rule. With the corrupt French generals, the Church, and the grandees all locked in a struggle for power, she vows to hold onto the King (and the kingdom) through the Queen, playing off the various factions against each other.

Marie-Louise returns, jealous that Philippe refused to stay when she asked but did so for Mme des Ursins. Although Marie-Louise insists she loves Philippe, she confesses that he is not the forceful prince of whom she has dreamed. Mme des Ursins advises her to see in him the attributes of his kingdom and to accept his inadequacies through invention: "raise your ambition, and you will have in excess all the rest . . ." (I, 20). As for power, adds Mme des Ursins, the Queen ought to use her sexual hold on the King and to invent lies; "Do you want to have a good time, or do you wish to dominate?" she asks (I, 22). According to Mme des Ursins, Marie-Louise will never fully possess the King until Louville is gone. She whispers to the Queen a plot for "une bonne farce" (I, 23) that will displace the general.

Through her influence on Marie-Louise, Mme des Ursins has been able to schedule the King's council meetings and to limit admission to the royal quarters. This very morning, both General Louville and Cardinal Porto-Carrero wait outside, having been denied entrance; Aubigny, a young man whom the Princess favors, is let in. Eventually she allows Louville (but not the Cardinal) to enter the Queen's chamber, where the General accuses Mme des Ursins of forgetting her loyalty to the French in Spain: "Up until now here they were giving us Frenchmen Jack-fuck!" (I, 29).[25] She convinces the general that Amirante, the powerful Castillian noble in the grandees' faction, whom the Cardinal has had appointed ambassador to France, is a spy for Holland and is now headed not for Versailles but for Portugal. She exhorts him to go after Amirante. The pair reach an "alliance sincère et complète," with Louville avowing, "Me, I'm being frank, madam"; "Me too," she answers, "I am frank, Monsieur de Louville . . . when it is necessary . . ." (I, 36).

Once Louville departs, the Princess opens Louville's confidential correspondence about to leave for France. She is amazed by his letter, in which he confides that he is sleeping with the Queen's attendants and accuses Mme des Ursins of plundering the treasury and conniving to set up Aubigny so that she can secretly marry him. With a few strokes of the pen, she rewrites the letter, then sends for the old Cardinal, whom she earlier refused to see. When he enters, the Princess begins plotting with him, promising that he will become governor of Spain when they are rid of Louville. She relates that even now the French general has sent musketeers after Amirante—an affront sure to enrage the grandees as much as it does the Cardinal. He leaves, proclaiming, "Quelle femme! Quelle femme!" (I, 42).

Enter the Spanish royal couple, he complaining of boredom and yearnings for France. Before the Queen can reveal the surprise she has planned as a diversion for him, a delegation of grandees arrives, protesting Louville (and "his dogs of musketeers from France" [I, 48]) "escorting" Amirante. A messenger announces that Amirante has, through forged papers, escaped into Portugal. Mme des Ursins urges Philippe to denounce Amirante while the grandees beg him not to condemn one of their own. The King tells them that he will consider; yet once the nobles have gone, he wavers. Only Marie-Louise, by playing upon his desire to see the surprise she has for him, can make him sign the order against Amirante and Louville, who has allowed this escape and must now be sent back to Versailles.

Mme des Ursins's joy over her victory is interrupted by the entrance of Aubigny, who has encountered yet another courier from France: the Princess, secretly accused of fornication, is about to be recalled as well. After a brief self-reproach ("Heedlessness, women's weakness!" [I, 64]), she summons up her spirit, determined to answer all charges before the Sun King. So ends Act I.

We might pause a moment here to reflect that more than half a century after the play was first produced, the first part of this long script may easily seem, as Beauvoir put it, "neither ridiculous, nor clumsy, nor even very boring; but despite a certain liveliness of the dialogue . . . dreadfully flat." Even the occasional risqué references—to mooning a cleric or "Jack-fuck" ("Jean-Foutre")—do not prevent the play, with its laboriously twisting plot and long (despite many cuts) monologues, from appearing over-written. The opening of *The Princess of Ursins*, and indeed the play as a whole, through its excesses and repetitiveness, may clarify Beauvoir's final comment to Sartre that "one can't conceive why it was ever written."

Still, this Prologue and first act, even in synopsis, illustrate Jollivet's world view. Ever the provocateuse, she seems to enjoy the vulgarity of the streets. The profanity (of which a few critics, back when *Plutus* opened, had complained) and the relatively modern slang seem out of place yet somehow daring. Men, including Louis XIV, Louville, Philippe, and Aubigny, are easily led and misled, even as they are cajoled into believing themselves to be in charge. Indeed, Albéroni's fawning and literal as well as figurative ass-kissing behavior parodies masculine power relationships: All men are rather like commedia buffoons. In reality, in the Jollivet universe, women rule—deftly, through manipulation and seduction, not performing at the center of the world stage but carefully working from the wings.

Because the central character in the play is a woman, the protagonist's attempt to gain complete and overt control becomes all the more difficult—perhaps, Jollivet seems to insinuate, impossible. Nonetheless, Mme des Ursins's deviousness is again and again justified simply by the ongoing "truth" that, in the world depicted, women are publicly relegated to second-class positions and privately must rely on their ability to manipulate men in order to have any power at all. This "truth," which Jollivet had learned from everything around her and had largely accepted, is illustrated throughout the early part of the play: Louis XIV is the acknowledged monarch but Mme de Maintenon makes his decisions; first the Princess and then Marie-Louise control Philippe; and the Princess, who is generally acknowledged to be a mere advisor to the

Queen, is able to dominate a general, a cardinal, and a host of nobles, all males whom the world at large recognizes as powerful. What choice does an ambitious woman have, Jollivet seems to ask, but to move behind the scenes?

There are, perhaps, in Mme des Ursins's unscrupulous determination hints of a very tangible energy and charm. Her steadfastness in her attempt for power may not appear exactly admirable, and yet those who fall into her traps always seem to deserve their fates. Indeed, unlike the machinations of Shakespeare's Richard III, which often crush the innocent and the good, the Princess's plots are aimed at those who seem no better, and occasionally even somewhat worse, than she herself and who, furthermore, if they were more intelligent, would dispose of her as readily as she is able to dispose of them. As the high and low moral grounds are, respectively, lowered and raised, her bid for power is played on a more level field.

Yet history tells us, as it told Jollivet, that the Princess would have to end not the victor but the vanquished. Even though, in the ensuing acts, the protagonist capably defends herself at Versailles, Mme des Ursins must return to Spain to fight a fearless and cunning battle. Most of the men she encounters are easily confused and surprised. Yet the script's example of the quintessentially stupid subordinate male, Albéroni, proves her undoing. Through a series of his deceptions, the Princess is ultimately forced to flee to Italy, where she later dies a tired old woman. In a sense, her nemesis, Albéroni, has learned to appear harmless, witless, and pliable, but, like the Princess herself, the crafty cleric has been busy behind the scenes even as he has clowned before the footlights. In this respect, Dullin in the role as Albéroni was especially poignant: The veteran director-actor seemed to tolerate and appease his bullying mistress, and yet ultimately, Dullin, like Albéroni, remained in control.

Certainly on one level the play, with its demands of space, its use of lavish sets and costumes, and its need for many actors, was written to take advantage of Dullin's new theatre and its substantial funding, a substantial amount of which came from Vichy itself.[26] Of course, *Princess* was begun around the start of the drôle de guerre and probably completed before or shortly after the Defeat. Thus, on quite another level, the author's initial thematic intention was probably not very different from what it had been when she had written her earlier play, *The Shadow*: to express as provocatively as she knew how her own peculiar vision of life (and thereby achieve fame as a dramatist). Yet by the time Jollivet came to write the later play, this vision had altered with the author, who had ceased to be the stunning young woman who had swept Sartre and Dullin (and many others) off their feet; the offensive opportunist whom Beauvoir recalls during the Occupation was an aging and abusive drunk who gave reporters fifteen-year-old photographs of herself and mistakenly imagined that she could, while the Nazis ruled Paris, make her mark as a playwright.

By the time the War came, Jollivet's future had been for many years tied to Dullin. The ambitious Toulouse, against whom Sartre had compared Beauvoir, had long accepted (although she could never have admitted it) that she could make it only via her lover.[27] Even her own self-serving publicity does not hide her dependence on the great director. Through Dullin, she believed, she would receive the recognition she felt she deserved. Through his production of her play, she hoped that the new order, which in reality could not have been any friendlier to her efforts than the order that had come before, would allow her to (as Beauvoir paraphrases Camille in *The Prime of Life*) "use her own epoch as a pedestal."

In terms of individual authorial intention, then, the recurring patterns in *The Princess of Ursins*, because of both when the play was written and who had written it, comment not on the historical past or present nor on the general topic of the role of women in society but on the play's inevitable subject, namely Simone Jollivet. The egocentric author found in her aging title character an ideal vehicle for expressing her personal philosophy; the practice of grabbing all one can, no matter how one goes about grabbing, is repeatedly romanticized, even glorified.

Yet, even though, as I have suggested, the logical way to regard the author's intentions would be to view the play as a statement by the dramatist about herself and about the universe as she construed it, Jollivet's ideas about her own script may have altered as the Occupation wore on. As an avid theatregoer, she no doubt had a growing awareness that plays by Spanish authors or with Spanish themes were in vogue[28]; she may well have believed that her pseudo-Nietschean historical drama would capture the hearts of the master race[29]; perhaps she hoped that the brilliantly staged production and skillful acting would seal the play's success.[30] I seriously doubt that Simone Jollivet—who in her calculatedly self-effacing apologia in *La Gerbe* makes herself more the discoverer of the plot than its creator—had the faintest idea that at the heart of her play was an obsession, not merely hers but of the culture at large, with the increasing powerlessness of women under the Occupation.

And yet, her play may be easily read that way. In the world of *The Princess of Ursins*, as in the world decreed by the Nazi occupiers and the weakening regime at Vichy, women were relegated to the role of wives (and with it, the role of mothers) and not only excluded from any type of work through which they might achieve autonomy and influence but discouraged from work in general. As Sweets reminds us, in wartime France the campaign to keep women entirely out of the work place may have been no more successful than the campaigns to eradicate prostitution and abortion, but Cobb's list of what jobs women could and did hold indicates a serious lack of equity between the sexes. Similarly, in *The Princess of Ursins*, women may be officially engaged as consorts (like Mme de Maintenon and Marie-Louise) or behind-the-scenes advisors (like Mme des Ursins), but they, regardless of their capabilities, can never hope to attain the powerful and publicly recognized positions allotted to men.

Given the reactionary turn against females, which emerged in France during the early 1940s and official sanctions of the repression of more than half the population, women with talent and ambition faced incredible obstacles. Schwartz makes clear that the only situation in which women worked with some equality with men was in the Résistance. Those who, like Beauvoir, prior to the war had struggled for prominence and who, for different reasons, chose not to fight the new order directly were compelled to learn firsthand the effects of day-to-day life imposed on women in general.

Only a few, such as Arletty, whose film career flourished during the Occupation, actually used the "epoch as a pedestal" to climb upward.[31] Like Arletty, who had made her way onto stage and screen through a career of posing for and sleeping with a number of successful artists, Jollivet was highly skilled at playing by the rules drawn up by a male-dominated culture. Her seemingly amoral attitude toward sex, which had once so fascinated both Sartre and Beauvoir, was simply the means to an end. This end, which continued to elude her but almost always found Dullin, was her own worldly (and by virtue of that, artistic) success.

Oddly, *The Princess of Ursins* prophesies not Jollivet's triumph but the failure that women playing by the Occupiers' rules would inevitably encounter (including Arletty, who was sitting in jail when *Les Enfants du Paradis* finally premiered). Although Mme des Ursins puts up a marvelous fight, in Act II, first defending herself at Versailles, then conniving with and then against the parties in Spain, in Act III she loses control of Spain, forfeits her lover, and is driven out of the country. In the play's epilogue, her rival, buffoonish Albéroni, whose genius she has been duped into overlooking, meets her by chance many years later in a garden in Rome. Albéroni, now a cardinal, asks the Princess if she has renounced all future projects, all ambition, to which she replies,

> You want a laugh! At my age! . . . Old coquettes make themselves pious, but what do we become, we others, when old age overtakes us? (III, 47)[32]

Humiliated in her defeat in war and love, thwarted in her bid for absolute power, Mme des Ursins has retired. Her cynical tranquility quietly foretells the alcoholic demise that awaited Jollivet after Dullin's death.

The ultimate lesson Jollivet had learned, the one she wrote about in this play and the one she lived, was not that the Princess was a victim of her times but that she herself was not entirely responsible for her downfall. There indeed stood against her a vast masculine conspiracy. Significantly, the conflict between what Jollivet knew to be true and what she hoped to accomplish through the production of this play infuse the ending with an unsettling calm. Having fought the battle of the sexes through manipulating the men in power, Mme des Ursins's only flaw was to seek power overtly for herself—openly, without the guise of submission. In a world in which women had to work behind the scenes, the Princess wanted to stand in the spotlight. Although Jollivet's experience had taught her that this aspiration was doomed to failure, her play does not really valorize the superiority of males, who are no better than the heroine. On the contrary, by focusing at the end on the defeated female protagonist, she destabilizes the fascist fable and questions the play's own moral. *The Princess of Ursins* may not be a proto-feminist play, but its characters and plot—indeed, its very composition—complicate what at first glance may seem a simple message.

Conclusion

As with Jollivet's first play, *The Shadow*, the press was not friendly to *Princess*. Jacques Berland in *Paris-Soir* praised Dullin's direction and acting but criticized the writing (by "Mme Simone Jollivet") as dramatically weak; Dullin's only error was in "the choice of the piece." Georges Ricou in *La France Socialiste* found the story too complicated and overpopulated with characters to interest the general public. Agreeing with Beauvoir's first impressions, Ricou concludes, "One feels, with the succession of tableaux, an impression of monotony, of boredom. . . ." Even *Paris-Midi*'s Maurice Rostand, whose review of the production and performance is largely positive, describes the play as "a little dull, a little gray, weighed down by the continual asides which suggest the old-fashioned repertory. . . ." And the dean of the collaborationist critics, Alain Laubreaux, whose *Les Pirates de Paris* would open at the Ambigu that spring, held up Aristotle's rule requiring the unity of time and place to Jollivet's untidy script.

Reviewers tried to maintain their respect for Dullin even as they attacked Jollivet's play. "Let's wait for some very lively and durable play from him," advised Armory in *Les Nouveaux Temps*. Charles Quinet in *Le Matin* politely damned the play with the faint praise, "a beautiful effort of erudition, drawn from the encyclopedias," and called it, "un grand succès d'estime." André Castelot, whose critiques in *La Gerbe* usually dripped with venom, excused himself from reviewing the actor who played Philippe, the French king of Spain (his own brother, Jacques), complimented Dullin on both acting and directing, and offered a few admonishments to the playwright (he felt the third act digressed into a very conventional melodrama).

Although she had some success as a translator, Jollivet's work brought in, at best, mixed reviews. Her greatest commercial success, her adaptation

The Princess of Ursins meets her nemesis, the cleric Albéroni in Act I of The Princess of Ursins *(courtesy Association Charles Dullin).*

of Aristophanes' *Plutus*, which opened in 1938 (and was revived during the Occupation), was seen by many as a ribald updating of a great comedy, but for that very reason, Robert Brasillach in *Candide* and Laubreaux in *Je suis partout* had protested that she had vulgarized and distorted a classic that ought to have been a vehicle for lampooning liberals.[33] After the War, when Dullin and Jollivet were attacked in the press over the production of *King Lear*, Jollivet's translation of which, many felt, grossly misrepresented Shakespeare's text, Beauvoir came to their defense with a review of her own in *Action* in which she accused the attackers not only of disliking Shakespeare but of following Brasillach and Laubreaux, who were by now both infamously hated collaborators. Fliers with testimonials by Louis Jouvet, Gaston Bâty, Armand Salacrou, and Pierre Renoir urged spectators to come see for themselves.[34] The play, however, did not find an audience, and eventually Dullin had to abandon the again renamed Théâtre Sarah Bernhardt.

What about Jollivet's politics? The evidence we have for her chilling statements has been cited above from the descriptions of incidents that Beauvoir included in her correspondence and memoir. Indeed, if we are to trust Beauvoir's descriptions of what Jollivet did and said, and there is no reason we should not, then we ought to ask whether or not Jollivet was a Nazi sympathizer.

Clearly, Jollivet's words are hideous. Still the insinuation that she was in some way a collaborator seems, even in the context of Beauvoir's writings, an overstatement. Toulouse was certainly a loud-mouthed, bullying, alcoholic opportunist who liked to outrage her listeners and perhaps, if given the chance, would have done whatever she thought necessary to succeed. Of course, for reasons implied by her own play, actual opportunities for her to collaborate were difficult to find. This, of course, does not make Jollivet's remarks any nicer, but to describe her differences with Beauvoir during the Occupation, as does one editor, as genuinely "political" (Hoare 38 n63) is to misrepresent Jollivet; in Beauvoir's memoirs and letters, in spite of one Simone's repeated condemnations of the other, Camille emerges not so much as a proto-fascist but as a would-be self-promoter.

It is important to recall how in 1945, when Dullin and Jollivet were both accused of collaboration, Beauvoir took the opportunity to rise to their defenses in *Action* (Francis and Gontier 135). At worst, perhaps, Simone Jollivet was a bigoted opportunist and not a successful one at that. If she had collaborated horizontally, Beauvoir would no doubt have mentioned it. In existentialist terms, Jollivet's words may have signified a pro-Nazi attitude, but her actions spoke far more softly: The only thing she might have done for the fascist cause was *The Princess of Ursins*, which all the fascists around her rejected.

According to Beauvoir, the only writer who had, after the premiere of *The Shadow*, come up to Jollivet, "clasped Camille's hands and talked of a masterpiece" (*Prime of Life* 108), was the visionary Antonin Artaud, who after the War would be regarded as a major figure in the theatre. Artaud unfortunately was not able to attend *Princess*; he had been committed to the asylum at Rodez, having been diagnosed as insane. Perhaps he would have appreciated Jollivet's second effort as a dramatist although I suspect he would have found it too talky, too long, and rather short on spectacle.

Georges Pioch observed, in his lukewarm notice in *L'Œuvre*, that we see in the play the plain truth about the protagonist, "of the intrigues, the triumphs, and finally, of the defeat of her wholly virile ambition"; he was referring, of course, to the character of the Princess, but he might just as well have been describing the author, whose own values were founded upon those of the male-centered culture around her.

Nonetheless, Jollivet was herself too much the narcissist to believe she could be at fault. Her statement to Beavoir around Christmas 1940 says it all: "People with something inside them will always get it out, persecutions or no persecutions." Unlike the Princess herself, the playwright might project her ultimate failures on those around her, especially on Dullin. Her descent into alcoholism to some degree represented her escape from any recognition that she might have acknowledged that women, not unlike the Jews, had become objects of persecution.

5

The Politics of Intention:
Jean Anouilh's *Antigone* via *Oreste*

Introduction

When critics and historians try to classify the politics of plays written and produced during the Occupation, they inevitably operate between those polar opposites, "resistance" and "collaboration" and attempt to identify how a playwright intended his or her work to be construed. Collaboration, as I have used it in the previous chapter, implies more than just a sympathy for the Germans and their policies; it carries the idea of some actual participation on their behalf. Simone Jollivet, for example, may have made remarks that indicated her support of the Nazis, but we have no evidence that she in fact did anything to help their cause. True, her sympathies were deplorable, but how and with whom did she actively collaborate? Even if we wish to regard *The Princess of Ursins* as in some way vindicating a fascist view of womanhood, which at best it does only in part and which the collaborationist press certainly failed to grasp, we must remember too that the script was probably completed before the Occupation began.

With regard to "resistance," I have noted in this book's overture, John F. Sweets's proposal to move the definition beyond "the activities of the organized resistance movements" to one that takes into account the general atmosphere that nurtured and encouraged such activities. "A broader construction of the term *resistance*, involving *active opposition* to the Vichy regime and the Germans, is admittedly unwieldy," Sweets concludes. "But it is also truer to the complex reality of the resistance in France" (224). Clearly Sweets is suggesting that "the resistance in France" is not the same as "the Résistance in France."

Henry Rousso in his study of how France in the present has come to view the France of the past, *The Vichy Syndrome: History and Memory in France Since 1944*, discusses what he calls the "resistancialist myth," according to which the majority of those who remained in France between 1940 and 1944 were, whether or not they had actually worked for the Résistance, at least in sympathy with it. This idea of France as a nation of resistors, initiated by Charles De Gaulle in his speeches following the Liberation of Paris in 1944, began to decline in popularity only in the late 1960s (302–303), when, as Rousso tells us, "[h]istorians set out to penetrate the veils thrown up by Robert Aron . . ." (305). Rousso explains that "the intrinsically ideological nature of the resistancialist myth . . . accounts for its weakness . . ." for "[i]t was unable to accommodate experiences of the Occupation that had nothing to do with resistance" (303).

Two important works helped demolish resistancialism: Marcel Ophuls's searing 1971 documentary on French wartime anti-Semitism, *Le Chagrin et la pitié* (*The Sorrow and the Pity*), and Robert Paxton's 1972 unflinching reevaluation of the Pétain government, *Vichy France: Old Guard and New Order, 1940–1944*. As the resistantialist myth has receded, some historians and critics have gone back to take a look at all that has been made of the Occupation, while others have begun to examine those experiences from the period, which the myth could not, as Rousso puts it, "accommodate" and had thus excluded. The result has been a counter and far less flattering image of the role France played in the War, in the Occupation, and in the Holocaust.

A similar reversal may be detected in studies of the wartime stage. As I have previously mentioned, when the War ended, Philip Toynbee voiced the opinion that "[t]he Germans appear to have interfered very little with the freedom of the Paris stage, and there has been a varied and fertile dramatic activity" (156). Of course, in reality the Germans and the Vichy government had frequently interfered with "freedom of the stage," and as I have indicated earlier, the theatre under the Occupation was neither as varied nor as fertile as it had been before (and would be after) the War.

From the Liberation onward, many serious critics of stage literature and theatre historians avoided looking at the issue of "resistant" and/or "collaborationist" theatre by using lenses framed by what cinema critics would come to call "auteurism": By focusing their discussions on the body of work by a particular playwright or of a particular director, they could ignore the political and historical contexts and problems. For example, André Roussin, in an essay on Jean Anouilh published at the end of the War, examines the dramatist's scripts from 1932 to the present (being 1945) and examines their more formalistic elements (themes, characterization, plot structure, etc.). Through the 1990s, the standard French view of twentieth-century French drama and theatre follows the succession of directors, from Antoine to Copeau, and from his four protegés to Barrault, with Ariane Mnouchkine as their heir. Yet the passing of resistancialism began to open up the possibility of dismantling some of the associated myths that had operated within the theatre.

Passages from two British critics illustrate how resistancialism and the shift away from it have influenced their views on one of the major controversies within Occupation stage literature: the political orientation of Anouilh's *Antigone*. Although Sir Harold Hobson discusses the Occupation in *The French Theatre of To-day* (1953; I will later quote from this work), in *French Theatre Since 1830* (1978) he comes back to it, devoting an entire chapter to the period and in it goes to some length to summarize *Antigone*'s reception:

> The first reaction to *Antigone* in Paris in 1944 was one of indignation on the part of those sympathetic to Resistance. The word ran round that *Antigone* was a Nazi play. It was thought in the arguments between Antigone and Creon that Creon made out the better case. . . . [Hobson analyzes the plot to demonstrate the error in such an interpretation.] After a comparatively small number of performances Creon became identified in the popular view with the German Occupants: and to those Occupants Antigone was the indomitable rebel who, though routed in argument, still resolutely said No. Even before the end of 1944 the legend had become firmly established that in writing *Antigone* Anouilh had deliberately intended to present to the public a Resistance play. (204)

These events emerge with a very different emphasis in David Bradby's *Modern French Drama 1940–1980* (1984), also in a chapter on the Occupation:

> At the time of the play's first production the structure was sufficient and the emptiness [of the heroine's sacrifice] went unnoticed for the most part, since each member of the audience read into the play his own concrete difficulties—whether to resist, whether to collaborate. Anouilh's politics had always been rather ambiguous. His early plays had contained hints of social protest, but political choices were never presented in anything but the most personal terms. . . . *Antigone* was well reviewed in the Collaborationist press and was at first assumed to be on the Vichy side. But the progressive isolation of Antigone carries along with it a strong emotional charge when the play is being performed, leading an audience to sympathise with her much more strongly than might be evident from a reading of the play. Gradually the public came to identify more with Antigone and her uncompromising "No!" Creon came to be seen, not as the sensible compromiser but as the opportunistic collaborator. (35–36)

The difference between the two passages—written just six years apart—is remarkable. Hobson, who had covered the contemporary theatre in England and France for decades, articulates ideas that obviously stem from resistancialist mythology; in fact, his chapter on the Occupation is the final one in his 1978 book (which covers French theatre from 1830 to the "present"). Bradby, however, begins his book with his chapter on the Occupation and appears to come at the subject from a distinctly post-resistancialist point of view; his skepticism and distrust of Anouilh are palpable.

Neither critic claims that the play was *meant* to be construed in the way that pro-Résistance audience members did construe it; both acknowledge that the initial reaction in the press and public was toward Creon, but one identifies him with the Germans and the other with Vichy. They imply that the reception was due not to the dramatic text but to something else. Indeed, for both critics there remains the question of Anouilh's *intention*: "the legend had become firmly established," writes Hobson, "that in writing *Antigone* Anouilh had deliberately intended to present to the public a Resistance play"; because of the "emptiness" of the script, according to Bradby, "each member of the audience read into the play his own concrete difficulties—whether to resist, whether to collaborate," as if there had been no intent on Anouilh's part to signify.

This chapter examines the text of *Antigone* by viewing it through *Oreste*, a play that Jean Anouilh began in 1942 and then abandoned during the same year in order to write *Antigone*. The fragment *Oreste*, which was not published until 1945, retells the legend most often reenacted on the Occupation stage, the myth of the children of Agamemnon; it also sheds light on the play that succeeded it, offering a glimpse of the playwright's process in writing *Antigone*. Part of my goal here is to discuss Anouilh's work in the context of the Occupation—to see it amid the maddening contradictoriness of the period. Rather than regard the theatre as a force for resistance or for collaboration, which would ultimately force me into a premature judgment, I will attempt to look at the very ambiguity discernible in what Roderick Kedward calls "the inevitable compromises involved in fulfilling the demands of everyday life under the Occupation . . ." (7).

I will concentrate here on the politically motivated arguments that *Antigone* aroused when first produced in 1944. It is important to make sense of those arguments that seem to swirl around the debate as to this script's significance if only because *Antigone,* more than any other work, has provoked an ongoing dispute in many ways symptomatic of the general dispute over the role of the theatre during these four years. Moreover, this dispute has formed a major focus of discussion for those who have looked at the playscripts of the period, and this focal point has, in some ways, obscured other issues, such as the role of the stage in affirming and reshaping sexuality. My hope in this chapter is that an analysis of *Antigone* in light of *Oreste* may bring additional evidence to an ongoing controversy, and that once I have addressed the political arguments, I will be able to proceed, in the following chapter, to an examination of the staging of a politics of sexuality.

Atreus's Children in Occupied Paris

Postwar critical response to Anouilh's *Antigone* has, along with critical response to the Occupation theatre in general, undergone a major change. While a number of critics after the Second World War and members of the public at large acknowledged that the play contained an intended pro-Résistance subtext, more recent writers have doubted its existence. For example, Mary Ann Frese Witt, in *The Search for Modern Tragedy*, is able to link Anouilh's (and also Henry de Montherlant's) plays with fascist ideology. Through an analysis of the period and a perusal of both Anouilh's completed dramas and his contributions to the collaborationist press, Witt makes a convincing case that *Antigone* is "permeated by an ideological subtext informed by aspects of aesthetic fascism" (226) and that in spite of the lack of "overt political references" in this and other plays of the 1930s and 1940s, Anouilh's "articles for the German-sponsored papers, as well as his plays produced under the Occupation and in particular *Antigone*, all place him in a context of French fascist ideology of the period" (229). Such an interpretation, though well researched and intelligently argued, nevertheless seems to follow clearly a post-resistancialist approach to the Occupation.

Most critics do agree that during the period Antigone, like Jeanne d'Arc, became a familiar figure on the stage; there was a production of Sophocles' version at the Odéon in 1942, another version produced by Vichy (for the Chantiers de la jeunesse) in 1941, three reprises of the Cocteau-Honnegger Opera (1941, 1943, 1944), and in 1944, both Sophocles' version and Thierry Maulnier's adaptation of Garnier's. A veritable "crise d'antigonnite," wrote André Fraigneau in *Comœdia* in March 1944 (Witt 219).[1] This Antigone boom reflected, in part, a larger trend, the revival in the theatre of interest in plays with storylines derived from the Greeks.[2] Other notable examples include Jean-Louis Barrault's production of Aeschylus' *Les Suppliantes* in July 1941 at Roland-Garros Stadium (discussed in chapter 2), Anouilh's own *Eurydice*, which opened in December 1942 at the Atelier, and Racine's *Phèdre*, which received productions at the Comédie-Française beginning in March 1941 and at the Ambassadeurs in June of the same year. There were also several operas based on Greek myth.[3] Yet the most frequently seen classical characters on the Occupation stage were not Antigone and family but the children of Agamemnon.

The recurrence of characters drawn from the Oresteian legend is observable not only in the Comédie-Française's *Iphigénie à Aulis* (opened

November 1941), by Euripides, but also in its presentations of *Iphigénie en Tauride* by Goethe (opened April 1942) and *Iphigénie à Delphes* by Gerhardt Hauptmann (opened May 1943).[4] Orestes was kept alive in no fewer than three productions of Racine's *Andromaque*, the most important of which played at the Comédie-Française beginning in September 1941.[5] The revival of Giraudoux's *Electre* (at the Avenue in March 1943) and the premiere of Sartre's *Les Mouches* (at the Cité in June 1943) suggested that contemporary French dramatists might also take refuge in the classical past. Giraudoux's 1935 *La Guerre de Troie n'aura pas lieu* had used Hellenic legend to comment on twentieth-century diplomacy; in the context of the Occupation, however, his 1937 *Electre* was eagerly viewed by the Germans and their friends as what Agnes Raymond calls "a defense of order" (18) and "an apology for dictatorship" (118n); Alain Laubreaux in *Le Petit Parisien* led the collaborationist press in praise.[6] In contrast, Sartre's rendition of Orestes's return, generally panned by the collabo press (partly because of its "decadent" staging), might have been more likely to be interpreted (if audience members were inclined to interpret it so) as ridicule of Vichy and a depiction of the choice not to collaborate. *Les Mouches* ran only a few weeks in June 1943, but its reputation as a resistance play, which a retrospective reading certainly makes plausible, must be tempered with the knowledge that the German censors permitted it; therefore, whatever call to resistance was perceptible seems to have been evident only to like-minded French spectators.[7]

No matter what their sympathies, by the close of the 1942–1943 season, theatregoers had been deluged by the Agamemnon story. André Castelot, the vicious critic for the German-embassy-funded *La Gerbe*, diverged from fellow Nazi sympathizers with a negative review of Hauptmann's *Iphigénie à Delphes*. He had apparently had enough of the woes of the House of Atreus. Castelot cited the "innombrables Iphigénies" followed by the "reprise d'*Electre*" and the "création des *Mouches*," and confessed to a certain Atriedophobia—this a season before Fraigneau's "Antigone crisis"!

What about the Oresteian legend so appealed to Occupation playwrights, producers, and audiences? Certainly, its sanctioned antiquity was important, but so was its potential for ambiguity; Sartre, after the Liberation, would say that the myth behind *Les Mouches* had been a useful vehicle: "Why stage declamatory Greeks . . . , unless to disguise what one was thinking about under a fascist regime?" (*Sartre on Theatre* 188) Thus, a dramatist (or director) might be able to articulate all sorts of statements through a retelling of what French and German censors saw as a legitimate part of traditionalist culture. Certainly, as the extant scripts of the Attic tragedians demonstrate, no other myth had proven an ability to be reenacted on stage with such utterly different meanings. Perhaps this last factor, more than any other, accounts for the wide use of this legend, exceeding even the recycling of the Antigone legend.

I suppose too that in the Oresteian myth itself—or, to put this in structuralist terms, among the essential components of the Oresteian story, which cannot change from rendition to rendition—lie particular narrative figures that resonate throughout the period. One might, for example, associate the link between power and fatherhood (both true fatherhood and false) with the paternalism of Pétain, or catch in the theme of sacrifice for the future a glimpse of Vichy's National Revolution or of the Résistance.[8] Still, as I note above, this myth seems highly capable of conveying multiple meanings, a property that in itself would have recommended its use.

No doubt, in the highly charged and constantly changing political atmosphere of the Occupation, the stage, like the culture as a whole, seemed fraught with shifting values and varying significances; ambiguous itself, it was drawn to ambiguity. Witt emphasizes how fascist "Parisian theatre reviewers tended to look with disfavour on plays that were overtly propagandistic for the Vichy cause" (191). Moreover, *Les Pirates de Paris*, the one French play that was blatantly anti-Semitic and profascist, was decried by critics (except by Alain Laubreaux). Unlike Germany, where a monolithic political ideology might be readily inscribed into a new script or imposed upon an otherwise ambiguous classic (like *The Merchant of Venice* or *Woyzeck*[9]), France—or French critics—seemed to prefer a high degree of obliqueness. Perhaps such a preference for ambiguity reflected the taste of a right-wing elite whose bias against propaganda had been formed during the Third Republic, when most propaganda art had come from the left. Or perhaps in this context, where varying right-wing ideologies competed with each other, these critics recognized the need to keep open the possibilities of representation.

Theatre Ambiguity/Audience Reception

The attraction of ambiguity to theatre artists—writers, directors, designers, and actors—perhaps derived less from a desire to please reviewers than from a firsthand knowledge of the heterogeneity of their audiences. The political spectrum, for example, consisted not merely of the varied and visible shadings of fascism[10] but of the less easily detectable tones of rightists and leftists working against Vichy and Berlin, of the skeptical who attempted to avoid helping the occupiers, and of the many whose invisible sympathies shifted as the War wore on. In this environment, it is no wonder that stage heroines such as Jeanne d'Arc and Antigone could be and were claimed by Pétainists and Gaullists alike, by pro- and anti-Germans, by reluctant resistors and fascist fellow travelers. Much of the ambiguity of the French stage was intended not only (as Sartre implied) to "disguise what one was thinking about under a fascist regime" but also (and perhaps more usually) to allow the material to appeal directly to as many spectators as possible, French fascists included (or, in more than a few cases, in particular). Even with the subsidies given by Vichy to private theatres, playhouses still worked to maximize their profits. The only way to continue production was to keep drawing houses from a divided general public.

Both the record-breaking rise in theatre profits and attendance during the period, far greater than before the Occupation,[11] show how well the Paris stage responded to the need for French entertainment, at a time when film fell more heavily under German control and movie houses became places where the Gestapo might "conscript" spectators for involuntary labor service in Germany. The theatre was less likely to sustain such raids and, with a few exceptions, carried a more dependably French product. As Patrick Marsh asserts, "on entering the theatre, one was among Frenchmen taking part in an essentially French experience which the horrors of war could not, temporarily at least, affect" ("The Theatre . . ." 143). As Marguerite Jamois told Célia Bertin during the Occupation, "In the theatre, you're never alone. You depend on each other" (176). And Bertin, recalling how, the Occupation theatre affected her as a teenager, notes:

> In those somber years, Parisians went to the theatre a lot to set aside, for an evening, their daily misfortunes. . . .
>
> Seated in the nearly dark room, I didn't really concentrate on what happened on stage. My spirit floated between what I heard and the questions I asked myself. Thoughts of oppression, of the war never left me. Still, in the theatre, they withdrew a little. The sound of the words alone existed and a certain tension. (235)[12]

Of course, it would be wrong to equate what Marsh calls "an essentially French experience" with being in solidarity with the Free French or the Résistance, for French fascists claimed, as much as the Gaullists, to represent the true France; the prototypical Vichy poster displayed the face of Pétain with the ostensibly incontrovertible question, "Are you more French than he?"

In this context, if only because of the audience's own concerns with identity, virtually any play presented during the Occupation, no matter when it was written and what its author's intent, was inevitably construed as defining what it meant to be French. Theatre artists, partially in an attempt to retain houses, offered, consciously or not, definitions that satisfied a broad range of spectators. Perhaps the best example was Claude Vermorel's *Jeanne avec nous*, which opened at the Théâtre des Champs-Élysées in January 1942 (and continued at other theatres until August), in which Joan emerged as a heroine for both collabo press and the Résistance. Gabriel Jacobs, examining the script, its production, and their reception, finds much in the text (written in 1938)[13] to explain not only the rightist critics' appreciation but also postwar assertions that audiences had decoded statements against the Germans. Jacobs notes how "much of the play could have been interpreted to suit one's own prejudices and preoccupations" (117). Witt, referring to Vermorel's writings for the fascist press, logically concludes, "It is indeed difficult to reconcile the Vermorel author of 'Théâtre de demain' in 1941 with the purported author and coproducer of a Résistance-oriented performance in 1942" (191–192 n4); yet many who attended the play during the Occupation (notably Simone de Beauvoir and Paul-Louis Mignon) would have no difficulty later recalling it as a compelling statement about France résistante.

Of course, such incongruity is endemic to the topic—to the times, place, and institution. We may look with irony on how Jean Marais, who was (via Cocteau) aided by the Nazis, who in the Reich exterminated homosexuals, eventually tried to enter an actor's unit of the Résistance; similarly, Paul Œttly, who directed and starred in Laubreaux's *The Pirates of Paris* in the winter of 1942, would appear in the spring of 1943 as the High Priest in *The Flies* (which even Added concludes was at least intended as anti-Vichy criticism, 259–260) and in the early summer of 1944 directed and acted in Albert Camus's *Misunderstanding*. The theatre, like fallen France, was marked by the contradiction inherent in Sartre's famous remark about the Occupation: "I wonder if I shall be understood if I say that it was both intolerable and at the same time we put up with it very well." Buried in this amiably stated paradox lies the terrible shame to which many in France admitted even while they denied it: that not until the War began to shift did they think that the Allies might win. As Witt maintains, many sources describe "the tendency of Resistance sympathizers in the audience to 'adopt' Anouilh's Antigone, while collaborationists applauded along with them" (221); however, such a phenomenon might not have occurred before the autumn of 1942.

Events in the latter part of 1942 strongly implied, in spite of censorship and an active collaborationist press, that Germany might not be the ultimate victor. True, De Gaulle had left in 1940, from which time The Free French in London were broadcasting their message of resistance; furthermore, the Nazi attack on the Soviet Union in June 1941 not only encouraged radical fascist groups (such as the Parti Populaire Française) to become wholehearted collaborators but, just as significantly, impelled many French Communists, who up until then had remained inactive, to resist the Occupier. Allied landings in French North Africa began at the close of November 1942, by which time the Germans had occupied the so-called Free Zone. The bloody siege of Stalingrad, which began in September 1942, dragged through the fall and into the winter of 1943, bringing the average French citizen some tangible evidence that Germany was not invincible. *Antigone* belongs to the latter part of 1942; *Oreste*, even in its incompleteness, is a statement on the first two years of the Occupation.

Thus, even though one may locate Anouilh and his plays in what Witt describes as "the context of French fascist ideology of the period," one must—in order to be fair to the dramatist and his work—struggle to identify and understand the ambiguities inherent in his dramatic and theatrical texts. For the sake of accuracy, I am proposing that the playscript that Anouilh never completed be viewed as a draft of the play that supplanted it, or at least as evidence of what he eventually chose to present publicly—and chose not to present. If nothing more, Anouilh's rejection of *Oreste* for *Antigone* suggests the dramatist's intention to increase the possibilities of interpretation, specifically of political interpretation, in his next script.

Antigone: *Script, Production, Response(s)*

In spite of the "Antigone crisis," Anouilh allowed his play to be produced near the end of the Occupation. As with many of the classical reworkings of the time, the playwright followed the prototype in a variety of ways. Essentially, Anouilh's retelling follows the plot laid down in the ancient tragedy: Polyneices and Eteocles, the sons of Oedipus, have killed each other in a battle over Thebes. Their uncle, Creon, king of the city-state, has ordered a state funeral for Eteocles, the brother who defended the city, but has decreed that the attacker, Polyneices, must remain unburied. Their sister, Antigone, daughter of Oedipus, niece of Creon, and fiancee of Creon's son, Haemon, buries her brother in spite of Creon's order that those honoring Polyneices will be executed. The characters from Sophocles are all present: Ismene, Antigone's sister who tries to dissuade her from the burial; Haemon, who once Antigone is sentenced takes his own life; Creon's wife, Eurydice, who on hearing of Haemon's death commits suicide; and the messenger who comes to deliver bad news.

Yet there are significant changes. To Sophocles' cast Anouilh has added a young page in Creon's retinue, a nurse who has raised Antigone, and a few more guards. And he has reduced the full Greek chorus to a one-man commentator, à la Shakespeare. The Chorus character serves as one of the devices that distance the audience from the story. "Well, here we are," he begins, addressing the house. "These people are about to act out the story of Antigone" (3)[14]. He introduces the characters and even describes their fates, both as characters and actors in the play. "What this [technique] achieves," asserts David Bradby, "is an effect of one and the same time of distance and emotional sympathy" (34).

Both in his opening monologue and throughout the script, The Chorus comments not only on the story (and characters and setting) represented in the play but on the play as play. After his introductory speech, The Chorus leaves the stage until the point when Creon is told by one of the guards stationed at the dead body that someone has buried Polyneices. Again, looking directly into the auditorium, he offers a long monologue on the difference between tragedy and melodrama, then provides a transition back to the action, and exits (23–24). Later, when Creon has sent Antigone out with guards, The Chorus returns, commenting and interjecting as Haemon pleads with his father to save Antigone (44–46); here, The Chorus partially fulfills the role of the Greek prototype, but at the same time, he retains full awareness of the narrative. As Antigone exits to her death, The Chorus quips to the audience, "And now it's Creon's turn" (50). After the plot has reached its denouement, he summarizes, "It is all over. Antigone is calm tonight, and we shall never know the name of the fever that consumed her. She has played her part" (53). Even as he enters into the play and recounts (and thus creates or at least dramatizes) events, The Chorus never completely loses his identity of metatheatrical reporter.

In addition, in the play's dialogue between protagonist and antagonist, the latter resorts at particular moments to theatrical imagery: "You have cast me for the villain in this little play of yours, and yourself for the heroine" (33), Creon chastises his niece; "My part is not an heroic one, but I shall play my part" (37) he later warns; and in explaining what really happened between the two brothers, he adds, "I want you to know what took place in the wings of this drama in which you are burning to play a part" (39). We may recall how Jean Giraudoux, who was no stranger to such metatheatrics ("Let's pretend that what happens in a traditional play happens to us . . ." says the Man from Marsac to Agnès), had integrated this sort of innuendo into *The Apollo of Marsac*; still, few have made much of this association between Giraudoux and Anouilh. Most critics tend to link Anouilh's work to that of Luigi Pirandello, the brilliant fascist Italian playwright, many of whose dramas were produced in Paris before the War. Ironically, because Pirandello's French translator was Jewish, there were only two productions of Pirandello scripts in Paris during the Occupation: *La Volupté de l'honneur*, adapted by C. Mallarmé, at the Théâtre de la Cité in 1941, directed by Charles Dullin. *Vetir ceux qui sont nus* at Dullin's former playhouse, the Atelier, was directed by—and supposedly translated by—André Barsacq (Witt 213), who would direct and design *Antigone*. Bradby attributes what he calls Anouilh's "reduction of characters to masks or roles" to the influence of Pirandello (37).

Yet even as this influence is clear, Giraudoux seems to have contributed heavily to Anouilh's development as a playwright. Early in his career, Anouilh had worked as the secretary for Giraudoux's director and mentor, Louis Jouvet (who, while Anouilh was drafting and discarding *Oreste* and then writing *Antigone*, was touring Latin America with *Apollo* as part of his repertoire). Anouilh not only learned stagecraft from Jouvet, as had Giraudoux, but had worked in their theatrical world and for a short time literally lived within it: Bettina Knapp recalls how when Anouilh married Monelle Valentin (who would play the title role in *Antigone*), "he was so poor . . . that Jouvet lent him the sets for *Siegfried* to furnish his home" (*The French Theatre* . . . 143). In addition to the theatricalism, which marks both writers' work, the two share a thematic device: In many of Giraudoux's plays, a central character chooses between ordinary life and the ideal, a process often personified by characters of the opposite sex. Thus Hans must choose between Berthe and Ondine; The Président chooses Agnès over Thérèse, and Agnès selects the Man from Marsac over Apollo. Anouilh's plays frequently turn on the same motif. For example, in his first play to be produced under the Occupation, *Léocadia* (written before the Defeat), Prince Albert must decide whether he prefers the memory of his late fiancee, the etherial ballerina Léocadia, who drank only champagne and ate only orchids, or her physical double, a charming but mundane seamstress, Amanda. This legacy of Giraudoux is apparent also in *Antigone*.

The same dichotomy between life and the ideal, which pleasantly runs through *Léocadia,* is greatly widened and darkened in *Antigone*. Even as the dualism apparent in Sophocles' tragedy, between the practical sister and the visionary, remains in Anouilh's version, eventually the opposition between the idealistic Antigone and the rest of the world—embodied by the other characters—expands. Early in the play, The Chorus tells us in notably theatrical terms that Antigone is fated to do what she does: "When your name is Antigone, there is only one part you can play; and she will have to play hers through to the end" (3). Yet despite this pronouncement and despite critical complaints that the characters here are little more than predestined masks, the notion of choice remains strong in Anouilh's reenactment, even stronger perhaps than in Sophocles' original, in which Antigone never seems to think twice about what she has chosen to do. The Occupation Antigone, however, is deeply affected by Creon's admission that his honoring one brother and denying burial to the other was arbitrary: "everything that Polyneices did, Eteocles planned to do," he tells her. The corpses "were mashed to a pulp. . . . I had the prettier of the two carcasses brought in and gave it a state funeral; and I left the other to rot. I don't know which was which" (41). At this point, Antigone decides not to die, or rather to compromise by accepting that life to which she has been bidding farewell throughout the play. Yet when Creon goes on to summarize cynically how life is an inevitably compromised affair, Antigone once again rejects it. Hence, at least in this play, a range of characters represents the ordinary world, which Antigone rejects, while the ideal, which Antigone ultimately chooses, remains abstract, even obscure.

I noted in chapter 3 how in *The Apollo of Marsac* there are traces of the then-current day-to-day circumstances and observed that in its own way, the script Giraudoux sent to Jouvet in 1942 was not a "comédie sans tickets." In *Antigone*, the text seems to oscillate between language devoid of modern reference and slangy, seemingly contemporary allusion. After a conversation between Antigone and her nurse, which at first seems to be taking place in a quasi-classical world or at least one without time, the Nurse exits with, "I've made you some coffee and toast and jam" (14). Amid the long argument between protagonist and antagonist, with all its theatrical imagery, the latter tells the former that Polyneices was "[a] little beast with just wit enough to drive a car faster," and that, after Polyneices struck his father for refusing to pay a gambling debt, the young man stood in a corner of Oedipus's study "sneering and lighting a cigarette" (39). And the tobacco-chewing Guard who comes to take Antigone to her death, tells her that the advantage to being a guard, rather than a soldier, is, "You get a house, coal, rations, extras for the wife and kids" (48). Quite noticeably, the sudden jumps into the modern world are not to the Occupation, where there was little if any coffee, gasoline for cars, tobacco, or coal, but to a world in which shortages were easily remedied, a world without commercial restriction, a world (as Robert Brasillach might say) "sans tickets." Consequently, the shifts from a pseudo-ancient time to the present and vice versa are doubly estranging. Even as the audience—the original actual audience as well as the intended audience—had to separate the "classical" from the contemporary, they were also forced to distinguish between their own hard times and a materially better epoch.

The deliberate use of the narrator-chorus, the methodical insertion into the speeches of both chorus and characters of theatrical reference, and the calculated shifting of time through anachronisms within the dialogue, all contribute to the play's ambiguity; that is, they widen the possibility of varied audience response. As I have observed above, ambiguity was not only a question of taste—even the critic-ideologues in the collaborationist press preferred a play that at least appeared subtle—but a matter of necessity. The text of *Antigone* and its production had to pass the censor and at the same time to appeal to diverse critics and audience members. Thus, Antigone's refusal to cooperate, midway through her long argument with Creon, appears vague, perhaps even arbitrary and ridiculous:

Creon: The whole thing is absurd!

Antigone: Yes, it's absurd.

Creon: Then why, Antigone, why? For whose sake? For the sake of them that believe it? To raise them against me?

Antigone: No.

> Creon: For whom then if not for them and not for Polyneices either?
>
> Antigone: For nobody. For myself. (32–33)

This oft-quoted exchange is not entirely Anouilh; indeed, it seems to have been inspired by a passage in Sophocles' *Antigone* (lines 904–920), part of the protagonist's long epode, in which she exclaims that she would not have committed this act for a husband or child but only for a brother because:

> . . . once a brother's lost
> (Mother and father dead and buried too)
> No other brother can be born or grows again. (Roche 195)

Many scholars reject this speech as an interpolation by an actor or by an inferior poet and argue that the lines are spurious, offering as proof Antigone's rather unexpected and illogical rationalization. Genuinely Sophoclean or not, however, the lines are almost always included in the Greek text and in translations (sometimes bracketed) because they have been attributed to the play for so long; "Aristotle," notes M.A. Bayfield in his edition, ". . . was acquainted with the passage in its entirety" (n. on lines 904–920, 116–117). In any case, the notion of Antigone offering an "absurd" explanation for her actions is in fact present in Sophocles' version and thus not a total invention by Anouilh.

At the same time, Creon's and Antigone's "absurd" may—in fact, should— remind us of Jean-Paul Sartre's use of that term. Significantly, in a 1946 lecture in New York, entitled "Forgers of Myths" (and later printed under that title), Sartre describes the new form of drama coming out of France:

> Our plays are violent and brief, centered around one single event; there are few players and the story is compressed within a short space of time. . . . A single set, a few entrances, a few exits, intense arguments among the characters who defend their individual rights with passion—this is what sets our plays at a great distance from the brilliant fantasies of Broadway. (*Sartre on Theatre* 41)

Sartre's first example of such a play, in fact, his paradigmatic instance for his discussion of existentialist theatre, is Anouilh's *Antigone*. The heroine, he tells us,

> may have seemed abstract because she was not portrayed as a young Greek princess, formed by certain influences and some ghastly memories, but rather as a free woman without any features at all

until she chooses them for herself in the moment when she asserts her freedom to die despite the triumphant tyrant. (35)

In other words, Sartre presents Antigone as the prototypical existential protagonist. His description of her as a "free woman" is something to which we must return in the next chapter, but for now, Sartre's discussion of Anouilh's text is important.

Important, perhaps, merely because Sartre (for many reasons) was widely viewed as a postwar voice for the Résistance. Subsequent critics have found it difficult to accept his endorsement of Anouilh's play and have struggled to explain why Sartre said and wrote as he did. Thus, David Bradby, argues that Anouilh's plays are all form without substance: "His characters reduce the Existentialist concepts of choice and responsibility to an appeal to their role. . . . [Anouilh] is here appealing to a traditional structure of experience, but emptying it of its traditional significance." He then adds, "For the experience to be at its most intense, the choice must be a hopeless one, the diametrical opposite of commitment" (35). In other words, for Bradby, Anouilh's *Antigone* is not truly existential because it is not théâtre engagé.

Yet the real problem for many critics with regard to this play lies not so much in the script, nor in its theatrical text, but in its reception in Paris before the Liberation and in how its reception has been remembered. There is some evidence that some spectators did in fact experience the play as a statement of sympathy with the Résistance. Yet with the rise of the resistancialist myth once Paris was freed, the idea that *Antigone* was an anti-Collaborationist play became popular, even generally accepted not just in France but around the world. Sartre, though, never professed this notion; what he in fact said was that "Anouilh stirred up a storm of discussion with *Antigone*, being charged on the one hand with being a Nazi, on the other with being an anarchist" (40).

On the one hand, Sartre is referring to the only review of *Antigone* that appeared in the underground press. Added quotes from Claude Roy's critique in the underground Communist resistance journal, *Les Lettres Françaises* of March 1944, entitled "Their Antigone and Ours" (Witt 60):

> Anouilh's *Antigone* remains ever free due to that supreme liberty: suicide. When Creon asks her why, in the final count, she would die, she answers: "For me." This speech rings lugubriously at a time when, on the whole continent, in the whole world, men and women are dying who could, in response to Creon's question, answer: "For us, for Man! [Pour nous, pour les hommes!]" (Added 257)[15]

Added uses Roy's invective to support his claim that the play was not a work of "resistance theatre." Yet, Sartre has clearly referred to Roy's response.

Moreover, Witt notes the praise of the Occupation press for *Antigone*, that "a few collaborationist writers take the part of Créon's 'order' against Antigone's 'anarchy'..." (as Sartre has already told us). Witt also reveals that the majority of critics in the press during the Occupation "agree with Laubreaux that both antagonists are in a fundamental sense right" (227). If there were charges that Anouilh was a "Nazi" or "anarchist," the prevalent public and collaborationist opinion seems to have been less extreme.

The creation of the myth of Antigone *résistante* was publicly generated only after the Liberation. Witt deftly traces its genesis from the autumn of 1944 (228ff). The press is in part responsible, but so is the anecdotal evidence. For instance, Harold Hobson quotes (and translates) from Béatrix Dussane, of the Comédie-Française, who in *Nôtes de Théâtre* discusses her responses to the Occupation *Antigone*:

> Antigone's refusal became the symbol and the sublimation of the personal refusals of all and every one. Her stubbornness, her "I am not here to understand, I am here to say no," may seem inexplicable to audiences in happier times, but they struck to the heart people watched by the Gestapo, and familiar with every misery. And each time she declared or let it be understood that no argument or force should prevent her from burying her brother, the public exulted in its heart, You shall not prevent us from helping the men hidden in the wood behind the farm.

Dussane goes on to explain how after the Germans left Paris, she brought friends, who had recently returned to the city, to see a performance:

> I was astonished to feel no longer the same tension between stage and audience. . . . Certain parts of the public continued to follow the play with enthusiasm, but others fell away. The explanation is that with the Liberation the tension between constraint and clandestinity suddenly vanished. It was now necessary to sympathize with *Antigone* by an intellectual effort, whereas formerly one had been in a conspiracy with it. (Hobson, *French Theatre of To-day* 45)

Dussane, who sympathized with the Résistance, was a longtime member of the theatre community. That she describes in such terms the audience's response during her first visit fits in very neatly with the reinvention of the theatre to suit resistancialism, and so does the response she describes during her second visit, after Paris had been liberated, which implies that the performances during the Occupation did not receive the diverse response Sartre describes and that the absence of the Nazis made the play less relevant.

Perhaps, unwittingly, Dussane is revealing her own sudden uneasiness with the playwright: As Galster adds, *Antigone* may have reopened on September 27, 1944, but early in October, the Commission responsible for the "épuration" (or the purging) of the theatre demanded the immediate suppression of the piece (278).[16]

Bradby explains the before-and-after phenomenon in a manner that supports his notion that *Antigone* is all traditional form without traditional substance: "In Anouilh's play the structure of self-sacrifice is enacted, but all the informing elements of love, patriotism, devotion, that might give meaning to this sacrifice are carefully rinsed out." He further attributes the play's initial success to its "structure [which] was sufficient and the emptiness went unnoticed for the most part, since each member of the audience read into the play his own concrete difficulties—whether to resist, whether to collaborate" (35). Bradby's distaste for the play itself and/or for the myth of its resistance message causes him to blame, as it were, the audience for seeing in the play what they did. The more serious implication of Bradby's assertion, however, is that the play itself had a rather minor, unintended role in its reception by those sympathetic to the Résistance; we must come back to the question of intent shortly, but for now, the matter of *Antigone*'s reception remains before us.

Witt too feels uncomfortable with the resistancialist view of Anouilh's drama. As I note above, she does an admirable job of discussing the history of its reception. Nonetheless, her conclusion, based on her careful survey on how the playwright's articles in the collaborationist press are "permeated by an ideological subtext informed by aspects of aesthetic fascism" and how his journalism and plays "place him in a context of French fascist ideology of the period," seems somehow to diminish the actual experience of the spectators. "It is surely time," she concludes, "to dispel once and for all the notion that Antigone represents the Résistance and Créon the collaborationist government, or rather that particular response should be seen as a reading of spectators conditioned by highly charged circumstances of reception" (229). But does one then make sense of the responses to this play by seeing them as incidental accidents of a particular historical situation?

Ultimately, the argument about *Antigone* hinges on the issue of authorial intent. The dispute is not really over what the play means but what and how it was intended to mean. Some critics tend to diminish some of the evidence of the play's reception because it does not entirely fit with their theses. Thus Bradby describes *Antigone* as an empty structure that allowed audiences to project their own choices on it, and Witt isolates the play's wartime reception as "conditioned" by certain "circumstances." Both are striving to smash the mythic image of this play as resistance theatre, as is Added, who with Roy's review contradicts and discounts the anecdotal evidence of reception. Yet audience response is far more problematic to analyze.

A play's meaning is not limited to a finite set of ideas. Interpretation is rather a continuum, comprised of what the play has been previously thought to mean and what it may presently be construed to mean. A play's meaning is a history of its different and varied receptions. As for intent, we may only guess at that. As Witt convincingly proves, an examination of Anouilh's contemporary press writings may be helpful. Nevertheless, the most persuasive piece of literary evidence might be that draft for a play that Anouilh had discarded just before writing *Antigone*.

Oreste *as Pre-Text for* Antigone

Oreste begins in a manner we may easily recognize from *Antigone*: The style is obviously presentational, with all the characters on stage. There is no chorus or narrator, but much of what is said by individual characters is also directed to the house. At rise, Egisthe faces the audience and explains that the four are here, within the walls of Argos, "to play the game of Electre and Oreste—the game of Egisthe and Clytemnestre" (55)[17], in which a red ball, thrown among the players, scorches the actor-characters' hands. He eventually reveals how, as death approaches, he has surprisingly once more been able to sleep (68). Oreste tells the house that under this unmoving sun he must commit an evil act because, in spite of Clytemnestre's skeptical objections to the contrary, he has endured much evil (58).

Throughout, Electre bitterly complains—to the audience, to her brother, and to Egisthe—about her loneliness and her squalid life (and as with Euripides' Electra, her abasement is largely her own doing). Argos's king and his stepdaughter frequently resort to animal imagery, Egisthe while referring to Oreste, Electre while referring to Egisthe. Although Egisthe recognizes that his murder and Clytemnestre's are fated, Electre fears that his calm acceptance of destiny will dissuade Oreste from revenge. Egisthe (unlike his wife) readily admits to the murder of Agamemnon, but he also confesses that he could not bring himself to kill Agamemnon's children. Electre, though striving for what is right, remains throughout self-righteous and egocentric in her drive for revenge; her long, shrill, unrelenting harangues (to both her brother and stepfather) say more about her deprivations than any desire for justice. At the very end of the fragment, as Electre continues to cry out and Oreste faces Egisthe, the older killer stoically addresses his own murderer familiarly: "Tu n'as que moi, Oreste, malgré ses cris. Et je crois bien que je n'ai que toi" ["You only have me, Oreste, despite her cries. And I know well that I only have you"] (79). Locked in this game, the characters can continue only as long as none of the action— no matter how inevitable it may be—occurs. Once events start to unfold and things begin to happen, this world will completely fall apart.

There are some striking similarities that may be drawn between the fragment and *Antigone*. In addition to the presentational style shared by both, the juxtaposition of the young girl and the older monarch, for example, is prominent. As Kathleen Kelly notes, the pair "are comparable to the two central characters in . . . *Antigone*" with Egisthe a "realist" like Creon (16) and Electre bent on an act that is inevitable and thus necessary but meaningless. Moreover, Egisthe, like Creon, is a complex villain and seems both cognizant of his crime and ready to pay for it, while the heroine Electre, like the uncooperative Antigone, frequently seems less than sympathetic. The myth in the fragment has been, like the myth in *Antigone*, problematized, with a complicated and ambivalent reworking.

Indeed, for the most part, what little critical evaluation there is of *Oreste* quite logically likens it to *Antigone*.[18] While the general lack of discussion of the fragment may be attributed to *Oreste*'s brevity (a mere twenty-six pages in its original large-type printing), the few critics to examine it have seen in it either, as Edward Marsh (in accord with Kelly) writes, a "trial run for *Antigone*" (106) with Electre anticipating Antigone and Egisthe prefiguring Creon (107) or, as Alba della Fazia suggests, a work in the same category as *Antigone*—a " 'costumed' play" with " 'savage' hero and heroine" (10).[19] Of course, because *Oreste* was written during the same year as *Antigone*, critics are understandably prompted to make such comparisons. Yet there is one dissenting critical voice: Instead of linking Anouilh's fragment to *Antigone*, John Harvey likens *Oreste* not to another play by Anouilh but to Sartre's *No Exit*. The characters, Harvey asserts,

> already cognizant of the outcome and significance of their acts, . . . are doomed to replay their lives forever. As everything has already happened, characters and spectators alike freely accept their roles as inevitable. But by the same token, the characters are so firmly rooted in their present condition that they are unable to break away and relive their pasts. Consequently, the slightest dramatic disclosure is inconceivable: Oreste cannot, in the heat of confrontation, suddenly discover that he will kill (or has killed) Egisthe not out of revenge but out of desire for purity. (94)

In a sense, suggests Harvey, *Oreste* was doomed to remain a draft, never to become a play. Once the action demanded by the myth began, the play would have lost its point; imagine a *No Exit* in which the Hell-bound trio were allowed to undo some of what they had done during their lives. While Sartre's play was built on characters that Sartre himself had created (characters who could remain eternally inactive in Hell), Anouilh took his characters from a myth, which demanded that something in particular happen. Perhaps Anouilh felt that *Oreste*, as a vehicle for dramatic performance, could not move very far.

Nonetheless, Harvey's idea points to an aspect of *Oreste* that no one else has noted. Unlike Anouilh's completed plays from the period, which may be re-created in the present, *Oreste* itself, like the characters it contains, remains stuck in time. The fragment and its implied drama is fixed midway through the Occupation. In this "situation-limite," where the most important actions are not the result of choice, small, seemingly irrelevant acts take on enormous significance. Electre's decision to sleep in the attic and work in the kitchen, though ridiculous, becomes an expression of who she is, even as life itself comes to resemble a game. We may detect, in the apparent futility and arbitrariness of such choices, a glimpse of Antigone's ultimate explanation for her refusal. Yet, unlike Electre's familial opposition, Antigone's "No," as private and personal as it may seem, is clearly articulated to the head of state.

Despite any similarity between the Argos of *Oreste* and the Thebes of *Antigone*, there is a vital difference: Argos is a claustrophobic, private world, devoid of social consequence; Egisthe's murder of Agamemnon and Oreste's revenge seem, despite potential political implications, highly personal, without group resonance; there is little hint of anyone beyond the foursome. The Oreste game features four characters; the Antigone game is far larger, and even demands the mediation of a one-person chorus. In putting aside *Oreste* for *Antigone*, Anouilh chose to apply more widely many of the ideas that remain in the fragment, to contextualize the central drama in a deliberately civic setting, and to emphasize how the heroine's choices alter the workings of the state. Perhaps these changes are simply the inevitable result of choosing the Antigone myth over the Orestes myth, but this choice in itself perhaps offers a hint of the playwright's motivations: Rather than add an intensely personalized drama to the current glut of Atriadaen adaptations, Anouilh opted for a more implicitly political work.

Argos embodies the first two years of the Occupation: the world following the Defeat and the isolation of the Occupied Zone. The world of Argos is a world of shortages, of denials, of hopelessness. To many Parisians, Germany seemed unstoppable; even with the entry of the United States into the War at the end of 1941, the Axis appeared on the verge of victory, with Britain the only European power still engaged in combat. In January 1942, Germany set about planning its "final solution," and in the spring and summer, Jews—now compelled to wear the yellow star—were rounded up, sent to Drancy and from there on to the East. Paris had become a frightening place, one to which many closed their eyes. This attempt to exclude the realm of public events from one's consciousness led to a stronger focus on the private, the personal world of surviving, sustaining, getting through. Of course complete escape was impossible. As Célia Bertin has already told us, the theatre could serve only as partial diversion.

As if to ensure the insularity of Argos, Anouilh denies the text of *Oreste* references to modern life. There are no automobiles, no cigarettes or chewing tobacco, no cosmetics, no coffee or coal. This exclusion of contemporary allusion, common to classical French drama, does not prevent the characters from speaking in the very genuine, conversational language common to Anouilh's plays. Yet even while the characters break the fourth wall, between the stage and the auditorium, they never confuse house time with stage time. For all its direct appeals to the house, *Oreste* remains an island distinctly separated from its audience.

Harvey's comparison of Anouilh's fragment to *No Exit* is particularly apt for another reason: the use of characters in each is similar. Sartre's play contains three souls consigned to an existentialist's hell. Although the drama may momentarily rest on one of them, the very premise of the piece is that they can never escape each other's presence. *No Exit* is clearly not "about" one character. The same goes for *Oreste*: the four participants are stuck in a hermetically sealed, eternal deadlock; their situation can only be rectified by a violent act that they are unwilling to commit and that will terminate all the characters' lives, or to put it another way, will terminate the play itself. Even though the title of the play, or rather of the draft, is *Oreste*, Oreste is never its sole focus. But in Anoulh's *Antigone*, there is a clear protagonist. "Anouilh's model," writes Bradby, "the *Antigone* of Sophocles, is about Creon and the rest of the royal house of Thebes as much as it is about Antigone. Anouilh changes that focus, keeping our gaze firmly fixed on Antigone's moment of self-destruction up to the very end of the play" (35). We are asked to follow Antigone as she progresses through the un-Argive, wide world of Thebes.

The result of such a focus is that *Antigone*, without including overt political references, manages to take on political implications. To keep the audience from identifying too closely with Antigone, the playwright has created devices to distance them; lest they mistake the play for yet another classical revival, Anouilh adds the alienating mechanism of modern, though clearly not immediately contemporary, references. Of course, spectators are free to make of a play what they will. As Witt asserts, in the same houses in which some audience members saw Antigone as the Résistance and Creon as Vichy, there were fascist sympathizers who saw Creon as a necessary force against the anarchist Antigone, and many more who recognized both as being equal forces that were both "in a fundamental sense right." There were also those who viewed Antigone's rejection of Creon's compromised bourgeois world as a celebration of revolutionary fascist values. These last two interpretations seem every bit as conditioned by the circumstances of the Occupation as the one championed by those seeking to praise the French theatre during the War. (In fact, these last two focusing on Creon, which appear to ignore much of Anouilh's attempts to concentrate the audience's attention on the protagonist, in many ways may seem even more incongruous than the resistancialist view.)

In any case, whatever he may have said or written elsewhere, it is difficult not to see Anouilh's desertion of *Oreste* for *Antigone* as a move to write about individual actions in the context of society as it was experienced in the latter part of 1942. If *Antigone* seems today, as it does to a significant number, to lack the messages about the Résistance that were once perceived in it, the play, at least when contrasted with *Oreste*, appears to become more consciously concerned with its times and circumstances. While one may concur with Witt that *Antigone* is "permeated by an ideological subtext informed by aspects of aesthetic fascism" and that the playwright's journalism and plays, "place him in a context of French fascist ideology of the period," one may still feel drawn to the idea—particularly after examining *Oreste*—that *Antigone* (with its apparent curious silence on political issues) was written, at least in part, to allow some reading by some spectators favoring some form of resistance.

Conclusion

To an enormous degree, the interpretation of dramatic literature is intimately linked with contemporary politics. During the resistancialist years, discussions of *Antigone* were influenced by the need to create the image of a resistant France, and these discussions in turn helped support such an image. With the decline of resistancialism, discussions of Occupation drama were guided by a consciousness of "The Vichy Years," and these discussions similarly expanded the notion that much of France had collaborated. The result of such a politicized interpretation of drama both simplifies a complex playscript politically and tends to marginalize as insignificant other kinds of discussion.

It may seem, at least at first glance, that the most evident fascistic aspect of Jean Anouilh's *Antigone* is its depiction, whether intended or not, of sexuality. Witt, to her credit, points out how, during the Occupation, the figure of Antigone was easily connected with Joan of Arc, who became a cultural icon for Vichy (and eventually for the Résistance). And just as Joan, with her male attire and short hair, her skill as strategist and warrior, might be viewed as a mannish woman, there was the tendency to view Antigone too as a masculinized heroine (220). Anouilh represents her as a male-identified protagonist: She defines herself as the daughter of Oedipus, the genuine father-king, and never even mentions her mother by name. Ismene is the more "feminine" of the sisters; Anouilh has Antigone put on Ismene's clothing, makeup, and perfume (almost like drag) when she wants Haemon to reassure her of his love. "Creon's solution to the Antigone problem," notes Witt, "is to reinstate her in the feminine role, to see her happily married to his son" (224). In Anouilh, then, Antigone seems to become spokesman for patriarchal society. It would indeed be easy to equate this patriarchy with Vichy's National Revolution or with the New Order that collaborationist writers, such as Alain Laubreaux and Robert Brasillach, hoped would evolve in France.

Witt picks up on the idea of the protagonist's gender, but her remarks are a means to an end: What she has to say about the heroine's sexuality is overshadowed by the larger political issues framing her thesis. Still, her commentary is unusual: Literary critics who explore the drama of the Occupation for the most part pay little attention to sexual-political issues, feeling instead obliged to offer more definitive pronouncements in conventional political terms.

For example, Serge Added brings to his analysis a wealth of important research. At the same time, readers may detect in his work a significant need to close a longtime debate rather than to reopen an ongoing inquiry. None of his arguments invalidate his research, but his research does not always support his arguments. As we have seen, Added's use of Roy's *Antigone* review, the only one published during the Occupation in the noncollaborationist press, is meaningful but not in itself definitive. In addition to ignoring the reviewer's motivations, Added discounts the reception not by critics but by viewers. Dussane and others give some testimony as to what the audience made of the play, and even if such personal narratives do not accurately describe the entire audience's response, they do at least convey some of what the specific spectators felt in the presence of the play. Of course, it would be as wrong to imagine that such testimony negated comments by critics as it would be to privilege the interpretations of any single critic. In order to appreciate reception, one must try to understand not "spectator response" but the responses of many differing spectators.

I have not attempted here to offer a final verdict on what *Antigone* signifies; I have tried rather to introduce into the ongoing dispute *Oreste*, one more piece of evidence, and to integrate that evidence into a larger discussion. If I have proven anything, it is perhaps only that in the face of conventional political contentions, we may fail to consider what I view as the stronger and more insidious political power of Occupation drama: its ability to argue, to reconstruct, and to confirm subtly but palpably the politics of sexuality. Such concerns are taken up more directly in the following chapter.

6

The Politics of Reception:
Jean-Paul Sartre's *The Flies*

Introduction

Claude Roy's critical comments about Antigone, to which I refer in the previous chapter, illustrate just how deeply cultural (rather than conventionally political) Anouilh's gender constructs are: Antigone's refusal to go along with Creon, asserts Roy, "rings lugubriously at a time when, on the whole continent, in the whole world, men and women are dying who could, in response to Creon's question, answer: 'For us, for Man!' " (Added 257). What I have translated as "Man" here, which might also mean "Mankind," is in the French, "Pour les hommes," literally, "For men." French, like English in this case, carries the notion that the world is populated by "men," and this assertion seems particularly noticeable because Roy has just indicated that "men and women" are sacrificing themselves for the greater good; the greater good and humanity itself are engendered as male. Like the practice in English of assuming that a third person singular unknown is masculine ("Someone left his coat in the hall"), the use of masculine and feminine linguistic elements in French often reflects and enforces cultural forces that shape the construct of sexuality.

If Roy, then, writing for the Communist Résistance, can use the same patriarchal words and phrases, such language is obviously not limited to profascist discourse. The notion of a phallocentric world is inscribed in most of the literature of the time. If Simone Jollivet's *Princess of Ursins* belittles the male-dominated world, it nonetheless depicts it as the ultimate victor against even its most wily opponent; if Jean Cocteau's *The Typewriter* questions the wisdom of the fathers (the town fathers, the actual father Didier, and the fatherly Fred), its only image for the future lies with the odd but ultimately conventionally heterosexual coupling of a zany orphan girl and an ex-con. And no matter what the intended and/or apparent political messages of *Eight Hundred Meters*, *The Apollo of Marsac*, and *Antigone*, their sexual-political agendas only bolster the very conservative and oppressive dominance of male-oriented culture.

As I suggest in chapter 4, the kind of sexual equality that women could not find under Vichy and the Occupation was available, to some degree, in the Résistance. The influence of women working against the Germans and collaborators influenced French politics after the War when women finally won the right to vote. Yet the sexual politics of the Pétain government (and for that matter, of the Résistance) did not come out of nowhere: Its attitude toward women, like its attitude toward homosexuals and children, was in large part a carryover from the Third Republic.

Significantly, Simone de Beauvoir's ground-breaking postwar analysis of male-dominated society is aimed not at the role of women during the War but over centuries. Beauvoir refuses to limit the source of the problem to a specific person or regime; her point in *The Second Sex* is that the oppression of women is so pervasive that one may see it throughout all time and everywhere. Although Beauvoir never throws the spotlight of feminist critique on the works of her close friend, Jean-Paul Sartre, his work too may easily be seen as conveying the same sort of cultural messages as other writers. Indeed, her references in *The Second Sex* to his writings are for the most part to his philosophical study, *Being and Nothingness*, published in 1943. She might have glimpsed a more concrete expression of his ideas about sexuality in his play published and produced in the same year, *Les Mouches* (*The Flies*).

There has been much debate since the play's first production over the meaning of *The Flies*.[1] During the War, Sartre spoke of this play in philosophical terms: "My intention," he told *Comœdia*'s Yvon Novy in April 1943, "was to consider the tragedy of freedom as contrasted with the tragedy of fate" (*Sartre on Theater* 187). Yet, a few months after the Liberation, Sartre indicated that rather than freeing him to write on resistance, the use of myth had been a constraint:

> Why stage declamatory Greeks . . . unless to disguise what one was thinking about under a fascist regime? . . .
> The real drama, the drama I should have liked to write, was that of a terrorist who by ambushing the Germans becomes the instrument for the execution of fifty hostages. (188)

Two decades later, in a tribute to Charles Dullin, who had directed and starred (as the king of the gods, Jupiter) in *The Flies*, Sartre would claim that the play's "political tone was not calculated to please the critics, all of whom were collaborating with the Occupying Power" (189). Many who have written on the drama have argued that Sartre's intended message was realized in and through the production, and that, as Dorothy McCall puts it, "The audience of *The Flies* in 1943 was less interested in the philosophical problems . . . than in its clear political meaning" (15). Others, such as Heidi Stull, tend to overstate the play's significance: "It [*The Flies*] was Sartre's most forceful contribution to the *résistance*, his powerful exhortation to action, any action, no matter how controversial or painful, against an intolerable political situation that threatened the very existence of an entire people" (72). Such writers tend not to mention that Sartre's play (much like Jollivet's) ran at the "aryanized" Théâtre Sarah–Bernhardt to low capacity houses for only a few weeks, opening on June 3, 1943 and closing on the 27th.[2]

In a section of *Le Théâtre dans les années Vichy* entitled "Théâtre Résistant: Mythe ou Réalité?" Serge Added discusses *The Flies*, which, he contends, was obviously intended to criticize collaboration and to support the Résistance. Written during the Occupation, Sartre's retelling of the Orestes myth depicts Argos's cult of guilt and the dead, clearly meant to ridicule Vichy's national campaign of guilt (which was perhaps best epitomized by the regime's own slogan, "la terre et les morts"), and there are numerous indications throughout the script that its author is advocating, through Orestes's murder of the heads of state and his subsequent acceptance of his crime, action against the regime in power and even the occupiers. Yet Added's ultimate conclusion is that, because his research cannot locate contemporary responses that acknowledge such an interpretation, such an interpretation did not take place (253–262). However, with all the circumstances under which *The Flies* was presented, there are good reasons for a lack of discussion of the play's subversive subtext. In direct contrast to Added's view of *Antigone*, which he concludes was, at best, construed as championing resistance in spite of the author's intentions, he suggests that *The Flies*, which was intended to advocate resistance, was never perceived as such during the Occupation.[3]

As I have remarked earlier, theatre reception is not as easily demonstrable as one may wish. As an example, we can return to the play discussed in chapter 1: The press notices and varied personal testimonies on the opening performance of *The Typewriter* give neither a clear nor a consistent account of the uproar that occurred in the auditorium; there is sound evidence that something happened but little to indicate what exactly that was. Furthermore, the absence of written records to support the idea that any of the spectators understood the play's gay subtext should not be taken to indicate that none of the audience received it. At best, surveying audience response is a necessary but highly speculative enterprise.

Moreover, intentionality is of less interest here if only because most of the plays produced during this period do not seem to have deliberately—or rather consciously—included sexual-political agendas. Politics remained conservative, not in the traditional sense, for we know there was increasing dissent as the Occupation wore on, but in the sense that those opposing the Vichy ideologues and the Paris fascists did not usually focus on sexual-political issues.

In terms of intent, Sartre's subtext appears to have been intended (and was probably received) as political. That Sartre was aware of this subtext at the time also appears quite likely. Yet the sexual politics of *The Flies*, which is fully consonant with the sexual-political messages in other plays of the period (no matter what their political affinities), and which seems to have been included without Sartre's complete awareness. Just as Beauvoir remained blind to the message behind *Princess*, she appears not to have noticed just what Sartre's play has to say about sexuality in general and about women in particular. Perhaps her silence on these matters is the result of her loyalty to Sartre, or perhaps the very obvious political message behind *The Flies* obscured its sexual-political issues. For whatever reasons, few have looked at how this drama both ridicules the conservative order and simultaneously upholds its basic sexist structure.

Sartre and Sexuality

In discussing Sartre's views on gender differentiation, Andrew Leak proposes that in *Being and Nothingness* the refutation of Freudian theory of sexual identity results in a reification of Freudian ideas: "The truly obsessive and persistent image of the feminine in Sartre's writing is . . . a supine, naked woman beckoning and threatening in one and the same gesture," Leak deduces and adds that "the threat is one of castration" (14–15). As I note above, Sartre's ideas, particularly as articulated in his 1943 philosophical book, had an enormous influence on Beauvoir's feminist examination of Western culture: The refusal to rely on Freudian theory enables her to move away from the assumption that psychology was a study that could not be questioned.

Yet, the contradiction that Leak locates in Sartre's discussion is pervasive throughout Sartre's work. His deliberately nonconformist life and his position toward the end of the War as a leading intellectual combined in peculiar ways. Just as his romance with Jollivet may have made him aware of just how wrong he was to want to possess another (as John Gerassi reveals; see chapter 4), his relationship with Beauvoir taught him numerous lessons as well. The publication of the correspondence between the father and mother of existentialism has disclosed that even as their physical affair with each other waned, their sexual involvements with others became part of their relationship. Each led separate sexual lives but seems to have shared those lives with the other. For example, many of the ostensibly innocent friendships with women that Beauvoir mentions in *The Prime of Life*, her memoir of the 1930s and 1940s, were in fact intimate. Beauvoir's letters to Sartre reflect this intimacy in detail. And although Sartre's ideas on gender and sexuality would expand over the postwar years, they remained, essentially and fundamentally, rather conventional (as well as patriarchal and sexist) despite their supposed unconventionality.

One of Sartre's frankest discussions about sex came toward the end of his life in an interview with Catherine Chaine. In addition to his numerous admissions here of being something of a male chauvinist, Sartre confessed to a preoccupation with females: "They have always been at the center of my thoughts," he revealed. "Even when I think of subjects not directly related to women, I am still thinking of women" (103). And in his explanation of women as equals, his imagery reveals just how exotic women are; he tells Chaine, "it was a question of overcoming a woman in almost the same way that one overcame a wild animal, but by wiles, smiles and ingenuity: to force her out of the wild state into one of equality with man" (104). Sometime later in the interview, in describing his relationship with Beauvoir, Sartre asserts that in her "I had found a woman who was the equal of what I was as a man—and it was that, I believe, that rescued me from out-and-out male chauvinism" (118). While this last statement sounds progressive, the earlier description of the female, the savage creature who must be forced out for "equality," suggests just how contradictory Sartre's notions are.

Sartre also described to Chaine his childhood, in which doting females surrounded him, in order to explain his sexuality.[4] Hence, although women other than Beauvoir remained secondary in his life, he preferred (or perhaps required) that he be the primary love in their lives (118). That he is strictly heterosexual is emphatically stated by his remark that as a boy "[t]enderness and love, as I saw them, meant two people clasping each other and kissing." He continues, "That's what it was and I couldn't enjoy it with boys because they were too coarse. Relations with boys meant a friendly exchange of fists and nothing else. No tenderness" (104). Thus, Sartre at least appears to have chosen to fill his life with women because early on he saw the world divided into male toughs and female sweeties; as a tough himself, albeit one in need of tenderness, he sought to hunt the heart, to capture his prey so that he might deliver it into freedom. Yet one of Sartre's later remarks suggests otherwise. "Often I love it," he confides to Chaine, "when a woman feels that, at least for a while, she owes *everything* to her relationship with me." Even as Sartre adds, "I realize it's *machismo*," his notion of sexuality has begun to sound familiar (239).

Did Sartre believe that one chooses one's gender, one's sexuality? When Beauvoir's biographer, Deirdre Bair, introduces *The Second Sex* by quoting Beauvoir's, "One is not born, but rather becomes a woman" (vii), we may begin to understand that a major idea that Sartre and Beauvoir shared was that life was a series of choices. Perhaps given what one has and what one can do, one makes certain choices that contribute to the creation of identity. Such a notion is of course intimately linked with the existentialism both espoused.

However, when Sartre articulated the belief, in his massive writing on and rewriting of the life of Jean Genet, *Saint Genet: Actor and Martyr*, that Genet had chosen to be homosexual, the implication was indeed that one's sexuality was a matter of choice. In his very last interview in February 1980, Sartre spoke with two gay writers from the newspaper *Le Gai Pied* about homosexuality and clarified some of his earlier assertions. After reiterating how "Genet was the very model of the man who creates himself in a situation," in other words, the very paradigm of existential man, Sartre concedes, "Naturally, Genet is a particular case. One can't say those things about just any homosexual . . ." (35). Still, Sartre shortly after does say a few things about "just any homosexual": "the homosexual is a potential traitor," "the homosexual tries to be a deep reality, very deep," and "[i]n the homosexual, there is a dark aspect that defines him, that reveals itself to him but not necessarily to others" (36). Moreover, that homosexuality might be chosen by someone, even if he (or she) is clearly not just any homosexual, continues to suggest that sexuality (in certain "situations") is a matter of preference and self-selection.

Women and homosexuals may appear romantic, if not totally sympathetic, figures to Sartre. In a way, they, as other groups of individuals who are distinct from the culture at large, have been oppressed and yet managed to survive, sometimes even flourish. In this light, in an interview with Madeleine Gobeil, published in the mid-1960s, Sartre praises the point of view of women— "from a woman you get the sensibility of a different being, an intelligence perhaps superior to a man's, and not hampered by the same preoccupations"— and says that it is formed at least in part by "the female predicament." He then compares women to another "different" group, the Jews:

> Similarly, what I particularly appreciate in my Jewish friends is a gentleness and subtlety that is certainly an outcome of anti-Semitism. . . . I like the Jews as they have been made by persecution. . . . A Jew, of course, might retort: "That's racial prejudice. It's up to you to like us as men, or as a religious community, but you shouldn't indulge in satisfactions of your sensibility or intellect just because we have managed to win through after starting with an intolerable handicap imposed on us by others."

As he shows throughout his interviews, Sartre is wonderfully gifted as a ventriloquist: He is able to speak in the voice of the Other and thus dismiss the other's response when it does not agree with his own. Jews are interesting not so much as "men" but as the recipients of "men's" abuse. Similarly, Genet is more interesting because he is a homosexual, which means that he, given his "situation," has chosen to embrace this ostracized sexual role. And, Sartre adds, a woman, who must cope with her allotted role, is interesting because she does not act as the empowered but as "a slave and an accomplice." Consequently, even as Sartre declares "I'm in favor of total female emancipation," he must emphasize that "when the day comes [of female emancipation], the special qualities of sensibility, for which I prefer the company of women, will be due purely to chance" (76).

Genet himself eventually drew away from Sartre's influence. The publication of *Saint Genet* in 1952 forced him to explore his own psyche. By 1964, Genet told the same interviewer to whom Sartre had made the above remarks about the Jews that he had always been aware of his attraction to boys: "It's only after I became conscious of this attraction that I 'decided,' 'chose' freely my pederasty,[5] in the Sartrian sense of the word. In other words, and more simply, I had to accommodate myself to it even though I knew that it was condemned by society" (qtd. by White 383). In his own view of himself, then, Genet ultimately disagreed with Sartre's paradigmatic tale based on Genet's life.

What then is Sartre actually referring to when he heroicizes Genet's choice? Is he merely appropriating his friend's unique circumstances and elevating them to existential situations and acts? Genet's reply offers an indication: he had had to "accommodate" himself to being homosexual, which was "condemned by society." Yet beyond that, as White admirably demonstrates, Genet did so in a way substantially different from other gay writers before him, who:

> almost always resort to an aetiology of homosexuality which functions as a plea for understanding, [while] Genet presents his characters in his novels without apology or psychoanalytic history. Whereas much homosexual fiction of the period shows the protagonist's slowly dawning awareness that his love is accursed, Genet's gay characters . . . never doubt for a moment the nature of their desires. (387)

Of course, it was no coincidence that such fiction should emerge from Genet, for his writing was obviously informed by his life. What Genet had chosen was not only to write as a homosexual but to live openly as one. In a world in which some gay writers, including André Gide and Marcel Jouhandeau, acknowledged their homosexuality but remained married, and others, such as Cocteau, playfully denied what most knew to be true, and others still, such as Henry de Montherlant, maintained a strict silence about their personal affairs, Genet was unique. Not only was he openly gay, but unlike Roger Peyrefitte (see chapter 7), Genet was unashamedly proletarian, a self-proclaimed member of the demi-monde, and sexually passive.

Genet's choice was to live as a homosexual in a world that condemned homosexuals. Genet had not chosen his sexuality but had deliberately chosen to link the way he lived with the way he loved. And even while Sartre was on some level aware of Genet's actual choice, it appeared to Sartre, whose scrutiny of French culture came through thick existentialist lenses, that Genet's courage lay not just in his refusal to conform to cultural conventions but in his determination to live outside of what the culture sanctioned, to create himself as an entirely new culture-free being through his acts. Yet Genet's work, rather than establishing an anti-culture or even a counter-culture, clearly looks back on conventional culture, exploring, ridiculing, critiquing it. Thus, as White contends (and as Kate Millet demonstrates), Genet separates an individual's physiological sex from his or her sexuality and gender, thus exposing the arbitrariness of such cultural constructs as masculinity and femininity (529).

Yet Sartre's blindness to Genet's real achievement was not due only to his need to view the poet-thief-homosexual as a primary example of existential philosophy; Genet also called into question many of the ideas on which Sartre seemed conflictedly fixed. Women and men were not necessarily one way or another, but Sartre enjoyed the company of women because they were in need—of love, of money, of emancipation. Men (except for Genet and a very few others) were dull for Sartre because they had nothing new to teach him—he was, after all, already a man. And Sartre's comparison of women to the Jews quite clearly implies that in some ways Sartre preferred the oppressed who had been formed by the experience of oppression to the genuinely liberated, or at least equalized, individual. For all his serious differences with French culture, Sartre remained in many ways a culturally conventional Frenchman. He had been raised by women and gone on to become something of a womanizer. Even while maintaining a central relationship with one woman, he had affairs with many others. He liked to have women focused on him and dependent on him, even as he maintained his own independence. Such a life is not in itself highly unusual in France. In short, Sartre's innovation was not that he chose to live such a life but that he chose to admit publicly to living it.

Sartre: Occupation Playwright

Sartre's career as a dramatist began during the Occupation. In fact, his first play was written and performed while he was a prisoner of war in Stalag XII D at Trier, in December 1940. This drama about the first Christmas carefully but noticeably leads its literally captive audience to the conviction that one must resist. Patrick Marsh identifies Sartre's *Bariona, ou le fils de tonnerre* (*Bariona, or the Son of Thunder*) as one of the Occupations's two examples of genuine anti-German, resistance drama (the other being Vermorel's *Jeanne avec nous*; "Le Théâtre . . ." 249).

In Sartre's initial effort as a playwright there is a clear intent to disguise by making the script resemble what seemed, at least to German prison camp authorities, a Christmas pageant devoid of subversive meaning and also, in spite of the play's benign appearance, a desire to communicate with the audience about their immediate circumstances: "This drama, biblical in appearance only, . . . was aimed exclusively at prisoners," described Sartre in 1946 (*Sartre on Theater* 39), and in a 1968 interview he asserted, "The script was full of allusions to the circumstances of the moment. . . . The envoy from Rome to Jerusalem [a character in the play] was in our minds the German. Our [German] guards saw him as the Englishman in the colonies" (185). Certainly, a reading of the play reveals many allusions and concerns to contemporary wartime events.

The script included, with good reason, only one female character, who comments to the men on stage and sometimes asks questions. Perhaps Sartre wanted to avoid the potential comedy that might come from the role of Sarah being performed by a male in drag, or perhaps he felt she played a necessary though minimal role in the action. For whatever reasons, the political message in *Bariona* seemed to overshadow not only issues of religion and history but of sexuality.

Although Sartre believed this drama had fulfilled its mission, his opinion of it was not very high. "Why did I not take up *Bariona* again later?" he mused in 1968. "Because the play was bad. It sacrificed too much to long expository speeches" (185). Indeed, it is the preachiest of Sartre's plays but in many ways the most endearing, for it has an almost austere innocence and a charm that, in the explicitness of its message, feels somewhat medieval. Still, quite unlike *The Flies*, *Bariona* has never transcended the immediate context in which it was presented. This pageant remains a relic of its time rather than a dramatic script that through revival has come to mean more and differently. *The Flies*, on the other hand, like Anouilh's *Antigone* and a few other plays of the Occupation, has remained a renewable text. Revivals have been brought to the stage, and students and critics of literature continue to discuss the work. The playtext, again like *Antigone*, may carry a substantial legacy from the Occupation, but readers and spectators continue to find present, rather than just historical, significance in it.[6]

Along with *Antigone* and a number of other plays from this period, the use of the classical past in *The Flies* has been much discussed. As mentioned in the previous chapter, there were several scripts based not just on Greek myth but specifically on the myth of the vengeance of Agamemnon's children. Sartre's version, like the one Anouilh never finished, deviates considerably from its Attic prototypes. Indeed, just by naming his work *The Flies* (rather than "Electra" or "Orestes" as others had done), Sartre seemed to be signaling to his audiences that this work was no mere resuscitation of Hellenic grandeur; in spite of some clear connections between *The Flies* and its tragic forbears, Sartre's Oresteia is in the end derailed by its author's enactment of his own philosophy. The power of the gods is negated in the script, and all is reduced to a drama about human acts within a set of peculiar circumstances, human choices in the context of what Sartre calls a "situation." The characters of the gods, in whom the Greeks genuinely believed, affect only those who believe in them, and the personifications who represent them—Jupiter, the Furies—articulate dramatically how their power derives from and serves to support those in political power on Earth. The rather cynical remarks of the King of the gods and the stinging nastiness of "the kindly ones" are clearly human, spoken in the same twentieth-century conversational French of the other, mortal characters. By the final curtain, Orestes has seemingly broken from the cultural conventions that previously might have identified (and thereby limited) him and thus has created himself.

Rather than with Pylades, Orestes arrives in Argos with his aging Tutor. A mysterious stranger, who is a disguised Jupiter, has been tailing them: He tries to dissuade Orestes from remaining in the city, and the dismal condition of the place seems to make Orestes eager to go. The town is like a rotting corpse, plagued by the flies that give their name to the play. Yet when Electra enters for what is traditionally the "recognition scene," Orestes has begun to accept that Argos is part of what must define him. As a wandering exile without family and friends, the dismal city is crucial to his identity. In the Greek versions, Electra eventually recognizes Orestes, but in *The Flies* recognition comes only later in the play; in the Greek versions, Clytemnestra meets Orestes only when she is about to die, and yet here, the queen enters while Electra questions him, and mother and daughter vie for his attentions.

The next act starts with what is perhaps Sartre's most interesting innovation: The local belief, established by Aegisthus when he assumed power by murdering Agamemnon, is that on one day each year the spirits of the dead emerge from their graves to reproach the living. This ceremony of guilt becomes a sometimes hilarious parody of the sort of reactionary breast-beating institutionalized by Pétain and Vichy. Throughout the play, Electra has criticized her mother and stepfather, and here too she launches into a tirade against them that ends in an extravagantly savage dance. Afterward, Orestes approaches her and reveals who he is. Although Electra tries to discourage him, he takes on vengeance as an act that will make him into the Orestes whom he believes he must become.

The murder scene that follows focuses not so much on Clytemnestra, the perpetrators' mother, as on Aegisthus, the political chief of Argos, who is killed on stage. Electra waits as Orestes climbs the stair to their mother, whose screams we hear. When he returns, Orestes proclaims that they are free. He suddenly seems different to his sister: he has now in fact become, through his acts, Orestes. Electra, however, is suddenly burdened by guilt, which will soon be personified by the Furies. In the following scene, as they seek refuge in Apollo's sanctuary, the Furies threaten both, but only Electra succumbs to their power. Jupiter enters and bargains with her, promising to assuage her punishment if she will acknowledge that she is merely another victim of Orestes's crime. Ultimately Electra accepts the power of the gods, but Orestes ends the play by addressing his new Argive subjects. Fearlessly, Orestes takes on their guilt, freeing them (as he has freed himself) from the terror of religion, and then exits like the Pied Piper, taking the flies with him.

Sartre uses the ancient myth to create a situation in which Orestes must choose what to do; in existential terms, Orestes's choices in this situation constitute who he is—his deeds, as the Greeks would say, not his words, have determined his identity. In so doing, however, Sartre does away with the religious and legal legacy of earlier versions: Orestes will not rush to Athens where Athena will absolve him of his crime. Instead, he seems supremely isolated—alienated and fated to wander alone, free and yet always an outsider, in short, a resistor.

Thus both the use of myth in *The Flies* and Sartre's own philosophical convictions lead back to the play's politics. Inevitably, as again with *Antigone*, the historical question of (conscious) conventional political intentions and audience reception of them may easily consume any discussion of *The Flies*. Yet an investigation of the sexism carried in the script has already been opened: As I indicate below, an astute critique of Sartre's patriarchal themes already exists. My goal here is to build on what has come before, perhaps to add to it, and to move the ongoing project toward some discussion of how the politics of sexuality in *The Flies* influences the sexuality of political discourse.

In her dissertation, "Postpaternalism and the Fear of the Feminine: The Economic and the Erotic in Strindberg, Brecht, Giraudoux, and Sartre," Hedwig Fraunhofer presents an extensive and a convincing exploration of how on an immediate level *The Flies* seems to depict the alliance of Electra and Orestes as a "society of siblings [that] opposes paternalistic authority of the gods and the king" (324), that is, the authority of Jupiter and Aegisthus. Yet, as Fraunhofer observes, by the end of the play Electra has gone over to the other side by falling prey to the threats of the gods—of Jupiter and the Furies; thus, through his murders of his mother and stepfather, Orestes "revenges the death of his and Electre's father, Agamemnon, and appears to be reestablishing paternal and royal authority, as well as metaphysical order" (335). In other words, "[t]he society of sons and fathers" has not been replaced by a society of (male and female) siblings but "by a society of (male) equals," a society of brothers (344).

Moreover, Fraunhofer emphasizes, as with Sartre's attempts to refute Freud in *Being and Nothingness*, this dramatic "critique of paternalistic authority" remains "a profoundly patriarchal play" (346) through what Fraunhofer calls "the negativization of the feminine, and the feminization of the negative" (347). Not only does Electra succumb to the gods of the patriarchy, but her entire being is predicated on the arrival of her male sibling. While Orestes finds freedom in embracing his criminal acts, thus becoming what he has done, Electra flees her own liberation and fades into the paternalistic culture in which women become representative of all that is bad.[7]

Electra, unlike her brother, is unable to reason. Fraunhofer asserts that Electra and all the other women of Argos, Clytemnestra included, are consistently compared to animals, wild creatures of feeling, governed largely by their instincts and lusts (355–368).[8] Fraunhofer's ultimate point is that in *The Flies* Orestes "assimilates Electre's, the Other's, freedom" and that "[h]is project of recovering himself is, ultimately, a project of absorbing the Other" (380). Indeed, Sartre, in his later interview tends to state this explicitly: "it was a question of overcoming a woman in almost the same way that one overcame a wild animal, but by wiles, smiles and ingenuity: to force her out of the wild state into one of equality with man" (Chaine 104). The implication is that one must seduce the female into her own equality: Sartre advocates a kind of horizontal liberation in which women, even when equal, remain, if not on the bottom, nonetheless bottoms. Not only are there no women who accept their freedom in *The Flies*, but there seem to be no individuated female characters; the second sex is generalized as second rate, conforming to a consistent set of characteristics. For whatever reasons Sartre compares women to the Jews in his interview with Gobeil (76), his attribution of certain traits to Jews, no matter how positive his intent, is racist and in some ways not very different from French anti-Semitism. Likewise, his attribution of specific traits to homosexuals in his last interview—"the homosexual is a potential traitor," "the homosexual tries to be a deep reality, very deep," and "[i]n the homosexual, there is a dark aspect that defines him, that reveals itself to him but not necessarily to others" (Le Bitoux and Barbadette 36)—supports the notion that in many ways Sartre's opinions are not entirely his own: quite often his presumptions have been fashioned by the surrounding culture against which he rebelled but within which he prospered.

Beauvoir's place in Sartre's world was apparently not of the woman who can prove the possibility of liberation but of the exception, the exceptional woman who demonstrates how most women seem incapable of rising to equality.[9] There is so minimal a use of women in *Bariona* that issues of sexuality hardly arise, but more significantly, none of the female characters—of which there are many—in *The Flies* can join Orestes's revolution. If we examine Sartre's first theatrical effort, we may easily accept, given its peculiar circumstances of composition and production, the singularly political nature of the prison-camp pageant; however, the conflict between politics and sexuality in Sartre's recasting of the Orestes myth remains difficult to ignore. In fact, the heroine of Giraudoux's *Electre* and even the Electre of Anouilh's unfinished *Oreste* seem stronger and far more liberated than the Electra in *The Flies*, who, as Fraunhofer observes, virtually becomes Clytemnestra (346ff). Only in Sartre's third play of the Occupation, *Huis Clos* (*No Exit*), does there emerge a female figure—one rumored to be based on Beauvoir herself—who appears to break free of or at least expand upon Sartre's concept of what women are.

Yet in *The Flies*, for all its implications with regard to self-liberation through acts of resistance, the paradigm is engendered as masculine. Sartre's choice here is especially significant in that, having read the classical plays based on this myth and more recent ones, he knew that he might have made the act of murder a joint effort and that the society of brothers, which Orestes calls into being at the end of the play, might very easily have become a society of brothers and sisters. Politics here, however, seems to be an exclusively male enterprise.

Thus we arrive at a peculiar impasse with regard to the way politics was thematized in sexual terms on the Occupation stage. In a way, it hardly mattered how the playwright chose to create a female protagonist: as a woman taking on a common enemy (such as Jeanne d'Arc), a woman taking on phallocentric culture (such as Antigone and the Princess of Ursins), or a woman trying to have power over her own destiny through exploiting her cultural role among men (such as Giraudoux's Agnès and Cocteau's Solange); the established cultural framework within which reception took place, as well as the conservative political control over censorship and virtually all media, tended to influence heavily the possibilities of interpretation.

Hence Jeanne and Antigone emerge as victorious over their own femininity—they are not quite male but just as good as (though, as with Sartre's elevation of Beauvoir, they are the exceptions that maintain the rule). The Princess of Ursins is nothing more than a manipulative madwoman, and one must admire Agnès for her ability to remain a Frenchwoman, just as one must pity Solange, whose impotence before the cruel town is made tragic in a romanticized way. No matter what heroines or female protagonists dramatists presented on stage, the culture was fully prepared to absorb them, even as the voices of authority championed or panned what appeared on stage. Indeed—and this appears to be one of Added's key points—given how the theatre was subsidized by Vichy and other right-wing entities, given its dependence on publicity in profascist publications, and given its need to please audiences sympathetic to Vichy and the occupiers, how can one imagine it to be anything more than part of the fascist culture at large?

My answer here, as earlier, derives from the very nature of theatre and audience. No matter how one tries, one cannot control the interpretation of stage texts any more than one can delimit responses to literary texts. The performance of the most didactic drama, such as Sartre's own *Bariona*, allowed for diverse reception, as Sartre himself describes. (Even the morality allegory *Everyman*, which appears to be so explicit that interpretation is not even required, holds sufficient ambiguity that it may be re-created again and again to varied reception.) There can be little doubt that in particular audiences of particular plays there sat particular spectators who were not only willing to read into a script their own subversive ideas but who accurately recognized the playwright's intent for them to do so. I believe this occurred with *Antigone* and *The Flies*. Moreover, those instances when spectators mistook the intent of the playwright—as with a specific line in Henry de Montherlant's *La Reine Morte* (*Queen After Death*; see chapter 7)—do not invalidate the possibility that genuinely (and sometimes consciously) intended significance was also construed.

Nonetheless, through many of the playscripts of the period the issue of sexuality flows at times almost unnoticeably. The politicization of interpretation of Occupation dramatic texts, not only of Sartre's 1943 play but indeed of all works, has traditionally excluded and minimized discussion of the culture's role in the formation and regulation of gender and identity on stage, and has thereby made invisible some of the more blatant political oppression advocated by the wartime stage. *The Flies* may advocate personal responsibility and resistance, but one is left asking, responsibility and resistance by whom?

Conclusion

In his next play, Sartre seems to counterpoise the seductive siren created by male-dominated culture with the woman who openly defies men and who does not define herself in what appear to be culturally acceptable terms. *No Exit*, which opened toward the end of the Occupation, a week or so before the Normandy invasion, depicts three people detained in Hell, which appears, quite unfrighteningly, to resemble a drab hotel sitting room furnished in the style of the Second Empire. Into this setting come Garcin, a selfish coward, Estelle, an ignorant but glamorous society girl who has killed her own illegitimate baby, and Inez, a lesbian postal clerk who has destroyed her cousin and his wife. The premise here in existential terms is that all three must spend eternity aware that they can never undo the acts they have previously committed.

Yet although the play would like to carry the notion that all three have been condemned to each other, the supreme torture is reserved for Garcin, stuck between the beautiful but vapid child-murderess and the resolutely hateful lesbian: While many see *No Exit* as exemplifying the play's famous line, "Hell is—other people," this existentialist inferno is perhaps better described as a case of "unlucky Pierre," where a man must endure the worst of all fates, trapped between two women. "Garcin," observes Leak, "is destined to pass eternity oscillating . . . between a 'conscience haineuse' (Inès), and a 'femme immobile' who threatens constant engulfment. In other words, . . . [he is caught] between two diametrically opposed images of the feminine" (31).

Unlike *The Flies*, *No Exit* was a hit—perhaps what we today would call a "fringe" hit but nonetheless a clear success—both before and after the Liberation. Its brevity (the play ran one hour, twenty minutes) and its use of space and time made it perhaps the one play of the Occupation that pointed to the stage works that would appear after the War, to what is now called the Theatre of the Absurd. Yet, as with *The Flies*, whose postwar renown was based on the play's identification (by Paul-Louis Mignon and others) as "théâtre résistant," Sartre's intense and often talky one-act inferno, even while it tries to deconstruct some of the fundamental values that support the culture at large, reinscribes and valorizes many of that same culture's sexual constructs, thus contradicting itself.

However, *No Exit* is no more contradictory than *The Flies*. Both come from a time when the world was polarized, when collaboration and resistance at least appeared to be rather straightforward choices. Of course, the two terms in reality never exactly constituted some simple antithetical pair; Sartre's own experience under the Occupation makes that much clear. Yet the illusion that life might be seen as a series of binary oppositions, which for the sake of artistic depiction runs through much Western literature, demands a consistent representation: good and bad, black and white, collaboration and resistance, man and woman. In Sartre's reconstructions of the world, in spite of all their promise of liberation, Self and Other only make sense if one is oneself male.

7

A Politics of Sexuality:
Henry de Montherlant's *Nobody's Son*

Introduction

If, as suggested in chapter 4, Simone Jollivet's representation of a repressively misogynistic culture in *The Princess of Ursins* was largely, if not entirely, unintended, the same may be said for Jean Cocteau's gay revisioning of heterosexual society in his pseudo-Boulevard potboiler, examined in chapter 1: In both cases, the playwrights simply painted the world as they saw it. Cocteau's sensibilities had shaped the point of view discernible in *The Typewriter*, just as Jollivet's cultural background and personal experiences had taught her the lessons of misogyny, which, without thinking, she inscribed into the text of her historical melodrama. Neither had set out expressly, he to write a gay suspense play, she to write a feminist tragedy. And with regard to *Princess*, no one at the time seems to have noticed its sexual-political implications, while the battle waged over *The Typewriter* appeared to most— including Cocteau himself—to have centered on neither the dramatic nor the theatrical text but on the playwright. Yet the whole notion of intentionality as a solely conscious act seems in retrospect rather narrow: As we have seen, writers write from a variety of intentions and are aware of only some of them.

However, with regard to an intentional sexual-political message, the Occupation plays of Henry Millon de Montherlant are significantly different in intent from Jollivet's and Cocteau's. In both *La Reine morte* (*Queen After Death*, written and produced in 1942) and *Fils de personne* (*Nobody's Son*, written 1942–1943 and produced in 1943) there is a deliberate subtext—even, arguably, a deliberately *subversive* subtext. Although one may (as I argue in the previous chapter) see the same in Jean-Paul Sartre's first publicly staged play, the intended political subtext in *The Flies* is political in conventional, contemporary terms—the politics of Vichy, of collaboration and resistance—and thus, at least in theory, would have been relatively accessible to audiences. At the same time, Sartre's sexual-political message seems clear enough to be intended though not necessarily consciously. Montherlant's plays, however, contain a subtext directly concerned with sexual politics. A carefully encoded commentary describing Montherlant's views on sexuality in general and declaring his own sexuality in particular is included in both his stage works of the period, and this commentary is articulated in unconventional, highly personal terms.

Nonetheless, access for audience members to this commentary was restricted. Only those "in" on Montherlant's message were meant to receive it, and those "in" people were to have included those few who shared the playwright's private view of the world—that is, those who both knew and partook of his sexuality. In his posthumously published letters (written before and during the Occupation) to Roger Peyrefitte, Montherlant, ostensibly to deceive those reading the mails, refers to these "in" people as members of a "Chivalric Order." As he implies in the essay, "Les Chevaleries," written in July 1940 and included as the opening piece in the 1941 collection *Le Solstice de Juin*, this is the Chivalric Order of adult men who, like Montherlant (and Peyrefitte and other men of their acquaintance) were pedophiles.

Although in more formal discourse the practice of identifying pederasty with homosexuality in France is on the wane, the confusion survives in spoken French: For example, in the French translation of *Angels in America: Part 1*, which opened at the Avignon Festival in July 1994, American slang pejoratives such as "fag" and "queer" were rendered as "pédé," the French pejorative derived from "pédéraste" and which is generally extended to all male homosexual practices between men. The implication is that all homosexuals are child molesters. As recently as 1989, Dominique Fernandez, perpetuated this belief in his survey of "culture homosexuelle," entitled *Le Rapt de Ganymède*; indeed, the very name of the work identifies homosexuality with pedophilia. As we will see, Montherlant sought to negate such an identification, not because he felt that homosexuals did not deserve to be thought of as pedophiles but because he found it vital to believe that pedophiles should not be thought of as "fags" and "queers."

Montherlant had for years practiced sexual acts—for the most part fondling and sodomy—with prepubescent boys, but his activities were conducted very discreetly until his acquaintance with then diplomat, later writer, Peyrefitte. Their relationship, which, as their extensive correspondence records, emphasized their many and varied encounters with boys, seems to have encouraged the previously circumspect and once remorseful Montherlant to express his sexuality not only in the coded format of their letters (where, for example, boys receive female pseudonyms and pedophilic acts are described in language customarily used for heterosexual intercourse) but also in his most public of works, his stage dramas, which in many ways utilize encoding strategies different from those deployed in the correspondence.

The critical hostility that *Princess* and *The Typewriter* drew merely because of the playwrights' identities (the former because Jollivet was a woman, the latter because Cocteau was a homosexual) offers a glimpse of how Montherlant and his works would have been received had his secret life been publicly acknowledged, either by himself or by others. Perhaps the first revealing piece that he wrote about his own sexuality was the 1940 essay on the "Chivalric Order," although earlier in his career he had dropped hints in his articles and novels regarding his preferences. Certainly, his macho public persona as harsh misogynist, athletics enthusiast,[1] lover of war, and avid bull fighting fan—roles that he had refined through his writings—had been carefully crafted to disguise those few hints of pederasty, which before, during, and after the Occupation was publicly perceived as less than masculine. There is, nonetheless, some evidence (his supposedly successful efforts to have sex with women and his struggle to form relationships with them) that long before the Occupation he had felt genuine ambivalence and remorse about his sexual interest in boys.

Nevertheless, by the time he met Peyrefitte, Montherlant seems to have accepted his own sexuality; with Peyrefitte as his confederate, he appears to have come to embrace it. Their correspondence solidified through writing Montherlant's growing identification of himself as pedophile: While his letters to Peyrefitte became opportunities for him to record the details of his sexuality, he found himself creating other pieces—essays and stories, some meant for Peyrefitte alone, some for the public—which in some way asserted more emphatically than before the precise nature of his sexual life. Indeed, as the friendship between the two men developed, Montherlant injected into his theatre projects statements about pedophilia that were his most direct but which remained deceptively indirect—indirect, yet, to those who were then or are now able to read them, statements that seem curiously, even outrageously obvious.

The outrageousness of these statements begins to emerge when the avoidance and denial of spectators (professional critics and ordinary theatregoers alike) becomes evident. To a certain degree, the Vichy regime, with an Education Ministry headed after 1942 by homosexual (and thus "pédé") Abel Bonnard, and its need to enlist influential artists, no matter what their private backgrounds, may be blamed. In spite of much public posturing to the contrary, enabling adult males to have sex with children, whether through active promotion or through silent compliance, ranks as one of the National Revolution's more revolting achievements. The Nazis too were happy to protect M. de Montherlant; the celebrated author was a perfect candidate to advance Himmler's plan to allow French culture to destroy itself from within. Nevertheless, more than any particular political regime, French culture itself as it existed before and during the Occupation and for a long time afterward was responsible for the supposed imperceptibility of Montherlant's allusions to pedophilia. Yet, that his revelations of his secret self should appear on the Occupation stage is no accident: It, indeed, was the most natural time for his message to emerge.

Henry de Who?

There is a certain justice that a writer who, during his own lifetime, delighted that his works provoked such angry response should today be so little known. Although in France Montherlant's novels sell a few copies and his plays are occasionally performed, he is no longer regarded as the great author many once held him to be. Students rarely study him, literary critics seldom argue about him, and the general public—who, while Montherlant was still alive, believed that in the year 2000 he of all their contemporaries would be the most widely read and appreciated—have pretty much forgotten him.

Information about the writer's hidden sexual life began to surface after his suicide in 1972. First came Peyrefitte's revealing memoir, *Propos secrets* in 1977, then in 1983 Montherlant's intimate correspondence with Peyrefitte, and finally in 1990 Pierre Sipriot's second volume of his extensive and detailed biography, *Montherlant sans masque*. This ongoing disclosure was not exactly unexpected (because after the War his work came much closer to depicting his sexuality), but many found it quite sensational if not shocking; still, the published revelations failed to reignite popular interest in his novels, essays, and plays, both those already published and those released posthumously. Perhaps the nature of the information itself was enough to repel potential new readers and make former readers feel somewhat betrayed (for Montherlant had always claimed, among other things, to have been brutally honest with his public). Yet, in the end, his written works themselves appear to have far less to say to readers today than to readers half a century earlier.

It is arguable that both Montherlant and his works anticipated the very disparity that eventually materialized, namely the considerable difference between the author's public and private selves. Indeed, a credible case may be made that Montherlant's writings in some way attempted to resolve, however unsuccessfully, the highly problematic conflict that pitted who Montherlant wished he was against who he actually was. Such a notion, which presumes some constant inner strife in the writer, though certainly accurate, nevertheless simplifies many of the larger moral complications and tends to ignore the significance of the sexual politics inherent in his writings.

Generally, the public saw the person that Montherlant wished and perhaps tried to be. The evolution of this image is visually documented in the photographs taken throughout his life. Indeed, the uncomfortable though proud school pictures, included in Sipriot's 1979 *Album Montherlant* (43, 51, 59), predict the later photographs: Henry at nineteen, in morning coat, arrogantly posed (head upturned) à la Maurice Barrès (72); Henry in the last year of the First World War, nearly strangled by his military gear but managing, in spite of his great coat and the blanket wound about his torso, to summon up (under his bowl-like helmet) some hauteur (75); and Henry at twenty-five, the robust sportsman, in jersey and shorts, a soccer ball tucked under his right armpit, his left hand at his hip, with a stance that looks seriously athletic and competitive (94). Yet between twenty-five and thirty years, Henry's portraits have clearly given way to Montherlant's; the frown has deepened, the seriousness has turned grave, even grim, and as the hair cut becomes shorter and the forehead climbs, the ears achieve noticeable prominence (85, 89, 95, 100). This face, into which an expression of brooding, of tortured inner struggle has been clearly etched, Montherlant continues to wear until his death.[2]

How Montherlant appeared in his portraits was, of course, not necessarily who Montherlant really was. Photos with Véra Korène at the Comédie-Française in 1953 (129), with Maurice Genevoix welcoming him at the Académie Française in 1957 (211), and in the same year at a bullfight in Toulouse (216), actually show him smiling. Still these shots are noticeable exceptions; the solo portraits, many of them posed, clearly reflect how Montherlant was (and wished to be) seen. In time, the somber visage came to resemble the ancient military mask, worn by Roman officers for combat and burial, which Montherlant had purchased for his antiquarian collection and in which he wanted to be entombed (182–183). Like the pictures taken for public dissemination, his writing served as a mask, demolishing Henry and creating Montherlant, simultaneously obscuring one identity while defining another. In the arena of open controversy and intellectual combat, he was Henry de Montherlant, the writer, but on the street, in a park, outside a movie theatre, he was someone very different.

Through writing, he fashioned Montherlant, weaving throughout his career a myth of identity that he was able to hold in place until his self-inflicted annihilation. For example, although he was born on April 20, 1895, he maintained in print that his birth occurred on April 21, 1896; the latter date, according to legend, marked the anniversary of the founding of Rome, and the year 1896 was the same in which Henryk Sienkiewicz's *Quo Vadis*, which profoundly influenced his childhood interest in Rome, was published.[3] This myth of origin eventually led into his own myth of becoming. Montherlant had survived an estranged though privileged childhood with a distant father who spent little time with and emotion on his wife and son, and an invalid mother whose intense but often misguided affections were oppressive. Then, at sixteen he entered Sainte-Croix de Neuilly, an exclusive Catholic school, in preparation for the baccalaureate, but a year and three months later, in March 1912, he was expelled, supposedly for his intense romantic friendship with a younger school fellow. Montherlant told Peyrefitte that sodomy among the boys was widespread (*Propos Secrets* 65) and mentioned too the secret club—"The Family"—comprised of boys engaged in sex. Indeed, "The Family" appears as the name of the group described in Peyrefitte's own retelling of Montherlant's tale in the novel, *Les Amitiés particulières* (*Special Friendships*); the name also occurs in the essay on the chivalric order, in which Montherlant recalls the tight group of youths at the school Sainte-Croix de Neuilly and proposes it as the model for his new order of knighthood (858). A year later (Robichez 9), Montherlant had begun to transform the events surrounding the breakup of what he now regarded as the most important relationship in his life into what would become two works of literature.

At least during his own lifetime, the play and novel that he based upon this early sexual experience (works that he revised throughout his career) formed Montherlant's most overt admissions regarding his covert sexual life. Both works were printed relatively late in his career: The play, *La Ville dont le prince est un enfant* (*The City Whose Prince is a Child*), was not published until 1951 and not performed until 1967, and the novel, *Les Garçons* (*The Boys*), did not appear until 1969 (and then only in an edited form). These belated disclosures give some indication of Montherlant's intense ambivalence in submitting before his audience an explicit exploration of his own sexuality.[4]

In transforming his experience into a play, then a novel, Montherlant created three major characters: Alban,[5] an intelligent sixteen year old, who is captivated by one of his younger classmates; Serge, a mischievous but engaging fourteen year old, who eventually returns Alban's feelings; and the Abbé de Pradts, a teacher at the school who is himself drawn to Serge and whose jealousy causes Alban's expulsion. Thus, as Josephine Arnold acutely surmises, "The author has split himself in two and shown us the pain of thwarted pederastic love in both its formative and culminating phase" (196). The disclosure through the fictive representations, then, concerns what Montherlant regarded as the origin (the sixteen year old's love for a younger boy) and the present state (the older man's pursuit of prepubescent boys) of his sexuality. Yet, typically, this latter aspect of the disclosure is subverted by the absence of sexual motives on the part of the adult—never, Arnold acknowledges, "does the author suggest even remotely that the Abbé de Pradts has sexual designs on the younger boy" (195)—so the narrative's emphasis falls on the more socially acceptable sexual love between the two boys. Montherlant was writing, in part, to give substance to his own myth of origin: For him it seemed that pedophilia was the result of his failed love experience (and hence its cause) and that performing sexual acts with a boy who was about the same age as the one from whom he had been separated was the only way he could find satisfaction—or so he believed.

Such a belief, of course, is in itself a self-justification. In reality, most practitioners of psychology and psychiatry, both now and during Montherlant's lifetime, have maintained that pedophilia originates in a perpetrator earlier than adolescence, indeed sometime during childhood or even earlier. No doubt some incident or series of incidents that had occurred long before Montherlant began at Sainte-Croix de Neuilly precipitated this adolescent obsession and contained the formative influence on his sexuality. Certainly the distant father and passionate mother contributed to his intolerance for intimacy and his desperate longing for love. Yet the event that seemed at least for his own purposes to be responsible for his sexual orientation was the ill-fated school affair. By locating his sexuality in this event, Montherlant was eventually able to sanction and even glorify his pursuit of boys.

Une Correspondance Particulière: The Language of the Letters

In his revealing 1977 memoir, *Propos secrets*, in which he devotes a chapter to his relationship with Montherlant, Peyrefitte indicates that before their meeting, only three people knew of Montherlant's pedophilia: André Gide, himself a pedophile, who had encountered him in North Africa; a boy in a local café who found boys for Montherlant; and Pierre de Massot, who (like Gide) knew Montherlant from his own pedophilic excursions in North Africa. Massot told his friend Henri d'Amfreville (also a pedophile), who, while lunching with his friend Peyrefitte, noticed Montherlant at another table and confided to Peyrefitte that the famed writer shared their sexual tastes.[6] Just back from his post at Athens, from which he had been removed for his scandalous affair with a young servant, Peyrefitte now frequented various pickup spots and spied the author one afternoon at the "kermesse" ("village fair" or in this case, "street fair") in Clichy. After some initial reticence, Montherlant, aware that he was in the presence of a fellow pedophile, began a friendly conversation (62–63).

Prior to this, Montherlant seems to have operated solitarily. The boy at the café who procured for him was the only youth who knew his true identity (64). Montherlant would introduce himself as Monsieur Millon (significantly, Millon was his father's surname), commercial representative, under which name he rented a small flat ("une garçonnière"), where he would go for sex. As their friendship grew, Montherlant let Peyrefitte use the apartment once or twice (66), and in addition they not only shared some of the same boys but were intimate with two brothers, Montherlant taking the older and Peyrefitte the younger (although some switching apparently went on). In spite of the differences in ages (when they first met in April 1938, Montherlant was 43, Peyrefitte 31), the two men had much in common: Both led secret lives, felt relatively isolated in their pursuit of sexual pleasure, and had a genuine interest in literature. When the "street fairs" were closed with the onset of war in 1939, Montherlant was ready to share other pickup spots and new cruising strategies with his friend (65). While Peyrefitte, who would soon leave the Foreign Office to take up writing, relished his acquaintance with the author— after first meeting Montherlant in Clichy, Peyrefitte read all his works (64)— the older man, who had led such a covert sex life, began to write about his sexuality, first in his extensive correspondence with Peyrefitte, then in his published and performed works.

On one level, then, the letters served as communication between the two men not only when they were geographically distant but, because Peyrefitte did not have a telephone, when both were in Paris. On another level, however, the correspondence provided a safe forum in which Montherlant for the first time might write of a part of his life about which he had previously only hinted. Yet, as noted earlier, even as their correspondence quite openly discussed their sexual exploits, Montherlant inscribed his conflicts regarding his own sexuality into every letter. The two used what Peyrefitte calls their "jargon" (*Correspondance* 42 n3), of which the following paragraph, taken from an early letter (dated "Sunday," 1938), serves as a good example:

> Je viens de découronner ou coronner une pouliche dodue, parfaitement complaisante, à la vulve élastique et *qui promet* (la vulve). Elle s'est laissé faire avec courage. Par ailleurs, elle a fait marcher ses grandes eaux deux fois en trois quart d'heure, ce qui est très bien. (42)

> [I came to decrown or crown a plump filly, perfectly complacent, in her elastic and promising vulva. She allowed this to happen with courage. What's more, she caused her great waters to flow twice in three-quarters of an hour, which is all quite good.][7]

In a series of notes, Peyrefitte translates the jargon, explaining that "la couronne" ("the crown") meant a boy's anus (and thus the verb form means "to sodomize") and that "ses grandes eaux" ("her great waters") were "[s]permatiques." At the same time, Peyrefitte points to an even more pervasive trend: Throughout the passage Montherlant has substituted feminine nouns and pronouns for masculine; thus, notes Peyrefitte, "la pouliche" ("the filly") should be read as "le poulain" ("the colt"); indeed, Peyrefitte adds, all of Montherlant's correspondence on this subject was written "au féminin" (to which Peyrefitte replied using the same convention); "la vulve élastique" ("the elastic vulva") should be construed as "l'anus élastique" (42–43 n3–6), just as "Elle" ("She") should be read as "Il" ("He"). This linguistic strategy of replacing male with female seems at first glance intended to give any unauthorized reader the impression that both men were discussing their physical relations with girls.[8]

Although this code, which, Peyrefitte admits, Montherlant inaugurated (42 n4), sought to disguise their clandestine activities, its deployment presents a series of contradictory implications. The first involves the extent of Montherlant's awareness of societal responses to his sexuality; he knew, having had as early as 1938 at least one brush with the law,[9] that the legal consequences of his activities could be very serious and damaging. Indeed, even the statutes that would be passed by Vichy in 1942 (described in chapter 1) against homosexual acts between an adult and a minor (between the ages of seventeen and twenty-one years) would not apply to Montherlant's conduct because his sexual partners were invariably younger—usually much younger— than seventeen. If Montherlant's actual concern was to avoid prosecution, then why, rather than altering his partners' sex, did he not change their ages, for acts with a minor (someone under seventeen), male or female, were in fact punishable?

This question can be answered but only by a second contradiction: As much as Montherlant despised women—to whom in his correspondence he refers as "l'autre race" (54)—his misogyny was superseded by his homophobia. While sex with prepubescent boys became for Montherlant an increasing obsession, he remained staunchly intolerant of adult homosexual males whose partners were other adult males; such men he considered effeminate and thus (because women were hideous to him) loathsome. Although he was quite convinced that his sexuality was sharply distinct from homosexuality, Montherlant obviously did not wish to run the risk of being taken (by an ignorant general public who confused homosexuals with pederasts) for a homosexual. Hence, to insure that a stranger reading these letters would not take Montherlant for an invert, he ironically had—quite literally—to effeminize the masculine nouns and pronouns.

In fact, Montherlant had gone so far as to create for himself a definition of sex with boys that entirely (though illogically) circumvented homosexuality—a definition that in itself presents a third contradiction. As Sipriot explains in his Préface to the *Correspondance*, Montherlant believed that sexual love for male children or adolescents who had not yet grown facial hair was really the love of the feminine in them and thus was hardly different from heterosexual love (19).[10] Of course, such a rationalization is revealing: why would anyone intent on embracing the feminine resort to males? Uninterested in women and contemptuous of men who sought other men, Montherlant validated what he believed to be his unconventional sexuality by explaining it in the most conventionalized (that is, heterosexual) terms; the letters, with their consistent switches in gender, linguistically do the same.

There are in the correspondence, however, moments when the substitution of one gender for another does not successfully help Montherlant either to express or to mask what he is trying to convey. For example, in a letter from April 1941 from Grasse, Montherlant describes an encounter in a cinema where he became excited while touching a boy beside him. "O mon cher," he tells Peyrefitte, "je m'arrête, pour sentir à l'index et au pouce de ma senestre cette affolante odeur de glu féminine" ["O, my dear, I stopped myself to smell on the index finger and thumb of my left hand that distracting odor of feminine glue"] (265). Here, Montherlant would have denied that "féminine" should be read to mean "masculin" because he denied (although clearly too fervently) any interest in members of his own sex. One might argue that here "féminine" means just what it ordinarily means: After all, if he rationalized that what he loved in boys was their femininity, then why should "féminine" not simply mean "féminine"?

The answer here reflects a final twist in Montherlant's mythologizing of his own sexuality: As Arnold notes, he had earlier, in *Les Olympiques* (1924), "expressed a marked admiration for athletic young women who appeared to be neither male nor female but examples of what he called a 'third sex' "; it was easy to see prepubescent boys, who had yet to develop secondary male characteristics, similarly (192). Thus, in the sentence quoted above, "féminine" means neither masculine nor feminine: Montherlant himself, then, might translate it as "pedophiliac," but only if that could mean "a sex apart from the usual two."

Montherlant's "admiration for athletic young women" may have been "marked" when he first wrote *Les Olympiques* in 1924, but fifteen years later his tastes had noticeably changed or perhaps clarified. Having reissued this book in 1938, he sought to accompany it with a series of photographs; as corroborated by the correspondence, during the following year he spent many hours working with photographer Karel Egermeier, selecting pictures to illustrate the most recent edition. The result was *Paysage des Olympiques*, completed in December 1939 (47) and published on May 21, 1940. The album was introduced by Montherlant and featured Egermeier's photos.[11] As Montherlant explains, "il ne s'agit pas ici, à quelques exceptions près, d'athlètes adultes, mais de «juniors» et de «cadets»" ["it is not a matter here, with a few exceptions, of adult athletes, but of "juniors" and "cadets" (both masculine forms in the original) and not a question of performances but of atmosphere] (8). "L'essence du sport," he continues, "est mouvement, mais ici, comme dans les *Olympiques*, c'est un *état* qui nous a séduits et retenus" ["The essence of sport is movement, but here, as in the *Olympics*, this is a *state* that seduces and engages us"] (9).

Although the 1938 text of *Les Olympiques* (passages from which, along with page numbers, accompany the photos) retains Montherlant's adulation for "femmes sportives" (*Paysages* 46), the great majority of photographs are not of female athletes; indeed, there are only twenty-six (clustered together, 30–52) of young athletic women (late adolescents who have passed through puberty) as opposed to sixty of males. Of these sixty (which sandwich those of the young women), all but four (66, 67, 68,[12] 70) appear to be of young (prepubescent) boys. Nineteen of these pictures depict boys with naked chests, twenty-four show boys with bare legs, and two represent boys with no clothes at all. A number of shots emphasize boys' feet, and several others have the boy staring longingly into the lens. In a particularly revealing picture, a foregrounded boy in soccer gear gazes into the eyes of an adult male statue, somewhat blurred in the background but clearly nude; the caption reads:

> Le Génie du stade, qui tient de ses deux bras de pierre les tables où flambent les nom de nos tués, avec un geste d'aînesse et comme on tient deux jeunes épaules . . .

> [The Spirit of the stadium, which holds in its two arms of stone the tablets on which burn the names of those killed, with a gesture of seniority and as one holds two young shoulders . . .] (22)[13]

Of course, Montherlant did not take the photos, but the letters (and captions) make it evident that he selected them. All the pictures are tastefully done— not even the nude shots seem particularly pornographic. Yet this album, about which Montherlant eagerly wrote to Peyrefitte during 1939, seems the most graphic indication[14] up until this time of the allegedly macho author's actual interest in sex with male children.

L'Amitié de la Chasse: The Content of the Letters

On one level, the letters between the two men represent much of what occurred during the course of their daily lives; on another, however, the letters are themselves what occurred. Montherlant's growing need to write about his sexuality, even when his writing remained encoded in jargon and inverted in gender, was as significant as any of the events described in the correspondence, and Peyrefitte's role in this was formidable. Not only do Peyrefitte's letters—many of them longer and less inhibited than Montherlant's—promote Montherlant's increasing frankness, but apparently in spoken conversations the younger man exhorted the older, at times through irony, at times through reproach, to throw off his mask and write more directly about his passions (*Propos secrets* 78). Early in the relationship, Peyrefitte told Montherlant that he had done nothing to advance the much maligned cause of pederasty (79).[15] Thus, from the first years of their friendship, Montherlant began to view his more public writing as a medium for affirming his ideas about his own sexuality and for protesting what he viewed as a campaign against pederasty. Of course, Montherlant's affirmations and protests during the Occupation were intended to be clearly discernible only to those predisposed to deciphering his ambiguous messages.

Montherlant began his letters to Peyrefitte in the spring of 1938. The following August, Montherlant picked up a fourteen year old named Edmond N. (nicknamed Doudou, and in the letters rechristened Coré), a boy from Montmartre. After attending the Munich Conference, he returned to Paris, where, in December, he set up Peyrefitte with Edmond's eleven-year-old brother, Roland, (nicknamed Roro, and in the letters rechristened Eos or Aurore). The men's sexual adventures with these children were permitted, if not promoted, by Mme N., the boys' mother. Over the next three years, Montherlant and Peyrefitte contributed financially and in other ways to maintain the working-class N. family.

At the same time Montherlant also continued writing and publishing. His collection of essays (some criticizing the deals made at Munich), *L'équinoxe de septembre*, was released by Grasset at the end of 1938, and in the beginning of 1939, he completed at Peira-Cava his tetrology of bitterly misogynistic novels, *Les Jeunes filles*, with *Les Lépreuses* (which would be serialized in *Marianne* in May and published by Grasset in September). Then, fighting a bout of pulmonary congestion, he went on to Nice. Later that same year, he worked with Egermeier on selecting the photos for *Paysage des Olympiques*. That summer, Peyrefitte took Roland N. with him on vacation to his parents' large home in Alet. In this Montherlant (playing the great man of literature) assisted by sending Peyrefitte's aged father a cordial though formal letter thanking the old man for allowing his young nephew, Roland, to spend his holidays at the estate; the letter to the father, as Peyrefitte acknowledges, carries many doubl'entendres for the son (60 n1).

During the years with Doudou and Roro, both men had sexual relations with numerous other boys, sometimes one passing on a particular boy to the other. In December 1939, Peyrefitte came up with the idea of a chivalric order dedicated to heroes of pedophilia—an idea that would eventually surface publicly in Montherlant's essay (which I will discuss below) eight months later. After another winter stay at Peira-Cava, Montherlant returned to Paris, and eventually, just as Grasset was releasing *Paysages des Olympiques*, he left for the front as correspondent for *Marianne*. As conditions deteriorated and Parisians fled the capital, Montherlant made his way to Marseille, where, alone, he worried at the lack of news from Peyrefitte and the N. family.

According to Sipriot, however, in *Montherlant sans masque*, these worries did not inhibit Montherlant's pedophilic urges: On the contrary, as June turned into July, he cruised cinemas but found the creaking seats and floorboards unsuited to his escapades and the newsreels (of the Defeat and its aftermath) depressing. In a public square, he risked touching a boy sitting beside him on a bench, but the boy stood and shouted. A policeman asked the boy to explain what had happened; when he said Montherlant had given him an electric shock, the officer took the boy for crazy and let the author go (140). Montherlant again came close to arrest after being interrupted during sex with a young male prostitute on a boat in the boat basin (141).

But when the author invited to his hotel room the son of a Polish family whom he had befriended, he showed the boy his journal and revealed, for amusement, how all the "shes" should have been "hes" (*Propos secrets* 92). The boy told Montherlant that his mother knew all about him and that he should change his hotel because she was going to start a scandal. Montherlant ignored him; three days later, the police ordered him to appear for interrogation the next day. The following morning, Montherlant sent his notebooks, filled with details of his pedophilic adventures, to Peyrefitte's family and then reported to the police. The interview lasted the afternoon. For a time Montherlant was held in a jail cell but was eventually brought to a prosecutor, who said that men such as he were the reason France had fallen. The judge set him free on the condition that he remain in Marseille, but back at his hotel, he saw that his papers had been seized. The following day (July 12), the commissioner refused to return the missing papers (the boy had confessed the gender switch), but the judge, who had never before read Montherlant's work, now tackled several of his books and was so pleased by them that he asked the author to autograph them. The affair was quickly settled: The threatened letter to the Légion d'Honneur was never sent, and Montherlant left for Nice (*Montherlant sans masque* 141–143).

These three incidents suggest a pattern of obsessive behavior, which was perhaps more evident in Montherlant's later life. After the war, through his old age, and until his suicide, the author seemed to become increasingly controlled by his sexual impulses. Arnold identifies the classic "paraphile" symptoms he exhibited while cruising, his "fugue or trancelike state" and his utter inability to keep himself from leaving his apartment despite efforts to confine himself there (200).[16] Yet his correspondence from this period reveals a far more conscious, even a calculated acceptance of what, in current popular terminology, would be termed a sexual addiction. Perhaps the sudden shock of the Defeat occasioned this heedless pursuit of boys. Yet what is particularly clear from all three of these incidents is that Montherlant was not merely compulsively following his desires for sex but was seemingly trying to get caught in the act.

Montherlant had already written his essay on the "Chivalric Order," but it would not appear in print until the release of the first issue of what had become a pro-Nazi *Nouvelle Revue Française (NRF)* (January 1941) and then later that same year in *Le Solstice de Juin*. Of course, with the *NRF* now headed by French fascist Pierre Drieu la Rochelle, who hated homosexuals as much as he hated Jews, Montherlant's essay could not overtly espouse pederasty (which for Drieu would have been the same as homosexuality, if not worse). An ordinary reader probably saw in Montherlant's "Les Chevaleries" a piece typical of the author of *Les Olympiques* and *Les Jeunes filles*. The author called for the establishment of a group that would rejuvenate the dissipated France that had led to the Defeat. This Chivalric Order's exclusion of women and inclusion of adolescent boys and a few men nearly fades, almost unobtrusively, into the ultra-macho and misogynistic image Montherlant had already created for himself.

Yet there are important clues to the genuine nature of his subject. For example, he claims that this "Order" was founded at the end of the First World War by himself and another man whom he calls P. (whom we may identify as Peyrefitte), who first came up with the idea and whose thoughts on the subject are reflected (and possibly quoted) in the essay. And Montherlant emphasizes how the order was modeled on a particular organization of boys at the school of Sainte-Croix de Neuilly—The Family (858). Although we may easily identify such references, most of Montherlant's public could not. Nonetheless, a perceptive (and not necessarily pedophilic) reader might easily discern the real message: Sipriot notes that after reading "Les Chevaleries," Jean Guéhenno wrote in his diary on January 11, 1941, that Montherlant was placing himself at the head of a Teutonic order and of the Knights Templar (long reputed to be pederasts; *Montherlant sans masque* 147).[17]

Privately, however, Montherlant responded to the humiliation from the police through what appears to be a story, "Oblomov à Nijni-Novgorod," which he sent to Peyrefitte (*Correspondance* 83–90), who received it by July 15 (96). Allegedly written by Dostoyevski and translated/adapted by "N. Galitzine," this short fiction is a thinly disguised account of what Montherlant felt he had suffered in Marseille; as in the letters, the reversal of gender (the boy in the incident becomes a girl) conceals from the mail censor the true nature of the "tale," in which the reader—that is, Peyrefitte—himself figures as a character (named Sergueiev). The terminology of the "Order" and of chivalry had originally been injected into the correspondence by Peyrefitte in a letter sent in December 1939 (which does not survive though Montherlant's reply does: 70 n1); however, when Montherlant wrote Peyrefitte from Nice, on July 21, 1940, to comment on the events to which the encoded "Oblomov" referred (94–95), he repeatedly made use of the term "ordre" as his means to signify "pédérastie" (95 n5, n7, n15). His own suffering before the authorities and his extensive use of terminology derived from chivalry lend his letter a certain tone of nobility.

This nobility derived from what Montherlant now saw as a growing persecution of "knights"; indeed, he alludes in "Oblomov à Nijni-Novgorod" to how Sergueiev (Peyrefitte) had also been recently apprehended. This had occurred in April 1940 in the Jardin du Luxembourg and was Peyrefitte's second arrest on charges of pedophilia. Although the police released him, the presiding official told Peyrefitte that his file indicated his previous run-in and that if there were a third transgression, he would pay the penalty (88 n1). Peyrefitte was stopped yet again, first in June (96ff) and then in July, this time in Vichy (108). As a result, he was forced to resign officially from the Foreign Office in October, at which time Montherlant encouraged him to become a writer. Fittingly, Peyrefitte's first novel, published during the Occupation, *Special Friendships*, re-creates much of the story of adolescent love and separation that Montherlant had told him. But even as one of the founders of the "Order" was able to publish such a novel during this period, other "chevaliers" were being arrested and detained.

Thus, pedophilia was for Montherlant more than just his sexuality: It became his identity, his cause, his politics. Many have commented on the political implications of one of the famous lines in *Queen After Death*: "En prison se trouve la fine fleur du royaume" ["The finest flower of the kingdom finds itself in prison"]. Serge Added, for example, astutely observes that this statement was often construed by audiences (who sometimes cheered or applauded) as referring to contemporary political events in France (257). But the line, with all its noble, chivalric implications, has little to do with conventional politics.

Indeed, Added is right to be skeptical of any intended implication of resistance, at least in the conventional political sense of the term, for the line did not pertain to the Germans. It referred instead to that regime that was currently imprisoning members of the "Order." As Richard J. Golsan reminds us, Montherlant, rising to his own defense against postwar charges of collaboration, would declare that the only group he belonged to during the early part of the Occupation was a minority that "resisted the politics of Vichy." The "Order," which appeared in his correspondence with Peyrefitte and in the pages of the *NRF*, was the only group that fits this description (148–149).

Ironically, Peyrefitte tries to explain away *Le Solstice de Juin*, which includes a welcome for the Germans (who banned the book but later lifted the ban), by insisting that in all political matters Montherlant was completely childish and lacked any adult judgment (*Propos secrets* 79). Still, at least early in the war, Montherlant, who eventually left Nice and the Free Zone and returned to Paris, saw Vichy as far worse than the Nazis.

Queen After Death: *Hints to the House*

Although Montherlant had, over the 1920s and 1930s, acquired a substantial readership, he seems to have regarded his plays in performance as the most public of his works. This interpretation of events would at least explain his willingness to publish in 1951 the dramatization of the experiences that made their way into Peyrefitte's first novel but to refuse all requests to perform the play for more than fifteen years.[18] Jean Meyer at the Comédie-Française and Jean-Louis Barrault and Madeleine Renaud, now at the Marigny, wished to produce it, and yet Montherlant hesitated and submitted *The City Whose Prince is a Child* to Archbishop Feltin, who told Montherlant it should not be performed (Robichez 56–57). "A book," concludes Arnold, "was safe; the theater was not" (194). No doubt the very real presence of living spectators— who might react immediately and even disfavorably—must have frightened this author who had spent so much of his literary career protecting himself against detection and ridicule.

Yet the theatre became for Montherlant, especially during the Occupation, perhaps the most effective forum in which he could present his sexuality to a smaller though certainly more educated audience. True, he ran the risk of incurring the hostility of the public, who were in fact there, but at the same time Montherlant as playwright probably delighted in watching his own work come alive in the theatre. Actual performers enacting on stage a fictive script can bring the relative distance of literature excitingly, even dangerously, close to both author and spectator. To achieve a theatrical success and in the midst of such popular recognition to be able to celebrate that which virtually all condemned—Montherlant could rise to both.

Montherlant made his mark as a dramatist during the Occupation. True, he had published two plays before the War, *L'Exil*, written in 1914, printed in 1929, but never professionally performed in his lifetime; and *Pasiphaé*, written in 1928, printed in 1936, and performed at the Pigalle in 1938 (Robichez 13–18). However, neither of these scripts enjoyed the welcoming reception that many of his novels found. In April 1940 Montherlant began work on *Port-Royal*, but he eventually destroyed this draft and more than a decade later resumed it from scratch. A year and a half later, Jean-Louis Vaudoyer, head of the Comédie-Française, asked him to peruse with an eye for translation and adaptation several scripts from Spain's golden age. Among them, Montherlant discovered Luis Velez de Guevara's *Reinar después de morir*, written in 1604. However, rather than simply adapt it, he created his own play (Robichez 19–25).

As noted earlier, Spain's golden age was very much in vogue on the wartime stage. Indeed, from the time of Corneille's *Le Cid*, there had always been a French fascination with staging Spain and all things Spanish, but during the Occupation there was something more than merely exotic about that land beyond the Pyrenees. Montherlant had spent time in Spain—his glorification of bull fighting came from his visits to Spain with his grand-mother—and certainly Spanish pride and honor (not to mention its fascistic government) were close to his own sense of self. Moreover, he was by tem-perament an excellent candidate to write a tragedy.[19]

Queen After Death loosely follows the older play but becomes, in a variety of ways, uniquely Montherlant's. Ferrante, King of Portugal, is about to marry his rather submissive son and heir, Prince Don Pedro, to the very assertive, even aggressive Infanta of Navarre. He is unaware that Pedro—for whom he has felt a great indifference for years—has secretly married the illegitimate (and foreign) Inès de Castro, who is now carrying Pedro's child. Gradually, the truth about Pedro's relationship with Inès emerges; to ensure peace between Portugal and Navarre, Ferrante arrives at the decision that Inès must be put to death. Although Ferrante is reluctant to pursue such a plan, Inès's own refusal to leave Portugal because of her love for Pedro leaves him little choice. The inevitability of this awful act, in spite of the unwillingness of all parties involved to commit it, seems unavoidable.

The premiere of *Queen After Death* in December 1942 at the Comédie-Française was one of the most important theatre events of the Occupation: Montherlant, hitherto appreciated as novelist and essayist, emerged as a major playwright. In spite of the audience's inclination to savor what they might occasionally perceive as references to contemporary problems, most specta-tors were probably pleased to see the play as pure and rather traditional tragedy, divorced from and well above the banal concerns of everyday life. As Golsan eloquently demonstrates, there have been various attempts to in-terpret the play politically, but *Queen After Death* is complex and not easily reduced to some readily comprehensible statement about conventional poli-tics (161–162). The tragedy seems almost neoclassical in its apparent sepa-ration from the world in which it came to light.

Very few who have read or seen this play, perhaps Montherlant's best but certainly his best known, would think of it as in some way dramatizing the playwright's sexuality. However, Arnold offers a very convincing inter-pretation, which decodes the commentary that Montherlant intended for his fellow pedophiles. She points to two of his changes from Guevara's script, first, the expanded role of the aged king, and second, the creation of a new character, a young page, Dino del Moro. As usual, her analysis yields a startling glimpse of Montherlant's pedophilic subtext:

> In the last scene the dying king selects Dino out of all his entourage and clasps him to his breast in the hope that the child's innocence will somehow wash away his sins. The function of the page in this scene might well be questioned by spectators who barely have had occasion to notice this minor character. . . . Having just destroyed one innocent child [the one Inès was carrying], the dying monarch hopes to be saved by the innocence of another. . . . [T]he young page, who is the last and only courtier to linger near the dead king's body, finally abandons it in order to kneel near the corpse of Inès. Her husband places a crown not on her head but on her belly. The object of veneration is not the dead woman but the dead child. (193)[20]

The question Arnold implies—Did the spectators question the use of Dino at the end of the play?—is a crucial one. There is no evidence that anyone saw past the immediate story. Maybe because Montherlant so effectively has inserted so much heavy emotion into this final scene, audiences simply accepted Dino's sudden and unpredictable importance as part of Montherlant's peculiar dramaturgy. Spectators became caught up in the utter sadness and defeat suffered by all in the play, perhaps even followed without question some of the symbolism in which the young page figures.

Similarly, one may further ask about what audience members made of Ferrante's explanation of his feelings toward his son. The speech occurs early in Act I, as the King confronts Pedro:

> . . . As a baby, I confess, you scarcely held my attention. Then, from five to thirteen years old, I loved you tenderly. . . . Thirteen was the year of your great glory; you had at thirteen a grace, a gentleness, a delicacy, an intelligence that you have never recovered since; it was the last, marvelous ray of the setting sun; only one knows that, within twelve hours, the sun will reappear, whereas the genius of childhood, when it goes out, has gone forever. They always say that the butterfly comes from a worm; with man it's the butterfly that turns into a worm. At fourteen it was all over, you had gone out; you had become mediocre and coarse. Before then, God forgive me, I used sometimes to be almost jealous of your tutor; jealous at seeing you take seriously the things said to you by that old fool Don Christoval, more so than the things I said to you myself, I used to think, too: "Because of the business of the State, I shall be forced to lose my child: I haven't time to devote myself to him." From the moment you were fourteen, I was

delighted for your tutor to relieve me of you. I no longer looked for you, I avoided you. You are now twenty-six: for thirteen years I have had nothing more to say to you. (8)[21]

Naturally, anyone who has read Montherlant's correspondence with Peyrefitte and is familiar with his life can easily discern in this speech a perfectly clear statement about the author's sexual preference for boys. But how did Occupation audiences perceive this monologue? Did they detect in it anything strangely peculiar, if not troublingly suggestive?

Or were they, as suggested above, perhaps distracted by the story itself or the symbolism at play throughout the drama? The child inside Ferrante has long ago died. But the King's inner child came alive again through Pedro's youth. As Pedro grew to adolescence, Ferrante seemed to thrive once more; the onset of Pedro's adulthood destroyed that. Yet even though Ferrante discards his own image of renewal ("one knows that, within twelve hours, the sun will reappear, whereas the genius of childhood, when it goes out, has gone forever"), the cycle appears to continue: Thirteen years after Pedro's charms have faded, the King sees in his page the same innocence and other qualities he observed in his son. Thus, if childhood has been blotted out forever, Ferrante himself has been the cause: the child who would have, thirteen years later, succeeded the page (i.e., the child of Inès and Pedro) dies with Inès. Those familiar with the posthumously released information on the playwright may read this in a particular way—Ferrante, like Montherlant himself, is forever seeking what he will inevitably destroy—but to a general public during the Occupation, whose knowledge of Montherlant was limited to the mask that he wore, such a theme might still make sense.

Still, my query about the highly idiosyncratic and very disturbing insinuations raised by Ferrante's speech has yet to be resolved. Even with the script's elegantly high tragedy, exciting intrigue, extraordinary dialogue, and wonderful characters, and even with a superb production and stunning performances at the Comédie-Française, was there no one to whom Ferrante's description of his own fatherhood sounded extremely odd? Whoever heard of discarding a son at fourteen simply because he had turned fourteen? Was this consonant with the experience of fatherhood that audience members knew? Again, although spectators might easily have questioned this, there appears to have been a lack of criticism and concern.

Perhaps to premise a characterization on such a definition of paternity may have been manageably reconciled; after all, spectators might have accepted that Ferrante was in some way eccentric or exceptional. The oddness of the explanation (which we can see would have been understood—or was at least meant to have been recognized—by members of Montherlant's "Order") would thus not have disrupted the appreciation of the play by the majority of spectators.

Yet to premise an entire play on such a definition of fatherhood—what might audiences make of that? To take this one disturbing aspect of *Queen After Death* and make it the prime theme of a drama might challenge audience members to wonder about what in fact was being perpetrated before them on stage. Indeed, in his next play, Montherlant would pull out more stops: True to his changing behavior, he would try to reveal more of himself even as he attempted to mask his revelations. Perhaps, in art as in life, Montherlant wanted to be apprehended.

Nobody's Son: *The Politics of Pedophilia*

Montherlant came closer to revealing the truth about himself in his next play. Unlike the grandeur of golden-age Iberia in *Queen After Death*, *Nobody's Son* is mundanely set in the present—or at least in the very near present: The play opens in 1940, in a furnished villa at Cannes in the autumn after the Defeat, and by the close of Act IV, four months have passed. Here is a script written around the same time as *Antigone*, only in this case the playwright very explicitly looks backward from the second half of the Occupation to the early days. We may recall Montherlant's problems in Marseille during this time— and the main character of this play, a successful middle-aged attorney named Georges Carrion, presently lives in Marseille, shuttling between his Marseille law office and the house in Cannes where he has set up his former mistress, Marie, and their son, Gillou. For those "in-the-know" friends of Montherlant who were aware of his personal life—those men like himself in whom he had confided and whom in his previous play he had called France's "finest flower"—a very clear message about pedophilia was easily identifiable.

True to Montherlant's life and art, of course, even these disclosures, which were originally intended for the "knights" of his chivalric order and which now seem much clearer to readers familiar with Montherlant's personal history, were masked. Here is how the dramatist rewrites his own past: Georges abandoned Marie before she gave birth to Gillou and only twelve years later does he see the child, when he runs into Marie and the boy on the Paris métro. Georges is thrilled to meet his adolescent son and provides support for both Marie and the child (whom he maintains in a house of their own), but when Georges is called up for the War, he is separated from them. He becomes a prisoner of war, and Marie and Gillou flee Paris and settle temporarily among the refugees in Angoulême. Georges escapes the detention camp and, because escapees are arrested in the Occupied Zone, comes to Marseille where he sets up his practice (and finds a mistress). After weeks of waiting, he receives a letter from Marie, and mother and son are soon resettled, first in Marseille (again in separate quarters from Georges), then in Cannes.

Act I begins about two weeks after their move to Cannes. Georges, who comes once a week to see the boy, arrives late in the evening. Although Marie is self-centered and tawdry, Georges reveals himself to be a sullen perfection-ist with a terrible weakness for his son. Yet from the start of the play, he is wary of his devotion. "I had measured my affection, and its obstacles, and I had accepted them," he confides to Marie. "As for him, I had measured his failings and his gaps, and I had accepted them too" (186). This early confes-sion articulates the central conflict in the protagonist and in the play: Georges is unable to love Gillou for who he is; what Georges adores is Gillou's potential, or rather his own imaginings of the boy's potential, and his desire to make Gillou become his ideal. By the end of the play, Georges has rec-ognized that his son is incapable of the kind of "moral courage" that he wants from him; Georges allows Gillou to leave with Marie for Le Havre (where Marie's lover has gone) in the Occupied Zone while he remains in the south, no longer a father.

The premise here can be traced back to *Queen After Death*. Georges's renunciation of Gillou reflects the King's description of his rejection of his son. In the later play, however, Gillou is at the very age of Pedro when Ferrante ceased to be interested in him. Thus, in *Nobody's Son* Montherlant actually dramatizes (rather than having a character describe in words) his own ambivalence, his intense attraction to a boy and his extreme distaste for the child as child. Montherlant created, like Georges, fantasies in which ide-alized children bloomed into miniature replicas of himself. Thus, he was incapable of accepting for very long actual boys, whose genuine potential was in any case to grow into men, whom Montherlant abhorred as sexual objects and who could never be what Montherlant believed he wanted.

The dramatization of pedophilia is in theatrical terms surprisingly per-vasive in *Nobody's Son*. Here, Montherlant reduces the role of woman to that of the manipulative birthing mother. While Inès's loyalty to Pedro is posed in noble terms, Marie is little more than a controling bitch, content to use her son and even sacrifice him to her own comfort. The playing field is thereby left open to the older man and the boy. In Act I, Gillou, alone with his father, tries to take Georges's arm and shortly after, as he starts to doze, the boy attempts to embrace him. Georges repulses both acts of tenderness. Yet later, watching Gillou asleep, he begins to weep openly, and when Marie tries to convince him that slumbering Gillou is weeping too, Georges retorts:

> So you don't know, even now, that when he's asleep, the sweat comes out on his face while his body remains dry? No, you didn't know! Any more than you had noticed, during twelve years, that

he had a little stain, as of wine, on the bend of his left knee. It needed more to reveal that to you, the third day after I found you again. (189)

Georges's keen interest in the boy's body might perhaps seem understandable if we accept that he is speaking of his son, and so perhaps is the final action before the first-act curtain, as Georges carries Gillou off to his bedroom.

At the same time, the parents' physical intimacy with the child is demonstrated. When Marie kisses, touches, and smells the boy in Act II (195), there is a very palpable air of seduction. Indeed, she is attempting to get Gillou to seduce Georges into allowing them to leave for Le Havre. Once Georges enters and Marie leaves, Gillou sets about getting his father to kiss him; he even tries to manipulate his father with the very words his mother has used on him: "D'you love me? I love you more every day. I've never loved you as much as today." Playfully and a little too forcefully, Gillou elbows his father's ribs (199). Forgiving the rough play, Georges passes his hand through the boy's hair (200). By Act III, however, the two are embroiled in constant argument and do not touch. In Act IV, Georges insinuates that Gillou's attachment to Marie is unnatural. His confession of jealousy over the hours the boy has spent in his mother's bedroom (226) hints that on some level Georges suspects the two of incest. Yet even without physical contact, the original production concluded not with George's monologue, as originally planned by the playwright, but with Gillou's body language.[22]

In the end, the son disappoints the father: Georges is unable to get Gillou to reveal the identity of his mother's lover, such a confession being a sign that the boy trusts and values him more than he does Marie. The play closes with Gillou's failed attempt to win back his father:

Gillou: You'll send for me to come back at Easter, eh? Promise?

Georges: I never make promises.

Gillou: You must! You must! I want to go back with you. Poor Papa, I know I made you fed up. But now, when I come back, you'll see, I'll be good.

Georges: My little, big boy!

Gillou: Give me a kiss!

Georges: (at the end of his strength, pushes him away) No, on the platform, soon . . . Let me go . . .

(He goes out into the hall. Gilles, left alone, hesitates for a moment, then goes to look for his coat, toward the right, throws it over his arm, and goes out slowly, through the same door as the others.)

Georges, Marie, and Gillou, near the final curtain in Nobody's Son,
(Bibliotheque Nationale de France).

This stark image of desertion, of Georges's relinquishing his love for his son
for some vague but lofty principles (which will be discussed below), recalls
Ferrante's sacrifice of the unborn grandson he feels he must destroy in order
to keep afloat the ship of state. As Montherlant went on to write for the
theatre, such a climax of resignation became characteristic of his dramaturgy,
or as some put it, of his tragedy.

Because of the disclosures about the author's life made after his death,
modern readers may easily identify Georges as the author and Gillou as Doudou.
They may further suppose that M. de Montherlant's arguments with Mme N.
were the basis for Georges's disputes with Marie. They may even conclude
with some confidence that the enactment of this play was, in its own peculiar
way, another attempt by the playwright to expose his sexuality, to make public
that secret identity, which had begun to consume his personal and artistic life,
and to champion its cause, even as he tried to disguise his revelations.

Modern readers may even feel uncertain as to just how successful the
author's disguises may have proved. Indeed, even without knowledge of
Montherlant's actual past, they may discern a number of aspects of *Nobody's
Son* that suggest that circumstances are not exactly normal here. Not only do
both Georges's and Marie's physical and emotional involvement with Gillou
appear disturbing, but the physical intimacies that father lavishes on son seem

inappropriate in context of their relationship: Indeed, the entire contrivance of the plot—Georges readily abandons Marie and child without compunction, then conveniently meets them a dozen years later on the métro, at which time he immediately experiences passionate love for his son—suggests that while Georges may be Gillou's biological parent, he is in no way the boy's father. When Marie tells Georges, "You took your son as a man takes a mistress, just like that, for his nice looks, at a subway station" (215), the submerged subject matter almost seems to break through the dialogue. Similarly, a little earlier, Georges reproaches Gillou, "If I were a stranger in the house, you'd listen to me. I should be the unknown, the seductive, the dangerous" (205); again, the dialogue appears to expose the underlying truth, for this is exactly who Georges, who comes once a week and acts like a distant, disdaining outsider, indeed is.

Of course, all of this might make sense if the play attempted to paint Georges as the troubled man he obviously is: His lecturing, which literally puts Gillou to sleep, his continuous pontifications, which gesture vaguely toward some desire for national perfection, his coldness and desperate need to feel, make for rather deep flaws, which, in the tradition of neoclassical French tragedy, may allow Georges to be seen at least by some as a heroic figure.

However, the central subterfuge in the text, the intellectual thread woven through the script and responsible for distracting critics and audiences from the pedophilic subtext, requires that they identify with Georges and see such apparent failings as his strength. Indeed, what seems to be a pitiful personality disorder is intended to be read, ultimately, as Georges's heroism. Consequently, his eventual "victory" over human feelings in Act IV is anticipated in Act III when, after Marie has described his constant contempt as pathological, Georges replies, "If only I could inoculate my country with that disease. I should like to serve it as a master of contempt" (212). The resonance of such cruelty rings in political terms throughout the dialogue: In Act II, the attorney proclaims, "I prefer, if I must choose, a nation of toughs to a nation of ninnies" (199) and in the next act asserts, "A nation isn't made out of affectionate men" (213). Georges's psychological failings, then, like the author's, are translated into virtues, and the fantasized idealizations of youth, which manifest themselves physically, if not sexually, are elevated to an outwardly conventional, fascist political proposition. The play thus begins to have the sound, if not the look, of a drama of ideas.

The ideas, which appear to be contained in the script, are particularly pointed toward current affairs. As noted earlier, the play is actually set during the Occupation. As if to demonstrate that he is not writing a comédie sans tickets, Montherlant has Marie praise Gillou's shrewdness in contemporary terms: "Of all the household, including the cook, he is the one who manages best with food tickets." Georges soon replies that his son is "a mediocrity" (213). His response here is exemplary not merely of his disgust for his son but for the state of France. To Gillou's joke that if he were a woman, he would "get out of" military service, Georges declaims, " 'To get out of something': that's your whole ambition, all you boys of 1940" (200). His remarks about the boy seem to be directed toward an entire generation: "You are a deserted child," he tells Gillou. "That's your destiny. Indeed, most of the children in France are deserted children" (220). They are also, like Georges's own son, rather ordinary, which is bad, for "there's nothing left in France today to save honor except individuals, and individuals verging on the exceptional" (215). Gillou, who gets through the difficult present by holding onto being a child, perhaps the ordinary mama's boy who barters ration coupons with the butcher, has all the attributes needed for survival under Vichy—rather average attributes as Georges and Montherlant see them.

Significantly, Montherlant's portrait of the child is indeed that of a rape survivor: Gillou's incessant flirtatiousness, his limited attention span, his continuous need for affection, and his keen desire for and profound fear of Georges's approval are accurate signs of a boy who has experienced sexual abuse. Georges's treatment of his son may seem, even with the elaborate pretexts of plot and theme, bizarre if not inexplicable, but Gillou's behavior conforms to that of a minor who has been violated. Thus, even with the exposition of Georges's sexual interest in women (which of course is never dramatized) and the political rationales through which Georges's words and actions intentionally take on a symbolic significance (the honor of France and a rejection of the mediocre 1940 generation), there are ample clues as to what might really be at the bottom of this script—at least for modern readers, who may be astonished that the original audiences could not recognize the play for what it was.

Obviously, the original context formed an important frame through which the play might be viewed. For contemporary critics *Nobody's Son* arrived as the new drama by the maverick novelist, now playwright, who just a season before had stunned audiences with *Queen After Death*. His second play was inevitably compared with the more classic piece and was thought by all to be expectedly inferior. I use "expectedly" because unlike his hit at the Comédie-Française, *Nobody's Son* was preceded by a number of articles and interviews and even a preface by Montherlant (printed in *Comœdia*)[23] that all talked up the problems of France that the dramatist wanted spectators to see as the play's theme. Thus Alain Laubreaux, who understandably found much to praise in the play, noted in *Je suis partout* that reviewers "no longer had the right to ignore any of the intentions of M. Henry de Montherlant" and Georges Ricou in *La France Socialiste* hinted that Montherlant's advance publicity made interpretation (by critics and audience) unnecessary; in *Le Pays Libre*, Jean Faydit de Terssac, referring to the play's "Preface" written by Montherlant, wondered whether Georges's speeches should be taken as the author's own.

In this context, many reviewers saw the play as Nietzschean, construing in the father's rejection of his son the need for the superior man to sacrifice what is inferior.

Still, a number of theatre critics detected something odd in the whole conceptualization of the play. At least two—François Charles-Bauer in *L'Echo de la France* and Georges Chaperot in *Le Cri de Peuple*—actually quoted the barb Marie throws at Georges regarding his involvement with Gillou: "You took your son as a man takes a mistress, just like that, for his nice looks, at a subway station"; yet the point made by each is merely that Georges deserves to be the target of Marie's insult. Many reviewers described the play as cruel or found its depiction of family life improbable; yet here again the image of the author and his advance publicity seems to have done its job, for everyone concludes, like Marcel Lapierre in *L'Atelier*, that Georges's harsh words for his son are not his at all but rather Montherlant's harsh words for his audience. In other words, the press's general response was that the paradoxical and rigid view of the world contained in *Nobody's Son* was just another example of its author's idiosyncratic and contradictory outlook on life.

Earlier in 1943, several months before *Nobody's Son* premiered, the great theatre director, Jacques Copeau, had read a manuscript copy of the play. At the end of April he returned it to Montherlant along with a politely critical letter.[24] The gist of Copeau's critique questions the plausibility of Georges's rejection of Gillou and his lack of consideration and of respect for others. "I'm not familiar with anything like these [characters]," he complained. "They've fallen from the moon." He found the way that Georges spoke to Gillou as without "common sense" and "wholly unrealistic" (667). Still, Copeau's skepticism about the play's premise never goes beyond the problems in the script. After all, he was addressing one of France's greatest writers, a popular novelist who was now a rising star in the theatre, and a man whose fierce reputation for privacy was well known.

Copeau's carefully worded response shows that Montherlant was an acquaintance, not a friend. Still, as Arnold reveals, even good friends, such as "Jean Cocteau and Colette[,] were able to guess the nature of Montherlant's sexuality but never dared to broach the subject in his presence" because "[a] mere hint would have sufficed to destroy the friendship" (189). In the spring of 1942, Colette told Cocteau that she was sure Montherlant was hiding something. Cocteau noted in his journal that it was "un secret de polichinelle" ["A secret everyone knew and the one he would wish were kept secret"] (52), and a year later Colette was calling Montherlant by that very phrase (289). After Paris had been liberated, Cocteau reflected that *Les Parents Terribles* had angered people not because of its scandalous ideas but because it had required them to think. On the other hand, "the public adopted an immoral play by Montherlant, *Nobody's Son*, because it had a thesis" and they found in it the simple-minded pleasures they had known in older message-heavy scripts (547). "Immoral" is an adjective not often used by Cocteau; here was at least one spectator who had read the play's pedophilic subtext and saw past its pretexts.

Some may argue that during the Occupation the press and even academic writers were unable to comment on the pedophilic overtones in Montherlant's work due to German and Vichy control. Yet, after the war, when fascist censorship was no longer in effect, cultural pressures remained intact: One simply did not write about such subjects. Merrill Rosenberg describes how Montherlant, accused by the Résistance of collaborating with the Germans, was in fact found guilty and censured, kept from publishing for a year ("Montherlant and the Critics" 841); thus, that none of his post-Liberation critics vilified him for his sexual crimes is notable. Moreover, in *The Second Sex* (1949), in her scathing analysis of Montherlant's literary misogyny, Simone de Beauvoir only insinuates the nature of Montherlant's sexuality—her quote from *Les Jeunes Filles*, "Costals confides to us that young boys' hair smells better and more strongly than women's" (203) and the subsequent commentary are suggestive, but she never offers a direct statement. Only after the publication of *The City Whose Prince is a Child* in 1951 did critics begin to refer to Montherlant's sexual orientation.

Even then, however, the discussion never seems to take into consideration exactly all that the author has actually disclosed. For example, John Cruickshank, in a pioneering 1964 British study, speaks extensively of the importance of sexuality in the works but even in this context avoids describing the author's sexuality in specific. After linking Montherlant to Oscar Wilde's famous line ("Each man kills the thing he loves") from "The Ballad of Reading Gaol," Cruickshank goes on to suggest that Montherlant's misogyny is perhaps due more to the "moral climate particularly dominant in France around the turn of the century" than to "homosexuality" (34). Likewise, Robert Emmet Jones, in a 1962 American monograph, acknowledges Montherlant's depiction of homosexual characters (30) and earlier explores his aristocratic heroes (17–26) but never connects the two, not even when he quotes the Pope accusing Malatesta, "You slept with your son-in-law Camerino when he was an adolescent" (23). Once again, pederasty becomes equated with homosexuality, a subject that was in itself unmentionable.

Nonetheless, what remained unspeakable did not necessarily remain unknowable. That Copeau failed to mention, even in his diary, the particular bent of *Nobody's Son* does not necessarily mean he did not, on some level, notice it. After all, Colette and Cocteau both guessed what Montherlant's obvious secret was, but neither seems to have articulated it explicitly: Colette (with characteristic irony) preferred to call it a "secret de polichinelle" while Cocteau talked around it in his private journal. That critics during and after the War avoided writing on the topic directly but hinted about it suggests that there was some need on their part to assure readers that the subtext that they sensed in the novels, essays, and plays was indeed present. Perhaps the best evidence that those talking and writing about Montherlant did have some knowledge about his sexuality may be glimpsed from the very little they said about it and the few questions they asked.

Conclusion

In truth, the unwillingness of various individuals to recognize what they saw reflects a larger societal dynamic. As noted in Chapter I, the Nazis believed that allowing men like Montherlant to maintain their authority in France would eventually lead to cultural decay from within; the Germans both knew about Montherlant's sexuality and protected him. And Vichy, which had tolerated Peyrefitte's indiscretions until they could no longer be ignored, went easy on Montherlant (in part because of the Germans) even when there was concrete evidence of his crimes. What in M. de Montherlant's writings persuaded the judge in Marseille to drop the charges against the author? No doubt many of the ideas his honor found in Montherlant's books echoed those of a good part of France herself. The author stood out as the conservative maverick he had fashioned himself to be. Indeed, the political implications of *Nobody's Son*, no matter how implausible its characters and plot, might easily be seen as provocative but also highly relevant. The judge, like much of the French public, was engaged by Montherlant and his works.

If Montherlant lost some of his popularity after the War, he nevertheless eventually gained entrance to the Académie Française. Such a reward not only sanctioned him culturally but legally: He no longer had to fear arrest while wandering the streets looking for prey. Yet in spite of his run-ins with the law and the substantial dossier that the Paris police had on him, M. de Montherlant had always been allowed to cruise alleys and cinemas. Not only the wartime regime but the post-Liberation government, which retained the Vichy sodomy laws, failed to end the practice of adult men molesting children, nor did the Fourth Republic work to eradicate what public acceptance there was of this practice. Hypocrisy may have been especially virulent under Vichy, but previous and successive regimes were hardly immune to the illness. The problem was cultural.

Nonetheless, Montherlant's point of view particularly suited occupied Paris. His idealization of masculinity and childhood, his glorification of sport and of war, his Nietzschean cruelty and contempt for women, all seemed consonant with fascist culture. And even as we must remember that Montherlant was perhaps most appreciated before the War and continued to be acclaimed well after it, the Occupation seemed to give Montherlant a unique opportunity to translate his personal experience to the stage. Both the Germans and Vichy found in him a right-wing voice from the past who might carry over into the new era. Vichy might frown on him privately but publicly the Comédie-Française, subsidized and censored by the French State, was proud to debut *Queen After Death*. The collaborationist reviewers, with a few exceptions, rather than completely dismissing *Nobody's Son*, praised what they could and in spite of their criticisms recommended the play.

Consciously, Montherlant had linked his message of individual integrity with pedophilia. He was clearly aware of (and no doubt took great delight in) the subversiveness of the script's underlying theme. Unlike Jollivet's and Cocteau's plays, *Nobody's Son* actively seeks to deliver its sexual-political message, though its delivery was intended to reach only a few. And while *Princess* and *The Typewriter* characterized and critiqued the dominant heterosexist culture, Montherlant's play wholeheartedly endorsed and glorified it. His ultimate goal, of course, was to depict the perpetrator as victim, the empowered as powerless.

"I, who so love childhood, find that childhood, through him, disgusts me," laments Georges Carrion about Gillou (210). Could the dramatist have been any clearer? Montherlant had little real interest in real children, whom he violated and of whom he eventually tired. It was a fantasy of childhood and nothing less than the cultural dream of the patriarchal world that he had internalized and learned (or to put this in his own terminology, chosen) to cherish. Did the idealization of childhood in fact precede and form his sexuality, or did his sexual compulsion for children find refuge in highly traditionalist ideals? I suspect both occurred and simultaneously. In any case, in a desperate move to feel in control of a destiny that appeared quite beyond his control, Henry Millon de Montherlant suffered terribly; yet he did so by making others—for the most part helpless others—suffer worse. Much of his writing attempted to justify their suffering.

8

The Politics of Impersonation:
Casting and Recasting Paul Claudel's
The Satin Slipper

Introduction

Changes in the cultural constructs of gender and sexuality during the Occupation years are reflected in the decline of the "trouser role." Although a few prominent nineteenth- and twentieth-century actresses had found acclaim through playing male protagonists, this stage convention waned after the Defeat; after the Liberation, it all but disappeared.

To a degree, at least during the Occupation, the roles themselves and the plays from which they came were partially to blame: Alfred de Musset's hero in *Lorenzaccio*, who rid Florence of its internal and external enemies, was far too subversive for Vichy and the occupiers. Likewise, Edmond Rostand's *L'Aiglon*, which depicted the captivity of Napoleon's heir in imperial Austria, perhaps suggested too many current political issues.[1] Both plays had been star vehicles for Sarah Bernhardt (Rostand's had been especially written for her), who declared that there were too few leading roles for women and that she was certainly great enough to play such heroes; in her lifetime, she played more than a score of male roles. Other women followed as male protagonists, including Renée Maria Falconetti and Marguerite Jamois.

Both Bernhardt and Jamois successfully appeared as Hamlet. Nevertheless, when the Comédie-Française mounted Shakespeare's tragedy, in March 1942, the title character was played not by a woman but by the company's Wunderkind, Jean-Louis Barrault. Barrault, even during the Occupation, was known less for his Vichy spectacles (*Eight Hundred Meters* had appeared at Roland-Garros the summer before *Hamlet* opened) than for his experimental stage work from the 1930s (which, along with his pro-Spanish-Republic

Numance, would incite profascist critics to condemn his work). Yet even as he, as director of *Hamlet*, had cast himself as the Prince, Barrault's interest in and sensitivity to issues of sexuality and gender remained acute: The use of male and female bodies in *The Suppliant Women* might have reified the traditional sexual roles that Vichy promoted and toward which it legislated, but at the same time the very palpable displays of human flesh turned the austere Aschylean drama into a sensual (perhaps for some even an erotic) spectacle that was curiously at odds with the philosophy of the play's prudish governmental benefactors.

Still, the production at the Comédie-Française for which Barrault would best be remembered was not *Hamlet* but Paul Claudel's *Le Soulier de Satin (The Satin Slipper)*. The premiere of *The Satin Slipper* late in November 1943 is regarded as one of the high points of French theatre under the German Occupation. Its long-awaited opening received mixed notices. In the collaborationist press, critics who hated conservative but anti-German Claudel and his avant-garde co-adaptor, director, and lead actor, Barrault, did not hesitate to castigate the production. After the War, some—including Merrill Rosenberg ("Vichy's Theatrical Venture" 139–140) and Patrick Marsh ("Le Théâtre . . ." 351–353)—would claim that the piece was pulled from the repertory in May 1944 because it was seen as a resistance play, a view that the condemnation of the French fascist press helps substantiate, as does the praise of Communist resistance reviewer Claude Roy (Joubert 324, 328). (In contrast, Marie-Agnès Joubert [322], in her insightful *La Comédie Française sous l'Occupation*, and Christopher Flood [18] blame the electricity shortages; Flood also offers an extensive exploration of how to locate Claudel between the seemingly polar opposites of collaboration and resistance.)

Yet amid the more conventional political controversies of the time, the production of *The Satin Slipper* was also the site of a more subtle conflict involving the stage representation of gender. This conflict emerged in performance, much as it did through many of the plays of the Occupation, indirectly. The years between when the script was completed (1924) and when the play, in a version "pour la scène," finally premiered (1943), widened the gap between its author's intent and its director's vision. Although spectators were aware of this disparity, they could only comprehend it within the context of the times. As a result, this landmark production has remained suspended not merely in time but in part in significance.

In the previous chapter, I discussed how Montherlant's notions about sexuality, which in present-day terms appear obvious (as well as repellant), managed to pass for, if not conventional cultural constructs, then at least for acceptably unconventional ones. That *Nobody's Son* was performed during the Occupation and in a theatre directly subsidized (and to some degree controlled) by Vichy and censored by the Germans, implied some acceptance of

Montherlant's point of view. The Nazis, who (like officials in Vichy) were well aware of the writer's obsession for boys, no doubt enjoyed watching him pollute the defeated French nation, but those critics who sympathized with the enemy and wrote for publications supported by German money, were on the whole deferential to Montherlant's plays, both the celebrated tragedy presented at the Comédie-Française and the smaller drama at the private theatre.

Yet Montherlant's ideas about the similarities between boys and women were not all that far from what traditional French culture (even as articulated by Vichy) had in some ways already accepted. Indeed, as farfetched as Montherlant's beliefs may seem to readers more than fifty years later, his writings, although thought to be provocative and controversial, were never regarded as completely outlandish. Montherlant's texts, while serving their own private purposes for their author, drew on and valorized several existing constructs of gender and sexuality that we have glimpsed from another angle and in a very different guise: The transformation of female to male, which historically in France begins with Joan of Arc, who donned manly attire to save the nation, clearly re-emerged during the Occupation in the stage characterization of Joan (in Claude Vermorel's *Joan Among Us* and in other works) and in Jean Anouilh's *Antigone* (and even, though briefly, in Jean-Paul Sartre's *Electra*). The cultural belief that a girl (never a woman) might assume a heroic role befitting a man (always a young man), materializes in the French theatre through the custom of allowing women—not ingenues but more experienced actresses—to play male juveniles. Joan, the heroine of France (both of Vichy and the Résistance) and Antigone (simultaneously approved by collaborationist critics and Gaullists), depict on stage what Bernhardt and Jamois actually did on stage. This connection is perhaps best embodied by Falconetti, who gained fame on stage as Musset's Lorenzo and on screen as Karl Dreyer's Joan of Arc.

In this chapter I examine the conventions of representation in the original staging of *The Satin Slipper*. My primary focus will be on the ways in which gender was enacted on stage: Claudel, in his text, provided one female characterization that called for cross-dressing, and Barrault, through cross-casting one of the male roles, occasioned another instance of it. There was also, implied in Claudel's script, a character that embodied the ambiguity of human sexuality, and Barrault did not shrink from fully representing this figure on stage. Thus, contrary to the representation of male and female in Barrault's double bill at Roland Garros, in which masculinity was incarnated as glorified beefcake and femininity through the absolute absence of masculinity, *The Satin Slipper* raised the possibility of one sex being somehow similar to the other.

While this possibility was implicit in *Joan Among Us* and *Antigone*, the act of impersonation—both dramatic and theatrical—was not. I choose "impersonation" deliberately: Indeed, *The Satin Slipper* contains much impersonation, not just examples of female actors impersonating male characters but also of French, and since the Comédie-Française had been purged of Jews, Aryan, or at least Aryanized,[2] actors impersonating characters of "other races." Although this production was not the last in which a woman would play the role of a man, it is perhaps the final instance for many years of the creative and significant use of such casting in France.

From Page to Stage

One reason that the first production of *The Satin Slipper* was so long-awaited is that the play was generally considered, and with good reason, unstageable. It had a huge cast and four extremely long acts, or as Claudel called them, "days," each consisting of numerous and often lengthy scenes. There was a heavy demand on lighting, sets, costumes, makeup, and special effects. Even if the play could be mounted successfully, there was the more serious issue of whether or not an audience could sit through all nine hours of it.

When Barrault first approached Claudel for permission to produce the script, the playwright remained adamant that it must be performed in its entirety and all in one sitting. Eventually, Barrault convinced Claudel that France needed the play and that they could transform it into a more workable text; once the play had been trimmed, reordered, and rewritten, Claudel even agreed to dividing the four-and-a-half-hour performance in half, allowing the audience a dinner break. Still, the progression of scenes, each with its own elaborate or fantastical scenery, the huge cast, and much of the characteristically "Claudelien" dialogue, in long poetic lines and with many monologues and soliloquies, posed a considerable obstacle to any director.

In the stage version ("pour la scène"), the plot remained as complex as in the original, perhaps even a little more so because of the removal of some of the scenes that were less important to the main action but which explained some of its arcane twists. To try to describe what happens in *The Satin Slipper* leads unavoidably to reduction, and yet I will endeavor to offer the reader some sense of what is commonly acknowledged by playgoers as "the story." Sometime in the sixteenth century, before the play opens, a soldier, Rodrigue, and a woman, Prouhèze, have met in Morocco, where Prouhèze lives with her husband, the elderly Spanish governor of the colony. The two instantly fall in love, but devout Prouhèze, faithful to her husband, is prevented from acting on her passion.

The play proceeds from the hero's and heroine's mutual but ungratified longing. Their conflict is articulated in the opening scene, in which Rodrigue's brother, a Jesuit priest adrift somewhere in the South Atlantic, prays that Rodrigue will be able to transcend his hopeless passion. In Morocco, Prouhèze is sent by her husband on a journey; she has been entrusted to one of his retainers and begs the man to protect her, not from others but from herself. We have seen her before leaving, in the garden, flirting with Camillo, a Moor who is much taken by her. Now, on the road, she pauses at a shrine and begs the Virgin to keep her from straying from the righteous path. She removes one of her slippers, vowing, "when I try to rush to evil let it be with limping foot" (23).[3] Rodrigue, trying to evade the King, who wishes to send him as Viceroy to the American colonies, has camped with his Chinese servant near the inn where Prouhèze is staying. The servant tells Jobarbara, Prouhèze's African maid, that Rodrigue has been badly wounded in a duel and that if he is to live, Prouhèze must find a way to see him.

Thus, dressed as a boy, Prouhèze escapes. As she makes her way alone, her Guardian Angel speaks with her. Though she implores him to keep her from going to Rodrigue, he is able only to make her aware of what she is doing. At one point, she falls to the ground, and the Angel places his foot on her heart:

THE GUARDIAN ANGEL
It would be easy to keep thee here if I would.

PROUHÈZE
(*very low*.) Rodrigo is calling me.

THE GUARDIAN ANGEL
Bring him that heart, then, on which my foot is planted.

Despite her misgivings, Prouhèze wishes to bring Rodrigue her entire self, not merely her heart, to give herself to him body and soul. "One cannot get this idea out of her silly little head," comments the Angel to Prouhèze's insistence that she belongs to her lover (57).

At the castle in which Rodrigue lies near death, his mother argues with Prouhèze's husband. He believes that it would be bad for his wife to see Rodrigue, but the mother desperately hopes that Prouhèze's presence will help in her son's recovery. In the end, Prouhèze is confronted by her husband: She is to be sent as governor to the fortress rock of Mogador, where she must protect the African possessions of the Spanish King. Although unwilling to go, she eventually leaves the castle without seeing Rodrigue. Months later, after recovering, Rodrigue sets out for Mogador, in spite of the King's command that he head for America. His approach to the fortress is greeted by canon fire, and when he finally enters the walls, he is greeted by Camillo, the Moor, who is captain under Prouhèze and who still longs for her. Camillo produces a note from Prouhèze: "I stay, you go" (118). Defeated, Rodrigue sails for the New World. Projected upon a screen, The Double Shadow, which represents in silhouette the single entity comprised by Rodrigue and Prouhèze, now protests that it is being torn asunder.

After a decade as Viceroy in Central America, Rodrigue has succeeded but still cannot conquer his desire for Prouhèze; she has remained at Mogador, where Camillo has become her husband, and she has given birth to a child. In a dream, Prouhèze hears Rodrigue on the other side of the globe, in Panama, calling her. Her Guardian Angel appears and tells her that she has been the bait with which God will eventually hook Rodrigue and that, through his intense love for her, Rodrigue will learn to love others. Across the Atlantic, a courtier gives the Viceroy a letter that Prouhèze sent years before, when Rodrigue left Europe. Now, aware that he must return for her, Rodrigue sails again for Mogador. In their only scene together in the entire play, Prouhèze, convinced that Rodrigue's soul cannot be saved without her own sacrifice, arrives on his ship: having married Camillo, she must return to the fortress, but she leaves their child in Rodrigue's protection.

So follows the main action up to the Fourth (and final) Day, which was cut from the performance script except for the last scene, in which a ruined Rodrigue, ten years later, is held captive on a small boat. Afraid that his adopted daughter, Mary Sevenswords, the child whom the now dead Prouhèze left with him, has drowned trying to escape their captivity, he allows himself to be sold into slavery to the nuns of Saint Teresa. He is content to let himself be used to build convents for this new holy order, but when Rodrigue arrives on the nuns' boat, he hears the happy news that Mary has survived.

Although this synopsis is faithful to the principal plot, there are many additional and connected subplots involving a host of other major characters. Even the cut version of The Satin Slipper presents a plethora of scenes that on the surface appear digressive, even trivial, yet they illustrate how significant even the smallest actions by seemingly irrelevant characters do contribute to what happens. Some of what was cut—scenes from the first three Days and the bulk of Day Four—is explained by a narrator character, an Announcer devised by Claudel in the original full-length text but greatly expanded "pour la scène." The Announcer directly addressed the audience, referring in his speeches not just to the play and its story but to the ordinary events of daily life that spectators experienced in these last days of the Occupation. Although the entire play would take more than nine hours to perform, the cut version was still long. In a sense the duration, along with the large number of characters and many diverse settings, helped preserve the vast scope that Claudel had tried to depict: The work aspires to nothing less than a universal perspective.

Implicit in the text is Claudel's deeply reverent and yet highly peculiar Christianity. The wide perspective is both Catholic and catholic, and themes already familiar to the pious abound: All is included in God's plan, we are all connected spiritually, suffering makes us better people, in spite of our earthly lives we must ultimately defer to heaven, and true love between man and woman makes of them one flesh. At the same time, the almost tortuous romance throughout the play and the intense longing of each main character for the other remain central. The immaterial but nonetheless tangible figure of The Double Shadow thus becomes a vivid image of gender, and of sexuality as well, that for the audience may well transcend and contradict the intended Catholic message.

Moreover, while Claudel's original version was highly theatrical, the revision for performance heightened its use of spectacle. Barrault, through production, added even more. His interest in engaging the human body in "Total Theatre" was evident as early as 1935 with *Autour d'une mère* (his adaptation of Faulkner's *As I Lay Dying*). On an empty stage, the actors (scantily clad) became the scenery "through physical language, miming the sun, a river, rain, the flood, fire, buzzards, fish, a city, the circulation of traffic" (Brown 385). Similarly, in *The Satin Slipper* Barrault used his players' arms and legs as the brambles that separated lovers and made their entire bodies undulate as the waves carrying ships out to sea. The production was, moreover, rich in explicitly physical imagery. There was the scene (in Day One) in which Prouhèze's African servant, Jobarbara, danced with bare breasts in the moonlight, and in the tableau that closes Day Two (as well as Part I in the stage version), the Moon herself appeared to be nude. The glamorous costumes, many of them fantastic and carnival-like, as well as revealing, along with the appearance of nakedness, led critic Jacques Berland to compare the play's visual images to what one saw at the Casino de Paris, the Folies-Bergère, and the Folies-Wagram.[4] To those, like the eternally noxious Alain Laubreaux, who claimed to be devout worshippers, if not of God, then of the Comédie-Française, such theatre was sacrilegious.

Therefore, while *The Satin Slipper* articulately preached to the converted, the imagery in Claudel's script and the spectacle of Barrault's staging invited others who were not among the faithful to glimpse the world incarnated in images that swelled with eros. The play might be viewed as a religious vehicle, but it equally conjured up a far more carnal dimension of the world. Indeed, like many of the successes of the Occupation, *The Satin Slipper* offered its audiences an intensely ambiguous and problematic stage experience.

From Stage to Audience

Even by 1949, with the advent of postwar feminism, the sexual ambiguities and problems of the 1943 production of *The Satin Slipper* lay beyond what might be addressed. One of the more literate and sensitive viewers of theatre during the war, and a writer who learned during the Occupation first-hand what it meant to be a French woman, seemed unable to grasp just how ambivalent a playwright Claudel actually was. Simone de Beauvoir, in *The Second Sex*, declared, taking the original printed text as one of her primary examples:

> Claudel does no more than express poetically the Catholic tradition. . . . Venerating woman *in God*, men treat her in this world as a servant, even holding that the more one demands complete submission of her, the more surely one will advance her along the road of her salvation. . . . To sanctify this ranking in the name of the divine will is not at all to modify it, but on the contrary to intend its eternal fixation. (231)

Yet the same Beauvoir a decade later, in *The Prime of Life*, remembered in very different terms the performance of 1943:

> We had objected to a good many things in [*The Satin Slipper*] when we read it a few years before; but we had admired Claudel for successfully containing heaven and earth in a love affair. . . . The show . . . lasted for over four hours, yet it held us absolutely breathless. . . . . . . I was captivated by [Marie Bell's] speaking voice: she encompassed all Africa and the Americas, the desert and the oceans, in her vocal range; she seared one's very heart. Barrault was a frail Rodrigo indeed beside this burning bush. (564)

What had made this production of so "sexist" a drama so appealing? How would Beauvoir have justified her inconsistent responses? Although capable of making such discriminating and contradictory remarks, Beauvoir never reconciled them.

Beauvoir, however, might have admitted that the play she *saw* was different from the one she had read (and which she and Sartre had "objected to"); the play in performance was, according to her memoir, dominated by its mighty heroine, Doña Prouhèze, personified by Marie Bell. The pre-eminence of this female figure was made all the more emphatic, first, by the stage script's cutting of Day Four of the original text, in which Rodrigue must live on without Prouhèze, and, second, by the larger-than-life acting of its star.

Bell, in performance style, belonged to a line of Comédiennes whose training was (by modern standards) almost operatic. Like Rachel and Bernhardt, she was a member of that sorority of vocal sorceresses who could command the vast stage and auditorium in the house of Molière. If, as Beauvoir comments, Barrault's Rodrigue was "frail" in comparison, his frailty was in part due to his own acting background, which had been developed in the studio of Charles Dullin and in much smaller houses and which differed from the broad grandeur of classical French tradition.

In his role as director, Barrault did curtail a particular aspect of Prouhèze's character, one that in fact was implicit in Claudel's original script. He sought to suppress what Frederick Brown calls, "the bisexual nature of a heroine modeled on Saint Joan" (435); the reference here is most pointedly to Scene XII of Day One, in which Prouhèze, having donned boys' clothing to escape her husband's protectors, encounters her Guardian Angel. Indeed, Beauvoir recalled, "Marie Bell in male attire I found embarrassing: I had imagined Doña Prouhèze as endowed with more boyish charm" (*Prime* 564). One implication here is that Bell's style of performance could not in 1943 accomplish the sort of transcendence over gender that such roles, which had been part of the French theatre for centuries, required. The diva simply did not make a credible boy.

Yet the more obvious attempts at impersonation, which were never completely "successful" (perhaps the point was less to convince the audience that Prouhèze could pass as a male than to make clear that she was trying to do so), point, in consonance with the extensive theatricality throughout the production, to Barrault's principal object of interest even in this highly didactic and devotional work: theatre itself. What preserved Barrault's reputation after the war was, in large part, the notion that he had not been interested in the philosophy of his Vichy employers, merely in working with and on their stages. Jean Cocteau and Sacha Guitry, among others, would be remembered in the company of Germans, at the Ritz, at Maxim's, at the German Institute, at theatre and art openings; Barrault would be remembered being busy at his craft.

The hallmark of Barrault's wartime work was its clear meta-theatricality. Beauvoir and Sartre had followed Barrault's career, and though he was "a frail Rodrigo," they were drawn to his innovative staging and his "wonderful medley of styles" in *The Satin Slipper*. The use of actors' arms to portray the sea was "a happily inspired borrowing from Chinese theatrical convention." At the same time, Beauvoir observes that some of the many sets were depressingly conventional and concludes, "We walked out afterwards asking each other what line [Barrault] would ultimately decide to follow" (564).[5]

For Beauvoir, then, as for many others, the author of the first production of *The Satin Slipper* was just as much its director as its dramatist. Beauvoir's disdain for Claudel himself ("Ever since he had written his 'Ode au maréchal' we had found him utterly sickening" [564]) is counterbalanced by her clear respect for Barrault as an artist. It may seem odd that although she was one of the major proponents after the War of *engagement*, Beauvoir seemed able to sustain an appreciation of art for art's sake. Her judgment of Henri-Georges Clouzot's *Le Corbeau*, a film based on the same incidents that inspired Cocteau to write *The Typewriter* and which many read as an act of collaboration because it was made for a German-funded film company and appeared to denigrate life in the provinces, sounds remarkably apolitical: "We ourselves did not feel that *Le Corbeau* carried any moral message; on the other hand, there seemed no reason for it to arouse patriotic indignation. All we noted was that Clouzot had talent" (565). Personal loyalties also counted in such a critique: When Simone Jollivet, whose wartime political sentiments Beauvoir deplored, came (along with Dullin) under attack after the War, Beauvoir rose to defend her.

Playing the Other

The company of the Comédie-Française possessed renowned impersonation skills. In fact, as noted earlier, all roles in the cast of *Le Soulier* had to be performed by actors who, according to Vichy law, were Aryan. Thus Asian, African, and Semitic characters were represented by certifiable Frenchmen or -women. (The one Jewish character in the original script appeared in Day Four and thus had been cut with the rest of the act.) The actress appearing as Prouhèze's African maid, Jobarbara, for instance, wore heavy dark makeup, while Rodrigue's Chinese servant and Japanese secretary were painted yellow and had, thanks to pencil, slanting eyes; Don Camille, Prouhèze's Islamic husband, with the aid of putty and pancake, resembled a Moor.

Reviews of the 1943 production of *Le Soulier* reveal that some of these portrayals were considered convincing. Julien Berthau, claimed a skeptical Jean Sylvain in *L'Appel*, was surprisingly realistic (63) as the farcical Chinese. Yet photos of Berthau as the servant betray to present-day viewers that his make-up was in keeping with Claudel's conceptualization of the role itself, which, like the comical "Negress" Jobarbara, was demeaningly farcical and highly stereotyped—a racist caricature. In contemporary terms, these impersonations may have been construed as credible, but they still remained stagy: the European, who was playing the "foreigner," was always peeking out from behind the exotic mask. The same might have been said of Bell as Prouhèze masquerading as a boy, yet the mask that Bell provided Prouhèze was far less diverting and convincing.

Although Beauvoir clearly remembered Scene XII in Day One and Bell's unsuccessful impersonation, she fails to mention the other actor on stage at the same time. The Guardian Angel, whose first appearance comes in this scene, was in fact played by Mary Marquet, a pensionnaire then in her late forties, who was well known as a tragedienne with a stately figure and a great voice.[6] Claudel had apparently objected to this cross casting: The Angel was male, and he had written the part for a man. In fact, when the casting was first submitted to the playwright, in February 1943, the company had double-cast this one role, with Marquet and a younger male actor, Jacques Dacqmine as Guardian Angel (Joubert 321, 410–411n). Eventually, the handsome Dacqmine, whom some (including Cocteau) felt had been brought in as a replacement when Jean Marais had left the company, was reassigned (as I mention later), and so in the actual production only Marquet appeared as the Angel.

The cross-dressing scene itself is of particular interest, not only because of the way the Occupation production had been cast and acted, but because it becomes pivotal to the main plot. On a narrative level, Scene XII suggests, through the Angel's arguments with the heroine, heaven's view of Prouhèze's flight. More profoundly, however, as the Angel hints at his own similarity to Prouhèze, the scene sets up an analogy of sorts: The Guardian is to the travestied heroine as Prouhèze herself ought to be to Rodrigue. This analogy is later reiterated in Day Three, when The Angel explains that Prouhèze has been used to hook Rodrigue—the fishing imagery is especially appropriate both for its Christian undertones and for its place in the context of the play itself, so much of which is set near or on the seas. Indeed, Barrault's staging of the water, as a literal ocean of humanity, realized Claudel's symbolism.

Of course, what The Guardian Angel tells Prouhèze about angling for Rodrigue easily falls into what Beauvoir viewed as the height of Claudel's misogyny. In *The Second Sex* she notes:

> *Le Soulier de Satin* is the epic of Rodrigue's salvation. The drama begins with the prayer that his brother addresses to God in his favor; it ends with the death of Rodrigue, whom Prouhèze has led into sanctity. . . . [H]er mission is within her, and, accomplishing the salvation of a man or serving as an example for him, she accomplishes in solitude her own salvation. (230)

Woman is thus subordinated and dedicated to service "to children, husband, home, estate, Country, Church—this is her lot, the lot which the bourgeoisie has always assigned to her" (231). Even in their first encounter, The Angel's remark, "One cannot get this idea out of her silly little head," smacks of male condescension. In Beauvoir's terms, the intervention of the Guardian supports the Claudelian view, which, although it appears to differ from traditional Catholic belief, in reality sanctifies the ranking of man over women and "intend[s] its eternal fixation" (231). But in the first production The Guardian Angel's lines were spoken not by a male but by a woman playing a male. Barrault had, for perhaps the first time on the stage of the Comédie-Française, counterpoised a female actor who was playing a female character who is impersonating a male with a female actor who was impersonating a male character. He thus called into question the very act of impersonation that is the essence of acting and at the heart of stage representation.

In the scene in which Bell, as the cross-dressing Prouhèze, and Marquet, as the male Guardian Angel, first meet, Barrault's staging thus problemitizes what others might hear as simple male chauvinism in the script. If the Angel were acted by a male, the portrayal of the role becomes consistent with the sexist theme that women exist to submit to men. Yet, uttered by a woman playing a male, lines that might otherwise support this theme are delivered to the audience in a very different manner. When, for example, Marquet spoke the line, "One cannot get this idea out of her silly little head," spectators could suddenly hear it not simply as typically masculine ridicule of women, for it was articulated by a woman, albeit one who was impersonating a male, to another woman, who was incidentally impersonating a woman who was also impersonating a male. There was now the dimension of irony, of ambiguity, and the opportunity for interpretation. On some level then, audience members were offered complications in receiving the message that Claudel hoped to transmit; the playwright's preference for Jacques Dacqmine as The Guardian would have come from his desire to preserve his intended significance. In Barrault's production of *The Satin Slipper*, that intended significance was complicated.

The critics' responses reflected their own ambivalence about Marquet's casting and about the production as a whole. On the positive side, some, like Roland Purnal in *Comœdia*, commended her strong presence, while others, like Charles Méré in *Aujourd'hui*, praised her voice or, like Maurice Rostand in *Paris-Midi*, her diction. Armory in *Les Nouveaux Temps* found her black costume and mask-like face sent out shivers, and François Ribadeau Dumas in *Semaine à Paris* called her "a very beautiful black angel." The photo of Marquet that ran with the review in *Vedettes* supported Jean Laurent's description of her: a Guardian Angel "as sombre as the night." On the negative side, there was (as usual) Alain Laubreaux. In *Le Petit Parisien* he called the cast "machines for declaiming" and found Marquet (along with Barrault himself) the worst. He restated this sentiment in his much longer review in *Je suis partout*, saying she spoke the Guardian Angel with the accent of a policeman. And in an extensive and overly critical review printed in the artbook serial, *Hier et Demain*, François Le Grix complained that Marquet was dressed up like Mephisto: "In such a costume there is a determinism which does not allow the actor the liberty of her talents" (166).[7]

Implicit in all the criticism, both positive and negative, is the belief that Marquet was clearly identifiable as herself throughout her performance. Indeed, the photograph accompanying the notice in *Vedettes* depicts her as a sombre, dark, and obviously female presence. No one complimented her on (nor complained about) her impersonation, as they did the actors playing the "non-Aryan" roles; the discrepancy between the gender of the actor and the gender of the character goes unmentioned. For the Occupation French audiences, watching an adult woman play a beautiful young man fell within a recognizable convention in which impersonation was no more significant than it was for American audiences watching an adult woman (Maude Adams, Jean Arthur, Mary Martin, or Kathy Rigby) play Peter Pan.

The convergence of the two conventions—the cross-dressing of a character and the cross-casting of an actor—mark a confrontation of different theatrical styles. Yet as Barrault proved, especially in this production, he was a master of incorporating varied styles within one frame and creating from them something strikingly new.

Conclusion

Claudel had conceived the image that symbolizes the unity of the doomed couple: The Double Shadow, whose singularity is wrenched apart by the separation of Prouhèze and Rodrigue, appears in his original script. The Shadow, a single figure composed of two figures, recalls both Plato's double-creatures in the *Symposium* and his descriptions in the *Republic* of life as shadows cast upon a cave wall. While the Platonic associations serve Claudel's Christian theme and supposedly bolster his championship of heterosexuality, The Double Shadow carries with it a certain ambiguity. As brought to life on stage by Barrault, the ambiguity became highly noticeable.

I noted earlier that Jacques Dacqmine, the company's replacement for Jean Marais, was initially cast to alternate in the role of The Guardian Angel with Mary Marquet and that he was recast sometime before the actual opening. My photocopy of the program[8] of this production lists him in the role of Almagro, a minor character. Yet, a notice in *Comœdia* on November 15, 1943 reveals that he also appeared as the "body" of The Double Shadow—that is, his body was the one projected onto the screen to form this figure—*and* that Mlle L. Conte spoke The Double Shadow's voice.

Few commented on the image; in his largely negative review in *L'Oeuvre*, Jean-Michel Renaitour reported that at the moment the projected shadow began to draw apart, he could see a pair of woman's arms detaching from the silhouetted form (which he regarded as yet another instance of stage gimmickry). Yet this casting is significant: The juvenile and the ingenue are actually combined into a unique figure that incarnates human love. Love itself appears bisexual or ambisexual, transcending sexuality by incorporating it entirely. Before its disembodiment into male and female components, human love was personified through that which, in part, characterized the glory of Joan and the heroism of Antigone. The figure—in lieu of the character of Prouhèze—corporally represents a concept about gender that would fade after the Liberation.

After the War, with what came to be called "The Consecration of Paul Claudel," literary critics would proclaim the author the great Catholic playwright and *Le Soulier* his wartime gift to France. Yet, during the Occupation itself, in this era when many of the values of the Church were supposed to have been incorporated directly into the state, *Le Soulier de Satin* had proven very problematic. Only when France had once again become La République Française were commentators and reviewers able to appreciate Claudel's dramas for what the playwright presumably had wanted them to be. Jacques Guicharnaud, for example, insisted that Claudel's "works are didactic—not demonstrations but pure and simple affirmations" that operate for a Catholic audience as "the only true explanation" of the world. In spite of Guicharnaud's assertion that "faith does not allow of discussion" (67), drama certainly does. Indeed, one reason that drama was expelled from the church was that it was too difficult to regulate: Even the simplest faithful allegories gave rise to dangerous implications. All the same, to imagine a script as long and as convoluted as *Le Soulier* as a "simple" anything is not easy. To regard the message of this play as something other than the work in totality—to privilege those pieces of it that heavily promote the Church's prescribed constructs of sexuality and to discount all others—is to ignore the greater part of the play. The model of reception implicit in Guicharnaud's statement (and which coincides with Beauvoir's in *The Second Sex*) overlooks the complexity of the playscript.

Response to *Le Soulier* was politically motivated both during the Occupation and after the Liberation. Laubreaux's attacks on Claudel and Barrault were grounded in his fascist beliefs, but then Beauvoir's condemnation also stemmed from an ideology—from postwar feminism. In her wake, others have tried varied approaches to make sense of Claudel's contradictory figuration of women. "In every [play]," notes Jacques Lefebvre philosophically, "woman seems created for man, but in order to inflame in him a sorrowful desire" (57), as if to make consistent the ambivalent portrayal of sexuality. Michel Malicet's careful Freudian analysis imposes the logic of psychology upon the uncomfortably paradoxical: "le '*mystère*' du personnage fèminin" is solved through the "explications dans la théorie psychoanalytique" (120). Dominique Millet-Gérard, through a Marxist-inspired vocabulary proposes, "la feminité claudelienne est essentiellement double et révèle son sens le plus profond à travers une dialectique spirituelle qui transcende la singularité des 'rôles' " (17). In all three instances, critics deploy sophisticated means to harmonize what seems to them a distinct thematic dissonance.

Bettina Knapp, one of the very few to note an apparent discontinuity between written and performance texts, grounds her conclusions in a psychological discussion of the author: "Claudel's theological ideas are apparently an outgrowth of his inability to reconcile his sexual drive with his spiritual values" (*Paul Claudel* 140). "Yet," she continues, "as produced by Barrault, and when viewed symbolically as a dramatization of a vital theological problem, it neatly sets forth Claudel's viewpoint" (140–141). The most troubling word here, perhaps, is "neatly": In the end, Knapp agrees with Guicharnaud that Claudel is a successful (and "simple") "message" playwright.

The 1943 production of *Le Soulier* both promoted and denied Doña Prouhèze as heroine. Marie Bell's Prouhèze, unlike Antigone and Jeanne d'Arc, remained "all woman." The "bisexual nature of a heroine modeled on Saint Joan," as Brown puts it, might have led spectators to the notion that Prouhèze transcended sexuality and called into question the constructs solidified by the occupiers and by Vichy. Instead, Mary Marquet stepped into the male role of The Guardian Angel and thus blunted some of Claudel's idiosyncratic justification of male supremacy. Indeed, Beauvoir and other critics might have argued that Barrault's own wilting performance as Rodrigue also dampened the ultimately orthodox notions of sexuality to which Claudel subscribed. And the curious Double Shadow, with its final division into antithetical opponents, prefigures the postwar abandonment of cross-casting.

One of Barrault's contributions to the changes regarding who played what was to eclipse Mme Sarah as Hamlet after the Defeat; it was his amazing debut as a sociétaire. And while his staging of *The Satin Slipper* may have explored sexuality through casting, it never completely challenged Claudel's ideas of what constituted male and female. At best, Barrault mitigated Claudel's notions of sexuality but at a great cost: The device of the trouser role, of both the travesty written as part of the character and the travesty caused by casting a woman as a male, was virtually nullified as a meaningful theatrical convention after the War.

In the first season after the Peace, Marguerite Jamois would play Lorenzo as "the Maquis member, the resistance fighter who mixed with the occupiers in order to seize their secrets and plans and deliver them to his own chiefs" in an act of " 'engagement' " (Gastinel 352). But the actor whose postwar portrayal of Lorenzo would be remembered most was Gérard Philipe, who passed in life for the character whom Musset created. No longer would French audiences watch actresses move easily into male roles.

The waning of female-to-male cross-casting in French theatre is an indication of how deeply the Occupation influenced the major tenets underlying French culture. Barrault's staging of *The Satin Slipper* illuminates a moment when the great interpreter of the great playwright in the great theatre of France pulled back from what had come to be an accepted stage practice; thus, in his own small way and no doubt quite unknowingly, Barrault helped reconfigure French notions of gender in order to make them consonant with the constructs upheld in Nazi Germany.

Epilogue

Catching *The Last Métro*:
François Truffaut's Portrayal of Occupation Drama and Sexuality

Perhaps the best known representation of the Occupation stage, François Truffaut's 1980 *Le Dernier Métro* (*The Last Métro*) is, like most movies, composed of a series of erasures, reinscriptions, and constructs. Rather than re-create the past, the director and screenwriters (knowingly or unknowingly, but in either case, inevitably) deploy dramatic and cinematic conventions to forge a world, based on the wartime theatre culture of Paris, as background for a love story. Nonetheless, as almost always happens, audiences tend to (mis)take filmed fiction for fact and to confuse that which has been invented for that which was or is real.

This observation about *The Last Métro* derives, at least in part, from the ongoing discussion of how the French, through the intervention of postwar politics, have come to regard the Occupation. As noted in chapter 5, after Paris was liberated, the French view of the Occupation was guided by Charles De Gaulle and notable historians and journalists (among them Robert Aron): The "resistancialist myth" held that France had been a nation of resistors. Indeed, the very use of the term "Occupation" conveyed the notion that France had been the (defiant) victim of the Nazi occupier. However, with Marcel Ophuls's *The Sorrow and The Pity* and Robert O. Paxton's careful inquiry into the Vichy regime, this view began to change; more and more frequently, the name of that place where Pétain and his government established themselves appeared in the titles of works about that period between the Defeat and the Liberation. "Vichy" came to stand for the idea that France, on the whole, had not resisted and that the regime that strove to represent the French was in itself both an entity that collaborated with the Germans and that actively pursued its own fascistic agenda.

191

Thus, in a political analysis of postwar films about the Occupation, Naomi Greene asserts that *The Last Métro* suffers from this "Gaullist vision of the Occupation that came under scrutiny in the 1970s," and thus, the Occupation, she insists, figures in the film largely as an exotic, and at the same time a familiar, setting, almost at times as mere backdrop, and as "a source of conventional images" (292). Thus, charges Greene, through its romanticization, the film represses genuine memory of the Occupation, replacing it with romantic images gleaned from Hollywood movies and trivializing the period's more significant problems (291–292). Perhaps most tellingly, Greene observes, except for the film's villain, a collaborationist drama critic, all the characters involved in the French theatre are depicted as anti-German. This last aspect of the film strikes Greene as especially ironic, for the theatre, she writes, was "a world hardly noted for courage and resistance during the Occupation" (293).

Although Greene quite soundly identifies Truffaut's nostalgia and romanticism in his portrayal of the Occupation and presents a convincing critique of what at least appears to be the film's political grounding, her very discussion of *The Last Métro* emerges as equally, if not similarly, biased. Her remark about the French theatre world during the War—"hardly noted for courage and resistance during the Occupation"—betrays a tendency perhaps as reductive as resistancialism: Rather than subscribe to the myth that the French were at heart a nation of resistors, she appears to regard collaboration as the paradigmatic mode of French (or at least of French show people's) behavior; indeed, her evaluation even hints that this new myth has for some replaced the one propagated by DeGaulle. And although Greene may be right in her criticism of the film, her conclusions about Truffaut and his intentions ultimately simplify a work whose implications are far more problematic.

I do not wish to focus directly on the more conventional political implications of *The Last Métro*; others have done so and certainly will continue to do so. Instead, I seek to examine what the film makes of the Occupation theatre and of its dramatic repertory, in order to consider how Truffaut (re)presents the role of the stage during this bleak period and how he makes the staged performances relevant to constructs and reconstructions of Occupation sexuality.

Indeed, if *The Last Métro* on the surface seems to be a film about "France résistante," on a deeper level it raises some serious and difficult questions about the cultural role of dramatic spectacle. The film depicts the fictive story of actress Marion Steiner (Catherine Deneuve), whose refugee, Jewish husband, Lucas (Heinz Bennent), has supposedly left Paris, and follows her efforts to mount a stage production at the Théâtre Montmartre. Unknown to all except Marion, Lucas has actually remained in Paris, hidden in the theatre's basement, and through his wife (who in turn works through

Jean-Luc Cottins, the stand-in director), he is able to direct the play, a drama entitled *La Disparue* (in English, something like *The Vanished Woman*). During the course of the production, Marion falls in love with her co-star, Bernard Granger (played by Gérard Depardieu), who eventually leaves the cast to join the Résistance full time. As the Occupation ends, the film draws away from the characters' story, widening to a documentary-like narration about what happens to the characters, and then concludes with a deliberately ambiguous scene, that calls attention to the differences between art (in this case, drama and theatre) and life. Even while the film's spectators may relish both the film's intriguing fictive inventions and the abundance of period detail, they may notice, in the very play that lies at the center of the world depicted, an apparent weakness, what seems (at least at first glance) to be a bland core where the very heart of the screenplay logically ought to be.

Like Lucas and Marion Steiner, Bernard Granger and the Théâtre Montmartre, the play-within-the-film has been invented by screenwriters François Truffaut, Suzanne Schiffman, and Jean-Claude Grumberg. Similarly, in order to convince the film's audience that a real full-length dramatic work is being rehearsed and performed, the authors have created *La Disparue* as a series of small sketches—mere fragments of scenes—around which much of the action of *The Last Métro* revolves. Like the film-within-the-film in *Day for Night* (*La Nuit américaine*), the alleged *Meet Pamela*, also glimpsed only in small pieces, *La Disparue* has been deliberately made to seem, if not vapid, then largely conventional, even predictable, especially in contrast to the depicted "life" surrounding the production of the "play."

La Disparue does appear to have a coherent storyline; I can sketch out a "plot" synopsis: Hélène (played by Marion) has been widowed and left with a young son. A tutor, Carl (played by Bernard), arrives to care for the boy and proceeds to solve the mysterious death of Hélène's husband. In so doing, Carl exposes Dr. Sanders (played by *La Disparue*'s homosexual director, Jean-Loup Cottins, who in turn is played by Jean Poiret), who has convinced Hélène that she herself has killed her husband but has, due to amnesia, been unable to remember the crime. Under the guise of protecting her, Sanders, the real murderer, has kept Hélène a prisoner in her own home. I offer this summary with caution, for there are only a handful of short fragments to suggest the "play" in the film, and these are presented out of order and with few strands of narrative.

Some critics manage to make sense of this indistinct core by regarding the fragments of *La Disparue* as "scenes from what looks and sounds . . . [like] a pretty bad play" that is somehow appropriate to its historical context: "racially impeccable," notes Julian Jebb (210); "trivial 'Norwegian' (i.e., Nordic, non-Jewish) or pseudo-Ibsenian," insists Geoffrey Hartman (823); "conventionally romantic," write Leonard and Barbara Quart, who add that "the play's banality is so powerful that it threatens to flatten the film" (137). Thus, concludes Richard Combs, "in its carefully abstract, non-political, Ibsenesque way, it might be a typical artefact of the Occupation" (136).

However, if we stop to consider, the little we see of *La Disparue* presents an extremely atypical example of Occupation drama. Far more recognizable and characteristic would have been (1) a comédie sans tickets; or (2) a revival (a very large proportion of the scripts staged during the period were reprises); or (3) a work that reflected the influence of classical myth, which was apparent in many new French works (such as Jean Anouilh's *Antigone* or Jean-Paul Sartre's *Les Mouches*) and in revivals of Greek tragedies (such as André Obey's translation of Aeschylus' *Les Suppliantes*) or foreign pieces (such as Gerhart Hauptman's *Iphigenia auf Delphi*); or (4) a script inspired by Spain's Golden age (such as Henry de Montherlant's *La Reine Morte*, Paul Claudel's *Le Soulier de Satin*, or Simone Jollivet's *La Princesse des Ursins*), or a revival of Caldéron or Lope de Vega, or even a foreign play on a Spanish theme (such as Schiller's *Don Carlos*). In addition, very much unlike these previously mentioned plays, many of which (even in the face of rationing and dire shortages) were produced in grandiose period style, *La Disparue* is austerely set and dressed in simple (though clearly stylized), early twentieth-century style.

Also quite atypically, this unpublished script produced at Lucas Steiner's Théâtre Montmartre has, we are told, been written by a Norwegian. Scandinavian plays, in spite of any claims regarding their racial purity, were in fact relatively rare. The more rebellious works written by the major Northern dramatists might not have easily passed the censors. Over the four years of the Occupation, the private theatres produced only four plays by Ibsen (*Maison de Poupée* at the Ambassadeurs, 1940–1941, *Les Revenants* at the Jeune Colombier and then the Œuvre, 1942–1943, *Solness le constructeur* at the Mathurin, also 1942–1943, and *Hedda Gabler* at the Montparnasse, 1943–1944) and just three by Strindberg (*Orage* and *La Plus forte* at the Poche and *Danse de la Mort* at the Œuvre, all 1943–1944). Indeed, the period witnessed only a few productions of Scandinavian drama perhaps because, in the highly charged atmosphere of the times, the majority of the works by the great "Nordic" playwrights probably seemed too politically and ideologically dangerous.[1]

Also rare during this period were works by female dramatists. As suggested in chapter 4, one of the more notable Occupation productions by a female playwright was the extremely obscure *Princesse des Ursins*, written by Charles Dullin's turbulent companion, Simone Jollivet (the notorious "Camille" of Beauvoir's *Force de l'Age*), and produced by Dullin in 1942 at the Théâtre de la Cité (née Bernhardt). In accord with Nazi and Vichy doctrine, women, though certainly permitted *on* stage, were not frequently encouraged as playwrights. Hence, *La Disparue*, the French translation of a supposedly unknown, early twentieth century, Norwegian drama, by a woman, is in many ways alien to the Paris theatre of the period that *The Last Métro* purports to represent and is an inappropriate candidate for "a typical artefact of the Occupation."

Another approach to understanding *La Disparue*—one that conscientiously avoids caricaturing or categorizing the "play" and tries instead to locate it in the film as a whole—is offered by Michael Kline and Nancy Mellerski. In discussing the structures of ambiguity in *The Last Métro*, Kline and Mellerski suggest that the play-within-the-film is intended, at least at first glance, to seem "an empty vehicle" and that the play's title, "*La Disparue*, to some degree speaks for the status of art, which in occupied France was permitted to have form but no substance" (92). To support this notion, Kline and Mellerski allude to a passage from Truffaut's introduction to a collection of the wartime writings of André Bazin, the great French film critic and Truffaut's mentor. Here are some of Truffaut's more significant and revealingly anti-resistancialist remarks on Occupation cinema:

> There was no place for subversion or protest in the film of this period; the sanctions imposed would have gone beyond the Commission de Censure. . . . It is therefore understandable that cinema took refuge in historical films and films of fantasy and enchantment. . . .
> . . . I cannot accept the sometimes espoused patriotic theory that the historical or fantasy films made during this period deliberately delivered a courageous message coded in favor of the Resistance. . . . (18–19)

Having agreed that Occupation films were devoid of subversive intent, Kline and Mellerski argue that in the world created by the film, where "incompatibilities . . . have become daily patterns of life" (94), "the seemingly bland dialogue of *La Disparue* can now take on a number of suggestive meanings in the context of the Occupation." They even propose that, as the film delivers a stronger sense of the highly ambiguous context surrounding the "play," this "vehicle," which they initially described as empty, suddenly begins to take on significance: "The play within the film," they tell us, "refers to the search for truth, to the presence of contradictory lies, to a heightened sense of unreality, and to selective historical amnesia," although they concede that meaning remains "elusive" and "problematic" (95). Thus, rather than regarding the play-within-the-film as some meaningless art-substitute, these critics suggest that the nonexistent "script" clearly reflects Truffaut's postresistancialist point of view, so clearly articulated in his comments on Occupation cinema.

Of course, *La Disparue* is not now nor ever really was a play. Truffaut's purpose is merely to represent a play, and this "play" is intended as a figure or series of figures that can in some way stand in for an Occupation theatrical drama (and/or for stage drama itself). Although Kline and Mellerski, as critics of the film, may not be able to refrain from interpreting *La Disparue*, the real reason that the so-called play itself remains so "elusive" and "problematic" is because it is not in itself meant to be interpreted as a play by those who watch the film. Indeed, the fact that it appears in obscure fragments, which are deliberately out of sequence, makes interpretation by those watching *The Last Métro* extremely difficult, if not impossible. Perhaps the only ones genuinely empowered to interpret *La Disparue* are those who actually get to see enough of the fictive play to make any sense of it, and these can only be the fictive audiences who are shown watching *La Disparue* in performances in the film (and whom I will discuss later in this chapter).

In any case, Truffaut's comments on the cinema of the Occupation, contrary to Greene's assertions, clearly challenge resistancialist assumptions. The probable reason Truffaut felt obliged to voice such a vehement denial of the "theory that the historical or fantasy films made during this period deliberately delivered a courageous message coded in favor of the Resistance," is that, as Evelyn Ehrlich observes in *Cinema of Paradox*, "the view that these films [like *Les Visiteurs du Soir*] were allegories [with resistance themes] became so commonly held" (215n17). This phenomenon parallels the one with which Truffaut had to grapple in *The Last Métro*. Even if it is true that the fantasy and historical films of the period were so strictly censored as to be incapable of transmitting subversion or protest, many of those who watched them during the Occupation remembered receiving from them "a courageous message coded in favor of the Résistance. . . ." Likewise, as Truffaut himself was very much aware, an even stronger view had pervaded postwar criticism of French drama: Although strict censorship by the German Propaganda Staffel and/or by the Vichy government carefully restricted what was performed on stage, many who had gone to the theatre before the Liberation insisted that the fantasy and historical plays that they had attended had intentionally transmitted messages of resistance; as noted earlier, Sartre's *Les Mouches*, Claude Vermorel's *Jeanne avec Nous*, and Anouilh's *Antigone* have at various times been viewed as intentionally proresistance and have continued to spark debate.

Still, Truffaut himself has left us little about the actual stage drama of the actual Occupation; would he have detected any more subversion or protest in the plays of the period than he had done in the films? In a 1981 *New York Times* interview, he admitted to Annette Insdorf that if the film had " 'come out a few years ago, it would have been attacked for being very tolerant of the characters and expressing sympathy for everyone, including those "show people" who continued to perform during the war. But now,' he added . . . 'since Mao's death, the invasion of Afghanistan, and the upheaval

in Iran, it's once again possible to accept the idea that life is paradoxical' "
(175). These comments suggest a move beyond the postresistancialist comments Truffaut made about Occupation cinema. Rather than accept the view
of Occupation theatre expressed by Greene and others, Truffaut appears at
least here to embrace the contradictions of the period, to accept the "paradoxical" nature of his subject matter. He seems more interested, perhaps, to
borrow the very words Kline and Mellerski use to explain *La Disparue*, in
"the search for truth, . . . the presence of contradictory lies, . . . a heightened
sense of unreality, and . . . selective historical amnesia."

Thus, the film itself never makes clear whether or not Truffaut believes
the French stage "delivered a courageous message coded in favor of the
Résistance." Rather, *The Last Métro* avoids this issue, most noticeably through
its depiction of *La Disparue* itself, which in its fragmentary form seems to
pre-empt interpretation, at least by the audience of *The Last Métro*, and which
in its rather stylized presentation quite literally pales beside the scenes in the
film that purport to be depicting the characters' "real" lives. It is almost as
if, on one level, Truffaut is telling the film's audience that the drama of
surviving the Occupation was far more interesting and meaningful than anything mounted on stage.

I will return to this discussion of the cinematic role of the play-within-
the-film but must first focus on the dramatic role of *La Disparue*. The very
name of the "play"—"disparue" a word that in French means not merely
"vanished" (and "gone," hence "dead") but also "missing," as in missing in
action—suggests a woman who is not there; of course, the most obvious
candidate is Marion Steiner. In another language, such as English, it might be
construed as relevant to the most conspicuous absentee, Lucas Steiner, who
is hiding in the cellar, but French makes it quite clear that this absentee is
female. Indeed, Marion Steiner plays the title role in the "play" and is thus
as central to *La Disparue* as Catherine Deneuve is to *The Last Métro*. (In fact,
one of Truffaut's goals in making the film, according to his own pressbook,
was apparently "to give Catherine Deneuve the role of a responsible woman"
[Insdorf 1989, 232].) Thus, though she appears throughout the film, Marion
is frequently absent, both literally, as Insdorf points out ("under the stage"),
and figuratively: Her aloofness is witnessed and remarked upon by a number
of characters, her reticence and withdrawal is called even by the smitten
Bernard (the saboteur résistant) "intimidating," and she is and appears not so
much present as preoccupied (with her subterranean husband). Perhaps on a
deeper level, Deneuve plays not just Marion but Marianne, the symbolic
image of La Belle France, which, Truffaut heavily implies, is what is most
conspicuously missing.

Of course, the "play" scenes relate in a variety of ways to the scenes
that depict the "actual lives" of the actor-characters. In scenes between characters from *La Disparue*, Hélène (acted by Marion) and Carl (acted by Bernard)

put into words the unspoken attraction developing between the two actors; Carl's remarks on Hélène's isolation (88–89) ironically express the growing distrust (of prisoner and keeper) between Lucas and Marion, and Carl's departure from the house echoes Bernard's decision to leave the production. Yet these intermittent signals point more clearly to the film's most striking similarity between art and life, the construction in both of a three-sided structure: Carl, Hélène, and Dr. Sanders in the former and Bernard, Marion, and Lucas in the latter. The link joining the hidden Lucas with the actor playing Sanders has been forged early in the film, when Jean-Loup is made the substitute director due to Lucas's sudden "departure"; through most of the script, only the audience watching *The Last Métro* and Marion know in fact that Lucas is listening to rehearsals from the basement and providing notes (allegedly written by Lucas before his departure) that Jean-Loup is following.

The use of this isosceles figure—male-female-male—ought to be familiar to those who have followed Truffaut's career. Its most memorable appearance in French film—perhaps in all of modern film—comes in *Jules et Jim* (1961), set in Paris just before the First World War, in which two best friends, one French (Jim), the other German (Jules), fall in love with the same woman (Catherine), only to be reunited after the war through death. More subtly drawn, however, is the triangle in Truffaut's first feature, *Les Quatre Cents Coups* (1959), in which young Antoine Doinel's mother is caught between her adolescent son and her new husband. (Perhaps this earlier autobiographical film gives a psychological clue as to the reason for the director's attraction to the novel on which the film *Jules et Jim* was based.) True, as Truffaut went on scripting and producing, the legs of the triangle became markedly feminine, as illustrated through the sequels to *Les Quatre Cents Coups*, *Baisers Volés* (1968) and its sequels, *Domicile Conjugale* (1970) and *L'Amour en Fuite* (1979), and in *Deux Anglaises et le Continent* (1971), in which Jean-Pierre Léaud (the actor who played Antoine Doinel in all four of these films) is also cast as the lover caught between two sisters. Yet *The Last Métro* reverts to the earlier triangle, perhaps because, like *Jules et Jim*, the 1980 film takes place during a major war, or because, like *Les Quatre Cents Coups*, it is set (at least in terms of the director-writer's own life) during the Occupation.

Early in her study, *Between Men: English Literature and Male Homosocial Desire*, Eve Kosofsky Sedgwick examines René Girard's *Deceit, Desire, and the Novel* and sums up one of the book's major themes as follows: "in any erotic rivalry, the bond that links the two rivals is as intense and potent as the bond of either of the rivals to the beloved," and the "bonds of 'rivalry' and 'love,' differently as they are experienced, are equally powerful and in many senses equivalent" (21). Sedgwick's description of the male-male bond within an ostensibly heterosexual love triangle is dramatized clearly in *Jules et Jim*, where the romantic love/death finale is consummated by the two men (whose names entitle the film) as well as by the heroine. Similarly, in *Les Quatre Cents Coups* the connection between young Antoine and his stepfather takes on primal, even Oedipal, significance. In *The Last Métro*, as noted earlier, the triangle is doubly inscribed, once in the "lives" of the characters who are putting on the play and again in the "play" itself. Although Marion, "Catherine Deneuve [in] the role of a responsible woman," appears to be at the center of both the film and the play-within-the-film, Bernard and Lucas, rivals for her attention and affection, are the active forces within one three-sided relationship, just as Karl (Bernard) and Dr. Sanders (Jean-Loup, Lucas's stand-in) are vying for Hélène.

This competitive link between the two pairs of men, or rather the two pairs of male characters, is especially interesting in consort with the film's more discernible development of notions of sexuality, especially in light of its depiction of homosexuality. In fact, *The Last Métro* constructs sexuality in a highly traditional way: men are dynamic and assertive while women bravely do what they can. Thus, Bernard, the heterosexual Frenchman par excellence, unknowingly flirts with *La Disparue*'s lesbian designer, Arlette, and after her sexual orientation has been revealed to him, explains, "I just wanted to be with her. I don't know why. It was like wanting a warm croissant" (106). This hunger seems to extend to other women too, to Marion, to the woman he brings to the nightclub, and even to Martine, the black marketeer who will soon steal from the cast and end up as paid informant at the German propaganda bureau. His vain struggle to bed the unresponsive Arlette—"I simply have to make it with this woman before the dress rehearsal!" (78)—reveals his own predictable homophobia: "I can't stand to have a man touch me," he tells her while he is being fitted for costumes, asking this unattainable woman to take his measurements (to which she laughingly replies, "What if I hate to touch men?") (86). Later, describing his attempt to reclaim his stolen bicycle, Bernard tells how the thief publicly accused Bernard of having molested him, at which point in shame and fear Bernard backed off (94). In spite of his omnivorous womanizing, however, Bernard is repelled by Nadine, the opportunistic young actress whose active seductiveness seems out of keeping with what a masculine young Frenchman ought to want.

Not only is Nadine aggressive in her sexuality, but she is also rather versatile: Marion somewhat disgustedly discovers Nadine exiting an embrace with Bernard's "warm croissant." Of course, we have already seen Nadine arriving late to a rehearsal, surrounded by Nazi soldiers in a German jeep; her opportunism (and herein perhaps lies what Truffaut calls his tolerance "of the characters and expressing sympathy for everyone, including those 'show people' who continued to perform during the war") is, quite naturally, the basis for her collaboration with anyone who will advance her career. Thus, she has also been speaking over the (presumably Vichy- or Nazi-subsidized) radio and auditioning for roles in film productions (which, as Truffaut has already told us, were not resistance vehicles). She is the only character who is not nauseated by the critic Daxiat, whose profascist, anti-Semitic views permeate his theatre reviews. Her mercenary opportunism is neatly expressed in a rather theatrical monologue (58), and rather than evoking sympathy for her, the speech, which ends with a reference to Sacha Guitry (whose activities were labeled collaborationist well before the War ended), brands Nadine as a collaboratrice.

If the sexually unorthodox actress is linked with the enemy, the behavior of the supposed director of *La Disparue*, Jean-Loup Cottins, seems somehow murky too. Cottins is a homosexual—we are no doubt invited to suspect this when, in an early interchange with Marion, he admits that the collabo critic, Daxiat, has called a recent staging of *Britannicus* "an effeminate production" (27). As the film progresses, we meet his live-in partner, Marc (a cross between stage manager and gofer, who goes on to play a walk-on in *La Disparue*). Simultaneously, our understanding of Jean-Loup and his sexuality is seemingly guided by a series of subtle signs. In the first scene between Marion and Lucas, Marion discusses why she prefers not to tell Jean-Loup that Lucas is in hiding: "He knows too many people. He goes everywhere, he talks, he fools around" (60).[2] Later in the same conversation, Marion remarks to Lucas, "I was very pleased to see that [Jean-Loup] is capable of getting angry." The film then cuts away to Marc picking up the telephone (Daxiat has called) in Jean-Loup's "handsomely appointed apartment" (62). Like the homosexual Jean Cocteau (who after the War would, like Jean-Loup, go through a series of arrests and releases for suspected collaboration), Jean-Loup seems to use drugs, apparently asking the little boy next door to the theatre (who will soon be cast as the child in *La Disparue*) to grow some marijuana seeds (or are they for poppies?); "soon," he tells Jacquot, "we'll have a smoke" (75).[3] Although he pragmatically tells Marion (as he says Lucas would have done), "Give the best seats to your enemies," Jean-Loup listens to (Nazi-run) Radio Paris (113–114). Significantly, it is Jean-Loup who deals with fascist Daxiat, on the phone and in person.

While Daxiat's sexuality remains obscure throughout the film, the predatory Nadine articulates what the audience might have already inferred: "Doesn't he like women, your Daxiat?" she asks Jean-Loup (68). The possessive pronoun only adds to our suspicions. Certainly the critic's appearance, fat, insolent, self-important, might indicate that he is asexual, but his affectations, his prissiness and delicacy, in spite of—or rather because of—his disdain of effeminacy, suggest that he is homosexual. Indeed, except for Arlette (who by the end, in fact, seems to have found work in a film starring Nadine), those who desire their own sex—male and female—are prone to collaboration with the Nazis. Such a connection, which Andrew Hewitt describes as "homo-fascism," "a recurrent conflation and/or association of homosexuality and fascism" (2), has been traditional from the 1930s onward. That it should appear in a Truffaut film about the Occupation ought to offer little surprise; much of this director's opus is consumed with his cinematic reinscription of heterosexual desire, which is portrayed with so much intensity and fervor that we might construe that he fears that if he fails to re-create reality in such colors, the world may emerge in tones of pink and lavender.

As must occur in trigonometric equations, the most important moment in *The Last Métro* is not the one in which Marion and Bernard consummate their relationship (which transpires in Bernard's tiny dressing room) but in the brief confrontation between Lucas and Bernard in the basement:

Lucas: That's that. They're gone until next time.

Bernard: Being shut up down here is no life.

Lucas: It is a life. It's my life.

Bernard: Couldn't a better hiding place be found, a safer one?

Lucas: I'm not looking for a hiding place. This is my home.
           And no one will make me leave. (153)

Their argument is about the nature of masculinity. Is the man who defensively hides and operates from afar any less of a man than he who joins the resistance and plants bombs, who opposes the prevalent anti-Semitism and avoids and later physically attacks the fascist critic? Certainly, *The Last Métro* depicts Lucas Steiner as brave, even foolish at times, in his desire to come out of the basement, and uneasy about being able to do so little. Even his wife's attempts to play a proper wife—in an appropriately feminine way, the great Marion Steiner descends to cook dinner for her husband, have sex with him, even cut his hair—amount to little consolation. Bernard, equally foolhardy but admirably idealistic (almost the doglike man for whom Agnès longs in Giraudoux's *Apollo of Marsac*), defines manhood in this film.

Some viewers, unaware of the stuff from which this film has been put together, might accuse Truffaut of inventing a variety of improbable events. Yet the director and screenwriters, who were children during the war and not immediately involved in the theatre, have done some research. One Occupation theatre and film celebrity, whose autobiography was published in 1975, seems to have inspired parts of the filmscript: Jean Marais, the companion of Jean Cocteau and a notable actor during the period. Jean-Loup's allusion to Daxiat's contempt for an "effeminate production" of Racine's *Britannicus* is in fact a reference to the production that Marais directed and in which he starred (although in 1944, not 1942). And when Arlette remarks to Jean-Loup that Daxiat "couldn't help us keep the epilepsy scene" (50), *The Last Métro* once again touches on Marais, whose epileptic seizure in Cocteau's *The Typewriter* was cut from the script by the censors. Although chapter 1 looks at this play and its rather violent reception, what appears to be the most unlikely scene in the film, Bernard thrashing Daxiat, is also drawn from Marais's brawl with the critic who in panning *The Typewriter* also slandered Cocteau's sexuality and by implication Marais's.

Similarly, we may recall, that peculiar name, "Daxiat," was the nom de plume for the collaborationist drama critic for *Je suis partout*: Alain Laubreaux continued to write theatre criticism throughout the war, but when his script, *The Pirates of Paris*, the only French play that explicitly glorified anti-Semitism, appeared at Théâtre de l'Ambigu, he signed himself Michel Daxiat.[4] Even in the captive press, reviews were negative, except in *Je suis partout*, in which Laubreaux gave a positive review to his own—that is, to Daxiat's—melodrama based on the Stavisky affair of the 1930s. It was Laubreaux (among others) who branded Marais's *Britannicus* effeminate and who had much earlier repeatedly made fun of Cocteau's homosexuality; thus, Marais assaulted Laubreaux outside a restaurant in the spring of 1941. Yet Laubreaux, unlike the fictional Daxiat, was not suspected of being homosexual. In fact, the Daxiat of the film seems more powerful than Laubreaux, perhaps a combination between the theatre reviewer of *Je suis partout* and its highly influential profascist editor (and sometime drama critic), Robert Brasillach, who was indeed accused by some of being a homosexual.

Thus, through the pretext of a heterosexual love story, Truffaut manages to stage a showdown between Bernard, the resistor (a well-intended terrorist and saboteur, an endearingly idealistic artist driven to clandestine heroism), and Lucas, the man in hiding (le disparu) who survives without fighting. At this level, perhaps Greene's notions about the resistancialist posturings of *The Last Métro* are not so far off the mark, except that the allegory of political ideology in the film is enacted with extraordinary simplification: We never have a clear sense of what motivates Bernard to fight for the resistance, whether he is a Communist or a Gaullist, a man driven by his own past or the past of France, or perhaps by his existentialist leanings. Just as *La Disparue* is a stand-in for a play, Bernard Granger is a stand-in for a resistor. He is more a movie character than a depiction of a person.

In other words, the ostensibly political face-off between the resistor and the man in hiding is in itself a pretext for the rearrangement of acts that conform better to Truffaut's sense of what life is really about. The collabo critic becomes gay. The deeds of the gay Jean Marais are reassigned to the straight resistor. Homosexuality is exposed as a collaborationist condition. The now powerless Lucas Steiner is represented in *La Disparue* by Jean-Loup, a homosexual actor/director, who is in turn represented by a Jean

Poiret, the man who created and starred in the stage version of *La Cage aux Folles*. The relationship between Jean-Loup and Marc is continuously depicted as a master/houseboy situation. Arlette is hypersensitive and so desperate for love that she would even consort with Nadine, whose perverseness has obviously contributed to her sleeping with the enemy. Contrary to what history might have taught him—and Truffaut had seen Ophuls's *Sorrow and the Pity* and thus knew of Denys Price, the drag queen who determined to prove himself man enough to resist the enemy—the director/writer of *The Last Métro* is drearily insistent that anyone varying from the sexual norm is suspect. And Truffaut's ultimate goal has less to do with portraying the German Occupation of France than with recasting events to conform with his own beliefs on the nature of sexuality.

Earlier, I differentiated between the dramatic role of the play-within-the-film and its cinematic role. Perhaps now is a good time to consider how staged drama (represented by *La Disparue* and also by the unnamed "play" that ends the film) figures in *The Last Métro*. Kline and Mellerski offer a way into such a discussion by focusing on those later scenes in the film when *La Disparue* (initially glimpsed in rehearsal) is shown in performance before an audience (95). But how these critics interpret this so-called play ("to the search for truth, to the presence of contradictory lies, to a heightened sense of unreality, and to selective historical amnesia") appears to say more about what *they* as critics see in the film, for their interpretation does not adequately account for what the play means to the various audience members whom we see, such as the Jewish seamstress and the fireman, the collaborationist critic Daxiat and the rows of German soldiers seated in the house. The film asks us to watch these and other spectators responding to something that we ourselves are incapable of judging and interpreting and to learn from this interaction—which, except for the evil Daxiat, who pans the play in hopes of gaining control of the theatre, seems deeply felt and appreciated by the theatre audience.

The audience of *The Last Métro* is prevented from "reading" *La Disparue* from the point of view of the play's audience: not only are we repeatedly kept from viewing enough of the play and seeing it in any logical (or chronological) order, but the play is never offered to us, as are the musical numbers in a traditional Hollywood backstage musical, directly, for our own appreciation. Unlike a dance number in a Busby Berkeley movie, for example, in which an allegedly theatrical scene places the cinema audience where the theatre audience would be thus privileges the moviegoers' point of view, the fragments of *La Disparue* are served up from a distance or from an angle, on a stage that is set with exaggeratedly sharp angles and painted muted, unusual colors—peach, salmon, and pink (119)—and with obviously stagy, though realistic, acting; in other words, the film's audience is repeatedly alienated in its attempts to become or even to identify with *La Disparue*'s audience.

Thus, the film audience must retreat and is perhaps only able to construe the little bits of *La Disparue* as relating to the events that occur in the "real world" of the film. As discussed above, connections between the "play" and the "lives" are most evident. Thus, the play-within-the-film tends to direct us not to itself but to the larger action in the fictive "world" created by the film; in this manner, and in conjunction with extensive references to numerous other films (from *La Règle du Jeu* to *Belle de Jour*),[5] *The Last Métro* comments on itself and announces again and again that it is a film.

And an awareness that this film is a film becomes important to understanding the film: As previously noted, although the plot is invented, much of the action is based on real events or rather actual incidents. Moreover, in spite of the extensive use of the studio soundstage (except for the scene in which Nadine rides in with les Boches, the entire film—even the supposedly "exterior" shots—seems to have been shot indoors), *The Last Métro*, with its wealth of details of sight and sound, bears a frightening yet studied and deliberate resemblance to genuine artifacts of the Occupation, such as the color photographs and phonograph records of the period. For the French, the period remains today, even as it did in 1980, when the film premiered, extremely problematic, a still volatile and highly partisan topic of debate. Perhaps for this reason the final scenes of *The Last Métro* attempt to distill the lessons on spectatorship that the film as a whole has struggled to express.

In the final scene of the film, we watch what we believe to be Marion and Bernard in what we are told is late in the summer of 1944. He is seated in a wheelchair in what appears to be a hospital ward; through windows we glimpse nurses and patients across a courtyard. From the plot of the film, we have construed that he has been injured while working in the Résistance. She tells him that she has given up everything now that "he" has died—and from this we are led to infer that she has abandoned her life in the theatre now that Lucas has passed away. Bernard, however, appears to reject her, and she pulls away to leave. Yet during the scene, the camera too has pulled back: the walls of the ward are suddenly shown to be flats, and the windows now look out on a painted scene; once Marion has gone and he has buried his face in his hands, stage curtains draw together, and the sounds of an audience applauding are heard. There is a curtain call, and along with Bernard and Marion, Lucas appears on stage.

So at the conclusion of the film, we are confronted by a deliberate turnabout, a cinematic trompe l'oeil, in which we first find ourselves, at least for a short time, tricked into occupying the place of the theatre audience and then suddenly estranged, yanked back to our roles as spectators of *The Last Métro*. One of the lessons reinforced here is that theatre performance (whether stage or cinema) necessarily relies on context and that without a clear knowledge of the context, we are bound to misinterpret. Another lesson, then, is that we spectators should defer interpretation or, more significantly, delay judgment until our sense of context is complete. Yet another lesson is that we, quite startlingly, as audience, may be more than capable of finding meaning whether or not such meaning may have been intentionally transmitted by the theatrical art object.

In this way, Truffaut is able to suggest a great deal. First, the film implies that for one to judge the film without having a clear sense of the ambiguities and complications of the Occupation is a gross simplification (just as judging the Occupation without a clear sense of its complexity is insufficient). Second, the film seeks to expand the viewer's sense of the world of the Occupation, rather than to delimit or close it, to encourage further exploration, and to pre-empt or at least postpone a final black-and-white judgment. Finally, rather than delineate just how far the French theatre of the period went toward delivering a coded message of resistance, *The Last Métro* insinuates that whatever the capability of the theatre of the time to send such messages, audiences were certainly eager to receive them—so eager that they were perhaps capable of seeing things that we might deny were ever there (although by the end of the film, we ought to know better).

For Truffaut the affective fallacy is not apparent. What the author (in this case, the auteur-director) intends is clearly determinable and, moreover, distinct from what the audience makes of the author's work. Ironically, as Truffaut himself confessed, when Michel Mardore in *Le Nouvel Observateur* misinterpreted the naming of the play in the film *La Disparue* and pointed to the character Marc dressed as a gamekeeper (intended as a reference to *La Règle de Jeu* but reminiscent also of *Lady Chatterly's Lover*) on stage, it was partly Truffaut's own authorial fault (*Letters* 530); he had not meant any such reference. But audiences, the cinematic auteur seems to insist, through a twist of intentions in his film's final scene, can be wrong as well.

Greene's postresistancialist criticisms are useful and indeed valid, up to a point. Yet her characterization of *The Last Métro* as "a rose-tinted, comforting, and totally unreal portrait of *les années noires*" reflects an inevitably reductive reading of the film. Truffaut's intentions do not seem to have been to make, as Greene quotes one critic, "the negative image of the film by Marcel Ophuls [*Le Chagrin et la pitié*]" (293); indeed, such a formulation reveals a rather binary approach to a far more complex problem. If anything, *Le Dernier Métro* tries to avoid taking either the resistancialist or post-resistancialist position, striving instead to synthesize the two extremes; whether or not it is completely successful in doing so is quite another issue.

Yet the final frames of the film—the curtain call of the dramatic piece that ends the film—betray a much deeper intent. The tableau of Lucas, Marion, and Bernard receiving ovations brings us back to Truffaut's serious purpose, not only in this film but in all his work, differentiation between the sexes, differentiation between sexualities (gay and straight), and valorization of sexual identities. With the Occupation as backdrop for this ménage, the compelling force of nostalgia (apparent in scenes in which Marion draws stocking seams with eye pencil and buys a ham off the black market) becomes potent. In the tradition of that soundstage masterpiece, *Casablanca* and Dooley Wilson's song, even (or especially) in the bleakest of times, "Woman needs man, and man must have his mate. That no one can deny." The real political agenda of *The Last Métro* is neither to excuse nor accuse the wartime Paris theatre of collaboration but to commend it for its preservation of eternal, "cherchez la femme" sexuality; in this the film's revision of sexuality during the Occupation is reductive and, moreover, unmistakably wrong.

Finale

    In the end, the traditionally political questions about the role of the theatre in wartime Paris tend to be reductive: Was the French stage under the German Occupation collaborationist or was it resistant? The complicated evidence suggests that it was sometimes both, sometimes even simultaneously so. How and why this was possible make for answers that are far more interesting than a simple political categorization may allow. The disturbing fact that on the whole the Paris theatre does appear to have collaborated with those in power, and very well at that, perhaps, makes those moments when it provided some message of resistance all the more significant.

    Intent or lack thereof is difficult to ascertain. Jean Anouilh, following the War, apparently denied knowing anything about the Résistance during the time that he wrote *Antigone*. Even if that were true—and given Anouilh's postwar activities, one ought to apply some skepticism to such a statement—by the time the play came to the stage, both the dramatist and the director probably knew something about what was happening. After all, Claude Vermorel, who had contributed many articles to the fascist press, had allowed *Joan Among Us*, written in the 1930s ostensibly to condemn the Soviet purge trials, to be presented in a way that some in the audience discerned as condemning the Germans. Could he have been completely oblivious to the production's implications? Was he, like the fascist critics who praised the play, unintentionally or deliberately blind to what others might be seeing?

    Fascist critics, of course, were not blind: Lucien Rebatet saw in Jean Cocteau's *The Typewriter* indications regarding the author's sexuality. Unfortunately, what Rebatet chose to do with that observation was to use it as a smear, but what is equally meaningful here is that he did in fact see what was there. There may be all sorts of reasons why a play with an apparently noticeable political message, such as Jean-Paul Sartre's *The Flies*, was rejected by the collaborationist press: The staging, the corruption of the myth,

207

the leftist sympathies of the author himself—all these and more offered critics with fascistic values something about which to complain. However, the notices themselves never touch on what appears obvious today, that is, the anti-Vichy satire in the script itself. Were these reviewers unable to grasp Sartre's message or was their silence about it highly calculated? By denouncing the production and helping to doom the play to a very short run, were they not effectively censuring the ideas in *The Flies*? Perhaps what irked Brasillach most about Sartre's next play, *No Exit*, was that in spite of who wrote it and what it said, it was still—even in fascist terms—surprisingly excellent drama.

In the first season after the Defeat, Jean Marais had been somewhat smeared in the press for his sexuality. His guilt by association with Cocteau and his own "perverse" portrayal in *The Typewriter* had made him the target of collaborationist critics, especially of Alain Laubreaux, who accused him of effeminacy and much worse. The issue of homosexuality was, of course, complicated by the worship of the male physique that was already concomitant with fascism. Without separating the homosocial drive, supposedly embodied in images of male beauty, from homoeroticism, the fascist risked subjecting himself to the very degeneracy that he sought to destroy. Thus, Laubreaux's editor at *Je suis partout*, Robert Brasillach, would rhapsodize about masculinity and then castigate homosexuals as pederasts, just as he himself was accuesd of being sexually attracted to males. In order to support the purported visual symbolism of male power, the fascist had to distinguish himself from the fairy.

Jean Marais physically attacked Brasillach's representative in the theatre, Laubreaux. He further repudiated Laubreaux's negative characterization of him by appearing as the front runner in *Eight Hundred Meters* a few months later. As some of the notables watched from the stands, including playwrights Jean Giraudoux and Henry de Montherlant, the crowd was treated to an all-male racing event comprising Europeans (or at least of Aryans, for there was an Anglo-Saxon American included among the characters), under the subsidy of Vichy. Giraudoux, who witnessed the beefcake, would later have his Agnès compare men to big, good-natured dogs, a singularly unsexy and thoroughly conventional male-centered and heterosexist view; no man, Giraudoux assumed, really wanted (or needed) to be as gorgeous as The Apollo of Marsac or Bellac, even if that were possible. Montherlant, however, probably relished the show at Roland-Garros, even though the young men on display were far too old for him. The triumphant display of muscled bodies readily fit his sense of sport as masculine spectacle.

The homosexual anti-hero would eventually materialize in Jean Genet. Both Cocteau, who admired and feared him, and Sartre, who would see in him an otherness that he struggled to explain and thus contain, recognized that Genet was grappling with some of the crucial issues surrounding sexuality on which they themselves had only touched. But neither the gay Cocteau nor the nonconformist but straight Sartre could go very far beyond the constraints of their middle-class sensibilities and values. For all their unconventional yearnings, they, like Montherlant, produced works, which, in spite of their innovation, could easily fit into the theatre literature of their times. Yet Genet, who wrote the first draft of *The Maids* during the Occupation, would not emerge as a dramatist until after the War (and then, quite ironically, in the company of the highly conventional sexuality of Giraudoux's *Apollo* and Jouvet); The Dark Years had very little patience for any play that did not care to pass for what good theatre was supposed to look and sound like, even when, as in the case of Laubreaux's *Pirates of Paris*, it assumed the guise of blatant right-wing anti-Semitic propaganda.

Perhaps this was why Simone Jollivet's *The Princess of Ursins* was consigned to oblivion. With its raw and sometimes inappropriate writing and its twisted sense of history, the script was remembered as a vanity piece. True, Jollivet's script might never have found a production without her connection to Dullin, but still the wonderfully grotesque vitality in *Princess*, the world turned (for a time) upside down by the conniving of a strong, ruthless, and mature woman, anticipates some of what would follow. The image of an empowered evil woman captured the imaginations of Broadway and Hollywood after the War. The anachronisms and vulgarities of Jollivet's dialogue occasionally recall Alfred Jarry's *Ubu* and anticipate the savagery of Genet. (It was no wonder that Artaud had admired her early work.)

Beauvoir, for understandable personal reasons, would remain oblivious to Jollivet's merits, few though they might be. Even later, when Sartre had loosened his hold over Beauvoir (or Beauvoir had pried herself from Sartre) and when her own understanding of sexual politics had deepened, she would never quite be able to see past who Jollivet had been to her: That the other Simone was also a woman, was also entrapped by the same culture Beauvoir eventually recognized had trapped her as well, and that Jollivet's crazed play somehow, even in spite of itself, revealed traces of an existence bent and twisted by the same cultural constructs of sexuality that were unmasked in *The Second Sex*—all this seemed to be invisible to Beauvoir.

Perhaps Rebetat's response to *The Typewriter*—"inverted theatre"—may explain why it was only the most belligerent collaborationist writers, those whose zeal for the fascist revolution licensed them to use pugnacious, antibourgeois impoliteness, who expressed their rancorous criticism in such explicit and inflammatory terms. Just as Cocteau and Colette communicated about Montherlant's penchant for boys through code (as, of course, did Montherlant himself), the culture dictated that there were certain things about which one did not speak directly. Thus, just as fascist critics for other reasons kept silent about the anti-Vichy message in *The Flies*, they probably, like Cocteau and Copeau, were aware on some level of the pedophilic imagery in Montherlant's plays but were willing to overlook them.

"Resistance" and "collaboration" are not invalid terms but may become clichéed simplifications of what they actually do and may mean. Although the scripts included in this study may not be typical of the stage literature of the Occupation, they do share with the larger body of work certain similarities in composition, production, and reception that make them at least representative of the scripts of their time. None is completely "resistant" or "collaborationist"; rather, the circumstances under which these plays were written, staged, and witnessed suggest that, except for Laubreaux's extinct *Pirates of Paris* and Sartre's extant but incredibly turgid *Bariona*, all other plays seem to fall somewhere between these antithetical poles. If art is viewed merely as political expression and in binary political terms, the subtleties not only of the art work itself become reduced in significance but of the politics as well.

During my first visit to France, I had lunch with a young man who had befriended and later written extensively on one of the major entertainment personalities of the Occupation. He told me he was very pleased that I, an American, was writing on this period; in France, he confided, most books in the period were written by Jewish people who had something bad to say. This young man, whose grandmother had always lived in Vichy, had earlier mentioned what a wonderful town it was. It was too bad, he had insisted, that so many people, even today, could not think of Vichy without associating it with what it had been during the War, which he asserted was hardly the fault of the town itself. After I had gotten up from the table and left, I realized that my historical research, which for me was part of a somewhat distant and alien past, was for him terribly immediate and familiar, alive. The fact that I am Jewish made me stop eating the plat and pass on dessert; indeed, I had departed much sooner than I had planned. But it was at that point, while I waited for the métro at the Place de la Bastille, that I began to comprehend the terrible burden that the present places on the past.

Notes

_____

1. Mary Ann Frese Witt offers a fascinating discussion of Brasillach's ideas on drama and theatre in *The Search for Modern Tragedy: Aesthetic Fascism in Italy and France* (148–169).

Chapter 1

1. On the attacks on the revival of *Les Parents Terribles* in October 1941, Raymond Bach writes:

> This time the attacks began immediately and performances were interrupted by hecklers. The theater was temporarily closed by order of the French authorities, but was soon allowed to reopen. The attacks resumed with re-doubled violence: members of the Parti Populaire Français threw tear gas at the actors and ran onto the stage shouting derogatory comments about both Cocteau and his work. In the end, the play was definitively closed by the Germans. (29)

2. Translations from Marsh's "Le Théâtre Français . . ." are mine.

3. Translation mine.

4. This review is taken from the clipping scrapbook at the Bibliothèque de l'Arsenal. Except where specifically attributed and cited, all reviews are taken from *La Machine à écrire, pièce en trois actes de Jean Cocteau, répresenté pour la première fois au Théâtre Hébertot (sur la scène du Théâtre Batignolles) la 29-4-41.* [Press clipping scrapbook.] Paris: Bibliothèque de l'Arsenal, R. Supp. 735 [1941]. Unless otherwise noted, translations are mine.

5. Galster cites (22n197) for this her own paper, "Organisation et tâches de la Censure théâtrale allemande à Paris, sous l'occupation," which was presented at the international colloquium *La littérature française sous l'occupation*, 30 September–2 October, 1981 at Reims, and which appears in the "actes du colloque" (361).

6. *La France au Travail* (30 April 1941) indicates not only that Mme Abetz attended but also Edouard Bourdet, Sacha Guitry, M. Hartecœur, Mme Cécile Sorel, Mme Rosemonde Gérard, Maurice Rostand (who would review the play for *Paris-Midi*, 4 May 1941), and "vingt autres personalités marquantes."

Roger Sardou, in *Les Nouveaux Temps* (30 April 1941), adds Fernand de Brinon, and notes that with Sacha Guitry sat Guitry's wife, Geneviève, and Albert Willemetz (to whom *La Machine* was dedicated) and his wife; among the many notables attending were Serge Lifar, Arletty, playwright and critic H.-R. Lenormand, Colette, Roger Capgras, and Alain Laubreaux (who was reputed, at least by Jean Marais, never to have come at all).

7. Rousso recalls the Mouvement Populaire Français, which revived the fascist cause of the PPF during the French conflict over Algeria; this neofascist group "called for a war on both 'capitalist plutocracy' and the Marxist class struggle, conducted Nazi-style parades, and paid solemn homage 'to the great Europeans who knew how to live and die for the great cause of the white peoples of the world' " (78; Rousso quotes from Charles Luca, *Fidéléte*, February 1959, 344n8).

8. Laubreaux was the chief theatre critic for the weekly, but sometimes others wrote reviews (as with *The Typewriter*).

9. Translation mine. The original is stated thus:

> Problème sociologique: Pourquoi tant de pédérastes parmi les collaborateurs?
> C ..., F ..., M ..., D ... (qui, à ce qu'on dit, tâte de l'un et de l'autre).
> Attendent-ils de l'ordre nouveau la légitimation de leurs amours? (123)

I am indebted to George L. Mosse for this reference, which appears in *Nationalism and Sexuality*. As I indicate later in this chapter, the connections between homosexual and homosocial desire are important, especially in the French culture of the Occupation, but the connections are more complicated than Mosse seems to imply.

10. I suspect that the postwar conflation of fascism and homosexuality—what Hewitt calls "homo-fascism"—has made an already difficult subject for gay writers even more problematic. As a result, aside from texts that condemn homosexuals as fascist collaborators or commend them as resistors or martyrs, there are very few studies of the experience of homosexuals during the Occupation who are not easily categorized at either end of the spectrum. Revealingly, the bibliographical essay that closes *Gender and Fascism in Modern France*, the collection that includes Hewitt's essay on Genet, is conspicuously silent on the subject (Hawthorne & Golsan 179–181); not only does it fail to list any works on this topic, it never raises it.

11. In his preface to his 1981 history, *Le Mouvement homosexuel en France, 1945–1970*, Jacques Girard discusses the Nazi detention and extermination of German

homosexuals (he offers a long quote; 10–11) but is curiously silent on how gays fared during the war in France. In his "annexe" he lists only two dates from the Occupation:

1942   Pétain introduit dans le code pénal un délit d'homosexualité.

1943   Roger Peyrefitte publie ses *Amitiés particulières.*

Perhaps Girard viewed the conduct of gays who collaborated with a certain shame.

Similarly, writing nine years later, Dominique Fernandez, in the chapter of *Le Rapt de Ganymède,* which chronicles "Cent ans de misère," offers only two entries that pertain to the Occupation: one on Dr. A. Stocker's condemnation of homosexuality and another on Peyrefitte's novel (104). Moreover, although Fernandez discusses the portrayal of the male body by the Nazis during the 1930s (181–184), he seems to avoid any discussion of gay culture in Paris under the Occupation.

Any discussion of homosexuals and fascism must include an acknowledgment that the two have often been associated. Andrew Hewitt's *Political Inversions: Homosexuality, Fascism, and the Modernist Imaginary* explores the conflation of "homo-fascism" and credibly suggests that many of the connections drawn between the two have been erroneous. At the same time, Hewitt's analysis of how homosexuals have historically been linked to fascism may provide an explanation for the absence of such a discussion from the above. One may legitimately question to what extent Guéhenno's observation is based on a predisposition to seeing such a link and to what extent it is based on pure observation.

12. Homosexuals, apparently, in spite of their unnaturalness, seemed to be naturally occurring—or perhaps unnaturally occurring; in any case, even Himmler could not avoid the fact that homosexuals indeed continued to emerge, even among the Aryan races. Jews, on the other hand, Himmler reasoned, could be contained and even destroyed: Once there were no more Jews, he concluded, there would not be any more Jews.

13. I have begun using this term in this context largely to avoid repeating *homosexual.* I do not mean to imply that *gay* was used in its modern sense at the time of the Occupation; indeed, the word has taken much longer to catch on in France than in the United States and other English-speaking countries. Nonetheless, I have tried to reserve its use to describe, in some sense, a subcultural identity. Although during the Occupation one's *gay* identity would have meant something substantially different from what it does today, I believe, as suggested above, that such an identity had at the time at least begun to evolve.

14. After Vichy, this decree continued to operate under the Fourth Republic. Copley indicates that it "was confirmed by De Gaulle's post-Liberation administration, 8 February 1945" (204).

15. Nye, in an essay entitled "The Sexuality of Michel Foucault," qualifies White's view of Paris through Genet's eyes as "excursions through the twilight world of gay Paris as a kind of diorama of fascinating or tragic characters, a floating

opera unmoored from any position in the larger society"; he adds that the very detailed account of sexual activity in the biography "is a consequence of Genet's own choice to display [the activities of] his sex life . . . as open challenges to bourgeois sensibilities" (226).

16. Copley tells the following "salutary tale" of Maurice Sachs:

> Reading Gide's affirmation of pederasty in *Corydon* acted on Maurice Sachs as a liberation; it took him out of that oppressive climate of pre-war [World War I] France, one still perpetuated in the pages of Proust. Yet Sachs had also absorbed Nietzchean philosophy in Gide's writings, in particular the idea of the 'acte gratuit'—Lafcadio's mindless murder in the *Vatican cellars*—and this he was to apply with a fatal self-destructiveness during the Occupation. To survive he turned to the black market; he then chanced his luck as a foreign worker in Hamburg in 1942, only to drift into the role of police informer; his luck broke and he was arrested (as a petty crook rather than as a homosexual or as a Jew . . .). A similar opportunism in the camps in Alsace saw him through till the end of the war, but then enraged fellow prisoners were to lynch him in his cell. (178)

Steegmuller's story differs on a number of key points:

> After disposing of his grandmother's possessions when the old lady fled from Paris to Vichy—"she's playing bridge in the provinces, so I sold everything"—he was befriended by a German officer and lived with him in the rue de Rivoli: there are Parisians who remember Sachs's private horsecab [there being no automobiles except for the Germans, due to gasoline rationing] standing conspicuously before their house in that otherwise empty street. . . . Things went badly between Sachs and his German friend; for a time he played the black market with Violette Leduc, and then escaped deportation by volunteering for work in Germany, where for a time he operated a crane in Hamburg. Seeing possibilities in his charm and knowledge of several languages, the Gestapo invited him to leave the crane and circulate freely in the city, which swarmed with foreign workers, reporting to headquarters anything interesting that he might hear. This he willingly did—throughout the war he seems to have lived in an almost continuous state of sado-masochistic ecstasy—and succeeded in betraying a number of confidants to the Gestapo. But he overreached himself, invented accusations that he could not substantiate, and was sent to a Gestapo prison outside the town, where he was given drug and other privileges in return for reporting the conversation of his fellow inmates. When his prison was evacuated before the Allied advance, guards took him and others on a forced march toward Kiel; anyone who stumbled was eliminated; Sachs did not reach Kiel. . . . (446)

17. Copley includes case-study chapters on Gide (155–180) and Guérin (181–197).

18. When Genet's play, *Les Bonnes* (*The Maids*) premiered in 1947, Marais's portrait of Genet would accompany Roger Lannes's review (26 April 1947); see *Genêt (Jean) Les Bonnes, pièce en 1 acte; Giraudoux (Jean) L'Apollon de Marsac, comédie en 1 acte.* [Press clipping scrapbook.] Paris: Biobliothèque de l'Arsenal, R. Supp. 2069 [1947].

19. The same passage from which this is drawn is also quoted by Marsh ("Le Théâtre . . ." 232). The translation is mine.

20. Translation mine.

21. In two of the caricatures that accompanied press notices of *The Typewriter*, Marais is pictured as a frowning thug. In one cartoon, published with Pierre Malo's preview of the play in *Le Matin* (26 April 1941), Marais stands on stage, his arms crossed beneath his vast shoulders and a cross-eyed scowl across his lips while Cocteau, in overcoat and a scarf looks on, his right hand feyly extended holding a cigarette. In another, published with the short review (signed "Cl. C.") in *Beaux-Arts* (9 May 1941), he is surrounded by cast members: his arms flung into the air, he grimaces savagely.

22. A more detailed discussion of similarities between Nazi art and Vichy-financed spectacle appears in chapter 2.

One major difference between German and French art was their choice of objects. While Nazism was personified in the robust physiques of men, French artists (including Breker's mentor, Maillol) tended to focus on the female figure. "In both sculpture and painting," writes Michèle C. Cone in *Artists Under Vichy*, "youth [in Occupied France] tended to be signified by the bodies of preadolescent girls" (69). An exception was the "larger-than-life statue in bronze of a male nude entitled *The Perfect Athlete*," which its creator, Albert Bouquillon allowed "to be exhibited in the show Le Juif en France." This notorious exhibition at the Palais Berlitz during the fall of 1941 attempted to demonstrate the inferiority of Jews to Aryans (155).

23. As indicated in an earlier note, Guitry was present for the premiere of *The Typewriter*, as was his wife.

24. The program is included in the *La Machine* scrapbook at the Arsenal.

25. The promptbook is in the collection of the Bibliothèque Historique de la Ville de Paris, Code ART F201I. There are pages missing in the manuscript, some of which seem to have disappeared for no reason and others that appear to reflect cuts made by the censor (see note 26).

26. The mise en scène (118–121) reflects that this was later cut.

27. The program for *La Machine à écrire* features a full-page advertisement for the films distributed by Continental-Films, whose logo is linked with the German UFA.

28. Chauncey's reminder that the metaphor of the closet is a postwar phenomenon is significant here: "Gay people in the prewar years [in America] . . . did not speak of *coming out of* what we call the 'gay closet' but rather *coming out into* what

they called 'homosexual society' or 'the gay world' . . ." (7). At the same time, Cocteau, in spite of his denials and those of his friends, was "out" not only in the subculture of gay Paris but to many in the broader public as well, who perceived him as openly homosexual.

29. *Le Livre Blanc*, by modern standards, is rather soft-core. The illustrations range from suggestive to explicit, but again, they do not carry the same impact as today's homosexual pornography, which seems (as is implied in the next chapter) to have more in common with the fascist view of masculinity as symbolic of power than with Cocteau's playful drawings.

30. Robert Emmet Jones observes that in "the twenty years following the First World War France's theatre-going public saw four significant plays which dealt almost exclusively with homosexuality": H.-R. Lenormand's *L'Homme et ses fantômes*, Edouard Bourdet's *La Prisonnière* and *La Fleur des pois*, and Roger Martin du Gard's *Un Taciturne* (31–32). None of these plays were revived in Paris during the Occupation. As mentioned in an earlier note, both Lenormand and Bourdet attended the premiere of *The Typewriter*. When Marais attacked Laubveaux with his fists, he mentioned Bourdet as yet another innocent victim of the collabo critic.

31. Perhaps Maxim has read André Gide. In a way, the confession is reminiscent of *The Counterfeiters*.

32. See chapter 4.

Chapter 2

1. From the full-page advertisement describing the event in the weekly *Comœdia*, 5 July 1941. This advertisement and all other contemporary press references (unless otherwise noted) are taken from *Les Suppliantes d'Eschyle; 800 mètres, drame sportif d'André Obey, au stade Roland-Garros—les 5 et 6 Juillet 1941*. [Press clipping scrapbook.] Paris: Bibliothèque de l'Arsenal, R. Supp. 755 [1941].

2. The word in classical Greek may be applied to a variety of situations, including trials, battles, or sports, but in English (according to my *Webster's Ninth Collegiate Dictionary*) it can relate specifically to "the dramatic conflict between the chief characters in a literary work."

3. For Metheny, spectators (usually male) derive from sports the experience of the performer (also usually male) at the peak of his abilities; she sees the performers as providing "the spectators with symbolic evidence of the farthest reaches of man's ability to accomplish his human purposes" (80).

4. With regard to Breker's sculptures, writes George L. Mosse, in "Beauty Without Sensuality: The Exhibition *Entarte Kunst*" (included in the book that accompanied the Los Angeles County Museum exhibition about what the Nazis termed "Degenerate Art") their nudity "was an abstract, smooth, almost transparent nakedness and a frozen posture. . . ."

Referring to Hans Surén's *Gymnastik der Deutchen* (1938), which "advocated nearly complete nudity in the pursuit of sport or while roaming through the country-side," Mosse adds:

> but the male body had to be carefully prepared before it could be offered to public scrutiny: the skin had to be hairless, smooth, and bronzed. The body had become an abstract symbol of Aryan beauty, as it was in Leni Riefenstahl's film of the 1936 Olympic Games. (28)

5. For photographs of Occupation rallies, see N.A. Album 40, 243, 7 Zucca and N.A. Album 40, 243, 8 Zucca at the Bibliothèque Historique de la Ville de Paris, Paris; I would like to thank Liza Daum for showing me these albums of contact prints and others.

In N.A. Album 29/30 243 Zucca, there are photographs of a February 6, 1942 bullfight at the Vel d'Hiv as well as pictures taken in the Jewish ghetto of the Marais (only a few blocks from the Bibliothèque Historique) in 1941; see especially contacts 7284 ("Enterprise Juif") and 7293 ("Synagogue").

Another photograph of a bullfight in the Vel d'Hiv, dated September 6, 1942, is included in *Paris de la Vie Sportive 1940–1944*, the published version of the photo-graphic exhibition of the same name created by the Musée National du Sport in 1995–1996 (27). The book also includes a photo of the Sunday, July 6, 1942 performance of *Eight Hundred Meters* (43); in the picture, the bare-chested runners are led by Barrault, with Marais close behind, past one of the viewing stands. Male statues and Greek columns loom behind spectators or perhaps Le Choeur in bleacher seats.

6. While Borotra revered the memory of his late predecessor Lagrange, in a substantial athletic commemoration on October 5, 1941 (Gay-Lescott 89–90), he does not seem to have honored the man who had immediately preceded him, Jean Zay, who was Jewish and would eventually be murdered by the Milice.

Paxton notes that Borotra ("a fervent apostle of moral reeducation through sports") had been recruited by Basque sportsman Jean Ybarnégaray, Vichy's first minister of youth, the family, and sports.

7. Borotra's superior, Ybarnégaray, had a long history of right-wing affiliations and during the 1930s had admired what Paxton calls " 'that appeal of the race' that had been heard in Italy and Germany but not yet in France" (162). One of his goals as minister was to plan a campaign against "threatening 'sanitary and racial control' over immigration and naturalization" (167).

Race is not such an "un-French" issue if one looks to the French political far right. John Hoberman's *The Olympic Crisis: Sport, Politics and the Moral Order*, in addition to surveying the history of political responses to the Olympic games, offers a penetrating look at ultra-conservative views in France; see "Charles Maurras and the Neo-Fascist Critique of Olympia," 93–100. Of course, by mid-July 1941, when these plays were presented, the first series of Vichy's racial laws against Jews had already been passed.

8. See Robert Cardinne-Petit, *Les Secrets de la Comédie-Française* (Paris: Nouvelles Editions Latines, 1958), 256.

Brown comments on the quote, "Barrault omitted this episode from his memoirs, but the fact remains that he became a pageant master under Pétain long before he became a master of avant-garde ceremonies under Charles de Gaulle" (428).

9. Kenneth R. Dutton summarizes:

> Never before had the Western conception of physical development been turned to such blatantly political ends, or the idealized muscularity of classical art been so institutionalized to serve the purposes of the State. In the totalitarian climate of Hitler's Germany, the disparate fields of aesthetics, social morality, bodily development and political ambition were all brought together within a single theoretical framework which rendered all forms of expression subservient to the Nazi regime. (208)

Dutton's *The Perfectible Body*, though intentionally not a scholarly work, offers interesting photographs of nineteenth-century and early twentieth-century German weight lifters, nude exercisers, and bodybuilders; there was an obvious preoccupation with the male form in Prussia and Germany long before the Nazis came to power.

10. For more on Greek revivals and classically based contemporary dramas, see chapter 5.

11. The actors pictured in these photographs are actually Paris firemen who would also be performing in the half-time show.

12. The article first appeared in the 28 June 1941 issue and was reprinted verbatim in the same paper for the 7 July 1941 issue.

13. Barrault wrote an article, which appeared twice in *Comœdia* (21 June 1941 and again on 7 July 1941), in the same grandiose tone. Its title on both occasions, "Joie de l'effort," carries a disturbing echo of the Nazi program called "Strength through Joy."

14. Hoberman later goes on to observe, "Unlike Fascist Italy, the Third Reich could not display political athleticism at the top. Mussolini's physique was promoted as an unofficial ideal" (99). Indeed, the very top of the Nazi hierarchy—Hitler, Goebbels, Himmler, Göring—were hardly magnificent physical specimens.

15. Again, the source of the photograph is unclear; R. Supp. 755, page 30.

16. Some of the extracts by Giraudoux to which Marsh refers are included in R. Supp. 755, page 12. Others are listed by Marsh ("Le Théâtre . . ." 236); see chapter 3.

17. In writing on a 1990s expression of the cult of the body beautiful, Alan M. Klein notes:

> The mirroring so critical to both bodybuilding and narcissism is found in the relationship between fascist leader and "tamed" followers. With the body at the center of these displays, narcissism exists at a primitive level in which

exhibitionism, ideal mirroring, and object relations are pervasive, as well as somewhat unsophisticated. Politically, fascism has clutched to itself hegemonic masculinity, with its penchant for strength, aggression, lack of emotion, and like qualities, and encased it all in the male body. On an elemental level this is exhibited in the penchant for "virile posing," physical (including sexual) exploits of leaders, and the elevation of the athletic ideal (over other traits such as intellectualism) to center stage. (265)

Perhaps Barrault's inability to comprehend how the body, in 1941, signified with contemporary fascist beliefs was made possible by a willful act of ignorance.

18. As Richard J. Golsan notes, in *Le Solstice de juin* Montherlant "calls for France, like a vanquished athlete, to sit down at table with its conqueror and celebrate his victory. As painful as the debacle of 1940 was to the French, the metaphor of athletic competition employed by Montherlant is largely innocuous and in no way denigrates the loser" (149). Obey's drama, as we will see, does not entirely fit Montherlant's scenario. For a more detailed discussion of Montherlant during the Occupation, see chapter 8.

19. Indeed, a friend of mine who had worked in the theatre during the Occupation remarked to me that the suppliant maidens were naturally viewed as the prisoners of the Egyptians, just as the French had become the unwilling hosts of the Germans. My friend, however, had staunchly supported the Popular Front government and even after the Defeat remained sympathetic to its ideals.

20. I am going to refer to a version of the dramatic text, which Obey apparently updated for radio broadcast (which is the only version I could find). The script appears to have entered the collection of the Bibliothèque Nationale in 1964, which also seems to be the year of its broadcast; that same year, the Olympic games were held in Tokyo.

Entitled *Journée Olympique: Huit cents mètres*, the author is given as André Obey with "Réalisation Gilbert Caseneuve," and a rubber stamp at the upper righthand corner of the cover indicates that it was issued by "Compère, Agence Générale de Copies dramatiques et littéraires, 14, rue Henner, Paris IXe. . . ." See Bibliothèque Nationale 4oYa, 350, Radio.

Although this version of the script clearly incorporates techniques that were appropriate for radio drama but not for the stadium performance, the original text— as described by Occupation press notices and reviews—seems to remain intact.

No other text appears to have survived. The 1985 retrospective exhibition at the Bibliothèque Municipale de Douai (the town where Obey was born) offered a catalogue with a short bibliography (62–63); neither this bibliography nor the section of the catalogue describing artifacts associated with the production (37–38) refer to or cite an extant text of the play.

All quotes are my translations of this radio script.

21. Georges Pioch, in *L'Œuvre* (12 July 1941), includes the following: "Barrault, Cuny, Duphilo, Le Gentil, Poval, Verner et . . . Marais." Hervé Le Boterf includes Jean-Luis Barrault, Jean Marais, Alain Cuny, Georges Marchal, Roger Pigaut, and Michel Vitold (191).

22. Did Barrault step up to a microphone to reveal his character's inner thoughts? Although this was possible, I have no evidence that Jean actually spoke in the Roland-Garros production.

23. In his original piece on this incident, Obey makes it clear that the contestants are in fact not each from a different country. See Obey's "Le Huit Cents Mètres de Paul Martin," in *L'Orgue du Stade* (191–213).

24. Robert A. Nye provides information that helps explain why this fascistic combatative view of the world appears in the work of Obey, who was not a fascist. Nye sees the revival of sport in France as a postwar reaction to the Defeat of 1870 "to train the young to manifest the mental and physical courage needed for revenge." For those who revived traditional sport in France, "[s]port was not simply . . . the 'moral equivalent of war'; it was the means by which the moral and psychological conditions of the battlefield could be socially produced" (219). As someone growing up in the Third Republic, Obey was clearly influenced by the ideals of those nurtured by this revival, those "fin de siècle sportsmen [who] yoked the ethical ideal of an honorable amateurism—disinterestedness, the striving for 'pure' goals—to a doctrine of state service in the formation of military valor" (220).

25. Those who wished might, of course, equate the Finn with the German; Marsh offers the quote by Giraudoux, who made the same association under somewhat different circumstances: "Les peuples qui ont le pourcentage le plus considérable de revues d'art son ceux qui comptent le pourcentage le plus fort de gymnastes: l'Allemagne et la Finlande" ("Le Théâtre à Paris . . ." 158). (See chapter 3.)

Yet the Finns were not a "Nordic" people; their alliance with the Axis came principally from their enmity with the Soviet Union.

26. This excerpt is also cited by Marsh, in "Le Théâtre de Paris . . ." (236–237).

27. The considerable recent debate on whether or not Breker's sculptures (as well as other works of fascist art) are homoerotic seems to beg the question. A better question might be, Just how are they homoerotic? Hewitt illustrates the complexity of the issues involved (*Political Inversions* 25–29).

28. Mosse's *Nationalism and Sexuality* offers an extensive examination of Europe's sexual constructs from the late eighteenth century onward.

29. Marais was not the only homosexual actor in the cast of *Huit cents mètres*: Alain Cuny, a young performer, who the following April would begin work on one of the great films of the Occupation, Marcel Carné's *Les Visiteurs du soir*, also ran in the race.

Another runner-performer, who was not homosexual, Michel Vitold, also ran in *Huit cents mètres* and would go on to star in Jean-Paul Sartre's *Huis Clos* (*No Exit*) in the spring of 1944. He would also broadcast over Résistance radio (Cohn 47). Incidentally, *No Exit* would be directed by that "purveyor of pornography" who had directed *The Typewriter*, Raymond Rolleau.

30. Similarly, Beauvoir recalled that *Eight Hundred Meters* at least "gave us the chance to appreciate the technical skill of Barrault, Cuny, Dufilho, and Legentil—not to mention Jean Marais's good looks" (*Prime of Life* 485).

Chapter 3

1. These quotes are taken from *Les Suppliantes d'Eschyle; 800 mètres, drame sportif d'André Obey, au stade Roland-Garros—les 5 et 6 Juillet 1941.* [Press clipping scrapbook.] Paris: Bibliothèque de l'Arsenal, R. Supp. 755 [1941]. Translation mine.

2. Translation mine.

3. Translation mine.

4. Translation mine.

5. Giraudoux originally called the play *L'Apollon de Marsac*, and this was the title under which both the Latin American premiere (in Brazil in 1942) and French premiere (in Paris in 1947) were produced. However, sometime before his death in January 1944, the playwright revised the version sent to Rio, renaming the play *L'Apollon de Bellac* (Bellac being Giraudoux's native village in the Limousin); when the play was first published by Grasset, it was under this revised title.

Although the *Marsac* script was used for the two productions discussed in this chapter, the text of this version is not readily available. *L'Apollon de Marsac* was first published in French in Rio de Janeiro as a theatre supplement to the serial *Dom Casmurro*; see Jean Giraudoux, *L'Apollon de Marsac: comedia em um ado.* Another edition of the same text was apparently printed two years later in Mexico by Editorial Castillo; for a complete list of Giraudoux's published works through 1982, see Brett Dawson, *Bibliographie de l'ouevre de Jean Giraudoux: 1899–1982* . Because the *Bellac* script has become the standard version and is easily available, I refer to it (unless noted otherwise) as it appears in the now definitive Pléade edition of Giraudoux's plays, edited by Jacques Body; see Jean Giraudoux, *L'Apollon de Bellac* in *Théâtre Complet*, ed. Jacques Body.

In order to avoid using two names for what is essentially one work, in this study I will refer to this play as *Apollo*, and when necessary, will try to use the better known *Bellac* when a place name is required.

For a thorough discussion of the play's production and textual history, see Body's "Notice" and "Note sur la texte" in *Théâtre Complet*.

6. A. James Arnold examines the original version and notes some striking contrasts between it and the produced script.

7. Drama may, of course, be read without reference to its original context. Such a reading in itself carries with it an assumption that all contexts are basically enough alike that all literature may be read in the context of the present.

8. The breakup apparently began long before Jouvet, Ozeray, and the company left for Brazil. Evelyn Ehrlich explains:

Louis Jouvet took his company to Switzerland in January 1941 to make a film of their production of *l'Ecole des Femmes*. The film's director, Max Ophuls, offended the star by having an affair with his mistress, Madeleine Ozeray. [In a note here, the author cites Ozeray's *A Toujours Monsieur Jouvet* (Paris: Buchet/Castel, 1966) pp. 164–184.] Jouvet left Switzerland with the film uncompleted. He and his company had previously contracted for a South American tour and, once there, did not return. (9)

9. Léo Lapara in *Dix Ans Avec Jouvet* assigns the blame to Cocteau and his friends (192). For a detailed discussion of Cocteau's and Christian Bérard's role in getting Jouvet to produce *Les Bonnes*, see Edmund White's *Genet: a biography* (299–301).

10. Odette Aslan offers a detailed discussion of how the play changed and indicates Jouvet's influence on the early rewrites (38–43).

11. As indicated previously, here and throughout the plot summary, Bellac is used for the sake of readers who have come to know the play through its later form (both in French and translation). In the earlier edition, Marsac is used.

12. Readers familiar with the most readily available version in English, *The Apollo of Bellac*, adapted by Maurice Valency in *Four Plays* (73–101), will detect a different ending. Robert Cohen correctly observes that readers of the Valency version will notice that:

> Valency has . . . created a new character, "the Chairman of the Board," who is *really* handsome (in the eyes of the audience and Agnès), one to whom Agnès never needs to say the magic line ["How handsome you are"] in order to captivate. Valency also eliminates Apollo's remark about Agnès getting "a little fatter" after her conquest, and makes Thérèse [in this version the President's wife rather than his fiancée or mistress] return to the president after learning a lesson. Agnès then may wholesomely marry the Chairman. (9)

Ronald Duncan's abridged version, adapted from Valency's and offered in an abridged form, is in many ways truer to the original; see Jean Giraudoux, *The Apollo de Bellac*, trans. Ronald Duncan in *The Best One-Act Plays of 1956–57*, ed. Hugh Miller (9–35).

13. I examine the role of *The Maids* and its place in this peculiar double bill in the final chapter of my book on playreading, *Private Readings/Public Texts* (97–128).

14. As I have indicated, Lapara claims Jouvet was pressured by Cocteau and others to produce the play. He adds that the director knew the double bill "would not have a long run." Thus, he says, Jouvet began rehearsing Molière's *Dom Juan* two days after the first reading of *The Maids*, and, insists Lapara, "His presentiments proved exactly right" (195). Having defended the director, Lapara describes in some detail how the house reacted over the course of the plays' six-month engagement:

> The first few performances [the play opened on April 19, 1947] unrolled without incident. The audience contented itself with a show of hostility to Genêt's [sic] work—listened coldly and greeted the end with scarce and meager applause—and acclaiming more than reasonably the Giraudoux

play. . . . Starting with the eighth performance, things deteriorated. And then, up until the last, rare were the evenings on which *The Maids* was not the object, during the course of its performance, of jibes, jeers, snickers, or whistles. Finally, mixed in with the booing and whistling in response, there were a few bravos and some applause from Genêt's [sic] champions.

Each day carried with it a miniature version of the battle over *Hernani*. But the palm-branch of audience censure came back during the sixty-fourth performance, on Sunday, 21 September 1947, in the evening: the curtain fell on *The Maids* in a glacial silence which no applause came to break.

It did not rise again. (195–196)

The translation is mine. There is more than a detectable trace of defensiveness here: The audience's adoration for Giraudoux (Jouvet's favorite and author of the play in which Lapara himself was appearing) is contrasted with its loathing for Genet (of whom, we are told, Jouvet had been wary). Still, this account of the reception of the two plays seems consistent with the contemporary drama reviews.

15. With the exception of Ambriére's, every review of this double bill which I use here is listed in Richard Coe's excellent bibliography of the drama criticism of the first production of *The Maids* in "Unbalanced Opinions: A Study of Jean Genet and the French Critics Followed by a Checklist of Criticism in French" (67–68). Coe himself summarizes the coupling of the plays by remarking that *The Maids* premiered "in a perversely antithetical double-bill with Jean Giraudoux' precious-pastel-coloured *Apollon de Marsac . . .*" (36).

16. However, in a 1991 letter, Dr. Raymond wrote me that she thought the play "delightful."

17. As noted earlier, here and throughout, all references to the text of *Apollo* are to the 1983 (Pléade) edition. Subsequent references to this text utilize parenthetical citations. All translations are my own.

18. A facsimile of the first typescript page received by Jouvet in Rio is included in the program, which is included in *Genêt (Jean) Les Bonnes, pièce en 1 acte; Giraudoux (Jean) L'Apollon de Marsac, comédie en 1 acte*. [Press clipping scrapbook.] Paris: Bibliothèque de l'Arsenal, R. Supp. 2069 [1947]. Giraudoux's handwritten note appears at the top of it. On this page, instead of referring to Jouvet's character as M. DE MARSAC, he retains the use of "JOUVET."

19. It is tempting to speculate about Giraudoux's personal knowledge and meanings here. In light of the information summarized previously in the note on Ozeray, we may wonder whether the playwright was commenting, through Agnès, M. de Bellac, and the Président, on Ozeray's drift away from the brilliant but not remarkably handsome Jouvet and her attraction to Ophuls, the internationally known film director. Ozeray had the affair with Ophuls while she was playing Molière's Agnès. This reading of the play, coupled with the recollection that Ozeray as Giraudoux's Ondine had remarked how very handsome Jouvet (as Hans) appeared, might view *L'Apollon*, at least on one level, as a plea to Ozeray not to break with Jouvet.

20. Raymond quotes *Visitations*, pp. 128–129.

21. This line, changed by Giraudoux when he revised the play and retitled it *L'Apollon de Bellac*, remains in the Marsac version (18) and was thus part of the script for both the 1942 and 1947 productions. It is retained in the Ides et Calandes edition of Giraudoux's plays; see Jean Giraudoux, *Le Théâtre Complet de Jean Giraudoux*, Vol. 16 (181). The translation is my own.

22. The last page of the original printing of the play includes extracts from some of the reviews of the 1942 Rio premiere. Interestingly, the criticism reprinted from the review by Bandeira Duarte in *O Globo* does attempt to relate *L'Apollon de Marsac* to France's then current political situation. There is, however, no specific reference to the dialogue (24). I would like to thank Jordano Quaglia of the State University of New York's University at Albany for his enormous help in translating the extracts from the Portuguese and for his explanations about Brazilian culture during the Second World War.

The introduction to these extracts mistakenly states that Giraudoux was currently in exile (presumably in Switzerland; 24).

23. I quote from the *Dom Casmurro* printing (18). The translation is mine.

24. The review appeared 20–21 April 1947 (R. Supp 2069, 18).

25. Included on page 2 in *Dom Casmurro* printing; no photographer is given credit.

Chapter 4

1. See "*Jeanne d'Arc* Under the German Occupation" by Patrick Marsh, and "The Role of Joan of Arc on the Stage of Occupied Paris" by Garbiel Jacobs. "The Cult of Joan of Arc under the Vichy Régime," by Gerd Krumeich, discusses Pétain's government's use of Joan.

2. As indicated in the final chapter, when François Truffaut came to re-create on film the Occupation theatre world, he called the collaborationist critic character "Daxiat."

3. Laubreaux was not the only theatre critic to have his work produced during the Occupation. Rosenberg mentions that Jean-Michel Renaitour and Maurice Rostand also presented plays that he calls "pro-Vichy" ("The French Theatre . . ." 226).

4. "This booklet," explains Sweets, "was sent in late September 1943 to all teachers in the PDD with instructions to include the message conveyed to students on the family question."

5. For the law to which he refers, Paxton cites *Journal officiel*, 2–3 September 1941, 3694–3715.

6. Paxton refers to the law of October 11, 1941 and cites Jacques Desmarest, *La Politique de la main-d'ouevre en France* (Paris, 1946), 130–131.

7. Even after the Liberation and winning the right to vote, Frenchwomen's civil rights remained restricted under the law. Jane Jenson attests that "[o]nly mobilization in later decades would bring women onto the political scene as independent social actors" (284).

8. Translation mine.

9. Among the plays written by women and produced at the private theatres of Paris during the Occupation are the following: Noelle Verdier's *La Pension Farge* (at the Théâtre de l'Ambigu, 5/23/42–7/5/42); Suzanne Desty's *Taina* (at the Théâtre Charles de Rochefort, 9/26/41–10/26/41); Marcelle Maurette's *Le Roi Christine* (at the Théâtre Edouard VII, 3/3/44–4/18/44), her *Madame Capet* (at the Théâtre du Gymnase, 5/29/41–10/19/41 and 10/31/41–11/30/41 and then at the Théâtre Pigalle, 2/4/43–3/14/43), and her *Marie Stuart* (co-written with André Cadou, at the Théâtre Montparnasse-Gaston Bâty, 10/22/41–2/10/42); Simone May's *La Cinquième heure* (at the Théâtre de l'Œuvre, 12/2/42–1/24/43). This information is drawn from Merrill Rosenberg's list of the productions of the private theatres ("The French Theatre During the German Occupation, 1940–1944," 273–316).

10. In an unsigned, largely favorable review of *Princess* (perhaps attributable to Marcel Latriene), the critic began, "Le Théâtre de la Cité vient d'ouvrir ses portes. Sous la direction de Charles Dullin, le vieux Théâtre des Nations, qui porta longtemps le nom de Sarah-Bernhardt, a retrouvé une nouvelle jeunesse."

This review and all subsequent press references to *Princess* come from the clipping scrapbook, *La Princesse des Ursins, pièce en trois actes, un prologue et un epilogue, par Simone Jollivet*, Bibliothèque de l'Arsenal, R. Supp. 816 [1942]. The newspaper from which this review has been clipped is not identified.

11. Throughout my research, first in the United States and then later in France, I have been helped enormously by Edmond M. Desportes de Linières, founding president of the Association Charles Dullin in Paris; indeed, without M. Desportes de Linières's assistance, I would have been unable to write this chapter. It was he who (with the aid of Mme Cristou) located in the Bibliothèque Nationale Dullin collection a copy (virtually complete) of *La Princesse des Ursins*, a microfilm copy of which he kindly sent me. And it was he who, without compromising the Dullin correspondence, of which the Association is in possession, wrote for me two notes on Jollivet, the first on sources in French relating to her personality and the second, "Simone Jollivet, qui êtes-vous?"

M. Desportes de Linières has revealed that Jollivet was born in Toulouse in 1902. Thus, she was twenty-four when she first met Sartre (at the wedding of a mutual cousin) in 1926, about thirty when her first play (*L'Ombre*) opened in 1932, and nearly forty when *La Princesse* opened in 1942.

After Dullin died in 1949, she became more and more reclusive, drinking heavily in her isolation. Axel Madsen summarizes:

> Camille in the end had only Sartre and Beaver [the nickname under which Beauvoir wrote to Sartre]—Sartre to pay her debts, Simone to visit her in

her apartment where she lived as a perpetual drunk in her own filth, scraps of theatrical costumes and food brought up by the concierge and left to rot. When Simone and the concierge finally called the health department to have her taken to the hospital, the ambulance attendants found her in a semicoma on the floor covered with excrement—she even had it in her hair. When Simone visited her at the hospital, she apologized because her hair had been cut. She suffocated a few weeks later. (258)

Her death occurred on December 12, 1967, when Jollivet was 65. Beauvoir reports that the only mourners to attend the funeral were Sartre and herself, the Secretary of The Friends of Charles Dullin (Paul-Louis Mignon), the exectuor of Dullin's estate (and president of The Friends of Charles Dullin, Desportes de Linières), and Mme C., Jollivet's loyal concierge (*All Said and Done* 73–74).

12. This comes from Gerassi's interview with Sartre of February 26, 1971.

13. In spite of her extensive discussions about her very mixed feelings toward Jollivet, Beauvoir later denied her jealousy; see Francis and Gontier (xv).

14. This and subsequent reviews of *The Shadow* come from *Atelier* [Press Clipping Scrapbook: *L'Ombre*]. Bibliothèque Nationale, RT 3745, Tomc XI, 10-1 to 10-8; on the final page of this scrapbook, one may find an actual ticket from the production.

15. For example, in the autumn of 1936 he praises her adaptation of Shakespeare's *Julius Caesar* (73–74) and in 1939, after he has left Paris to serve in the army, writes her a friendly letter (293–294).

16. Here, as in the rest of this section of Beauvoir's memoir, the description in *The Prime of Life* is based on the entries in *Journal de Guerre*.

17. Toulouse in the former and Camille in the latter.

18. This incident does not appear in *Journal de Guerre*: Notebook number VI cuts off at 18 July 1940.

19. Curiously, the letters do not mention the Théâtre de Paris dinner, nor does the journal, upon which so much of *The Prime of Life* is based.

20. In examining the lives and writings of four French women writers during the Occupation, Elizabeth Houlding observes how for the first time the intellectual Beauvoir (like Colette) was forced to confront some of the day-to-day realities that she had previously been able to escape: "In their relative distance from active involvement in the war, neither resistance workers nor black-marketeers, Colette and Beauvoir are perhaps more representative of the vast majority of French women for whom the war years were largely a matter of getting by and making do" (39–40).

21. Patrick Marsh notes, "*Comœdia* stated that it was the duty of Vichy to make the theatre a fit part of the 'Révolution Nationale,' to rid it of all partisan ideology and

bourgeois ideas, 'de l'assasinir sans l'affadir, de le purifier sans le déviriliser' " ("The Theatre . . ." 156; qtd. from *Comœdia*, 13 November 1941).

22. Galster mentions how the following season (1942–1943), Novy would serve as Secretary General for Dullin's Théâtre de la Cité (151).

23. The copy of the playscript in my possession (as noted earlier, a microfilm of the text in the Bibliothèque Nationale) is marked with substantial cuts throughout. These handwritten edits have clearly been made (perhaps by Dullin himself, and certainly under his authority) on Jollivet's original typescript.

La Princesse des Ursins consists of a prologue and three separate acts (as well as ten tableaux), each of these divisions individually paginated.

24. A first scene, which gives Mme des Ursins a rather talky monologue about how she will control access to the new French monarchs of Spain, appears to have been cut entirely from the play.

25. An exchange about the Queen's dislike of Louville and then a short scene in which Marie-Louise enters, argues with the pair, and then exits, have been cut from the manuscript.

26. Added charts Dullin's subsidies quite clearly. Between 1937 and 1940 he was at the Atelier and received subsidies amounting to 23,750 francs. For the 1940–1941 season, he was at the Théâtre de Paris, which was funded by the city. For the latter half of 1941, at the Théâtre de la Cité, he received from the national government 287,500 francs; this rose to 400,000 for 1942 and 500,000 for 1943. He received 250,000 francs for the first half of 1944 (and apparently was then given an even larger amount by the government that replaced Vichy for the second half). From Added's chart, Dullin's company seems to have received more money than any other except for La Compagnie de la Regain, which was Vichy's official troupe in the Occupied zone (82).

27. Dullin had never divorced his wife and thus could not marry Jollivet. However, perhaps out of recognition of her place in Dullin's personal and professional lives, Jollivet was often referred to as "Mme Simone Jollivet" in notices and reviews.

28. Franco's nation, after June, 1940, became a neutral with friendly ties to Vichy. During the Occupation, Spain—especially in its golden age—figured prominently on the Parisian stage. Works by Lope de Vega and Caldéron were great successes (particularly at the Comédie-Française); the exotic and very Spanish themes of pride, honor, and heroism, which Merrill A. Rosenberg calls "a welcome antidote to the loss of national prestige which the French felt so acutely" ("Vichy's Theatrical Venture," 145) would emerge too in plays by French writers, particularly in two stage triumphs at the Comédie-Française, Claudel's *Le Soulier de satin* and Montherlant's *La Reine morte* (which is in fact set in Portugal but was inspired by a Spanish play that Montherlant had been asked to translate).

29. In *The Prime of Life* Beauvoir links Jollivet's sense of herself with what she had read of philosophy. She mentions how during the time Sartre was intimately

involved with Jollivet, Camille would "recite aloud from *Also sprach Zarathustra*—generally the passage which deals with the mastery of the body by the will" (68).

30. As it turned out, Jollivet did not play the title role, as Beauvoir tells us she hoped she would; the part of Mme des Ursins was given to Germain Kerjean (of whom Maurice Rostand in reviewing the play wrote "a tiré du rôle tout ce qu'on pouvait en tirer"). He praises the other actors, including Dullin as the ridiculous Albéroni ("une figure étonnante de Tartufe [sic] parmesan"), as well as N. Gontcharova's splendid scenery and costumes (photographs indicate that these were lavish for the Occupation) and George Auric's musical score.

On the whole, Maurice Rostand's review is positive. Ironically (as M. Desportes de Linières has pointed out), his own father, Edmond Rostand, had one of his great successes at this same theatre: *L'Aiglon*, which had starred Sarah Bernhardt, before the theatre's name had been changed to conform to the Occupation's racist policies.

31. Writes Evelyn Ehrlich:

> Arletty, whose crime consisted of having had an affair with a German officer[,] was imprisoned for four months and then placed under house arrest for an additional eighteen months before she was finally "purified" in November, 1946. . . . She is reported to have said at her trial, "My heart is French, but my ass belongs to the world." (174)

The argument for some was that Arletty's career during the Occupation was certainly not hurt by her relationship with the enemy.

32. This comes at the bottom of the last typescript page in the microfilm copy. There is evidence, however, that there was at least one other page, which has been either lost or cut from the manuscript. According to a letter (12 September 1994) from Mlle Cécile Pocheau of the Département des Arts du Spectacle at the Biobliothèque Nationale, the original from which the microfilm was made also ends on this page.

33. See Bibliothèque Nationale R. Supp. 145. Colette in *Le Journal* agreed that Jollivet had used too much argot and that the show seemed less Aristophanic than it ought to have.

34. Reviews are collected in the Arsenal scrapbook, *King Lear, trad. Simone Jollivet, mis en scène Charles Dullin, Théâtre Sarah-Bernhardt, 10 avril 1945.* [Press clipping scrapbook.] Paris: Biobliothèque de l'Arsenal, R. Supp. 1625 [1945]. The name of the theatre had been changed back to the Sarah-Bernhardt in 1944.

Chapter 5

1. Witt credits this information (and much more) to Manfred Flügge's exhaustive thesis, *Vereigrerung oder neue Ordnung: Jean Anouilhs 'Antigone' im politschen und ideologischen Kontext der Besatzungzeit 1940–1944.*

2. There had always been profound and complex connections between French culture and the classics, and these were compounded during the Occupation by German and French fascist interest in the Greeks; see George L. Mosse's *Nationalism and Sexuality*.

3. Among the productions, at the Paris Opéra and the Opéra Comique, of operas that were based on Greek myth were *Ariane à Naxos* by Richard Strauss and *Pénélope* by Gabriel Fauré and René Fauchois, both during the 1942–1943 season, and *Alceste* by Gluck, during the 1943–1944 season (Rocher 917–918).

4. In these two last cases, classicism helped soften the fact that the authors were German, just as the Spanish setting for the Odéon's production of *Don Carlos* muted the reality that the play was by Schiller.

5. Another production of *Andromaque* had already opened at the Ambassadeurs in May 1941, and a third at the Edward VII less than a month before D-Day (directed by Jean Marais). Perhaps the claustrophobia (a perfect image of the Occupation itself) of Racine's play, which has been compared to the inescapability of the hotel room in Sartre's *Huis Clos* (*No Exit*), contributed to the popularity of the play.

6. See *Electre pièce en deux actes de Jean Giraudoux, reprisé, au Théâtre de l'Avenue, la 30 [mars] 1943 (rép. gén le)*, R. Supp. 1220 [1943].

7. The case of *Les Mouches* remains hotly disputed. Serge Added allows that Sartre may have intended the play as criticism of Vichy and as a call to resistance but that no one (or virtually no one) received it that way. Ingrid Galster, Gabriel Jacobs, Patrick Marsh, and Merrill Rosenberg try to see the play as, at least in some way, gesturing toward resistance but disagree on the extent of audience comprehension.

8. I am indebted to my friend David N. Burke for his insights into the meanings of the Oresteia myth.

9. These two plays, which were produced in Nazi Germany, do not seem to have been performed in Paris during the Occupation.

10. Bertram M. Gordon, delineating the morphology of the French collaborator, describes a range of rightist figures, from extremists to moderates, each with a following. Even among those with nominal loyalty to Pétain, there were tremendous differences of opinion; many could claim to be for Vichy but against both the Free French *and* the Germans.

11. For a detailed and thoroughly researched discussion of audience attendance, subsidies, and profits, see Added.

12. Translation mine.

13. Serge Added mentioned to me, when I met with him in Reims, July 21, 1994, that Vermorel had said he had written *Jeanne avec nous* in 1938 to comment on the purge trials in the Soviet Union.

14. All quotes from the play have been translated by Louis Galantière (unless otherwise noted); page references refer to his version of the play.

15. Translation is mine.

16. Yet *Antigone*, if it did close, clearly reopened very soon after this declaration. Leo Forkey reports that the total run for the 1944–1945 production was 475 performances ("Paris Theatres During the Occupation" 305).

The Commission, according to Galster, had been influenced by the fact that Anouilh had not been part of a Résistance organization, had written for the collaborationist press, and his *Antigone* had been praised by the pro-German and Vichyite papers and condemned by Claude Roy (278).

Added notes that in spite of his contributions to fascist publications, the regional interprofessional "purge" commission passed Anouilh (321).

17. Translations from *Oreste* are mine.

18. A number of critics do mention *Oreste*. Among these are Archer, Beugnot, Borgal, della Fazia, Falb, Kelly, Luppé (who reprints the text from *La Table Ronde*), Pronko, Rombout, and Vier.

Only a few critics date the writing of the fragment; these include Harvey, Kelly, McIntyre, Marsh, and Smith; of these, all see it as "anterior to *Antigone*" (Harvey 94), and a few, notably Christopher Smith, identify its date of composition as 1942 (14).

Curiously, Manfred Flügge, whose exhaustive thesis on Anouilh's *Antigone* contains an extensive section on its genesis, seems not to know about *Oreste*. Along with Flügge's omission, Ingrid Galster (whose exhaustive book deals with critical response in the Occupation press to Sartre's wartime plays, including *Les Mouches*), Added, and Witt do not refer to *Oreste* either.

Moreover, in most references to the piece, little is said other than that it was drawn from the Oresteian story, appeared in print in 1945, and (from later writers) that it was incorporated into Anouilh's *Tu étais si gentil quand tu étais petit*, first performed in 1972.

19. And della Fazia concludes, as if the play had been finished, "Destiny demands that [Electre's and Oreste's] somewhat absurd concept of duty be played out to its tragic end" (11). Luppé mentions that the style of the piece is similar to that of *Antigone*, and adds, "C'est la même image familière du Destin . . ." (58).

Chapter 6

1. On the script, production, and critical reception of *The Flies*, Ingrid Galster provides an extremely detailed and thorough discussion (50–192).

2. Although Simone Jollivet's *The Princess of Ursins* in fact had a slightly longer run, Dullin (according to Beauvoir in *The Prime of Life*) apparently revived *The Flies* the following October and ran it for a season in repertory with other plays (539).

3. My friend, Dennis Gilbert, reminds me that Added's comments on *The Flies* are provoked largely by Ingrid Galster's excellent study of Sartre's wartime dramatic works and their critical reception.

4. During the years in which he was seen as the leading postwar French intellectual, Sartre in fact reestablished a large piece of his childhood: "After 1946 Sartre led a comfortable existence just around the corner of the [Café] Flore, at 42, rue Bonaparte, where he lived with his mother and played Shubert four-hand piano pieces with her, but this cozy home life remained hidden from most people's eyes" (White 268–269).

5. As noted in chapter 1, the word "pederasty" here does not actually mean that Genet had grown up interested in younger boys; the word is intended simply to mean "homosexual." More on this conflation may be found in chapter 7.

6. I would like to thank Dennis Gilbert for his help in locating critical material on this play.

7. A reader of *The Flies* today may easily discern Sartre's feelings about women, but of course such recognition has been made possible by more than three decades of feminist discourse on literature. I am not suggesting that Sartre's original audience recognized such misogynistic tendencies in the play, which for the most part conformed to the misogyny of the culture itself.

8. Electra, notes Nina Bailey, conforms to the stereotype of the temptress Eve (295).

9. Contrary to his later interviews, Sartre's sexist attitudes may, however, have changed as he grew older. Bernard Quinn tries to argue that, although the female characters from the Occupation seem to "engage in self-deception," three female characters from later plays—Hilda (in *The Devil and the Good Lord*), Anna (in *Kean*), and Véronique (in *Nekrassov*)—"attempt to live the authentic life" (39). In the end, however, "these three heroines have a liberating effect on the male protagonists" (44). This may remind readers of Fraunhofer's assertion that Orestes "assimilates Electre's, the Other's, freedom" and that "[h]is project of recovering himself is, ultimately, a project of absorbing the Other" (380).

Chapter 7

1. As noted in Chapter 2, Montherlant was among those who attended the double bill at Roland-Garros. His own interest in sports and his own writings on the subject make his presence, in the proximity of Borotra, symbolic.

2. The pictures included in the *Album Montherlant* end with shots from 1966 (220) and 1969 (222).

3. I would like to thank Dr. Josephine Arnold, not only for providing an explanation for Montherlant's change of birthdates but also for offering a brilliant psychosexual analysis of Montherlant and his work.

4. As indicated below, Peyrefitte published his version of Montherlant's experiences during the Occupation.

5. Montherlant retains the same characters in both the play, *The City Whose Prince is a Child* and the novel, *The Boys*. Alban is the younger version of a character about whom Montherlant previously wrote.

6. According to Peyrefitte, this occurred late in 1937 (*Propos Secrets* 62). However, Sipriot's chronology at the beginning of the *Correspondance* would suggest that it could only have occurred sometime after January 11, 1938 (the date on which Peyrefitte returned from his post in Athens).

7. Translations are mine.

8. Arnold notes a significant parallel: "The word *enfant* (child) is woven throughout the variegated tapestry of the writer's work." She goes on to explain how Montherlant made use of the ambiguity of the word—its ability to refer to both male and female, to "describe a very young person without specifying age," and to apply as an affectionate term in erotic situations—without being detected (192).

9. Sipriot, in his Preface to the *Correspondance*, notes how in December 1938, Montherlant was stopped at the kermesse Berlitz (near the Palais Berlitz) and questioned about caressing the knees of a fourteen-year-old boy in a movie theatre.

10. Sipriot quotes from Montherlant's posthumous *Tous feux éteints* (118), and I translate a paraphrase of the quote.

11. Although the book's cover indicates that eighty-seven of Egermeier's photos are included, I count eighty-six.

12. The photograph on page 68 shows young men (17 or older) running in the background while two young men sit talking in the foreground; this picture was also used for the book's cover.

13. The caption indicates that the passage appears in the 1938 *Les Olympiques* on page 104.

14. "Par quel hasard ce texte, qui dut passer totalement imperçu à sa parution, et n'a jamais été réprimé, tomba-t-il sous mes yeux?" asks Fernandez, who maintains that as a boy *Paysage des Olympiques* was the first book he encountered (other than books depicting classical statues) to show male nudity (103).

15. I am indebted (once more) to Josephine Arnold for these references.
In response to Peyrefitte's early admonitions, Montherlant retorted that his female readership would never stand for such admissions. Peyrefitte comments that, on the contrary, women could easily understand, because they themselves more or less felt amorous toward their sons, and concludes that this showed how childish Montherlant was in his judgment about life (*Propos Secrets* 79).

16. Arnold draws from John Money's *Gay, Straight and In-Between* (New York: Oxford UP, 1988).

17. Sipriot refers to Guéhenno's *Journal des années noires (1940–1944)*, entry dated January 10, 1941.

18. Robicher notes that in 1963, when *Fils de personne* was revived at the Mathurins, Montherlant allowed the first act of *La Ville dont le prince est un enfant* to be performed as a curtain raiser (57).

19. Mary Ann Frese Witt offers an excellent analysis of just how closely Montherlant's aesthetic impulses coincided with those of the fascist intellectuals and their notions on tragedy (195–211).

20. An additional implication of the ending of the play, as Arnold so insightfully describes it, is the misogyny in the closing tableau. Although the title speaks of the queen that Inès becomes through her martyrdom, her function as a woman seems, perhaps typically for Montherlant, to breed children.

21. This is taken from the English translation, *Queen After Death*, by Jonathan Griffen. Although, as indicated, this monologue has for the sake of brevity been edited for inclusion here, the deletions do not alter the remarks that appear.

22. The original production cut a final monologue by Georges and gave Gillou precise physical instructions on his exit, after which the curtain fell. See the prompt book of *Fils de Personne* in the Bibliothèque Historique de la Ville de Paris.

23. "Preface de *Fils de Personne*"; this and all other notices are found in *Le Fils de Personne, pièce en quatre actes d'Henry de Montherlant; L'Incompris, pièce en un acte du même auteur, représentée pour le premier fois le 17 XII 43 au Théâtre Saint Georges (rép. gen.le)*. [Press clipping scrapbook.] Paris: Biobliothèque de l'Arsenal, R. Supp. 1413 [1943–1944]. *L'Incompris*, a one-act play by Montherlant, was originally scheduled to appear with *Nobody's Son* but was cancelled before the premiere.

24. I am indebted to Serge Added for referring me to this extract from Copeau's journal. The translations here are mine.

Chapter 8

1. The arrival of the ashes of the King of Rome—or as the Germans preferred to call him, the Duke of Reichstadt—and their burial close to Napoleon's tomb at Les Invalides, prompted at least one Nazi official to encourage the Comédie–Française to stage *L'Aiglon*. This project never reached the stage, however.

2. The son of a Jewish father, Jean Yonnel, who played Prouhèze's husband, had been reinstated into the Comédie–Française (by order of German Ambassador Otto Abetz) in August 1941. His greatest role during the Occupation, however, would be as Ferrante, the protagonist in Montherlant's *La Reine Morte* (Added 48–49).

3. Quotes from the play that appear in English are drawn from John O'Connor's translation of the full text. Throughout the discussion, however, I retain the character names in the French (thus, "Rodrigue" for "Rodrigo").

4. Unless otherwise indicated, references to press notices are drawn from *Le Soulier de Satin: action espagnole en 2 parties de Paul Claudel, représenté pour la première fois, à la Comédie Française, le 27 Novembre 1943*. [Press clipping scrapbook.] Paris: Biobliothèque de l'Arsenal, R. Supp. 1453 [1943–1944]. Translations are mine.

5. Barrault had been Sartre's first choice as director of *The Flies*. His involvement in the Claudel project for the Comédie–Française inevitably precluded his participation in any other play. In addition, Beauvoir may not have known in 1943 (or 1944) where Barrault was headed, but when she came to write *The Prime of Life* she knew quite well that he would leave the Comédie–Française in 1946 and eventually form his own company with his wife, Madeleine Renaud.

6. I am indebted to Martha Walker of Mary Baldwin College, who, after I read a piece of what became this chapter, reminded me that the role of the Guardian Angel was played by Mary Marquet.

7. This review is not included in the Arsenal press scrapbook. However, a critique of Le Grix's critique is the last article in the scrapbook (101–103).

8. The program for the forty-eighth performance, on Thursday, March 16, 1944, several weeks before the end of the run, is included at the beginning of the Arsenal press scrapbook.

Epilogue

1. Le Boterf, whose work on the culture of the Occupation influenced Truffaut, notes also a production of "A Tragedy of Love," by Norwegian playwright Gunnar Heilberg, which Le Boterf does call "néo-ibsénien" (249). Perhaps this play inspired *La Disparue*.

2. As noted in chapter 1, when Jean Marais tried to join the Résistance, the same kinds of things (according to Louis Jourdan) were said about Jean Cocteau.

3. My friend Jocelyn Van Tuyl construes this plant to be tobacco, but both cannabis and poppies are better suited to the light and climate of Paris.

4. The *Annuaire Général du Spectacle en France* for 1942–1943, in its opening calendar section, clearly lists *Les Pirates de Paris ou «L'Affaire Stavisky»* as a play by Alain Laubreaux (38). However, in its synopses of plays of the season, the author is given as Michel Daxiat (73).

5. For some of these references, see the introductory section of the English translation of Truffaut's screenplay, especially "*The Last Metro* and the Cinema of the Occupation" by Mirella Jona Affron (3–8) and "*The Last Metro* and the Preoccupations of Cinema" by E. Rubenstein (11–22).

Bibliography

Added, Serge. *Le Théâtre dans les années Vichy, 1940–44*. Paris: Editions Ramsay, 1992.

Aeschylus. *The Suppliant Maidens*. S. G. Bernadette trans. *Aeschylus II*. David Grene and Richmond Lattimore, eds. New York: Washington Square Press, 1967, 5–42.

Allison, Lincoln. "Sport and Politics." *The Politics of Sport*. Lincoln Allison, ed. Manchester: Manchester UP, 1986.

Ambriére, Francis. Review in *L'Opéra*, 30 avril 1947, p. 1.

Anahory, Eduardo. Maquette pour *L'Apollon de Bellac*. In Jean Giraudoux, *Théâtre*. Vol. 2. Paris: Grasset, 1954, 433.

Anouilh, Jean. *Antigone. Nouvelles Pièces Noires*. Paris: La Table Ronde, 1945.

————. *Oreste: Fragments. La Table Ronde*, 3 (1945), 54–79.

————. *Tu Étais Si Gentil Quand Tu Étais Petit*. Paris: La Table Ronde, 1972.

Archer, Marguerite. *Jean Anouilh*. New York: Columbia UP, 1971.

Arnold, A. James, ed. *Caligula: Suivi de La Poetique du premier Caligula par A. James Arnold. From a 1941 Typescript*. Paris: Gallimard, 1981 [Cahiers Albert Camus, No. 4].

Arnold, Josephine. "Montherlant and the Problem of the Aging Pederast." *Aging and Gender in Literature: Studies in Creativity*. Anne M. Wyatt-Brown and Janice Rossen, eds. Charlottesville: Virginia UP, 1993.

Aslan, Odette. *Jean Genet*. Paris: Seghurs, 1973.

Atelier [Press Clipping Scrapbook: *L'Ombre*]. Bibliothèque Nationale, RT 3745, Tome XI, 10-1 to 10-8.

Azema, Jean-Pierre. *From Munich to the Liberation, 1938–1944*. Janet Lloyd trans. Cambridge: Cambridge UP, 1984.

Bach, Raymond. "Cocteau and Vichy: Familiy Disconnections." *L'Ésprit Créateur* 13.1 (Spring 1993), 29–37.

Bailey, Nina. "Le Mythe de la Féminité dans le Théâtre de Sartre." *French Studies* 31 (July 1977), 294–307.

Bair, Deirdre. "Introduction to the Vintage Edition." Beauvoir, Simone de. *The Second Sex*. New York: Vintage, 1989, vii–xviii.

Barthes, Roland. *Mythologies*. Annette Lavers trans. New York: Hill & Wang, 1972.

Beauvoir, Simone de. *Journal de guerre: septembre 1939–janvier 1941*. Sylvie Le Bon de Beauvoir, ed. Paris: Gallimard, 1990.

———. *Letters to Sartre*. Quentin Hoare ed. and trans. New York: Arcade, 1992.

———. *The Prime of Life*. Peter Green trans. New York: Viking-Penguin, 1965.

———. *The Second Sex*. New York: Vintage, 1989.

Bernadette, S. G. "Introduction to *The Suppliant Maidens*." *Aeschylus II*. David Grene and Richmond Lattimore, eds. New York: Washington Square Press, 1967.

Bertin, Célia. *Femmes sous l'Occupation*. Paris: Stock, 1993.

Beugnot, Bernard, ed. *Les Critiques de notre temps et Anouilh*. Paris: Garnier Frères, 1977.

Bibliothèque Municipale de Douai. *André Obey, Homme de Théâtre: Exposition*. Douai: Bibliothèque Municipale de Douai, 1985.

Body, Jacques. *Giraudoux et l'Allemagne*. Paris: Publications de la Sorbonne, 73 [1976].

———. "Notice" and "Note sur la texte" [of *L'Apollon de Bellac*]. *Théâtre Complet*. Ed. Jacques Body. Paris: Gallimard, 1983, 1702–1717 [Pléiade Edition].

Borgal, Clément. *Anouilh: la peine de vivre*. Editions du Centurion, 1966.

Bradby, David. *Modern French Drama 1940–1980*. Cambridge: Cambridge UP, 1984.

Breker, Arno. *Paris, Hitler, et Moi*. Paris: Presses de la Cité, 1970.

Brockett, Oscar G. and Robert R. Findlay. *Century of Innovation: A History of European and American Drama Since 1870*. Englewood Cliffs: Prentice-Hall, 1973.

Bronski, Michael. *Culture Clash: The Making of Gay Sensibility*. Boston: South End, 1984.

Brown, Frederick. *Theater and Revolution: The Culture of the French Stage*. New York: Random House, 1980.

Castelot, André. Review of Hauptman's *Iphigènie à Delphes*, *La Gérbe*, 10 juin 1943.

Chaine, Catherine. "A Conversation about Sex and Women with Jean-Paul Sartre." *Playboy* 25:1 (1978), 103–239.

Chauncey, George. *Gay New York: The Making of the Gay Male World*. London: Flamingo, 1995.

Chiari, Joseph. *The Contemporary French Theatre: The Flight from Naturalism*. New York: Macmillan, 1959.

Claudel, Paul. *Le Soulier de Satin*. *Théâtre II*. Ed. Jacques Madaule and Jacques Petit. Paris: Gallimard, 1965. [Pléiade Edition.]

———. *The Satin Slipper or The Worst is not the Surest*. Trans. John O'Connor. New York: Sheed & Ward, 1945.

Claudel, Paul and Jean-Louis Barrault. *Le Soulier de Satin: Edition pour la scène abrégée, notée et arrangée en collaboration avec Jean-Louis Barrault*. Paris: Gallimard, 1943.

Cobb, Richard. *French and Germans, Germans and French: A Personal Interpretation of France under Two Occupations 1914–1918/1940–1944*. Hanover, NH: New England UP, 1983.

Cobban, Alfred. *A History of Modern France. Volume 3: France of the Republics 1871–1962*. Baltimore: Penguin, 1965.

Cocteau, Jean. *Journal, 1942–1945*. Jean Touzot, ed. Paris: Gallimard, 1989.

———. *La Machine à écrire*. Mise en scène. Bibliothèque Historique de la Ville de Paris. [Prompt Book.]

———. *Théâtre II*. Paris: Gallimard, 1948, 91–192.

———. *The Typewriter*. Trans. Ronald Duncan. London: Dennis Dobson, 1947.

———. Preface. *The White Paper*. New York: Macaulay, 1958, 5–8.

Coe, Richard N. "Unbalanced Opinions: A Study of Jean Genet and the French Critics. Followed by a Checklist of Criticism in French." *Proceedings of the Leeds Philosophical and Literary Society*, 14.2 (June 1970).

Cohen, Robert. *Giraudoux: Two Faces of Destiny*. Chicago: Chicago UP, 1968.

Cohn, Ruby. *From Desire to Godot: Pocket Theater of Postwar Paris*. Berkeley: California UP, 1987.

Collins, Larry, and Dominque Lapierre. *Is Paris Burning?* New York: Simon & Schuster, 1965.

Combs, Richard. Review of *Le Dernier Métro*. *Monthly Film Bulletin*, 48 (July 1981), 135–136.

Comité d'Organisation des Entreprises de Spectacles. *Annuaire Général du Spectacle en France: 1942–1943.* Paris: Administration-Rédaction, 1943.

Cone, Michèle C. *Artists Under Vichy: A Case of Prejudice and Persecution.* Princeton: Princeton UP, 1992.

Copeau, Jacques. *Journal 1901–1948; Deuxième Partie: 1916–1948.* Claude Sucard, ed. Paris: Seghers, 1991.

Copley, Antony. *Sexual Moralities in France, 1780–1980: New ideas on the family, divorce, and homosexuality.* New York: Routledge, 1989.

Crosland, Margret. "Introduction." *The White Book* by Jean Cocteau. San Francisco: City Lights, 1989, 7–14.

Cruickshank, John. *Montherlant.* Edinburgh: Oliver and Boyd, 1964.

Dawson, Brett. *Bibliographie de l'ouevre de Jean Giraudoux: 1899–1982.* Bellac: Association des Amis de Jean Giraudoux, 1982.

Debusscher, Gilbert. "French Stoaways on an American Milk Train: Williams, Cocteau and Peyrefitte." *Modern Drama,* 25 (3 Sept. 1982): 399–408.

della Fazia, Alba. *Jean Anouilh.* New York: Twayne, 1969.

Dutton, Kenneth R. *The Perfectible Body: The Western Ideal of Male Physical Development.* New York: Continuum, 1995.

Electre pièce en deux actes de Jean Giraudoux, reprisé, au Théâtre de l'Avenue, la 30 [mars] 1943 (rép. gén le), R. Supp. 1220. Arsenal [1943].

Ehrlich, Evelyn. *Cinema of Paradox: French Filmmaking Under the German Occupation.* New York: Columbia UP, 1985.

Evleth, Donna. *France Under the German Occupation, 1940–1944: An Annotated Bibliography.* Westport, CT: Greenwood, 1991.

Falb, Lewis W. *Jean Anouilh.* New York: Ungar, 1977.

Fernandez, Dominique. *Le Rapt de Ganymède.* Paris: Grasset, 1989.

Flood, Christopher G. "Theatrical Triumph and Political Ambiguity: *Le Soulier de satin* at the Comédie Française in 1943–1944." *French Cultural Studies,* 3:17–30 (Feb. 1992).

Florisoone, Michel, Raymond Cogniat, Yves-Bonnat. *Un An de Théâtre 1940–1941.* Lyons: Editions de la France Nouvelle [1941].

Flügge, Manfred *Verweigerung oder neue Ordnung: Jean Anouilhs 'Antigone' im politschen und ideologischen Kontext der Besatzungzeit 1940–1944.* 2 vols. Rheinfelden: Schauble Verlag, 1982.

Forkey, Leo. "The Theatres of Paris During the Occupation." *The French Review* 22 (Feb. 1949), 299–305.

Fowlie, Wallace. *Dionysus in Paris: A Guide to Contemporary French Theatre*. London: Gollancz, 1961.

Fraigneau, Andre. *Cocteau*. New York: Grove, 1961.

Francis, Claude, and Fernande Gontier. *Simone de Bauvoir: A Life, A Love Story*. Lisa Nesselson, trans. New York: St. Martin's, 1987.

Fraunhofer, Hedwig. "Postpaternalism and the Fear of the Feminine: The Economic and the Erotic in Strindberg, Brecht, Giraudoux, and Sartre." Diss. U. of Oregon, 1995.

Galantière, Louis, trans. *Antigone. Five Plays* by Jean Anouilh. Volume I. New York: Hill & Wang, 1958, 1–53.

Galster, Ingrid. *Le Théâtre de Jean-Paul Sartre devant ses premiers critiques*. Paris: Jean-Michel Place, 1986.

Gastinel, Françoise. "Notice" to *Lorenzaccio*. Anna Gastinel, ed. *Comédies et proverbes* by Alfred de Musset, Vol. II. Paris: Société des Belles Lettres, 1952. 352–355.

Gay-Lescot, Jean-Louis. "La Politique sportive de Vichy." *La Vie culturelle sous Vichy*. Jean-Pierre Rioux, ed. Bruxelles: Editions Complexe, 1990, 83–115.

Genêt (Jean) Les Bonnes, pièce en 1 acte; Giraudoux (Jean) L'Apollon de Marsac, comédie en 1 acte. [Press clipping scrapbook.] Paris: Biobliothèque de l'Arsenal, R. Supp. 2069 [1947].

Gerassi, John. *Jean-Paul Sartre: Hated Conscience of His Century; Volume 1: Protestant or Protester?* Chicago: Chicago UP, 1989.

Girard, Jacques. *Le Mouvement homosexuel en France, 1945–1970*. Paris: Syros [1981].

Giraudoux, Jean. *The Apollo de Bellac*. English version by Ronald Duncan. *The Best One-Act Plays of 1956–57*. Hugh Miller, ed. London: Harrap, 1957, 9–35.

———. *The Apollo of Bellac*. Adapted by Maurice Valency. *Four Plays*. New York: Hill & Wang, 1958, 73–101.

———. *L'Apollon de Bellac. Théâtre Complet*. Ed. Jacques Body. Paris: Gallimard, 1983, 917–946 [Pléiade Edition].

———. *L'Apollon de Bellac. Le Théâtre Complet de Jean Giraudoux*. Vol. 16. Neuchatel: Ides et Calendes, 1951, 145–196.

———. *L'Apollon de Marsac: comedia em um ado*. Rio de Janeiro: Dom Casmuro, 1942 (theatre supplement 5).

———. *Souvenir de deux existences*. Paris: Grasset, 1973.

———. *Visitations*. Neuchatel: Ides et Calendes, 1947.

Giraudoux, Jean and Louis Jouvet. "Correspondence." *Cahiers de Jean Giraudoux, 9*. Paris: Grasset, 1980.

[Gobeil, Madeliene.] "Playboy Interview: Jean-Paul Sartre." *Playboy* 12:5 (1965), 69–76.

Golsan, Richard J. "Henry de Montherlant: Itinierary of an Ambivalent Fascist." Richard J. Golsan, ed. *Fascism, Aesthetics, and Culture*. Hanover, NH: New England UP, 1992.

———. "Literary Collaboration at *La Gerbe*." *Journal of European Studies* 23 (1993), 27–47.

Gordon, Bertram M. "The Morphology of the Collaborator: The French Case." *Journal of European Studies* 23 (1993), 1–25.

Greenblatt, Stephen. *Shakespearean Negotiations: The Circulation of Social Energy in Renaissance England*. Berkeley: California UP, 1989.

Griffen, Roger. "Staging the Nation's Rebirth: The Politics and Aesthetics of Performance in the Context of Fascist Studies." *Fascism and Theatre: Comparative Studies on the Aesthetics and Politics of Performance in Europe, 1925–1945*. Ed. Günter Berghaus. Providence: Berghan Books, 1996. 11–29.

Gruneau, Richard. *Sport, Culture, and the Modern State*. Hart Cantelon and Richard Gruneau, eds. Toronto: Toronto UP, 1982, 2–38.

Guéhenno, Jean. *Journal des années noires (1940–1944)*. Paris: Gallimard, 1947.

Guicharnaud, Jacques. *Modern French Theatre: From Giraudoux to Genet*. New Haven: Yale UP, 1967. (Yale Romanic Studies, 2nd Series, 7; rev. ed.)

Halls, W. D. *The Youth of Vichy France*. Oxford: Clarnedon Press, 1981.

Hartman, Geoffrey. "The Dubious Charm of M. Truffaut," *Partisan Review*, 51/52 (1984/5), 823–825.

Harvey, John. *Anouilh: A Study in Theatrics*. New Haven: Yale UP, 1964.

Hause, Steven C. "More Minerva than Mars: The French Women's Rights Campaign and the First World War." *Behind the Lines: Gender and the Two World Wars*. Margaret Randolph Higonnet, Jane Jenson, Sonya Michel, and Margret Collins Weitz, eds. New Haven: Yale UP, 1987.

Hewitt, Andrew. *Political Inversions: Homosexuality, Fascism, and the Modernist Imaginary*. Stanford: Stanford UP, 1996.

———. "Sleeping with the Enemy: Genet and the Fantasy of Homo-Fascism." Melanie Hawthorne and Richard J. Golsan, eds. *Gender and Fascism in Modern France*: Hanover, NH: Dartmouth College/New England UP, 1997.

Hirschfeld, Gerhard and Patrick Marsh, eds. *Collaboration in France: Politics and Culture During the Nazi Occupation, 1940–44*. New York: Berg, 1989.

Hoare, Quintin, ed. and trans. *Letters to Sartre*. New York: Arcade, 1992.

Hoberman, John M. *Olympic Crisis: Sport, Politics and the Moral Order*. New Rochelle, NY: Caratzas, 1986.

————. *Sport and Political Ideology*. Austin: Texas UP, 1984.

Hobson, Harold. *The French Theatre of To-day: An English View*. New York: Benjamin Bloom, 1953.

————. *French Theatre Since 1880*. Dallas: Riverrun Press, 1978.

Houlding, Elizabeth A. "Between the Lines: Women Writing the Occupation of France." Diss. Columbia U., 1991.

Insdorf, Annette. *François Truffaut*. New York: Simon & Schuster, 1989. [Rev. ed.]

————. "Interview with François Truffaut." In *The Last Métro*. Ed. Mirella Jona Affron and E. Rubinstein. New Brunswick, NJ: Rutgers UP, 1985, 173–179.

Inskip, Donald. *Jean Giraudoux: The Making of a Dramatist*. New York: Oxford UP, 1958.

Jacobs, Gabriel. "The Role of Joan of Arc on the Stage of Occupied Paris." *Vichy France and the Resistance: Culture and Ideology*. Roderick Kedward and Roger Austin, eds. London: Croom Helm, 1985, 106–121.

Jebb, Julian. "The Theatre of Occupied Paris," *Sight and Sound*, 50 (Summer 1981), 210–211.

Jenson, Jane. "The Liberation and New Rights for French Women." *Behind the Lines: Gender and the Two World Wars*. Margaret Randolph Higonnet, Jane Jenson, Sonya Michel, and Margret Collins Weitz, eds. New Haven: Yale UP, 1987.

Jollivet, Simone. *La Princesse des Ursins*. Manuscript in the Département des arts du spectacle, Charles Dullin Collection, Bibliothèque Nationale, Paris, France.

Jones, Robert Emmet. *The Alienated Hero in Modern French Drama*. Athens: Georgia UP, 1962 [Univeristy of Georgia Monographs, No 9].

Josephs, Jeremy. *Swastika Over Paris: The Fate of the Jews in France*. New York: Arcade, 1989.

Joubert, Marie-Agnès. *La Comédie Française sous l'Occupation*. Paris: Tallandier, 1998.

Kanters, Robert. Review in *Verger*, I, 3 (Nov. 1947), 85–90.

Kedward, Roderick. "Introduction: Ideologies and Ambiguities." Roderick Kedward and Roger Austin, eds. *Vichy France and the Resistance: Culture and Ideology*. London: Croom Helm, 1985.

Kedward, Roderick and Roger Austin, eds. *Vichy France and the Resistance: Culture and Ideology*. London: Croom Helm, 1985.

Kelly, Kathleen White. *Jean Anouilh: An Annotated Bibliography*. Metuchen, NJ: Sacrecrow Press, 1973.

King Lear, trad. Simone Jollivet, mis en scène Charles Dullin, Théâtre Sarah-Bernhardt, 10 avril 1945. [Press clipping scrapbook.] Paris: Biobliothèque de l'Arsenal, R. Supp. 1625 [1945].

Klein, Alan M. *Little Big Men: Bodybuilding Subculture and Gender Construction.* Albany: SUNY Press, 1993.

Kline, Michael B. and Nancy C. Mellerski. "Structures of Ambiguity in Truffaut's *Le Dernier Métro.*" *The French Review* 62.1 (Oct. 1988), 88–98.

Knapp, Bettina L. *French Theatre 1918–1939.* New York: Grove Press, 1985.

———. *Paul Claudel.* New York: Ungar, 1982.

Knox, Bernard. *Word and Action: Essays on the Ancient Theater.* Baltimore: Johns Hopkins UP, 1979.

Krauss, Kenneth. "Lorenzaccio, Castraccio, Lorenzetta." *George Sand Studies* 10 (1991), 18–27.

———. *Private Readings/Public Texts: Playreaders' Constructs of Theatre Audiences.* Rutherford, NJ: Fairleigh Dickinson UP, 1993.

———. "Probabilities of Collaboration, Possibilities of Resistance: Locating Anouilh's *Antigone* by Way of *Oreste.*" *New England Theatre Journal* 6 (1995), 19–32.

———. "Rewriting Gender in Time of War: The Stage Debut of *Le Soulier de Satin*" *Paul Claudel Papers* 1 (2001), 73–80.

———. "The Play Intended: Giraudoux's *Apollon.*" *Journal of Dramatic Theory and Criticism* 8:2 (Spring 1994), 59–76.

———. "Women in the Vichy Nightmare: Behind the Scenes in Simone Jollivet's *La Princesse des Ursins. Simone de Beauvoir Studies* 11 (1994), 88–103.

La Machine á écrire, pièce en trois actes de Jean Cocteau, répresenté pour la première fois au Théâtre Hébertot (sur la scène du Théâtre Batignolles) la 29-4-41. [Press clipping scrapbook.] Paris: Bibliothèque de l'Arsenal, R. Supp. 735 [1941].

La Princesse des Ursins, pièce en trois actes, un prologue et un epilogue, par Simone Jollivet. [Press clipping scrapbook.] Paris: Biobliothèque de l'Arsenal, R. Supp. 816 [1942].

Lacouture, Jean. *De Gaulle The Rebel, 1890–1944.* Patrick O'Brian, trans. New York: Norton, 1990.

Lalou, René. Review in *Gavroche.* 1 mai 1947.

Lannes, Roger. Review in *Le Figaro Littéraire*, 26 avril 1947, 6.

Lapara, Léo. *Dix Ans Avec Jouvet.* Paris: Editions France-Empire, 1975.

Laubreaux, Alain. Review of *La Machine à écrire. Je suis partout*, May 19, 1941, 9.

Le Bitoux, Jean and Gilles Barbedette. "Jean-Paul Sartre: The Final Interview." George Stambolian trans. *Christopher Street*, July/August 1980, 32–37.

Le Boterf, Hervé. *La Vie Parisienne sous l'occupation, 1940–1944.* Vol. I. Paris: Editions France-Empire, 1974.

Leak, Andrew. *The Perverted Consciousness: Sexuality and Sartre.* New York: St. Martin's Press, 1989.

Lefebvre, Jacques. "La Femme dans le théâtre de Claudel." *Revue Générale pour l'huministe des temps nouveaux*, 4 (Apr. 1983), 57–68.

Le Fils de Personne, pièce en quatre actes d'Henry de Montherlant; L'Incompris, pièce en un acte du même auteur, représentée pour le premier fois le 17 XII 43 au Théâtre Saint Georges (rép. gen.le). [Press clipping scrapbook.] Paris: Biobliothèque de l'Arsenal, R. Supp. 1413 [1943–1944].

Le Grix, François. "Le Théâtre: Remarques sur 'L'événement' du Soulier de Satin." *Baudelaire devant la douleur suivi de Quelques essais et Mises au point.* [*Hier et Demain*: 10.] Paris: Sequana, 1944.

Le Soulier de Satin: action espagnole en 2 parties de Paul Claudel, représenté pour la première fois, à la Comédie Française, le 27 Novembre 1943. [Press clipping scrapbook.] Paris: Bibliothèque de l'Arsenal, R. Supp. 1453 [1943–1944].

Les Suppliantes d'Eschyle; 800 mètres, drame sportif d'André Obey, au stade Roland-Garros—les 5 et 6 Juillet 1941. [Press clipping scrapbook.] Paris: Biobliothèque de l'Arsenal, R. Supp. 755 [1941].

Linières, Edmond Desportes de. "Sources d'Information—Bibliographie (en Français) sur la 'personalité de S.J.[']" [Paris: 1993; unpublished; handwritten ms. in possession of the author.]

————. "Simone Jollivet, qui êtes-vous?" [Paris: 1993; unpublished; handwritten ms. in possession of the author.]

Lottman, Herbert. *The Left Bank: Writers, Artists, and Politics from the Popular Front to the Cold War.* San Francisco: Halo Books, 1991 [rpt Houghton-Mifflin, 1981].

Lubetski, J. *La Condition des Juifs en France Sous l'Occupation Allemande, 1940–44: La Législation Raciale.* Paris: Centre de Documentation Juive Contemporaine, 1945.

Luppé, Robert de. *Jean Anouilh.* Paris: Editions Universal, 1959 [rep. 1964].

McCall, Dorothy. *The Theatre of Jean-Paul Sartre.* New York: Columbia UP, 1969.

McIntyre, H. G. *The Theatre of Jean Anouilh.* Totowa, NJ: Barnes & Noble, 1981.

Madsen, Axel. *Hearts and Minds: The Common Journey of Simone de Beauvoir and Jean-Paul Sartre.* Morrow: New York, 1977.

Malicet, Michel. "La Peur de la Femme dans *Le Soulier de Satin.*" *Paul Cladel 11 (1974): Les Images dans Le Soulier de Satin.* Jacques Petit, ed. *La Revue des*

Lettres Modernes, Nos. 391–397, 1974 (2). Paris: Lettres Modernes, Minard, 1974.

Marcel, Gabriel. Review in *Les Nouvelles Littéraires*, 1 mai 1947, 10.

Marais, Jean. "Confronting a Critic." François Truffaut et al. *The Last Métro*. Ed. Mirella Jona Affron and E. Rubenstein. New Brunswick, NJ: Rutgers UP, 1985. 182–184.

———. *Histoires de ma vie*. Paris: Albin Michel, 1975.

Marker, Chris. *Giraudoux par lui-même*. Paris: Editions de Seuil, 1957.

Marrus, Michael R. and Robert O. Paxton. *Vichy France and the Jews*. New York: Schocken, 1983.

Marsh, Edward Owens. *Jean Anouilh, poet of Pierrot and Pantaloon*. New York: Russell & Russell, 1968.

Marsh, Patrick. "Le Théâtre à Paris sous l'occupation allemande." *Revue de la Société d'histoire de Théâtre*, 33.3 (1981): 197–369.

———. "The Theatre: Compromise or Collaboration?" *Collaboration in France: Politics and Culture During the Nazi Occupation, 1940–44*. Gerhard Hirschfeld and Patrick Marsh, eds. New York: Berg, 1989, 142–161.

Maulnier, Thierry. Review in *Revue de la Pensée Française*, août 1947, 42.

May, Georges. "Jean Giraudoux, Diplomacy and Dramaturgy." *Yale French Studies* 5 (1950), 88–94.

Mayfield, M.A., ed. *The Antigone of Sophocles*. New York: St. Martin's, 1960.

Mehlman, Jeffrey. *Legacies of Anti-Semitism in France*. Minneapolis: Minnesota UP, 1983.

Metheny, Eleanor. *Movement and Meaning*. New York: McGraw Hill, 1968.

Millet-Gérard, Dominique. "La Figure féminine chez Claudel." *Claudel Studies*, 15:1 (1988), 17–28.

Montherlant, Henry de. "Les Chevaleries." *Les Solstice de juin. Essais*. Paris: Gallimard, 1963 [Pléiade Édition], 857–872.

———. *Fils de Personne*. Mise en scène de Pierre Dux. Relevé par Mr J. Faure. Bibliothèque Historique de la Ville de Paris. [Prompt Book.]

———. *Fils de Personne. Théâtre*. Paris: Gallimard, 1965. [Pléiade edition.] 275–346.

———. *Les Olympiques*. Paris: Grasset, 1938.

———. *Nobody's Child. The Master of Santiago and Four Other Plays*. Jonathan Griffen trans. New York: Knopf, 1951. 174–231.

———. *Paysage des Olympiques*. Illustrated with photographs by Karel Egermeier. Paris: Grasset, 1940.

———. *Queen After Death. The Master of Santiago and Four Other Plays.* Jonathan Griffen trans. New York: Knopf, 1951. 3–86.

———. *Tous feux éteints.* Paris: Gallimard, 1975.

Montherlant, Henry de and Roger Peyrefitte. *Correspondance.* Roger Peyrefitte and Pierre Sipriot, eds. Paris: Laffont, 1983.

Mosse, George L. "Beauty without Sensuality." *"Degenerate Art": The Fate of the Avant-Garde in Nazi Germany.* Los Angeles: Los Angeles County Museum of Art, 1991, 25–31.

———. *Nationalism and Sexuality.* New York: Howard Fertig, 1985.

Müller, Klaus. Introduction. Heinz Heger. *The Men with the Pink Triangles: The true, life-and-death story of homosexuals in the Nazi Death Camps.* David Fernbach trans. Boston: Alyson, 1994.

Musée National du Sport. *Paris de la Vie Sportive 1940–1944.* Paris: Ministere de la Jeunesse et des Sports, 1995.

Nye, Robert A. *Masculinity and Male Codes of Honor in Modern France.* New York: Oxford UP, 1993.

———. "The Sexuality of Michel Foucault." *Homosexuality in Modern France.* Jeffrey Merrick and Bryant T. Ragan, Jr., eds. New York: Oxford UP, 1996, 225–241.

Obey, André. "Le huits cents métres de Paul Martin." *L'Orgue du Stade.* Paris: Gallimard, 1924, 191–215.

———. *Journée Olympique: Huit cents mètres.* Paris: Bibliotheque Nationale, 4oYa, 350, Radio [1964].

O'Connor, John trans. *The Satin Slipper or The Worst is not the Surest* by Paul Claudel. New York: Sheed & Ward, 1945.

Oxenhandler, Neal. *Scandal and Parade: The Theater of Jean Cocteau.* New Brunswick: Rutgers UP, 1957.

Paxton, Robert O. *Vichy France: Old Guard and New Order, 1940–1944.* New York: Norton, 1972.

Perec, Georges. *W or The Memory of Childhood.* Trans. David Bellos. Boston: Godine, 1988.

Peyrefitte, Roger. "L'Après Midi de Deux Fauns." Henry de Montherlant and Roger Peyrefitte. *Correspondance.* Roger Peyrefitte and Pierre Sipriot, eds. Paris: Laffont, 1983, 7–10.

———. *Propos Secrets.* Paris: Albin Michel, 1977.

———. *Special Friendships.* Felix Giovanelli trans. New York: Vanguard, 1950.

Pronko, Louis Cabell. *The World of Jean Anouilh.* Berkeley: California UP, 1961.

Pronger, Brian. *The Arena of Masculinity: Sports, Homosexuality, and the Meaning of Sex.* New York: St. Martins, 1990.

Pryce-Jones, David. *Paris in the Third Reich: A History of the German Occupation, 1940–1944.* London: Collins, 1981.

Quart, Leonard and Barbara Quart. Review of *Le Dernier Métro. Socialist Review*, 2.1 [61] (Jan./Feb. 1982), 135–138.

Quinn, Bernard J. "The Authentic Woman in the Theater of Jean-Paul Sartre." *USF Language Quarterly* 10:3–4 (1972), 39–44.

Raymond, Agnes. *Jean Giraudoux: The Theatre of Victory and Defeat.* [Amherst:] Massachusetts UP, 1966.

[Rebetat, Lucien writing as] François Vinneuil. Review of *La Machine à écrire. Je suis partout*, May 12, 1941, 9, 21.

Rinieri, J.-J. Review in *La NEF*, 30 mai 1947, 158.

Robichez, Jacques. *Le Théâtre de Montherlant.* Paris: Société d'Édition d'Enseignment Supérior, 1973.

Roche, Paul, trans. *Antigone. The Oedipus Plays of Sophocles.* New York: New American Library, 1958.

Rocher, René. "Le Théâtre sous l'occupation." *La Vie de la France sous l'occupation (1940–1944).* Ed. Hoover Insitute. Stanford, CA, 11, 965–972, 1947.

Rombout, André François. *La Pureté dans le Théâtre de Jean Anouilh: amour et bonheur, ou l'anarchisme reactionaire: une analyse de la fonction 'mythique' de la virginité et de la pureté morale sur le comportement des indivdus en quête du bonheur.* Amsterdam: Holland Universiteits Pers, 1975.

Rosenberg, Merrill A. "Montherlant and the Critics of the French Resistance." *The French Review*, 44:5 (April 1971), 839–851.

———. "The French Theater During the German Occupation." Diss., Harvard, 1963.

———. "Vichy's Theatrical Venture." *Theatre Survey*, 11: 124–150, 1970.

Rousso, Henry. *The Vichy Syndrome: History and Memory in France Since 1944.* Arthur Goldhammer trans. Cambridge, MA: Harvard UP, 1994.

Sartre, Jean-Paul. *Bariona, or the Son of Thunder. The Writings of Jean-Paul Sartre.* Vol. II. Michel Contat and Michael Rybalka, eds. Richard McCleary trans. Evanston: Northwestern UP, 1974.

———. *Sartre on Theater.* Michel Contat and Michel Rybalka, eds. Frank Jellinek trans. New York: Pantheon, 1976.

———. *Witness to My Life: The Letters of Jean-Paul Sartre to Simone de Beauvoir 1926–1939.* Simone de Beauvoir ed. Lee Fahnestock and Norman MacAfee trans. New York: Scribners: 1992.

Sardou, Roger. "La répétition générale de 'La Machine à écrire." *Les Nouveaux Temps*, 30 April 1941. *La Machine á écrire, pièce en trois actes de Jean Cocteau, répresenté pour la première fois au Théâtre Hébertot (sur la scène du Théâtre Batignolles) la 29-4-41.* [Press clipping scrapbook.] Paris: Bibliothèque de l'Arsenal, R. Supp. 735 [1941], 13.

Schwartz, Paula. "Redefining Resistance: Women's Activism in Wartime France." *Behind the Lines: Gender and the Two World Wars.* Maragret Randolph Higonnet, Jane Jenson, Sonya Michel, and Margret Collins Weitz, eds. New Haven: Yale UP, 1987.

Sedgewick, Eve Kosofsky. *Between Men: English Literature and Male Homosocial Desire.* New York: Columbia UP, 1985.

Seel, Pierre. *Moi, Pierre Seel, déporté homosexuel.* Jean Le Bitoux, ed. Paris: Calmann-Lévy, 1994.

Sipriot, Pierre. *Album Montherlant.* Paris: Gallimard, 1979 [Pléiade edition].

———. *Montherlant sans masque: Biographie, 1895–1972.* Paris: Laffont, 1990.

———. Preface. Henry de Montherlant and Roger Peyrefitte. *Correspondance.* Roger Peyrefitte and Pierre Sipriot, eds. Paris: Laffont, 1983, 11–27.

Smith, Christopher. *Jean Anouilh: life, work, and criticism.* Fredericton, NB: York Press, 1985.

Steegmuller, Francis. *Cocteau: a Biography.* Boston: Godine, 1986.

Stull, Heidi I. "The Epic Theater in the Face of Political Oppression." *Myths and Realities in Contemporary French Theater: Comparative Views.* Patricia M. Hopkins and Wendell M. Aycock, eds. Lubbock: Texas Tech UP, 1985, 71–84.

Sweets, John F. *Choices in Vichy France: The French Under Nazi Occupation.* New York: Oxford UP, 1986.

Toynbee, Philip. "France: The Literary Situation." *The New Republic*, CXII (Jan. 29, 1945), 152–158.

Truffaut, François. *Le Dernier Métro. L'Avant Scène Cinéma*, 303–304 (1–15 Mar. 1983), 11–85.

———. *The Last Métro.* Ed. Mirella Jona Affron and E. Rubinstein. New Brunswick, NJ: Rutgers UP, 1985.

———. *Letters.* Ed. Gilles Jacob and Claude de Givray. Gilbert Adair trans. Boston: Faber, 1989.

———. Introduction to André Bazin's *French Cinema of the Occupation and Resistance: The Birth of a Critical Esthetic.* Ed. François Truffaut. Stanley Hochman trans. New York: Ungar, 1981.

Vier, Jacques. *Le Théâtre de Jean Anouilh.* Paris: Société d'Edition Supérior, 1976.

Voloinov, V. N. Appendix I: "Discourse in Life and Discourse in Art (Concerning Sociological Poetics)." *Freudianism: A Critical Sketch*. Bloomington: Indiana UP, 1976, 93–117.

White, Edmund. *Genet: A Biography*. New York: Vintage, 1993.

Witt, Mary Ann Frese. *The Search for Modern Tragedy:Aesthetic Facism in Itay and France*. Ithaca: Cornell UP, 2001.

Zucca, André. Photograph Album. N.A. Album 29/30 243 Zucca. Paris: Bibliothèque Historique de la Ville de Paris [c. 1942].

———. Photograph Album. N.A. Album 40, 243, 7 Zucca. Paris: Bibliothèque Historique de la Ville de Paris [c. 1943].

———. Photograph Album. N.A. Album 40, 243, 8 Zucca. Paris: Bibliothèque Historique de la Ville de Paris [c. 1943–1944].

Name Index and
Literary Works

―――

Abetz, Otto, 2, 6, 8, 22, 9; allows
Yonnel to stay in Comédie-Française,
233n2
Abetz, Suzanne, 2, 212n6
Achard, Marcel, 88
Adams, Maude, 187
Aeschylus, xix, 40, 45, 46, 51, 109, 194
L'Aiglon, 175; unrealized Occupation
revival, 233n1
Alceste [Gluck], 229n3
Alfa, Michèle, 14; caricature of, *xxiv*
All Said and Done, 226n11
Also sprach Zarathustra, 228n29
L'Amant de Bornéo, 72
Ambrière, Francis, 67, 223n14
Amfreville, Henri d', 151
*Les Amitiés particulières. See Special
Friendships.*
L'Amour en Fuite, 198
Anahory, Eduardo, 66, 75–77, *76*
Andromaque, 110
Angels in America, 146
Anouilh, Jean, xvii, 7, 8, 36, 64, 81,
106, 107–108, 194, 196, 207; his
Antigone, 113, 126–127; influences
on, 115–116; after war, 230n16
Antigone [Anouilh], xvii, xx, 36, 64,
81–82, 107–108, 129, 130, 131, 137,
139, 164, 177, 196, 194, 207; analy-
sis, 116–122; and *Oreste* 122–126;

heroine's sexuality, 126–127; postwar
run, 230n16
Antigone [Sophocles], 116; spurious
lines, 118
Antoine, André, 106
*L'Apollon de Bellac. See The Apollo of
Marsac.*
*L'Apollon de Marsac. See The Apollo
of Marsac.*
*The Apollo de Bellac [L'Apollon de
Bellac]. See The Apollo of Marsac.*
*The Apollo of Bellac [L'Apollon de
Bellac]. See The Apollo of Marsac.*
*The Apollo of Marsac [L'Apollon de
Marsac]*, xx, 2, 62, 64, 65–79, 130,
209; metatheatrics in, 70–71, 115;
topical references, 117; Rio produc-
tion, 221n5; English versions,
222n12
Ariane à Naxos, 229n3
Aristophanes, 40, 88
Aristotle, 39, 46
Arletty, 101, 212n6, 228n31
Armory, 33, 45, 51, 55, 56, 57, 102,
186
Aron, Robert, 191
Artaud, Antonin, 87, 88
Arthur, Jean, 187
As I Lay Dying, 181
Autour d'une mère, 181

Baisers Volés, 198
Le Balcon, 27, 28
"The Ballad of Reading Gaol," 171
Bariona, or the Son of Thunder,
    136–137, 140–141, 142, 210
Bariona, ou le fils de tonnerre. See
    Bariona, or the Son of Thunder.
Barrault, Jean-Louis, xxi, 15, 87, 107,
    109, 175–176, 177, 188, 189–190,
    218n8, 218n13, 219n17, 219n21,
    219n21, 220n22; and *Eight Hundred
    Meters-Suppliant Women*, 35, 36, 43,
    45, 47, 49, 52, 55; as Hamlet, 72;
    declines direction of *The Flies*, 234n5;
    adapting *Satin Slipper* script,
    178–181; staging *Satin Slipper*, 183,
    185, 186, 187; career, 175, 181
Barrés, Maurice, 149
Barsacq, André, 115
Barthélmy, Joseph, 85
Barthes, Roland, 38, 39
Bataille, Georges, 33
Bâty, Gaston, 3, 8
Baumer, Jacques, *xxiv*
Beauvoir, Simone de, xx, 33, 57, 72,
    82, 113, 133, 194, 209, 230n2; on
    Jollivet 88–93, 225n11, 226n13; and
    Sartre, 140; on Barrault, 182, 183,
    234n5; on *Le Corbeau*, 183–184; *The
    Second Sex*, 130, 171, 182, 185;
    during War, 226n20; on *Eight Hundred
    Meters*, 220n30.
Being and Nothingness, 130
Bell, Marie, 182, 183, 184, 185, 189
Belle du Jour, 204, 205
Bennent, Heinz, 192
Bérard, Christian, 75, 222n9
Berkeley, Busby, 41
Berland, Jacques, 33, 50, 102, 181
Bernhardt, Sarah, 175, 177, 182, 189
Bernstein, Henry, 33
Berthau, Julien, 15, 184
Le Bien-Aimé, 7
Blanchar, Dominique, 66
Bloch, J.R., 40, 41, 58
Blum, Léon, 41, 86

Boléro, 72
Bonnard, Abel, 12, 147
Les Bonnes. See *The Maids*.
Borgia, Lucretia, 30
Borotra, Jean, 43, 44, 45, 46, 51, 54,
    55, 56, 217n6, 231n1
Bouquillon, Albert, 215n22
Bourdet, Edouard, 15, 212n6, 216n30
The Boys, 150–151; characters in,
    232n5
Brasillach, Robert, xvii, xviii, xxii, 6,
    57, 103, 127, 208–209, 211n1; on
    Giraudoux, 78–79
Breker, Arno, 17, 21, 36, 41, 44, 47,
    54, 56, 58, 215n22, 216n4, 220n27;
    and Cocteau, 18–19, 21; exhibition at
    l'Orangerie, *37*
Brinon, Fernand de, 2, 8, 212n6
Britannicus, 201–202

Cadou, André, 225n9
La Cage aux Folles, 203
Calderon de la Barca, Pedro, 88, 194,
    227n28
Caligula, 64
Calsat, Jean-Henri, 49 set design
Camus, Albert, 64, 81, 113
Capgras, Roger, 8, 212n6
Carné, Marcel, 220n29
Casablanca, 205
Castelot, André, 7, 33, 102; "Atriedophobia,"
    110
La Chagrin et la pité. See *The Sorrow
    and the Pity*.
Champeaux, Georges, 33
Chaperot, Georges, 170
Charles-Bauer, François, 170
Charles-Henry, 90
Chateaubriant, Alphonse de, 6
Chavance, Louis, 25
Les Chemins de la Liberté, 18
"Les Chevaleries," 146, 158, 164
Le Cid, 161
La Cinquième heure, 225n9
The City Whose Prince is a Child,
    150–151, 160, 171; characters in,

232n5; 1963 performance of Act I, 233n18

Claudel, Paul, xxi, 70, 81, 176, 194, 227n28; religious ideals, 180–181, 188; characters in *Satin Slipper*, 177–178; revising *Satin Slipper*, 178–181; casitigated by Beauvoir, 182, 183

Clouzot, Henri-Georges, 25, 183

Cocéa, Alice, 8

Cocteau, Jean, xix, 1–34, 35, 56, 70, 72, 81, 82, 129, 135, 145, 183, 200, 202, 207, 208, 209–210, 211n1; caricature of, *xxiv*, 215n21; and Breker, 18–19, 21; during the Occupation, 19–23; opera of *Antigone*, 109; photo at l'Orangerie, *37*; poetry of theatre, 63; he and Colette on Montherlant, 170–171; on Dacqmine, 185; influence on Jouvet's *The Maids*, 222n9, 222n14

Colette, 209, 212n6; she and Cocteau on Montherlant, 170–171; during War, 226n20; on *The Shadow*, 228n33

Collamarini, René, 49 masks

Le Condamné à Mort. See *The Man Condemned to Death*.

Copeau, Jacques, 87, 106, 170, 210

Corneille, Pierre, 161

Corydon, 214n16

Le Corbeau, 25, 183

Couberton, Baron Pierre de, 45

The Counterfeiters, 216n31

Couquet, James de, 90

Cousins, Gabriel, 57

Coutaud, L., 49

Cuny, Alain, 52, 219n21, 220n29

Dacqmine, Jacques, 185, 186, 187

Daladier, Georges, 63

Darlan, François, 5

Dasté, Marie-Hélène, 49

Daudet, Léon, 42

Daxiat, Michel. See Laubreaux, Alain.

Day for Night, 193

De Gaulle, Charles, 4, 79, 106, 113, 191, 213n14

Dellanoy, Marcel, 50

Deneuve, Catherine, 192, 199

Depardieu, Gérard, 193

Le Dernier Métro. See *The Last Métro*.

Destry, Robert, 90

Desty, Suzanne, 225n9

Deux Anglaises et le Continent, 198

La Disparue, 193–194, 195–196, 197–198, 200, 203–204, 234n1

Dom Juan, 222n14

Domicille Conjugale, 198

Don Carlos, 72, 194, 229n4

Doriot, Jacques, 5, 13

Dorziat, Gabrielle, *xxiv*

Dostoyevski, F., 158

Dreyer, Karl, 177

Drieu La Rochelle, Pierre, 17, 158

Duarte, Bandeira, 223n22

La Duchesse de Langeais, 70

Dullin, Charles, xx, 8, 45, 72, 83, 86–87, 130, 183, 194, 225n11; and Jollivet 90–93, 99, 101, 115; acts in *Princess*, 225n10, 228n30; edits of *Princess*, 227n23; subsidies, 227n26; revives *The Flies*, 230n2

Dumas, François Ribadeau, 186

Duran, Michel, 72

Dussane, Béatrix, on *Antigone*, 120–121, 127

Eight Hundred Meters [Huit Cents Mètres], xix, xxi, 35, 36, 45, 46, 52–57, 58, 62, 64, 65, 130, 175, 208, 220n30

Electre [Giraudoux], 44, 201

Les Enfants du Paradis, 101

Epting, Karl, 8, 13

L'équinoxe de septembre, 156

L'Eternel Retour, 19

Euripides, 110

Eurydice, xvii, 109

L'Exil, 160

Falconetti, Renée Maria, 175

Fauchois, René, 229n3

Faulkner, William, 181

Fauré, Gabriel, 229n3
Faydit de Terssac, Jean, 169
Feltin, Archbishop, 160
Ferdinand, Roger, 72
Feuillère, Edwige, 70
Fils de Personne. See *Nobody's Son*.
La Fleur des pois, 216n30
The Flies [Les Mouches], xix, xx, 36,
    44–45, 90, 110, 145, 177, 194, 196,
    207, 210; analysis, 130–132, 137–
    142, 143; disputed interpretation,
    229n7; misogyny in, 231n7; wartime
    run, 230n2
La Folle de Chaillot. See *The Mad-
    woman of Chaillot*.
La Force de l'age. See *The Prime of
    Life*.
Ford, John, 88
"Forgers of Myth," 118–119
Foucault, Michel, 38
Fraigneau, André, 110
Franco, Francisco, 227n28
Freud, Sigmund, 10, 18, 28

Les Garçons. See *The Boys*.
Gémier, Firmin, 40, 50
Genet, Jean, xx, 9, 13, 14, 27, 28,
    31–32, 63, 67, 66, 208–209, 212n10,
    213n15, 215n18; and Sartre,
    134–136; and "pederasty," 231n5
Genevoix, Maurice, 149
Germain, José, 72
Gide, André, 13, 20, 135, 214n16,
    214n17, 216n31
Giraudoux, Jean, xix, xx, 44, 49, 51 61–
    66, 69–70, 73–75, 78–79, 117, 201,
    208, 209, 220n25; revival of *Electre*,
    110, 141; use of metatheatrics, 115–
    116; message to Jouvet in *Apollo*,
    223n14; references in *Apollo*, 224n2;
    presumed in exile, 224n22; naming
    Apollo, 221n5
Glantière, Louis, trans. *Antigone*, 230n14
Gluck, Christoph Willibald, 229n3
Goebels, Josef, 218n14
Goethe, Johann Wolfgang von, 44, 72

Göring, Hermann, 218n14
La Grande Pastorale, 40
Griffen, Jonathan, trans. *Queen After
    Death*, 233n21
Grumberg, Jean-Claude, 193
Guéhenno, Jean, 8, 9, 13, 158, 213n11,
    233n17
Guérin, Daniel, 13, 214n17
La Guerre de Troie n'aura pas lieu, 110
Guevara, Luis Velez de, 160
Guitry, Geneviève, 212n6, 215n23
Guitry, Sacha, 7, 21, 81, 183, 200,
    212n6, 215n23
Gymnastik der Deutchen, 217n4

Hamlet, 175–176
Hauptmann, Gerhardt, 44, 110, 194
Haute Surveillance, 27
Hébertot, Jacques, 2, 15
Heilberg, Gunnar, 234n1
Henriot, Philippe, 42
Himmler, Heinrich, 9, 17, 147, 213n12,
    218n14
Hirshfeld, Magnus, 11
Hitler, Adolf, 4, 5, 17, 21, 41, 218n9,
    218n14
Honegger, Arthur, 49; opera of *Antigone*,
    109
Huis Clos. See *No Exit*.
Huit Cents Mètres. See *Eight Hundred
    Meters*.
"Le huit cents mètres de Paul Martin,"
    52, 220n23

Ibsen, Henrik, Occupation productions,
    194
L'Impromptu de Paris. See *The Im-
    promptu of Paris*.
L'Impromptu de Versailles, 69
*The Impromptu of Paris [L'Impromptu
    de Paris]*, 69–70
L'Incompris, wartime prod. cancelled,
    233n23
Iphigénie à Aulis, 109
Iphigénie à Delphes, 44, 110, 194
Iphigénie en Tauride [Goethe], 44, 72

Jacob, Max, 22
Jamois, Marguerite, 112, 175, 177, 189
Jarry, Alfred, 209
Jeanne avec nous. See *Joan Among Us.*
Les Jeunes filles, 156, 158, 171
Joan Among Us [Jeanne avec nous],
　36, 72, 81, 111–112, 137, 177, 196,
　207; Vermorel's intent, 229n13
Joan of Arc [Dreyer], 177
Joan of Arc, 177, 183, 188, 189, 224n1;
　and *Antigone*, 126
Jollivet, Simone, xx, 72, 82, 102–104,
　105, 129, 145, 194, 209, 230n2; and
　Dullin 90–93, 99, 101; and Sartre,
　88–89; described by Beauvoir, 89–
　90, 91–94; photos, *95*; translations
　and scripts 88, 102–103; biographical
　details, 225n11; not cast in *Princess*,
　228n30; referred to as "Mme,"
　227n27; and Nietzsche, 227n29
Jouhandeau, Marcel, 13, 20, 135
Jourdan, Louis, 18, 234n2
Journal des années noires, 233n17
Journée Olympique: Huit cents mètres
　[Obey radio script], 219n20
Jouvet, Louis, xix–xx, 62, 65–66, 68,
　69–70, 71; influence on Anouilh,
　115–116; and Ozeray, 221n8,
　222n19; influence on *The Maids*,
　222n10; reception of *The Maids*,
　223n14; ms. of *Apollo*, 223n18.
Jules et Jim, 198–199
Julius Caesar [Jollivet trans.], 88,
　226n15
Jünger, Paul, 22

Kanters, Robert, 67
Kean, 231n9
Kerjean, Germaine, 228n30
King Lear [Jollivet trans.), 88
Korène, Véra, 149

Labiche, Eugène, 34
Labisse, F., 50
Lady Chatterly's Lover, 205
Lagrange, Léo, 42, 217n6

Lalou, René, 90
Lannes, Roger, 3, 215n18
Lapara, Léo, 67; on *The Maids*, 222n9,
　222n14
Lapierre, Marcel, 170
The Last Métro [Le Dernier Métro],
　xxi–xxii, 14, 15, 191–194, 195–198,
　199–206; see also *La Disparue.*
Latriene, Marcel, 225n910
Laubreaux, Alain (aka Michel Daxiat),
　6, 14–16, 17, 18, 20, 28, 34, 56, 82,
　103, 127, 169, 181, 186, 188, 208,
　210, 212n6, 224n3; attacked by
　Marais, 14–19, 216n30; on *Antigone*,
　120; on *Electre*, 110; *Pirates*, 72, 111,
　234n4
Laurent, Jean, 186
Laval, Pierre, 5
Le Grix, François, 186; attacks Claudel,
　234n7
Ledoux, Fernand, 52
Leduc, Violette, 214n16
Lefranc, Germaine, 72
Lehman-Haupt, Helmut, 58
Lenormand, H.-R., 212n6, 216n30
Léocadia [Time Remembered], xvii–
　xviii, 7, 116
Les Lépreuses, 156
L'Homme et ses fantômes, 216n30
Lifar, Serge, 212n6
Le Livre blanc. See *The White Book.*
Lorenzaccio, 175, 189
Louis XIV, 75, 83, 98

La Machine à Écrire. See *The Type-
　writer.*
La Machine Infernale, 19, 34
Madame Capet, 225n9
*The Madwoman of Chaillot [La Folle
　de Chaillot]*, 62, 63, 64, 79
The Maids [Les Bonnes], xx, 27, 209,
　215n18; with *Apollo* 66, 67, 68, 75
Maillol, Aristide, 215n22
Le Malentendu. See *The Misunder-
　standing.*
Malo, Pierre, 215n21

The Man Condemned to Death [Le Condamné à Mort], 31–32

Marais, Jean, 1, 2, 14–15, 16, 17, 18, 19, 20, 21, 33, 52, 55, 56, 57, 72, 82, 113, 208, 212n6, 212n8, 220n30; attacks Laubreaux, 14–19, 216n30; caricature of, *xxiv*; portrait of Genet, 215n18; prod. of *Andromaque*, 229n5; rejected by Résistance, 234n2; replaced by Dacqmine, 185, 187; directs *Britannicus*, 201–202; seizure in *Typewriter*, 202

La Marâitre [adapt. Jollivet], 88

Marcel, Gabriel, 67

Marché Noir, 8

Marie Stuart, 225n9

Marquet, Mary, 184–185, 186, 187, 189, 234n6

Martin du Gard, Roger, 216n30

Martin, Mary, 187

Martin, Paul, 52, 54

Massot, Pierre de, 151

Maulnier, Thierry, 67, 109

Maurette, Marcelle, 225n9

Maurras, Charles, 41, 42 , 58, 217n7

May, Simone, 225n9

Mein Kampf, 41

The Merchant of Venice, 111

Méré, Charles, 186

Mignon, Paul-Louis, 113, 143, 226n11

The Misunderstanding [Le Malentendu], 64; and Paul Œttly, 113

Mnouchkine, Ariane, 107

Molière, 69, 222n14

Montherlant, Henry Millon de, xxi, 12, 13, 20, 25, 51, 81, 109, 135, 142, 176, 194, 208, 209–210, 227n28; Occupation career, 145–148; sexuality, 146–148, 148–160, correspondence with Peyrefitte, 146, 148, 152–160; on defeated France, 219n18; at *Eight Hundred Meters*, 231n1; use of "enfant," 232n8; stopped by police in 1938, 232n9

Morihien, Paul, 14, 16, 20

Les Mouches. See *The Flies*.

Musset, Alfred de, 175, 177, 189

Mussolini, Benito, 4, 218n14

Mythologies, 38

La Naissance d'une cité, 40, 41, 58

Napoléon, 233n1

Nekrassov, 231n9

No Exit [Huis Clos], xviii, 26, 64; and *Oreste*, 123, 124, 125, 141, 142–143, 208, 220n29, 229n5

Nobody's Son [Fils de Personne], xxi, 12, 145, 176; analysis, 164–173; reception, 169–172; 1963 revival, 233n18; cuts in original script, 233n22

Notre Dame des fleurs. See *Our Lady of the Flowers*.

Novy, Yvon, 94; interview w. Sartre, 130; member of Dullin's company, 227n22

La Nuit américaine. See *Day for Night*.

Numance, 175

Obey, André, xix, 45, 64, 194, 219n18, 219n20, 220n23, 220n24

Oedipe [Cocteau], 20

Oedipus Rex [Gémier version], 40

Oedipus Rex [Sophocles], 40

Œttly, Paul, 82; director/actor, 113

Olympia, 41, 42, 47

Les Olympiques, 154–155, 158

L'Ombre. See *The Shadow*.

Ondine, 116, 223n14

Ophuls, Marcel, 106, 191, 203, 205

Ophuls, Max, 221n8, 222n19

Opium, 19

L'Orgue du Stade, 52, 220n23

Oreste, xx, 108, 114, 122–126; critical responses, 230n18, 230n19

Orphée, 19, 34

Our Lady of the Flowers [Notre Dame des fleurs], 14, 32

Ozeray, Madeleine, 63, 66, 68, 69–70, 71; and Jouvet, 221n8, 222n19; as Ondine 223n14

Parade, 34

Les Parents Terribles, 1, 2, 19, 22, 34, 72, 81, 211n1; Cocteau on, 170

Pasiphaé, 160

Passeur, Stève, 8, 88

Paysage des Olympiques, 154–155, 156, 158; nudity in, 232n14

Pellepoix, Darquier de, 42

Pénélope, 229n3

La Pension Farge, 225n9

The Perfect Athlete, 215n22

The Persians, 45, 46

Pétain, Philippe, 4, 5, 7, 43, 44, 73, 84, 85, 138, 213n11, 229n10; poster image, 112

Peyrefitte, Roger, 146, 147, 213n11; correspondance with Montherlant, 148, 152–160; *Special Friendships*, 150; first meetings w. Montherlant, 151–152; arrests, 159; on Montherlant's female readers, 232n15; writes Montherlant's experiences, 232n4; returns to Paris, 232n6

Phèdre, 109

Philippe, Gérard, 189

Piaf, Edith, 19

Pigaut, Roger, 219n21

Pioch, Georges, 47, 55, 56, 103, 219n20

Pirandello, Luigi, 33; use of metatheatrics, 115

Les Pirates de Paris: L'Affaire Stavisky. See *The Pirates of Paris: The Stavisky Affair*.

The Pirates of Paris: The Stavisky Affair [Les Pirates de Paris: L'Affaire Stavisky] 72, 82, 111, 202, 209, 210; and Paul Œttly, 113; Occupation attribution to Laubreaux, 234n4

Plato, 187

Plutus [trans. Jollivet], 88

Poetics, 39, 46

Poiret, Jean, 193, 203

Port-Royal, 160

Price, Denys, 203

The Prime of Life [La Force de l'age], 82, 89–93, 133, 182, 194, 227n29, 230n2; and *Journal de Guerre*, 226n16, 226n18, 226n19

La Princesse des Ursins. See *The Princess of Ursins*.

The Princess of Ursins [La Princesse des Ursins], xx, 72, 83, 94–102, 105, 129, 145, 147, 194, 209; reviews, 102; ms. of play, 227n23; run, 230n2

La Prisonnière, 216n30

Purnal, Roland, 50, 51, 55, 186

Les Quatre Cents Copus, 198

Queen After Death [La Reine Morte], 142, 145, 159; sexual depictions, 161–164, 165, 169, 194, 227n28

Quinet, Charles, 102

Quo Vadis, 149

Rachel, 182

Racine, Jean, 61, 109, 110, 201, 229n5

Rebatet, Lucien [aka François Vinneuil], 16, 22, 34, 207, 209

La Règle du Jeu, 204

Reichstadt, Duke of (Napoléon's son), 233n1

Reinar después de mourir, 160

La Reine Morte. See *Queen After Death*.

Renaitour, Jean-Michel, 187, 224n3

Renaud, Madeleine, 234n5

Le Rendez-vous à Senlis. See *The Rendez-vous at Senlis*.

The Rendez-vous at Senlis [Le Rendez-vous à Senlis], xvii, xx, 8

Renoir, Pierre, 8

The Republic, 187

Reynaud et Armide, 81

Ricou, Georges, 102, 169

Riefenstahl, Leni, 40–41, 44, 54, 56, 217n4

Rigby, Kathy, 187

Rinieri, J.J., 67

Roche, Jean-Marie, 46

Röhm, Ernst, 11, 18
Le Roi Chirstine, 225n9
Romains, Jules, 88
Rostand, Edmond, 175
Rostand, Maurice, 33, 55, 102, 186, 212n6; Occupation play produced, 224n3; on Princess, 228n30
Roulleau, Raymond, 16, 220n29
Roussin, André, 106
Roy, Claude, 230n16; review of Antigone, 119–120, 121, 127,129; on Claudel, 176

Sachs, Maurice, 13, 20, 214n16
Saint Genet, 134–135
Salacrou, Armand, 88
"Salute to Breker," 21
Le Sang d'un Poète, 19
Sans, Simone-Camille. See Jollivet, Simone.
Sardou, Roger, 2, 29, 212n6
Sarment, Jean, 72
Sartre, Jean-Paul, xviii, xix, xx, 9, 18, 26, 36, 44, 64, 81, 145, 183, 194, 207–209, 210, 220n29, 229n5; and Jollivet, 88–89, 225n11; on Antigone, 118–119; on Les Mouches, 110; remark on Occupation, 113; Being and Nothingness, 130; The Flies, 130–132, 137–142, 143, 177, 196; and sexuality, 132–136; and Genet, 134–136; No Exit, 141, 142–143; misogyny in The Flies, 231n7; female characters in postwar plays, 231n9; postwar life, 231n3
The Satin Slipper [Le Soulier de Satin], xxi, 81, 176, 177, 194, 227n28; stage adaptation, 178–181; interpretation and casting, 181–190
Schiffman, Suzanne, 193
Schiller, Friedrich, 72, 194, 229n4
The Second Sex, 130, 133, 171, 185, 209
Seé, Edmond, 90
Seel, Pierre, 10
Seigfried, set, 116
Seven Against Thebes, 46

The Shadow [L'Ombre], 88, 90, 94, 99, 102, 104, 226n14
Shakespeare, William, 88, 175; use of Chorus, 114
Sienkiewicz, Henryk, 149
Sodom and Gomorrah [Sodom et Gomorrah], 62; 69–70
Sodom et Gomorrah. See Sodom and Gomorrah.
Le Solstice de Juin, 146, 159, 219n18
Sophocles, Antigone, 40, 109, 116, 118; Creon in Antigone, 125
The Sorrow and The Pity, 106, 191, 203, 205
Le Soulier de Satin. See The Satin Slipper.
Special Friendships, 150, 159
Stavisky, Serge (Sacha), 82, 202
Strauss, Richard, 229n3
A Streetcar Named Desire, 27
Strindberg, August, 194
The Suppliant Women [Aeschylus], xix, 45–46, 51, 52, 109, 194
The Suppliant Women [Obey], 35, 36, 45, 46, 47–52, 58, 64, 65; photo spread, 48.
Les Suppliantes [Aeschylus]. See The Suppliant Women [Aeschylus].
Les Suppliantes [Obey]. See The Suppliant Women [Obey].
Surèn, Hans, 217n4
Sylvain, Jean, 184
The Symposium, 187

Une Taciturne, 216n30
Taina, 225n9
The Typewriter [La Machine à Écrire], xix, 1–34, 35, 56, 63, 65, 70, 72, 129, 131, 202, 145, 147, 207, 208, 209, 216n30, 220n29; analysis, 23–33; caricatures of production, xxiv, 215n21
Time Remembered. See Léocadia.
T'is Pity She's a Whore, 88
Tous feux éteints, 232n10
"A Tragedy of Love," 234n1

Triumph of the Will, 41, 51
Truffaut, François, xxi–xxii, 14, 15, 191–192, 193, 195–197, 205–206; on Occupation films, 195; other films by, 198–199; depiction of homosexuality in *The Last Métro*, 202–203; use of name "Daxiat," 224n2
Tu étais si gentil quand tu étais petit, 230n18

Ubu Roi, 209

Valentin, Monelle, 116
Vallat, Xavier, 42
The Vatican Cellars, 214n16
Vaudoyer, Jean-Louis, 51
Vega [Carpio], Lope de, 194, 227n28
Verdier, Noelle, 225n9
Vermorel, Claude, 36, 72, 81, 112, 177, 196, 207, 229n13
Vetir ceux qui sont nus, 115
La Ville dont le Prince est un enfant. See *The City Whose Prince is a Child.*

Vingt-cinq ans de Bonheur, 72
29 Degrés à l'Ombre, 34
Vinneuil, François. See Rebatet, Lucien.
Les Visiteurs du Soir, 196, 220n29
Vitold, Michel, 52, 219n21, 220n29
La Volupté de l'honneur, 115

The White Book [Le Livre blanc], 20–21, 28, 32, 216n29
Wilde, Oscar, 171
Willemetz, Albert, 212n6
Williams, Tennessee, 27
Wilson, Dooley, 206
Winckelmann, J.J., 44
Wisner, René, 90
"The World of Wrestling," 38
Woyzeck, 111

Ybarnégaray, Jean, 217n6, 217n7
Yonnel, Jean, 233n2

Zay, Jean, 42, 217n6
Zucca, André, 42, 217n5